ALSO BY RICHARD ENGEL

A Fist in the Hornet's Nest:
On the Ground in Baghdad Before, During, and After the War

WAR JOURNAL

My Five Years in Iraq

Richard Engel

SIMON & SCHUSTER
New York London Toronto Sydney

SIMON & SCHUSTER
Rockefeller Center
1230 Avenue of the Americas
New York, NY 10020

Copyright © 2008 by Richard Engel

First Simon & Schuster hardcover edition June 2008

SIMON & SCHUSTER and colophon are registered trademarks
of Simon & Schuster, Inc.

For information about special discounts for bulk purchases,
please contact Simon & Schuster Special Sales at
1-800-456-6798 or business@simonandschuster.com.

Designed by Jaime Putorti

Manufactured in the United States of America

10 9 8 7 6 5 4 3 2 1

Library of Congress Cataloging-in-Publication Data
Engel, Richard.
   War journal : my five years in Iraq / Richard Engel.
      p. cm.
   1. Iraq War, 2003–   I. Title.
   DS79.76.E543   2008
   956.7044'3092—dc22   2008013006

ISBN-13: 978-1-4165-6305-1

For Ali, Zohair, and the Iraqi staff of the NBC News Baghdad bureau

2003–2004

THE CALIPH IS CAPTURED

1

AD-DUR, IRAQ
DECEMBER 15, 2003

No one was to come in or out.

Dozens of American soldiers formed a defensive circle around the palm grove, silently keeping watch. Gunners in the turrets of Humvees parked next to the troops turned hand cranks at their waists to pan .50 caliber machine guns left and right, training the long gun barrels on the dense trees around the edges of the grove.

"Got to keep your eyes moving.

"Got to look out for snipers.

"Got to protect the circle.

"Nothing can go wrong today,

"Not in front of all these reporters."

It was a big day, and we all knew it. I was at the center of this defensive ring of American muscle and machines along with about a dozen other journalists. We probably looked ridiculous to the troops. They had their uniforms: khaki combat boots, M4 rifles, Kevlar helmets, and Wiley X ballistic sunglasses. We had our uniforms: brightly colored flak jackets (mine was sky blue), cameras, tripods, notebooks, khakis, and quick-dry synthetic shirts. The army had choppered us into this clearing on two Black Hawks to see what didn't look like much from the outside: a tiny cinder block farmhouse with a garden filled with sunflowers, oranges, and pomegranate trees. The fruit looked almost ripe on the cool bright December morning. But no one would be picking it. Not from this house. Not anymore.

"We have a cordon around the area, but it is still dangerous. Don't wander off," an army officer warned. My canvas hiking boots stuck in the soft black soil as I walked to the farmhouse and through its thatch gate.

But what I saw inside didn't make any sense to me. Military officials said Saddam Hussein was captured hiding in a hole. I didn't see any hole, but only a typical one-room Iraqi farmhouse with a cement patio in front where laundry and *basterma* (Arab pastrami) were drying on a line. One of the biggest manhunts in history had led the U.S. military here: Saddam's safe house where he slept and apparently cooked for himself. It seemed that he lived badly as a fugitive. My mother would have called the place, like my room growing up, "a pigsty." There were broken eggs on the floor, a dirty frying pan atop a gas burner, and a half-eaten Mars bar and an open bottle of moisturizer on a wooden stand next to a single, unmade twin bed. I imagined the dictator, who had lived in palaces with hundreds of servants, suddenly forced to fend for himself like a freshman in college who, no longer having his mother to pick up after him, eats junk food and doesn't clean up. It must have been a tough adjustment for Saddam. One of his private chefs told me the Iraqi leader was a finicky eater, often struggling with his weight; he always made himself a bit thinner in his statues. He liked vegetables and mutton stews, and would fine the chef if he used too much oil. Saddam would tip him if meals were particularly tasty and light. He liked things just so. One of Saddam's palace maids—like many, a Christian woman (Saddam thought Iraqi Christians to be especially honest and clean)—told me Saddam was also so fastidious about hygiene that she was required to take off her shoes and walk barefoot across a mat soaked in disinfectant before entering his bedroom. Saddam couldn't have liked living in this farmhouse, just three miles from his dusty home village, al-Ouja, which he hated for its poverty. The poor street thug who intimidated and killed his rivals until he became "al-Rais," Arabic for both head and president, had come full circle.

"But where's the hole?" I asked the officer. "Didn't you find Saddam in a hole?"

He led me back outside to the cement patio with the laundry line.

"At first we didn't see it either. A soldier was standing right here and didn't notice the hole until he kicked aside this mat," the officer said, pulling back a plastic tarp on the ground. Underneath was a Styrofoam cork in the cement about the size of a big fishing tackle box.

"When the soldier removed this Styrofoam cover," he said, "Saddam was inside. Saddam put his hands up and said, 'I am Saddam Hussein, president of Iraq, and I am ready to negotiate.' "

Saddam apparently lived in the farmhouse most of the time, and took refuge in the hole only when danger was close. Saddam also had a pistol, but didn't use it, and traveled in a beat-up white and orange taxi discovered nearby.

The soldiers were relaxed and joking with journalists. It was a "good news" day and this was the military's chance to play show-and-tell.

"And what did the soldiers say to Saddam?" one of us asked.

"President Bush sends his regards," an officer said.

We all laughed.

The scribblers among us frantically scratched notes into pads. Cameramen marked time codes so they could easily find the sound bite again, and the snappers took pictures of every angle, their big black cameras clicking like crickets.

The troops were playing it up. The soldiers from the 4th Infantry Division were the "landowners" here, in charge of the entire

Tikrit area. Their commander, Major General Raymond Odierno, an ogre of a man with a bald head and a no-nonsense personality, said, "Saddam was caught like a rat."

But in reality the elite U.S. Special Operations Forces code-named Task Force 121 did most of the work. U.S. officials said Saddam was located after the "hostile interrogations" of several of his relatives and bodyguards. Odierno said "five or ten" of them were arrested about ten days before Saddam's capture. On the day of the predawn raid, roughly six hundred soldiers from the 4th ID provided perimeter security to ensure no one escaped as members of Task Force 121 moved in, raided the farmhouse, grabbed Saddam, and choppered him south to a prison at the Baghdad airport, where he was identified by former aides, among them soft-spoken, gray-haired former deputy prime minister Tariq Aziz. But members of Task Force 121 don't give interviews, so to the 4th ID went the glory. Sorry, Task Force 121.

Looking back, it's easy to see why so many people, including me, were generally optimistic back then. Saddam was in custody. U.S. forces had killed his hated sons, Uday and Qusay, five months earlier. President George W. Bush had just stopped by Baghdad for a surprise Thanksgiving Day visit to the troops. U.S. military officials said at the time there were only about five hundred to seven hundred insurgents, many of them former Iraqi intelligence officers or members of Uday's paramilitary force, the Fedayeen, operating in about a dozen cells in the Baghdad area.

But even then, violence was starting to pick up. Two days before Saddam was captured, militants threw a grenade at a U.S. patrol in Baghdad carrying *Time* magazine writer Michael Weisskopf and photographer James Nachtwey. The grenade landed between the two journalists as they were stopped in traffic. Weisskopf reached down and threw the grenade out of the vehicle. It exploded in the air, blowing off his hand. Nachtwey was also wounded, but the veteran war photographer was able to keep taking pictures throughout the ordeal. Tough guy.

That's one of the reasons we liked Odd Job.

I had driven to Tikrit to cover Saddam's capture in Odd Job, the affectionate nickname for our homemade satellite truck. It's what Iraqis call a "bongo truck," a pickup with a rear cab covered in a canvas tarpaulin. Our engineers—the unsung heroes of the news business, our Task Force 121—fit it with a portable satellite dish, generators, tanks of diesel fuel, and enough cables to make it into a self-contained TV uplink. But it was Iraqi style. Unlike the white TV vans with telescopic dishes emblazoned with company logos that rush to crime scenes in the United States, Odd Job was rusted and painted to look like any other truck in Baghdad transporting onions or sheep. We liked it that way. Even back in December 2003, you didn't want to be seen. But stealth and discretion were our only defense at the time. Less than a year later, Iraq had become so dangerous we were forced to develop the most complex, expensive, and often inhibiting security procedures in the history of combat journalism.

The soldiers from the 4th ID gave us an hour to explore Saddam's hideout before heading back to their HQ, ironically in one of Saddam's most lavish palaces just a few miles away. The soldiers lived on green folding cots in the palace's huge rooms of green and white marble. Although the palaces looked impressive, like giant wedding cakes, the construction was shoddy. The crystals in the giant chandeliers were plastic. The toilets often didn't flush. The sinks with gold-plated faucets leaked. Hundreds of soldiers packed the building, nearly all of them young men away from their wives and girlfriends. You could almost smell the testosterone. A soldier told me that a few months earlier a visiting female reporter was sleeping topless on a cot, just covered with a white sheet.

"And it kept falling off!" he said.

It can reach over 120 degrees in the summer in Tikrit, so I can sympathize with the journalist trying to sleep. But she was such a distraction the military ordered her to leave the base.

I was in no rush to get back to the palace. I wanted to go in Saddam's hole. I was excited and must admit I was having fun. The entrance was smaller than a manhole cover, too small for me to fit through wearing my bulky blue flak jacket lined with ceramic strike plates. I ripped back the Velcro straps, put my hands on either side of the hole, and lowered myself inside.

When my feet landed on the floor, I switched on a flashlight and painted the walls with dim yellow light. The subterranean chamber was like a tomb: rectangular, about ten feet long, four feet high, and three feet wide. The walls were covered in rough concrete. The floor was lined with boards. A naked lightbulb and fan hung from the ceiling. The fan was attached to a plastic hose that ran through a hole drilled in the wall and led outside. It was a ventilation system and let Saddam breathe when the tomb was plugged with the Styrofoam cork.

It seemed odd to many people in the States that most Iraqis didn't celebrate the news of Saddam's capture. A few in Baghdad fired guns in the air, a dangerous celebratory tradition in the Arab world. (It was banned in Gaza after a gun-toting guest at a wedding accidentally gunned down both the bride and groom; but Gazans never stopped.)

The most common reaction in Iraq to the news of Saddam's capture was disbelief. Iraqi after Iraqi I interviewed insisted that the capture was a fake, a put-on by Saddam and the Americans to confuse them. I understood their skepticism. I also found the news hard to believe.

When I arrived in Baghdad in February 2003 about a month before the invasion, Saddam seemed in total control, ruling what I naively thought was in "the Iraqi way": the tradition of the ancient caliphs Haroun al-Rashid and Shahryar of the fabled *Arabian Nights*.

While working for a small newspaper in Cairo in the 1990s, I bought a paperback copy of the *Nights* at a used bookstore in Athens. I often traveled to Greece carrying transparencies of the weekly *Middle East Times*. We printed the paper abroad to avoid Egyptian censorship laws. The *Nights* I bought was a translation by Sir Richard Burton, the nineteenth-century British explorer, poet, adven-

turer, diplomat, soldier, archaeologist, swordsman, and writer
reputed to be fluent in twenty-nine languages. He became one of
my early idols, writer of some of my favorite lines, among them:

> Do what thy manhood bids thee do,
> from none but self expect applause;
> He noblest lives and noblest dies
> who makes and keeps his self-made laws.

In Burton's *Nights*, the caliph Shahryar murders his bride after
discovering her infidelity. Unable to trust another woman, the caliph then marries a series of virgins only to have them executed the
next day. The caliph's rampage stops when he meets the legendary
storyteller Scheherazade, who keeps herself alive by enthralling
him for 1001 straight nights with fantastic stories of jinn, giants,
and flying carpets, each one ending with the same phrase: "If you
let me live tonight I will tell you an even more fantastic tale tomorrow." So he does.

It was through this romantic haze that I saw Saddam, who I believe also fancied himself a natural heir to Iraq's grandiose rulers.
He rebuilt the ruins of Babylon and stamped his initials on every
brick. He commissioned a Koran handwritten in his own blood.
Saddam's word was law. If you crossed him you died. If you pleased
him you were rewarded with cars and villas. It was simple. Saddam
pardoned prisoners on his birthday, and sentenced men and
women to hang for insulting him. Blasphemy—publicly defaming
God or the Muslim Prophet Mohammed—was punishable by five
years in prison. Defaming Saddam carried a death sentence. Iraqis
said of their president, "If you raised your head, he cut it off."

Like his forebears, and many Iraqis today, Saddam was also an
ardent believer in fortune-tellers, oracles, and mystics. In August
2003, I met a jeweler from Baghdad's small Mandaean community, a dwindling religious order that follows John the Baptist. He
sold Saddam polished stones to protect him from evil. He told me
Saddam also took the advice of a twelve-year-old clairvoyant boy

who allegedly knew if a man was lying. After I drank several tiny, hourglass-shaped cups of strong, sweet tea in the jeweler's shop, which was filled with silver rings with red and green stones, I bought a lucky charm, a folded parchment inscribed with a hand-written Mandaean prayer wrapped in a stag's scrotum. I kept it in my shirt pocket for a year until I lost it. Fingers crossed.

Before the war there were giant photographs of Saddam on government buildings carrying bowls of rice (Saddam the Provider), brandishing rocket-propelled grenades (Saddam the Protector), eating bread with poor villagers (Saddam the Man of the People), and surrounded by adoring schoolchildren (Saddam the Father). All that was missing to complete the image was Saddam dressed in a caliph's robes and turban.

The caliph was now in American hands. Iraqis couldn't believe it.

This should have been a turning point. U.S. troops were still mostly greeted as liberators in December 2003. Despite much of the postwar rewriting of history, U.S. troops were welcomed when they first arrived. I saw Iraqis give flowers and bottles of whiskey to American soldiers in Baghdad in April 2003.

I ended my book *A Fist in the Hornet's Nest* with Saddam's capture. At the time I wrote that I didn't understand why the Bush administration wanted to invade Iraq. No one I spoke to in the Middle East was focused on Iraq in 2003. People in the region worried about Israeli-Palestinian fighting. Iraq was a nonissue. Nonetheless, I wrote that I supported the invasion, believing it had the potential to be the start of a radical plan to redesign and improve the modern Middle East, unstable since it was cobbled together by self-serving European powers from the debris of the Ottoman Empire defeated in World War I. But by late 2003, I was having serious doubts that creating a stable, democratic Middle East was possible—or being seriously pursued. President Bush invaded Iraq after having declared support for an independent Palestinian state. He called it Palestine, the first U.S. president to use the term. But then the Bush administration dropped diplomacy altogether.

2

Some of my most vivid memories from Iraq are personal and fleeting, like the taste of pacha, or sheep's-head soup. The wife of my fixer and friend Zohair made me this pungent Iraqi national dish when I was sick with a fever that made my temperature soar and my mouth taste like I'd been sucking on pennies.

Zohair, forty-six, gray-haired, with a sly smile and bright, mischievous eyes, has been my point man in Iraq since 2003. A former soldier once sentenced to death for going absent without leave from Saddam's army, Zohair is the ultimate inside man. At a moment's notice he can find a gun or set up an interview with the prime minister. If you are looking to interview an Iraqi family with a handicapped child that speaks English, just give him a few hours. If you need morphine, a counterfeit passport, or a meeting with a Sufi mystic, give him a day. But don't make the mistake of asking Zohair for pacha because he'll bring that too, complete with white floating dumplings of brain. Iraqis believe the soup makes you strong. It is even said to make men perform better in bed. "Good for a man," Zohair told me, standing at the foot of my bed, armed with an aluminum pot full of the witches' brew.

At the time, I couldn't even get out of the sweat-soaked sheets, let alone perform sheep's-head-Viagra-powered tricks in them. My doctor in New York told me colonies of amoebas and parasites were living happily in my gut, most likely breeding undisturbed there for nine months. I assume they had moved in during the Shock and Awe phase of the invasion when I drank mostly tap water from blue plastic jerry cans I stored under the sink in my room on the fourteenth floor of the Palestine hotel. American cruise missiles and JDAMs had destroyed so many pipes that Baghdad's already fragile and ill-maintained drinking water system mixed with raw sewage. It didn't taste bad, but I wouldn't recommend it. The doctor recommended a battery of antibiotics. Zohair recommended pacha. Neither worked.

I smile whenever I think of Zohair and his remedies. He brought me honey and cold-pressed olive oil from Kurdistan when I had a sore throat. He recommended I rub raw garlic cloves sliced in half on my face to grow a more even beard; mine comes in splotchy—not manly enough for Iraqi standards. That worked.

Like many Iraqis, Zohair doesn't want a civil war and couldn't care less if American troops are in his country. "We need an impartial U.S. military governor," he often says. "You let Iraqis rule, and it's all killing and infighting."

Zohair didn't support Saddam and doesn't want an Islamic regime. He drinks whiskey every night—now too much—smokes Dunhill cigarettes, and reads Karl Marx. Zohair doesn't want to die fighting for Iraq's honor and dignity against foreign occupation, or to claim the country for Sunnis or Shiites. He wants to buy a house. His attractive young wife, Shahid, Arabic for witness, wants a baby and has been struggling to get pregnant.

Other memories have left more of a scar, such as watching a group of Iraqi soldiers burn to death in front of me during a roadside bomb attack in Mosul.

This book is a string of these moments; it's how I will remember what happened in Iraq based on what I have seen here in places like Baghdad's Camp Falcon during Christmas 2003.

CHRISTMAS DAY, 2003
CAMP FALCON, SOUTH BAGHDAD

The music set the mood: festive, playful, and nostalgic. A band of uniformed paratroopers were entertaining the troops, playing Christmas carols on electric guitars and saxophones. They did solos and rocked out, as much as Christmas carols can be rocked out. The singer—peppy, young, and cute in a floppy camouflage hat— had a lot of sass. She was dancing, a big smile on her face, shaking her hips and standing right over the soldiers sitting in neat rows of folding chairs on a wide, dusty field. She was working the crowd, flirtatiously making eye contact and holding their gaze. The troops were having a good time, but no one was cheering and the music wasn't too loud. The soldiers had to make sure they could still hear the air raid siren in case of incoming rockets and mortars at this former Iraq army base; but that wasn't a big threat yet.

When the singer finished her final song, "Rockin' Around the Christmas Tree," a big burly commander took the stage. He looked like a character out of a Stanley Kubrick movie, the personification of a military man with hands big enough to rip phone books and who might have been born in a uniform. The general wasn't chewing on the stub of a cigar, but looked like he might have just put one out. He looked like the kind of man who could fix a pickup truck blindfolded and "tear you a new asshole" if you disobeyed an order. He looked like a man whose daughter you wouldn't want to date. The general swaggered onto the stage, took a microphone off a stand, and delivered a pep talk to the troops.

The general began by asking the soldiers to close their eyes and climb aboard his train of thought. "I want to just take you for a minute, and think back at that mall, where all your family members are shopping right now," he said.

The soldiers closed their eyes.

"You got that thought. See what it's like? A crowded shopping mall."

The general paused for emphasis. The soldiers got that thought.

"Well, guess what? Guess what that thought looks like to a terrorist? That terrorist wants to go ahead and drive a vehicle laden with all kinds of explosives into that mall back in the United States and disrupt our way of life.

"You're over here not letting that terrorist have the opportunity to do that."

The general went on to say that it was okay for soldiers to miss their families during the holidays, but to know they were in Iraq protecting them as part of the "most noble mission" in the world, "the global war on terrorism."

The speech, and so many I've heard like it in Iraq, bothered me. As I listened to it again in 2007, I kept thinking that the troops have been misled, right from the beginning. In the early days the message, the motivation for war, was simple and clear: fight in Iraq or your families at home will die. The terrorists are coming. The terrorists want you. Kill them in Iraq before they get you. Preemptive war. The speeches made me think of the McCarthy days of red scares and communist conspiracies to corrupt and overthrow the "American way of life." Those 1950s speeches sound so chilling, simplistic, and embarrassing now; so do the early speeches from Baghdad.

While terrorists undoubtedly do want to destroy shopping malls in the United States and kill Americans, the commanders in Iraq and at the White House have consistently used scare tactics that became increasingly hard to believe as the war progressed. By 2006, it was hard for a soldier trying to restrain Sunni and Shiite militias in Baghdad from drilling holes in each other to see how he was making his mother or sister any safer back in Texas or Florida.

Sitting in the back of a Humvee in 2007, a soldier gave what I think was the best summary of troop morale I've heard in Iraq: "There are three kinds of soldiers in Iraq. Those who believe in the mission, and believe we are here making America safer," he said.

"Then there are those who don't believe in the mission, and

think it's bullshit, but don't have a choice because they are in the army.

"And there's the third kind," said the soldier, on his third tour and about to get out of the army for good.

"These are the soldiers who don't care about the mission or really understand it, but are here to protect the guy on his left and right. I'd say 80 percent of the soldiers are like that. In the beginning there were more believers."

Some of the early believers thought they were in Iraq to avenge the terrorist attacks of 9/11, an eye for an eye. Luckily, the number of them dwindled over time.

After the Christmas show, our crew left Camp Falcon and drove back to our base at the Hamra hotel. Even by the end of 2003, security in Baghdad was starting to deteriorate rapidly. We'd made our hotel into a fort, surrounding it with checkpoints, walls, retractable spikes in the road called dragons' teeth, and armed Iraqi guards. NBC hired a former master sergeant from the British Royal Marines, Keith Rigby, as a consultant to design the perimeter wall. For two weeks, Rigby, a big red-faced man who seemed comfortable overseeing teams of workmen, managed the installation of tons of reinforced concrete slabs around the hotel and surrounding buildings. He closed two streets leading to the hotel. We didn't ask for permission. There was no government to ask. If you needed something you just did it. Other security companies took this anarchic freedom to murderous extremes, gunning down Iraqis who looked threatening.

We had no choice but to build the wall. Our first bureau had just been bombed. That bureau was in a small hotel called the Aike. It had no security infrastructure and was on a busy street corner. You could park a car right in front of it. I didn't worry much about that at first. Now, after five years in Iraq, alarm bells would ring in my head. Now I scrutinize building locations, vulnerabilities, entries, exits, and fire escapes, even when I visit relatives in the States. In restaurants at home I find myself scanning the room and sitting in the corner so I can watch the door. In Baghdad, we always back our cars into parking spaces, nose pointed out, so we can make a fast exit. We never stay too close to cars in traffic in front of us, always making sure we can see their tires, in case we need to escape. You never want to be blocked in. I catch myself doing the same when visiting my family in New York. It's hard to wind down from Iraq.

The bomb that destroyed our first bureau was hidden in a backpack behind a generator. It blew a hole in the wall and killed a cleaner from Somalia, crushing his head. Although it has become all too common for militant groups to target journalists in Iraq, I don't think we were attacked in 2003 because we were a news agency. We were bombed because of a stupid, baseless rumor.

A then little-known upstart Shiite cleric named Moqtada al-Sadr had distributed a pamphlet warning that Jews were buying up real estate in Baghdad. The leaflet, dropped on street corners and pasted to buildings, said Jews had set up headquarters in the Aike hotel. We were those Jews. Within days, the rumor was all over town. The Jews of Iraq were back and taking over.

After Saddam's government fell, there was an explosion of free press in Iraq. The Coalition Provisional Authority of U.S. administrator Paul Bremer bragged that while there were only a handful of state-controlled newspapers under Saddam, more than two hundred were in circulation just months after he was removed from power. There was press freedom, but also the freedom to print the lunacies that had been allowed to fester under Iraq's tyrannical regime, which, unfortunately, are also still common across much of the Middle East.

One of these new newspapers ran this cartoon on its front cover after Sadr and his new Mahdi Army started spreading rumors that the war was really a pretext for an invasion by Jewish settlers. I kept it because it was so comedic and disturbing.

There had been about 150,000 Jews in Iraq, but the vast majority of them left in the 1950s after a series of anti-Semitic attacks and the public execution of eleven Jews in Baghdad. After the 2003 invasion, there were only twenty-seven Jews remaining in Iraq and these last few were leaving the country, according to Emad Levi, the only rabbi still in Baghdad.

When I met Levi in his modest home in Baghdad's Betaween district, he was studying Hebrew for the first time. "Under Saddam Hussein, if you want to be safe, you must not know anything," he told me over coffee. "If someone asked you anything, you said, 'I don't know.'" It was self-defense through ignorance, real and feigned.

Levi was now frantically learning basic Hebrew phrases, numbers, and the names of colors because he wanted to move to Israel and find a wife. With fewer than thirty Jews in Iraq, and many of them septuagenarian women, the pickings were slim.

Levi said Jews in Iraq weren't directly persecuted under Saddam. They were just watched. Once Saddam's regime ended, however, they lost all official protection and fell victim to the crazed anti-Semitism that plagues Iraq and much of the Middle East. It was no longer safe. While it is tragic when any community is forced to leave its homeland—and Jews have been in Iraq for millennia—I have no doubt the Jews would've been killed if they stayed in Iraq while Moqtada al-Sadr and hundreds of other sectarian madmen, both Shiite and Sunni, ruled the streets and enforced their own brand of Islamic law.

I love the Middle East and have lived here for a dozen years. But I still cringe whenever I ride in taxis or sit in coffee shops and the subject of Jews comes up. The points are always the same:

- Jews are out to rule the world as they admitted in the *Protocols of the Elders of Zion.*
- Reporters are all spies, and work for the Mosad or the CIA.
- America has the power to fix all the world's problems but deliberately does not because it wants to keep Arabs and Muslims down to help Israel.

In cartoons in Egyptian newspapers Jews are often depicted with fangs and horns. I have been told several times that Jews deliberately brought AIDS to the Middle East. One of my favorite Jewish plots is that Jews exported bubble gum secretly laced with aphrodisiacs to rural areas in Egypt to corrupt women's morals and tear the fabric of traditional Muslim society. Egyptian police had discovered a group of young men and women having an orgy. Egyptians were shocked and outraged. It was a national scandal. The girls' families blamed Jews and their tainted chewing gum, and everyone felt better and moved on.

I have heard so many ridiculous theories, but only in Baghdad have I seen this worldview so extreme and armed. It's what blew up our first bureau. After that, we moved into the Hamra and made it into a fort; back then, it was a fun place to live.

When we returned from Camp Falcon, there was a Christmas party under way in the Chinese restaurant in the hotel lobby. My mother had sent by FedEx a honey-baked ham, rhubarb and apple pies, and baked Brie, a tradition she's kept every year. After NBC spent tens of thousands of dollars to fortify the Hamra, the hotel attracted dozens of freelance journalists, photographers, documentary filmmakers, human rights activists, and a few young American and Lebanese businessmen fishing for opportunities.

After security, the Hamra's other main attraction was its pool, the cleanest in Baghdad. Diplomats from the Australian embassy across the street would come by every day to enjoy a few beers on the pool deck. Spanish music played in speakers mounted on the walls. It was common to see foreign women in bikinis swimming laps. We played water polo at night. One reporter went Rollerblading in the neighborhood around the hotel, Karadah, a middle-class Shiite district of two-story cement homes, open fruit and vegetable markets, ice cream parlors, and family-owned grocery stores. Some journalists went jogging every morning. Five years later, we were living in such a different reality in the Hamra that I could hardly remember what it was like in the early days. About a year after we arrived, the leg of a suicide bomber would be floating in the pool, and all but a handful of reporters and human rights activists would be gone, or dead.

For years I've been talking about the Hamra, but still nobody believes we live there. As the war dragged into its second year, White House officials, American military commanders, and conservative pundits—particularly on the Fox television networks—began a campaign to criticize journalists for not going out in Iraq and reporting "good news." They said we were bunkered down in the Green Zone, the four-square-mile cluster of Saddam's former palaces and villas reserved for his politburo, reporting negative secondhand stories. The "real" story was out there, we just weren't looking hard enough to find it. The U.S. Army's 3rd Infantry Division captured the Green Zone in April 2003 and established it as the main, fortified American headquarters in downtown Baghdad. The military calls anything outside the Green Zone's wire the Red Zone. Most reporters have never lived in the Green Zone. We live in the Red Zone, but the myth has stuck. The spin has been powerful.

THE SHIITES RISE

3

A group of journalists decided to host a New Year's Eve 2004 party at the Nabil restaurant in Arasat, Baghdad's chicest neighborhood, full of cafés, boutiques selling knockoff Italian designer suits in garish greens and blues, and the bravest liquor store owner in the Middle East. During the 2003 American bombing raids, Miha moved his prized cases of Johnnie Walker, Stolichnaya, and Efes beer to his apartment around the corner from his shop so he could stay open for stressed-out reporters like me. I have found that no matter how war-torn a country becomes, liquor, Marlboros, prostitutes, guns, and pornography are never in short supply.

When I traveled in and out of Somalia for three months in 1999 to cover refugees from the civil war, there was no government—looters had even ripped down the phone lines to sell the wire—but there was a thriving black-market liquor trade. There were three cell phone providers, half a dozen currencies all claiming to be the official tender, but no police force, running water, or schools. It was easier to buy scotch than bread. An AK-47 cost $75. Prostitutes cost $5. Even in Yemen's lawless Marib province, where local tribesmen and Islamic hard-liners are so heavily armed I had to in-

terrupt my breakfast of eggs and stewed tomatoes to move a fellow
diner's AK-47 that was jabbing into my side—there were grenades
and rocket launchers on the table as if they were salt and pepper
shakers—it was easy to find Johnnie Walker Black Label. Black
Label is not even that good; it's just war fuel. I couldn't go to dinner
that New Year's Eve in Baghdad. I was busy filing from the bureau.
But I ended up at Nabil's anyway.

When the car bomb exploded, it destroyed about half of the restaurant. I saw overturned tables, a crater about six feet deep full of
water from broken pipes, downed power lines, smoking debris, and
cubes of chicken on the floor. A group of reporters from the *Los
Angeles Times* had been on the opposite side of the restaurant.
Shrapnel hit the newspaper's Mexico City bureau chief, Chris
Kraul, in the face, blinding his right eye. Eight others at the Nabil
restaurant lost their lives that night.

We no longer go to restaurants at all in Baghdad. It's not worth
it. They were never very good anyway, full of flies and hummus that
would be better used between bricks. I can understand why Saddam fined his chefs.

Over the years, there have been so many attacks like the one at
Nabil's that they have blended together into a hazy collage of blood
and screams. In five years in Iraq I have heard explosions or
gunfire almost every day. The sounds embed in your brain. You
can't shake them out. Sometimes I still hear them when I close
my eyes.

Baghdad is exceptionally quiet at night. Since it is often too dangerous to go out, there are no cars on the roads, no honking of
horns, no drunks leaving bars. No motorcycles. No ambulances. No
buses or subways. No street noise at all. Most Iraqis have bought
small generators to supplement rationed electricity. Their hum and
sputters are a constant noise in the city. But by 2007 gas had become so expensive, more than $2 a gallon, compared to around
$0.10 under Saddam, that most Iraqis could no longer afford to run

generators for long, so they're silent at night too. To fight the heat, Iraqis sleep on thin mats on the flat roofs of their homes, even though many have been killed and injured there by falling mortars and stray bullets.

Baghdad comes alive for a few minutes just before dawn when a chorus of muezzins summon the faithful with their hauntingly beautiful *fajr* calls to prayer. Their voices bounce off the cement buildings and seem to roll through the city. But sometimes, when the melodic songs go quiet, I am assaulted by memories of Baghdad's new music, the whooshing of outgoing mortars, the rat-a-tat-tat of assault rifles, the crashes of car bombs, and the buzzing of low-flying Black Hawks. I can pick them out like instruments in a terrible orchestra.

Military-grade high explosive in artillery shells and mortars emits shock waves that travel faster than the speed of sound and detonate with a sharp crash like breaking glass. They seem to splash when they explode. Car and truck bombs made of propane tanks or homemade bombs explode with a low, sucking thud. AK-47s yatter with a rhythmic pitter-patter, like a roll on a snare drum. Gatling guns mounted on American AC-130 Spectre gunships fire bullets so quickly you can't make out the individual shots, but hear only a loud grinding, as if an upstairs neighbor were dragging a heavy bed across a wooden floor. The AC-130 is essentially a C-130 Hercules cargo plane loaded with guns and 105mm howitzers that can be independently targeted and fired. A single AC-130 can suppress an entire battlefield and provide close air support to help extract troops or destroy tanks.

I listened to an AC-130 circle over the Hamra for an hour one night, firing rockets and a Gatling gun into a field that militants in the Dora neighborhood to the south had been using to launch mortars into the Green Zone. Anyone on that field of date palms would have been torn to pieces. Nothing would have been left of them. It was part of what the army called Operation Iron Hammer. It didn't work.

Oddly, I miss this orchestra of war, muezzins, and imposed silence when I am out of Iraq. I sleep well in Baghdad. It could be the stress, the heat, the dust, the feeling of always being on call, on the ready. But mostly, it just sounds like home.

I have a running joke with NBC's Middle East producer, Madeleine Haeringer. I am sure she is tired of it by now. Whenever there's a particularly big explosion or intense burst of gunfire near our bureau—sometimes two or three times a day—I turn to her and ask, "Do you hear that? That's the sound of freedom!" We laugh, but it is tragic. By 2007, anyone with $500 in his pocket was trying to escape the country.

Zohair always says the situation in Baghdad is *taabana*, Arabic for tired. "Baghdad is a little tired these days," he says, as if the city caught the flu. "There is only one hour of electricity a day, and the gas lines are long again, and there were twenty unidentified bodies found last week."

Zohair says Baghdad is tired. I'd say Baghdad is exhausted. I don't know how Zohair stays sane.

When I look back at the first few months of 2004, however, I don't remember the violence. I mainly think of it as the time when America's goal of bringing secular democracy to Iraq veered wildly off track. To a large degree it was the Shiite clerics who brought down the naive dream. They had their own plans for Iraq that the United States inadvertently supported and that are now dragging the region further into conflict.

In January 2007, Chris Matthews, the irascible, fast-talking host of MSNBC's *Hardball*, bluntly asked one of our correspondents on air: "So when did we become Shiites? We are Shiites now, right? When did this happen?" Chris was discussing the emergence of what Jordan's King Abdullah called the "Shiite Crescent," a growing Shiite power base stretching from Iran to Lebanon. Vali Nasr, author of *The Shia Revival*, one of the most important books on the Middle East after the U.S. invasion of Iraq, describes the rising power of Shiites in Iran, Iraq, and Lebanon as the most significant shift in the region in decades. It is certainly the biggest change I have seen since I moved here with a few thousand dollars in 1996, and is the most fundamental and dangerous shift in the Middle East since the 2003 invasion of Iraq.

So when did Americans become Shiites? The answer is January 2004.

NAJAF
JANUARY 13, 2004

If there is one word people need to know to understand what happened in Iraq after the fall of Saddam Hussein, it is howza. The howza is technically a network of Shiite religious seminaries. They are schools where scholars teach, study, and write religious doctrine and issue edicts, or fatwas. But the howza is much more than a fatwa academy; it is the real government in Iraq, and the United States brought it to power.

The howza in Iraq is based in Najaf, the spiritual center of the roughly 150 million Shiites around the world. Although Shiites are the majority in Iraq, they are only 10 to 15 percent of the overall Muslim population of more than one billion. But the Shiites' holy land is Iraq.

Najaf al-Ashraf, or Najaf the Most Holy, as it is known in Iraq, is built around the imposing and exquisite golden-domed, blue-tiled Markad Imam Ali, the shrine-tomb of Ali Ibn Abi Talib, the Prophet Mohammed's cousin, son-in-law, and eventual successor. I am often asked about the difference between the words "Shiite" and "Shia." They are basically synonymous. Shia is Arabic for Shiite. It is common, however, to use Shia as an adjective to describe the followers of the religion, the Shiites. There is a similar distinction between the words "Muslim" and "Islam." Muslims are the people. Islam is the religion. Ali is the patriarch of Shia Islam, the father of all Shiites. His tomb is under the domed Imam Ali shrine in Najaf, one hundred miles south of Baghdad.

When the Prophet Mohammed, an illiterate grain trader from Mecca raised by his uncle, died at the peak of his power in A.D. 632, he had no sons. His death left Islam and its new empire, the caliphate, with a strategic and ecumenical question: Who could lead the empire and replace a man chosen by God to deliver His final message, the Koran? Not surprisingly, the question was never answered to everyone's satisfaction.

As Mohammed's closest male relative and the husband of his youngest and favorite daughter, Fatma, Ali was an early contender to be the first caliph, or successor. Mohammed is said to have considered his young cousin Ali to be the son he never had. Ali was also one of the first converts to Islam, although some Sunnis say that since he was only ten years old at the time, his conversion doesn't carry much weight. Ali, they say, was just doing what he was told, unlike an adult who would have to change his religious convictions. Shiites stress Mohammed's affection for Ali, and quote him as having said, "I am the city of knowledge, and Ali is its gate."

But Ali lost the first power struggle after Mohammed's death. Instead, another early convert, Abu Bakr, the father of one of Mohammed's wives, Aisha, was chosen. But Ali would soon have his chance to be caliph, rising in a bloody coup. In 656, a group of rebellious Egyptian soldiers murdered the third caliph, Uthman, and installed Ali in his place. Shiites say Ali had nothing to do with the murder and initially refused to accept the position. But eventually he did, and early Shiites who supported Ali's initial succession finally had their way. But the outrage and demand for justice for Uthman's murder would escalate the battle for control of Islam.

Ali ruled the caliphate from the Iraqi city of Kufa near Najaf. Kufa, now just a suburb of modern Najaf, was a major city at the time in the Furat al-Awsat, or Euphrates River valley. Najaf was a nearby town of fairly minor significance. Ali had moved to Kufa because of Iraq's wealth, and to quell a rebellion led by Mohammed's widow Aisha. She was leading an army in Basra in southern Iraq determined to avenge Uthman and destroy Ali and the rebels who had brought him to power. But she wasn't Ali's only enemy. The governor of Syria, Mu'awiyya, one of Uthman's relatives, was also determined to unseat the new caliph. Ali now faced threats from both the north and the south.

In the end, however, Ali was murdered by a group originally from within his own camp, the Kharijites, religious radicals who believed Islam's new leaders had become more interested in power than in implementing God's will. In 661, a Kharijite assassin, Abd al-Rahman bin Muljam, slashed Ali with a poisoned sword while he was praying at a mosque in Kufa. Mu'awiyya quickly seized the caliphate and founded Islam's first royal dynasty, the Umayyads, based in Damascus. The early Sunnis were off and running.

Ali was buried in Najaf. His followers—the Shiat Ali, or partisans of Ali, later simplified to Shiites—never forgave the crime. They still believe that Muslims who would later be collectively known as Sunnis stole Islam's sacred leadership from the Prophet Mohammed's family. Najaf and Kufa today remain holy Shiite cities. It is the highest honor for Shiites to be buried like Ali in Najaf, in the city's sprawling Valley of Peace cemetery.

Shiites value this connection to Mohammed through his "perfect" family. Shiite friends of mine in Iraq call themselves members of the Ahl al-Kisa, or the "family of the cloak." Muslim texts say Mohammed once gathered his closest relatives: his daughter Fatma, her husband, Ali, and their sons Hassan and Hussein, and covered them under a single cloak. It was a sign of affection, and of his desire to protect and purify them.

> *"Allah only desires to take away any uncleanliness from you,*
> *O people of the household [Ahl al-Bayt], and purify you."*
> (KORAN, AYAT AL-TATHIR)

But the split between Sunnis and Shiites was still not complete after Ali's murder.

Ali's son Hussein tried to avenge his father and reclaim power for what Shiites collectively call Ahl al-Bayt, the Prophet's household. In 680, Hussein raised a small army and confronted Mu'awiyya's forces, now controlled by his son, the second Umayyad caliph, Yazid. Hussein's troops met Yazid's army on the dry plains of the Iraqi city of Karbala, forty-five miles northwest of Najaf. The ensuing battle set the tone for the emerging Shiite religion.

Yazid's troops besieged Hussein's band of seventy-two now legendary fighters. Shiite tradition says Hussein and his men were
surrounded, outmanned, and slaughtered after a valiant fight.
Yazid's soldiers then beheaded Hussein and carried his head to Damascus. The massacre at Karbala was too much for the early Shiites to bear. Sunnis had massacred Mohammed's close relatives.
There could be no reconciliation.

Every year in Karbala, Shiites commemorate Hussein's massacre during Ashura. The ceremonies are the most powerful and
emotive outpouring of grief, religious zeal, and passion I have ever
seen. During Ashura, hundreds of thousands of Shiites march to
Karbala, flailing their backs with bundles of chains called *zangeel*.
The worshippers cry and beat their chests while chanting, *"Ya Hussein! Ya Hussein!"* Oh Hussein! Oh Hussein! Some of the *zangeel*
are barbed to cut the men's backs. Other worshippers bow their
heads as an elder slices their scalp with a quick tap of sword. The
devotees let the blood run down their faces and onto their white
robes, offering clear proof that they are reliving the pain of their
martyr and hero, Hussein.

But the lamentations for Hussein are not merely religious.
They are how many Shiites see their return to power in Iraq after
the U.S. invasion. For Iraqi Shiites, their ascension to power has
been not just a political victory, but a moment of religious ecstasy,
the completion of Hussein's mission, which Americans troops unwittingly helped fulfill.

During a break in a meeting between American, Iraqi, and Iranian
diplomats in Baghdad in March 2007, I was sitting in a smoke-
filled waiting room in the Foreign Ministry watching al-Iraqiya,
the official television station of the U.S.-sponsored, democratically
elected Shiite-led government. It was the final day of Ashura and as
many as two million Shiite pilgrims were gathered in Karbala. The
television images showed the mourning rituals and a reenactment
of Hussein's battle. An actor in the passion play was dressed as
Hussein, complete with a sword, a flowing headdress, and a cape.

He was single-handedly fighting off the tyrant Yazid's troops until he was overwhelmed and heroically slain.

But the TV footage didn't stop there. The images from Karbala were intercut with current news footage of the aftermath of car bombings in Baghdad, wounded Iraqi women and children, and the destroyed Shiite al-Askari mosque in Samara, attacked by al-Qaeda militants in February 2006. The state-sponsored message was clear: the attacks on markets, Shiite mosques, restaurants, and university campuses, mostly carried out by Sunni radicals, are a continuation of the battle centuries ago between Sunni tyrants and Hussein.

As pilgrims carrying black and green flags marched by our Baghdad bureau on their way to Karbala I could hear them chant: *"Kul yom Ashura! Kul ard Karbala!"* or "Every day is Ashura! All land is Karbala!" Simply put, they were saying, every day and everywhere Shiites in Iraq are reliving Hussein's quest to reclaim Islam from the Sunnis. There was no talk of democracy, the Baath party, Saddam Hussein, the U.S. troop surge, or other subjects that dominated the coverage of Iraq in the United States. It seemed that many of Iraq's Shiites believed they were fighting a different war from the one most Americans believe we are engaged in in Iraq, and for different reasons.

On trips back to the States, I am often asked, "How is the war going in Iraq?" It is a deceptively difficult question to answer because there is no war in Iraq, but many wars, some centuries old, playing out on this ancient land. But this is not what we are most often led to believe. The common perception portrayed by both the White House and the Iraqi government, which is therefore commonly reflected in the media, is that the violence in Iraq is a fundamental struggle between two opposing teams: the Freedom Lovers and the Freedom Haters.

In this Manichaean, simplistic, and I believe deliberately misleading view of the war, the situation is as follows:

The Freedom Lovers: the twelve million Iraqis who plunged their fingers into purple ink on Election Day in December

2005 and chose freedom, democracy, and to definitively close the door on Saddam Hussein's dictatorship.

Team captains: the Iraqi government, the White House, the U.S.-trained Iraq security services, and the roughly 150,000 American troops in Iraq.

The Freedom Haters: Iraqi radicals, foreign jihadists, former Baath party members, and criminals supported by al-Qaeda, Syria, and Iran. They have formed an alliance of convenience to reject the democratization of Iraq. They don't want democracy to flourish in the Middle East because free people will choose to reject their backwardness and repression.

Team captains: al-Qaeda in Iraq and other Sunni militant groups, Iranian and Syrian agents, and, but not always, radical Shiite cleric Moqtada al-Sadr's Mahdi Army.

There are elements of truth to this narrative, but it is not why Shiites and Sunnis think they are fighting in Iraq. It is merely why the U.S. administration and Iraqi government say we are fighting in Iraq, and it is a fantasy. It's why I joke with Madeleine about "the sounds of freedom" outside our bureau. Four years into the war, if you asked most Iraqis if they believed they had been "liberated," you'd be met with a blank stare implying, "Are you crazy?" They were more frightened by the chaos than they were of Saddam. A year later, if you asked Iraqis the same question, they were more optimistic, but still nearly all of them wanted to leave the country.

The White House perpetuated the myth because it never wanted to admit the scale of the problem to the troops or the American people. The Iraqi government did not want to admit that it had no control over its own country. To admit there's a civil war is to declare failure. To claim there's only a terrorism problem implies there is a legitimate government fighting scattered outlaws.

Iraq has long been facing much more than just a terrorism

problem. A few bad apples are not ruining things for everyone. American officials and military commanders often stress that most Iraqis want only to raise their children in peace and would love to develop the economy and move on from their horrific past. The officials are correct, but the reality is there are large armed Sunni and Shiite factions fighting for power.

But I am not asked about the war as much when I go home now, and the people who do ask don't seem to really care. They know it's bad and don't want to hear about it. They ask, and then look behind me at a TV screen or rack of magazines. I used to launch into deep discussions about Shiites, Sunnis, and Kurds. I would draw maps on cocktail napkins to illustrate the shifting power plays, much to the amusement of NBC News anchor Brian Williams, who has kept a few of my scribbles. Now when most people in the States ask about the war, I simply say, "We are in over our heads. We started a war we were not qualified to deal with." We are in the middle of an ancient power struggle.

Sunnis believe that Shiites have long been rebels, heretics, and idol worshippers. Al-Qaeda in Iraq calls them the *rafida*, or refuters, because they refuse to accept what Sunnis consider the basic tenets of Islam and the historic progression of power through the caliphs. Sunnis are strict iconoclasts and forbid graven images.

Hard-line Sunnis believe creating images of Mohammed or God is punishable by death. Just ask the Danes. In September 2005, Denmark's largest newspaper, *Jyllands-Posten*, printed twelve insulting anti-Muslim cartoons, including one depicting Mohammed as a suicide bomber.

In January and February 2006, newspapers across Europe reprinted the cartoons. The editor of the daily Italian newspaper *La Stampa*, which also ran the drawings, told me he was sick of feeling bullied by Muslim radicals and was making a stance for freedom of expression. They knew they were picking a fight and wanted it.

The Swedish newspaper *Expressen* editorialized: "Defending freedom of expression against fundamentalist threats is a cause. It is a matter of principle, whether it involves [Salman] Rushdie's

Satanic Verses, a film about veils and the oppression of women or some clumsy drawings in a Danish newspaper."

The Danish newspaper that originally printed the cartoon received bomb threats. Danish embassies and cultural centers were ransacked and burned in Pakistan, Gaza, and Lebanon. Danish flags were torched in Cairo. Saudi Arabia and Libya pulled their ambassadors from Denmark. Danish goods were boycotted across the Middle East.

I was used to anti-American demonstrations. I was slapped around by an angry mob in Cairo during a protest against President Bill Clinton's little-remembered four-day war on Iraq, Operation Desert Fox. Those American air strikes were designed to punish Saddam for not cooperating with U.N. weapons inspectors and to "degrade" Iraq's ability to produce weapons of mass destruction. But why riot because of a cartoon? It seemed out of proportion.

But the uproar over the Danish cartoon pales when compared to the disdain radical Sunnis have for Shiites, an enemy of infidels from within. While Sunnis have no tolerance for graven images, it is common for Shiites to decorate their homes, cars, and shops with portraits of Ali and Hussein. The romantic images of the two men look almost identical, with thick lips, sensitive almond-shaped eyes, and black hair and beard.

For Shiites, Ali and Hussein are revered as saints. For Sunnis, even Mohammed was a mortal chosen by God to deliver His message. Sunnis consider the rituals in Karbala to be beyond sacrilege; they are blasphemous.

In an attempt to "wipe away" the Shiite heresy, in 2006 al-Qaeda in Iraq destroyed the al-Askari mosque in Samara, associated with the Shiite savior, Mohammed al-Mahdi, the Hidden Imam.

Shiites believe the Mahdi disappeared in the late ninth century, hidden by God, and will eventually return to usher in a new era of justice and salvation. By destroying the shrine in Samara, al-Qaeda was trying to say, "There is no Mahdi and he will not come, at least not on our watch." Al-Qaeda also wants to blow up the Imam Ali shrine in Najaf and Imam Hussein mosque in Karbala, built atop the site where Hussein fell in battle. If they succeed, we should prepare for sectarian violence the likes of which the Middle East has never seen. Shiites would turn on Americans. Militants would try to overrun American bases. I envision reporters being airlifted off hotel rooftops.

Najaf has always fascinated me. It is my favorite city in Iraq, and is by far its most international. It is also seductively attractive. Modern Baghdad is undeniably ugly, with hundreds of squat, boxy, socialist-style apartment buildings. Najaf's narrow streets and covered markets have the look and feel of an ancient Arab medina. The area around the Imam Ali shrine is packed with Persians, Afghans, money-changers, dragomen, and inns for pilgrims from across the Shiite world. Boys with wooden carts ferry the elderly and infirm to the holy shrine, surrounded by dozens of tiny shops and kiosks overflowing with books and DVDs of sermons in a dozen languages. Many of the kiosks hang speakers outside and play entrancing *lutumiya*, songs praising God, Ali, and Hussein set to the rhythmic beating of fists on chests and leather drums.

When I walked the streets of Najaf in January 2004, it felt as if I were exploring a sacred forbidden city. As I walked past the Imam Ali shrine carrying a tripod over my shoulder, I thought it might be one of my last trips to the city. No one was hostile, but I did not feel welcome. No one smiled or waved at me. I was met with cold stares. I felt like an infidel visiting a holy place. I wouldn't be surprised if one day Shiites declare Najaf off-limits to non-Muslims, as the holy cities of Mecca and Medina in Saudi Arabia are today.

I had driven from Baghdad to Najaf with Zohair, and we had linked up with a howza student named Sheikh Hassan al-Jarrah. The thirty-two-year-old junior cleric with a light beard and black robe had agreed to be our guide to the howza.

Sheikh Hassan wore a white turban, indicating he was not a descendant of the Prophet Mohammed's bloodline. Mohammed's descendants are called sayids and have the honor of wearing a black turban. There is a glass ceiling in Shiite Islam. The most senior Shiite leaders, including Iraq's Grand Ayatollah Ali al-Sistani, Iran's late Ayatollah Ruhollah Khomeini, and Hezbollah's Hassan Nasrallah, are all sayids. The news media often call the Hezbollah leader "Sheikh Nasrallah." It is incorrect. He is Sayid Nasrallah. By no coincidence, Iraq's first elected prime minister after the U.S. invasion, Ibrahim al-Jaafari, was a sayid.

Sheikh Hassan was studying Islamic jurisprudence at a howza led by Hojat al Islam Riad Mohammed Sayid al-Hakim, one of the leading clerics in Najaf and an ally of Sistani.

Each of the senior clerics in Najaf has his own howza. The cleric plays the role of grand master, setting the tone and the message that students learn, some more political than others. There are rivalries among the howzas as each competes for status, students, and funds. The more senior and popular a cleric becomes, the more students join his howza. It's a self-perpetuating process because the more students enroll in a particular howza, the more money the cleric's howza has to pay for charitable projects like health clinics and libraries, attracting even more followers.

There is no Sunni equivalent to the howza. Sunnis believe everyone has the ability to read the Koran and forge a direct relationship with God. The role of Sunni sheikhs is to help Muslims understand Islam for themselves. The former religious advisor to the late Egyptian president Anwar Sadat, Sheikh Mohammed Mutwali Shaarawi, remains after his death one of the Sunni world's most beloved clerics and televangelists.

Shaarawi was immensely charismatic. He had an avuncular, disarming look with a small, scrunched face and big ears. Shaarawi would sit cross-legged and rock back and forth while energetically explaining the Koran in simple language that every mechanic, butcher, and carpenter could understand. He would often break into a huge smile. Although Shaarawi died at eighty-seven in 1998, he remains an Egyptian and Sunni icon.

Umm Kulthum is Egypt's most famous singer, the matriarch of

modern Arab orchestra music. It is impossible to ride in a taxi in Cairo for half an hour and not hear one of her stately, poetic songs about love, religion, or patriotism.

"In the East, a day without Umm Kulthum would have no color."
(OMAR SHARIF)

Umm Kulthum is to Egypt what Edith Piaf represents to France, a national voice. Umm Kulthum's funeral in 1975 was said to have been bigger than the state burial of Egypt's hero of pan-Arabism, President Gamal Abdel Nasser.

It is equally impossible to ride in a taxi in Cairo and not hear one of Sheikh Shaarawi's sermons. After his death, Egyptian television ran a biography on his life, *The Imam of the Imams*, that was so fawning it embarrassed his children. A million people packed the streets for Shaarawi's funeral.

A few months before his death, I interviewed Shaarawi in his palatial villa on the desert road between Cairo and Alexandria. He told me, "The Koran is like the manual to a car. You want the car to work, just read the manual. When you need to fix a spark plug in a car, what do you do?" he asked me. Shaarawi was a master of the rhetorical.

"You read the manual?" I suggested.

"Exactly!" he said. "Allah's manual is the Koran!"

It was that simple. Shaarawi said he'd given up reading any books except the Koran. Sunni fundamentalist groups say the Koran is also the constitution.

Shiites take a more mystical approach and believe that only through immense study can the inner meanings of the Koran be understood, and that members of the Prophet's family, sayids, are especially attuned to understanding the message God handed down to one of their own. Ayatollahs are sometimes described as Shiite popes. They certainly have a hierarchy unrivaled by Sunnis, and a system to pay for it.

In addition to zakat, which is charity all Muslims must give to the poor, Shiites also pay khums, a direct contribution to the clergy, a howza tax. "Khums" comes from the Arabic word for one-fifth, and some Shiites contribute a fifth of the increase of their savings per lunar year to the howza. The howza dispenses the money to the poor, orphans, pilgrims, and its schools and social centers. The howza also administers the donations by pilgrims to the holy shrines. When Najaf opened after the fall of Saddam Hussein, tens of thousands of Iranian pilgrims started arriving, bringing with them millions of dollars. Saddam both banned Iranian pilgrims and allowed only the state to collect Islamic donations. Now the howza was collecting money directly.

In Najaf, Sheikh Hassan wanted to show off the city's revival and what the howza was doing with its restored power and wealth. "There were only a few hundred howza students under Saddam," he said. "Now there are already five or six thousand. The number is growing by the day."

Sheikh Hassan took us to his howza's main study hall in a five-story building on a tiny street crisscrossed with power lines. The building didn't look like a school. I didn't see any classrooms, desks, or blackboards. Instead, there were many small rooms where groups of five or six young men sat on carpets on the floor, quietly reading and discussing Islamic texts.

Howza students are peer taught. Senior students mentor younger ones. Once your peers have nothing else to teach you, you rise to the next level. The top clerics are the ones who can find no one more senior to teach them. "The howza in Najaf is now resuming its rightful place," Sheikh Hassan told me. "It will soon be bigger than the howza in Qom."

Hassan was bragging. He claimed that Qom, Iran's spiritual center ninety miles south of Tehran, had flourished only because Saddam repressed the howza in Najaf. In his interpretation, Qom had filled a void like a stand-in actor who had taken center stage only because the star was ill. Now Najaf was healthy again, and had begun to reclaim its leadership.

For centuries, Najaf has been closely tied to Iran and a destination for Iranian Shiite pilgrims. Although Najaf and Qom vie for dominance of the Shiite world much in the same way Rome and Constantinople competed for the leadership of early Christendom after the collapse of the Roman Empire, the two cities are cut from the same cloth. Iraqis, and Najafis in particular, do not want to be dominated by Iran or the clerics from Qom, but believe they are part of the same extended Shiite family persecuted by Sunnis.

The American media often lump Iraqi and Iranian Shiites together. While co-religionists, Iranians and Iraqi Shiites are not a unified bloc. Najafis believe they are the true standard-bearers of Shiites and should be leading Iran. And Iraqis, who are Arabs, accuse Iranians, who are ethnic Persians, of racism and arrogance. Most Iraqis, including most Shiites, are deeply suspicious of Iran and do not want to live in an Iranian-style theocracy.

The links between the Iranian and Iraqi howzas, and therefore the governments, are much deeper. This is what the United States wasn't counting on. American analysts, before the war, saw that Iraqi Shiites fought and killed fellow Shiites in Iran during the Iran-Iraq War in the 1980s. They chose to be Iraqi nationalists first, Shiites second. The United States assumed they would do the same after the invasion. But the war elevated and empowered the howza, which dates back to before the modern borders of Iraq and Iran. The howza is not Iraqi or even Iranian first and Shiite second. The howza is Shiite first and Shiite second.

For years I have been talking about the influence of the howza with the foreign editor of the *Nightly News*, Mary Laurence "ML" Flynn, the most dedicated editor I know in the news business, the woman I talk to nearly as much as my mother, who calls me every day. ML and I discuss ayatollah politics, the ups and downs of the clerics in Najaf. Sometimes when I get a little too swept away by Shiites, sayids, and their fatwas, ML in her typical brusqueness says, "Richard, I think this is all a little too inside-the-turban for us."

The expression has always made me laugh because it is similar to the reference to incestuous "inside-the-beltway" politics in Washington. If the maxim is true that all politics are local, the power plays within the howza are the local politics of Iraq. The rivalry between Najaf and Qom is real, but both are "inside-the-turban." America is now "inside-the-turban" too, like it or not.

Although Saddam was a Sunni, he repressed the howza mainly for political reasons. He did not want the clerics in Najaf to rival his power. Saddam's secular, pan-Arab Baath party was the only political party, the only source of authority. His crackdown on the howza, and Shiites in general, dramatically increased during Iraq's pointless war with Iran. Najaf's clerics were no longer just potential rivals, but possible collaborators with the enemy. Many of the howza's old guard, the Najaf elite, hail from Iran. The most senior cleric of all, Ali al-Sistani, was born in Iran and speaks Arabic with a Persian accent.

Sheikh Hassan showed me the apartment where Ayatollah Khomeni lived in Najaf before returning to Iran to topple the pro-Western Shah and lead the 1979 Islamic Revolution. He also took me to an exceptionally beautiful library packed with ancient tomes and parchments, and a communal study center full of men reading under ceiling fans.

Then Sheikh Hassan's cell phone rang. We had to rush off. Our appointment had come through to meet Hojat al Islam Riad Mohammed Sayid al-Hakim, son of a leading ayatollah, in the howza's equivalent of the dean's office.

But the cleric wasn't ready to meet me, so Sheikh Hassan gave me a tour of the howza's administration headquarters: howza central command. It was buzzing with activity. It didn't seem like a university, but more like a community center responsible for all matters of local government. It even had its own court, which was in session. I saw two families gathered in a room. There were no smiles. There had been a murder. The families of the accused and the victim had turned to the howza to find a solution and avoid a blood feud. They were in deep conversation and drinking lots of coffee. I didn't stay long.

I was most surprised, however, by the howza's computer room.

There were ten young men inside sitting in front of desktop termi-
nals connected to the Internet. The computer room operated
twenty-four hours a day, receiving e-mails in Arabic, Farsi, and English from around the world. The job of those in the computer room
was to reply to the e-mails, dispersing Sistani's rulings on topics
ranging from chess (forbidden) to masturbation (permissible if
done by your wife) to copyright laws (burning pirated DVDs is not
allowed). The Americans had freed Najaf from Saddam's repression. The Internet opened the howza to the world.

After about an hour, Hojat al Islam Riad al-Hakim was ready to
meet me, and I was led into a great hall that looked like a mosque.
Several dozen men in their sixties and seventies, some with long
white beards, sat against the walls. I took off my shoes and was
seated next to the cleric.

You don't just reach out and shake a hojat al Islam's hand,
pumping it as if he'd just sold you a used car. You raise your hand to
chin level, and then slowly put it over your heart while offering a
small bow. When you sit, always slowly, it is important never to
show the soles of your feet, which is considered offensive. The
proper way is to sit cross-legged, or—in a position that takes some
practice—with your knees together and both feet tucked under one
side.

Once we were settled, I sat for two full minutes in silence. The
cleric begins the conversation when he feels ready.

"We appreciate what the Americans have done," he eventually told me, breaking the silence. Although I don't work for the
government, I don't think he was able to see me as anything other
than an American. As far as I know, I was the first American he
had ever met. Hojat al Islam Riad chose his words carefully. Everything he says can be considered religious doctrine, every phrase
a fatwa.

"We could not have removed the tyrant Saddam Hussein alone.
Now we do not want to repeat the mistakes of the past," he said.

It was a simple statement, but it encapsulated the entire Shiite
vision for postwar Iraq. The hojat al Islam was referring to "past

mistakes" that had excluded Shiites from power in Iraq for nearly a century.

Iraqi Shiites were active in the 1920 revolt against British troops in Mesopotamia. In 1920, the Shiite Ayatollah Mohammed al-Shirazi issued a fatwa from Karbala declaring that working for the British was a sin. Shiites began to stage protests and demand elections for an independent government.

In June, the British civil commissioner, Arnold Wilson, agreed to elections for a "constituent assembly," but made the unpopular choice of Sunni Muslim, ex-Ottoman bureaucrats to organize the voting process. The Shiites continued to mount growing demonstrations, and by the end of June fighting broke out.

British political leaders at the time, including the desert explorer and Arabist Gertrude Bell, blamed Shiites for the revolt. British forces later handed power to the Sunni King Feisal, a friend and protégé of the talented British intelligence officer T. E. Lawrence, "Lawrence of Arabia," made famous by American journalist Lowell Thomas, who chronicled, and somewhat embellished, the 1916 "Revolt in the Desert" against Ottoman forces in the Arabian Peninsula.

Britain owed a favor to Feisal's family, the Hashimites, for their role in the 1916 Arab revolt in the Hijaz. Feisal and his descendants ruled Iraq for nearly four decades until the monarchy was deposed by a military coup in 1968 that eventually led Saddam Hussein to power.

I sat with Hojat al Islam Riad for about an hour. Most of our conversation focused on the meaning and significance of "democracy." It was the new buzzword in Najaf. "We fully support democracy," he told me. "But it should be real democracy, with every person, every Iraqi having a vote." He was outlining the vision set by Ayatollah Ali al-Sistani, the most powerful man in Iraq.

But Sistani's power is subtle and indirect. The grand ayatollah is almost never seen. There is only one official image of Sistani. In it, he has an almost expressionless gaze, like the Renaissance icons of Christ on the cross staring blankly at heaven. Sistani was the wizard behind the curtain, the opposite of Shaarawi, who was smiling on TV every week, explaining the simple life lessons of the Koran. Sistani speaks only through emissaries and is nearly impossible to meet, surrounded by layers of howza. But in 2004 Sistani was mobilizing his influence, as powerful, present, and invisible as the wind, against U.S. plans.

Paul Bremer, the counterterrorism expert turned American proconsul in Iraq, was advocating elections by caucuses to try to ensure that Shiites wouldn't sweep the vote and exclude Sunni and Kurdish minorities, which was exactly what would happen. The Bremer plan also envisioned a committee of Iraqi experts writing Iraq's new constitution with the assistance of Western academics and legal experts.

Sistani demanded direct elections by July 2004. It meant every Iraqi man and woman over eighteen would have an equally weighted vote. After the polls, elected Iraqi officials would write the constitution. Sistani was operating on the assumption that elections would bring Shiites to power and that Shiites would then write the constitution. He was correct.

On January 19, 2004, up to 100,000 of Sistani's supporters marched in Baghdad, chanting, "Real democracy means real elections."

I saw one sign that said, "Whither the hand that signs the constitution."

Sistani also turned the howza's infrastructure into a "democracy machine."

When I returned to Baghdad, I visited the Markad Sayid Idris, a husseiniya (in Arabic, Shiite mosques are called the "places of Hussein") near our bureau. The husseiniya had been transformed into a political headquarters. In a garage in a back room, a printing press was running off hundreds of posters of Sistani, along with copies of his fatwa calling for direct elections. Sistani first issued the fatwa

in June 2003, amid rumors, which turned out to be true, that
Bremer planned to choose a group of advisors to write the constitution and then hold elections. Sistani insisted it must be the other
way around. By November 2003, Sistani's fatwa was the Shiites'
rallying cry.

The "democratic" fatwa of Ayatollah Ali al-Sistani:

> *In the Name of the Almighty*
>
> *Those [occupation] forces have no jurisdiction whatsoever to
> appoint members of the constitution preparation assembly. Also
> there is no guarantee that this assembly will prepare a constitu-
> tion that either serves the best interests of the Iraqi people or ex-
> presses their national identity, whose backbone is sound Islamic
> religion and noble social values. The said plan is unacceptable
> from the outset. First of all there must be a general election so
> that every Iraqi citizen who is eligible to vote can choose some-
> one to represent him in a foundational constitution preparation
> assembly. Then the drafted constitution can be put to a referen-
> dum. All believers must insist on the accomplishment of this cru-
> cial matter and contribute to achieving it in the best way
> possible.*
>
> *May Allah the Blessed Almighty guide everyone to that which
> is good and beneficial.*
>
> *Signed and Sealed*
> *26 June 2003*
> *Ali al-Hussaini al-Sistani*

The local imam at the Sayid Idris husseiniya, Sayid Leith
al-Haideri, held weekly town meetings to explain the meaning of
democracy to his congregation. His job was to make sure Sistani's
fatwa was understood and implemented.

While Sistani was very clear about how elections and the drafting of the constitution should work, he never outlined his vision for
what democracy should ultimately bring to Iraq. The furthest he

would go was to say he opposed implementing a strict theocracy modeled on the Velayat-e Faqih, "the Guardianship of Clerics," implemented by Khomeini in Iran.

Sistani's calculations were more basic about overall Shiite empowerment. The details, he said, would be worked out later. His logic was straightforward: The United States brought elections to Iraq. Elections would bring Shiites to power. The Shiites would bring howza. Howza would set the moral and political baseline for Iraq. The howza would rule from the sidelines.

But clerics like Haideri, who unlike Sistani was in direct contact with his followers, had more specific ideas for the kind of state he wanted. "We must have free elections. Otherwise, it will be just as bad as Saddam's dictatorship," he told me. "Of course, our goal is to have an Islamic state."

It wasn't the only ominous sign of the Shiites' plans for the future. In Najaf I had passed two huge banners reading "The People of Najaf Demand Democracy!" and "Justice for the Baathists!"

Ali was the last Shiite ruler in Iraq. His son Hussein had tried to reclaim power, but was massacred, beginning a reign of repression Shiites believe continued through Saddam Hussein. Shiites were determined not to fail again 1,300 years later. Iraqi Sunnis were starting to realize their days were numbered, and that the Americans had unwittingly become Shiites.

4

BAGHDAD, GREEN ZONE CONVENTION CENTER

The American embassy in Baghdad summoned reporters to the convention center in the Green Zone for what was supposed to be the first of many historic moments.

The Iraqi Governing Council, an assembly of politicians U.S. officials handpicked to represent Iraqis even though most of them hadn't lived in Iraq for decades, had finally accepted and approved a temporary constitution. Many of the Governing Council members were the same Iraqi opposition leaders that American and British intelligence agencies had paid to supply ultimately incorrect information about Saddam's weapons of mass destruction programs and cheerlead the downfall of his regime. Most Iraqis had never heard of them. But today they were "heroes" because they had agreed to a temporary constitution that U.S. officials believed everyone could recognize as tangible progress in Iraq.

It wasn't the final draft of Iraq's new democracy, but it was a blueprint for how elections would take place and how the constitution would be written. The document also included an impressive bill of rights, abolishing "torture in all its forms, physical or mental," establishing "the right to a fair, speedy, and open trial," and declaring, "No one may be detained by reason of political or religious beliefs."

"The only thing I care about is the bill of rights. I am very proud of it," the respected elder statesman and Governing Council member Adnan al-Pachachi told me at his Baghdad villa the day before the signing ceremony. Pachachi, a Sunni and a former Iraqi foreign minister and ambassador to the United Nations before the 1968 Baathist coup, was seen by many Iraqis as a decent, secular moderate. He also had the advantage of looking like a president, with an avuncular face, hound-dog jowls, and brilliant silver hair. He looked like the Iraqi George Washington that U.S. officials were desperately trying to create. But at eighty-one, Pachachi wasn't up to countering the sharp elbows of his political rivals. He seemed to know it, and for two hours over tea he waxed on about the bill of rights. "If it can pass, at least it will be something concrete," he said.

But already guns, not laws, were starting to rule Baghdad. The bill of rights was meaningless even on the day it was to be signed.

As I was waiting at a checkpoint outside the convention center in the Green Zone, I watched an American soldier almost shoot dead an Iraqi man standing next to me. I was lined up with other reporters and Iraqi guests between two rows of concertina wire at Checkpoint 3. We were waiting for three American soldiers to call us forward to be inspected and patted down for bombs.

The Iraqi man was in his forties and wearing a white dishdasha, the flowing pajama robe common in rural areas of the Middle East. He broke out of the line and started walking to the American troops.

"Stop right there," a soldier yelled at him.

But the man didn't stop. He kept advancing toward the soldiers.

"Get your hand out of your pocket!" the soldier yelled, louder, more emphatically.

The man's right hand was tucked into the pocket of his dishdasha.

The soldier raised his M4 rifle at the man, who was now about twenty feet from the checkpoint and still advancing.

"Get your fucking hand out of your fucking pocket!" the soldier screamed. I heard the soldier pull and release his rifle's slingshot, loading a round in the chamber. It just takes a light pull with two fingers to draw back the slingshot, and then release it with a snap. Many soldiers cut off the fingertips of their gloves to get a better grip on the slingshot and the trigger. The soldier was now locked, loaded, and about to fire.

"Wait! Wait!" an old Iraqi man yelled in English, waving his arms. He rushed up and grabbed the man in the dishdasha by the shoulders.

"He is deaf!" the old man told the soldiers. The man in the white robe was also missing his right arm. His empty sleeve was fastened to his right pocket with a safety pin. He couldn't have moved it even if he'd heard the soldier yelling at him.

"Tell him he has got to be more careful!" barked the soldier, lowering his M4. "This stupid haji doesn't know how close he was to getting smoked."

"Do you mind if I move forward?" I asked the soldier. I didn't want to surprise him with any sudden moves.

"Yeah, yeah, come up," he instructed me, and gave a quick, annoyed wave.

You never want to rush a checkpoint. We carry American and British flags in our cars, and generally stop about a hundred yards away, put the flags in the front windshield, and wait to be waved forward. American troops at checkpoints nearly always have binoculars and usually see you before you notice them. But they are not always that professional and can be surprised.

A few days after the Iraqi man was almost killed at Checkpoint 3, one of our producers, Gene Choo, was also nearly shot there. Gene, like so many in the news business, is short-tempered, always in a hurry, and always on his cell phone. A soldier was busy talking to an attractive female Iraqi translator in tight jeans and bright makeup and didn't notice Gene until he was up close. The soldier raised his rifle, pulled back the slingshot, and let it fly, chambering a round. Snap! "Get the fuck back!"

"What the hell are you doing? Lower your weapon," Gene told him. Before joining NBC, Gene served several years in the Republic of Korea army, the very serious and very tough ROK.

The soldier took it as an affront, a personal insult to his authority and manhood.

"Back up, man, back up!" he yelled, and flicked off the rifle's safety with his thumb. It would just take a tiny squeeze to fire.

"I think he was trying to impress this female translator," Gene said, and filed complaints all the way up the chain of command. He later received an apologetic call from a commanding officer, saying the soldier had "violated the rules regarding escalation of force. He never should have locked and loaded on you." Iraqis don't get that kind of treatment.

I had to pass through two other checkpoints that morning so our camera gear could be sniffed by dogs and wiped for traces of explosives.

Over the years, I have gone through so many checkpoints and been patted down so many times, the submissive pose has become instinctive. You raise your arms to your sides, turn your back to the soldiers, and let them inspect the collar of your shirt; pat your back, sides, and chest; finger your belt line; and finally run their hands down the sides of your legs.

As I was standing at a checkpoint, arms akimbo, Tom Brokaw looked at me and said, "Richard, it's the pose of the post-9/11 generation." At airports and shopping malls, Americans were now getting used to it. In the prison-like Green Zone, it's the daily ritual, the Green Zone massage.

Many of the Iraqi politicians were already in the convention center when I arrived. They were smiling, shaking hands, and congratulating one another. Most of the twenty-one men and three women on the Governing Council were in their fifties and looked like typical Arab bureaucrats with dark oversized suits. The men had thick black mustaches and greased-down hair. The women's faces were caked with brown foundation makeup and blue eye shadow. A few of the men were fingering prayer beads. Others jingled keys and cigarette lighters in their pockets.

This was the group Bremer had chosen to rule Iraq until Iraqis elected their own leaders. They were mainly figureheads, the Iraqi face of the U.S. Coalition Provisional Authority. Bremer and Lieutenant General Rick Sanchez, the overall U.S. military commander, ran the country. Bremer even gave weekly TV addresses to the Iraqi people, his version of President Franklin D. Roosevelt's fireside chats. The speeches, most of them sermons about the virtues of democracy and the need to build a society free from tyranny, were simultaneously translated into Arabic. My Iraqi friends called it *televisyoun bremeriya*, Bremer TV.

Zohair, who is not easily offended, and never lived a day in a free society, found it patronizing. "Doesn't Bremer realize that we are the oldest culture in the world?" he asked me as we were watching Bremer TV in my office in the Hamra. I was surprised because Zohair liked Bremer. He didn't mind living under a foreign ruler. It was better, he thought, than empowering an Iraqi Shiite or Sunni with an agenda, scores to settle, and money to steal.

In Egypt, a man told me why he supported President Hosni Mubarak, even though he considered him to be like a pharaoh on his throne for decades, and surrounded by corrupt cronies. "He's been president so long, he's no longer *gaann* [Arabic for hungry]. He has eaten all that he needs, and is fat and full. If a new president is elected, he'll be hungry too at first and will have to eat. It is better to have someone who has eaten his fill."

For Zohair, a self-hating Shiite whose personal philosophy is a unique blend of Karl Marx and Islamic fatalism, the logic was similar. Bremer wasn't *gaann* and didn't have a religious agenda. Zohair had no confidence in his countrymen. His suspicions were understandable.

In early 1983, as the Iran-Iraq War was chewing through the armies on both sides, Zohair was summoned for military service. He had no interest in fighting Iran or anybody else. Zohair's mother was of Iranian descent, *tabaiya Iraniya*, and when the war started, Saddam's regime had nationalized her family's villas in Baghdad. The national theft gave Zohair even less incentive to fight in a war between Saddam and Ayatollah Khomeini. Zohair nonetheless reported for duty at a base near Baghdad, signed his name on a military roster. Afterward, Zohair stayed at home and hoped he'd be lost in the shuffle. There were evidently many Iraqis doing exactly the same thing.

In the same year, Saddam issued one of the most infamous declarations of his presidency, "The Day of Warning." He appeared on state television with a stern, clear message. Any soldier who did not report for duty within twenty-four hours would be sentenced to death and executed.

Zohair still wasn't interested in fighting. Khomeini's army wasn't as well equipped as Saddam's troops, but Khomeini was compensating for inferior technology with what Iran had in abundance, religious fervor. Khomeini, and the clergy ruling the Iranian military, had begun dispatching thousands of Koran-carrying zealots to rush and overrun Iraqi military positions in human wave attacks. Thousands were slaughtered on each side.

After Saddam's televised warning, Zohair decided to run. He hid in his uncle's factory in an industrial zone on the outskirts of Baghdad. But the secret security forces came looking for him.

"At two A.M. I saw several cars pull up outside the factory," he told me. "I could see their headlights outside a window. I had closed all the windows except for one up high by the ceiling. If I climbed up a ladder, I could see out of it, and no one could see in. But I panicked when I saw the cars pull up. I opened the window and climbed on the roof."

I had known Zohair for more than a year before he told me his story. I'd never asked, but one night over a bottle of scotch it finally came out. I thought it was impolite to ask our Iraqi staff about their pasts. Everyone had a dark history in Iraq. Everyone worked for the regime and informed on their neighbors. I didn't want to embarrass them by asking about it.

"I ran across the roof of the factory, but it was so dark and I tripped and fell hard on my knee. I fell right on a steel rod sticking out of the cement." Zohair pulled up his pant leg and showed me a triangle-shaped scar about two inches below his knee. "I think I broke my leg, but I was so scared I kept running. I climbed off the roof and kept running, limping down the road. I saw a neighbor and he stopped me.

" 'What are you doing running in the night?' my neighbor asked. Then he called over the secret police."

Zohair's uncle's neighbor and friend had turned him in. It was to be expected. The Iraqi security forces regularly used collective punishment to enforce the many laws. If your neighbor had a satellite dish (banned under Saddam), you were responsible if you didn't inform on him, and you would be similarly punished with five years in prison.

The secret police arrested Zohair and loaded him onto a bus to a military prison near Basra in southern Iraq.

"I was put in a jail cell on the base with forty other people. We weren't given any food or water for days, and then just a stale *samoun*," he said, referring to the white diamond-shaped loaves of pita bread popular across Iraq.

"After about a week, I don't know how long, maybe it was a month, I don't know, I was told I'd been sentenced to death. The officer said I needed to wait for the signed death sentence to arrive from Baghdad."

Zohair stayed another month in the cell, waiting for the execution orders to arrive. Then came the morning Zohair was supposed to die.

"They loaded us all on four buses. There were about a hundred of us, all sentenced to death. There were no trials, no judges, and.

no lawyers. No one even talked to us. The buses drove to Basra's main soccer stadium."

"They were going to do the executions there, in public?" I asked.

"Yes, in public. They had even arranged for families to line the road the bus was taking to the soccer stadium. They were insulting us as we drove by and throwing rotten fruit and garbage at the bus."

Zohair was getting more excited as he told the story. He poured himself another glass of Grant's whiskey with a splash of water.

"In the stadium there were poles in the ground," Zohair said, and stood up. "They were about this high," he said, raising his hand about five and a half feet from the floor. "They were thin wooden poles."

"How many were there?"

"About fifteen. They brought us out in batches of fifteen and tied our hands behind our backs around the poles like this." Zohair put his hands behind his back to show me how he was bound.

"There was a table behind the firing squad where three officers sat. There was a Russian phone on the table, the kind you wind up to make a call. The phone was there in case a senior officer called to call off the executions."

"So they tied all fifteen men to the poles at once? How many gunmen were there? How big was the firing squad?"

"There were forty-five gunmen."

"Forty-five?" I gasped. It seemed like a lot. I'd envisioned fifteen, one for each condemned man.

"Yes, there were forty-five, three for each man. One was lying on his stomach and would shoot from the legs down. Another was kneeling and would aim from the waist to the neck. The last gunman was standing and shot at the head. They each fired three shots."

"So each person was shot nine times?"

"Yes, nine times, and then the commanding officer would go up to each of the men with a pistol and shoot him in the head. They called that the *talkit al-rahma*, the mercy shot. Then your family was sent a bill for the bullets."

"And you watched this?"

"Yes, we had to watch. I watched two groups shot dead. Many of them were people I had met in my cell. I was in the third group."

Zohair and I both had another drink.

"After they were shot, a doctor would declare them dead. He would go up and put his hand in front of their mouths to see if they were breathing. He didn't bother to check them all.

"After the bodies were taken away, they brought me out to a pole and tied my hands behind my back. Then they took two pieces of tape, wrote my name on them, and stuck one to my leg, and the other on my shirt." Zohair tapped his right breast to show me where the tape was put.

"They put our names on the tape so they could identify the bodies. I couldn't even walk as they marched me to the pole. My legs were solid. I couldn't walk. Other people, you know, went to the bathroom in their pants." Zohair didn't like to curse. I could picture Zohair tied to a pole, standing in muddy pools of warm blood, the air thick with the smell of piss, blood, shit, and gunpowder. I have seen several videos of Saddam-era executions. Like the Nazis, Saddam's forces kept detailed records of almost everything they did, and videotaped many executions. The executions were not formal, or somber, or even especially well organized. There was no military precision. The executioners would talk and joke among themselves as they stood behind the firing squad. In one video, I could hear the executioners talking about what they would have for lunch. It was routine.

"They put a blindfold across my eyes and I waited. I couldn't think," Zohair said.

Then the phone rang.

"The commanding officer yelled 'Stop!' just as the gunmen were about to fire.

"Three of the people in my group were Shiites from Najaf. A cleric from the howza had asked for their pardon. Saddam had agreed. The commander in charge of the executions wanted to make sure he didn't accidentally kill the wrong people and pardoned the whole group, including me. Everyone in the third group was pardoned.

"They untied me and brought over the next group. I was pulling the tape off my leg when they were shot."

"They just let you go?"

"No, they brought me back to the cell and kept me for about another month. I had to wait until a written pardon came from Baghdad. The whole time I worried they would change their minds." I imagined Zohair's anxiety waiting in the cell, not sure if he would be sent back to the firing squad. When I am depressed or lonely in Baghdad, worried about a story, or frustrated because ML has just torn through a *Nightly News* script I have written and made a dozen changes, I often feel guilty. "Why should I worry about petty problems?" I ask myself. I have no right.

I looked at Zohair, sitting in a chair in front of a bucket of ice and an ashtray full of twisted-out cigarettes. We were both getting drunk. I was humbled by his ability to cope.

"So did they finally bring the letter?" I asked.

"Yes, an officer came in my cell and called my name, 'Zohair Shaaban al-Beyati!'

" 'Yes, sir,' I said.

" 'How do you feel today?' he asked.

" 'I don't know, sir.'

" 'Orders for your pardon have come. You will not be executed. How does that make you feel?'

" 'I don't know, sir,' I said. 'When can I go?' "

We both laughed.

" 'You can collect your clothing and leave now.'

"I didn't even go to the room where they stored our clothing. I just ran to the main road and kept running. I think I ran for four or five miles until I found a car. I asked the driver to take me all the way from Basra to Baghdad. I didn't care how much it cost.

"When I got home, my mother was sick. She had cancer. I think it was because she was so nervous. She died a short while later."

The experience armed Zohair for the anarchy of Baghdad after the American invasion. "I don't trust anybody," Zohair always tells me. "Don't I love you like a brother? Don't even trust me," he says. It worries me. "How can I live without any trust?" I wonder. I have become much more guarded over the years in Baghdad, but nothing like Zohair. He doesn't tell his family where he goes or where he's been. He gives false names to every person he meets. He changes his route to work every day. He's swapped his car every year so it doesn't get noticed.

Zohair certainly didn't trust the new Iraqi politicians, the members of the Governing Council. Most Iraqis I know agreed with him. I don't know why American officials put so much stock in the group. I think Bremer, under pressure from Washington, was so desperate to find "founding fathers" to complete the myth of democratic nation building in Iraq that he picked the wrong people, sharp operators who knew how to tell Americans what they wanted to hear. The first time I interviewed Ayad Allawi, a former spy who looked exactly like Tony Soprano and who would soon be tapped by the Americans to be interim prime minister, he sounded more like President Bush than Bush himself.

"The terrorists of 9/11 are the same terrorists we face here," he said. "We thank the American people for their sacrifices and know that Iraq is the front line in the war against terrorism. We are building a democracy here that will be the model for the Middle East."

Allawi and the other Governing Council members had experience lying to Americans from their days in opposition parties headquartered in Washington, London, Tehran, and Damascus. After the U.S. invasion, they'd all scrambled back to Baghdad, itching for power. Many had also worked for American, British, Syrian, Iranian, and even Saddam's intelligence and security agencies. The Governing Council was an odd collection of businessmen, con artists, mullahs, and warlords linked by a common avarice, ambition, and opportunism. Most also shared a hatred for Saddam and a belief that the Bush administration was the best tool to get them into power.

The men included:

Ahmed Chalabi (U.S. intelligence asset and accused con man wanted for arrest in Jordan for bank fraud)

Ayad Allawi (former British and American intelligence asset and a onetime Baath party member nearly assassinated by Saddam's henchmen)

Abdul Aziz al-Hakim (leader of the Badr Brigade, an armed branch of the Iranian Revolutionary Guards)

Ibrahim al-Jaafari (leader of the Dawa party, which pioneered the modern use of suicide bombings, dispatching militants to attack the Iraqi embassy in Beirut in 1981, killing thirty, and the American and French embassies in Kuwait City in 1983, killing six)

Masoud Barzani (Kurdish rebel leader)

Moufaq al-Rubaie (Shiite historian)

I didn't trust most of them individually. Together, I wouldn't have left my wallet unguarded in the same room with them.

Zohair described the Governing Council dismissively as "the men who came to Iraq riding American tanks." Ahmed Chalabi, who did actually accompany American forces on the march from Kuwait, would later claim he'd personally liberated Baghdad.

But today, assembled in the Green Zone, these men were America's champions of democracy, and the U.S. embassy had called in the press to make sure we got it all on tape.

It was supposed to be a mini-1777, when the American Second Continental Congress drafted the Articles of Confederation, the precursor to the U.S. Constitution. The convention center was decked out in full patriotic regalia. I watched a chorus on a stage lined with Iraqi flags warm up, singing "Moutni," "My Country," the Iraqi equivalent of "America the Beautiful." I walked over to a dark wood Victorian writing desk in the middle of the convention center's rotunda. On the desktop, twenty-five fountain pens were neatly arranged in a semicircle. These were the pens the Governing Council members were about to use to ratify the temporary constitution. The desk had once belonged to the first Iraqi king, Feisal I.

There were American troops in the building too, but in disguise. Soldiers and marines from the military's always optimistic, usually uninformed public relations department, the Combined Press Information Center (CPIC), were busily setting up microphones, running speaker cables, and adjusting the flags. But the troops were all wearing civilian clothing, jeans, khakis, and button-down shirts, so the TV cameras wouldn't show American soldiers in the room as Iraqis signed their first major legal document after the fall of Saddam Hussein.

But there was a big problem. Not everyone was there. Five Shiite politicians had left Baghdad unannounced to seek guidance from Iraq's real capital, Najaf. They wanted Sistani's approval before moving ahead.

As spelled out in his fatwa, Sistani opposed any document drawn up by U.S.-appointed Iraqi politicians. He wanted elections first, for Shiites to win them, and for the elected government to write the constitution. Bremer had repeatedly tried to visit Sistani, but the ayatollah refused. Sistani didn't want to be associated with the American occupiers, or to be strong-armed into accepting the American plan. But on February 12, 2004, U.N. envoy Lakhdar Brahimi, a respected fellow Muslim with a reputation as a negotiator, traveled to Najaf and convinced Sistani to allow the political process to go forward before holding elections. Brahimi explained that Iraq needed a law to define how Iraq's transition to democracy would take place. Sistani gave in, but wouldn't budge on his principle that only elected officials could write the constitution.

However, now that the time had come to actually sign the framework document, the Shiite politicians were balking. They traveled to Najaf to double-check they weren't contradicting the howza's wishes.

What the Americans and the Governing Council eventually devised to meet Sistani's criteria was an incredibly convoluted, drawn-out political road map, calling for several elections, each one having more significance. When NBC producers first arrived in Baghdad, I had to sit them down for at least an hour to try to explain the process. The perception in the United States was that Iraqis simply had one vote, dipped their fingers in purple ink, and chose their new leaders: democracy accomplished. The reality is that there were two elections and a referendum held over the course of a year. Looking back, I think the process took far too long and helped create the political vacuum that pushed the country to civil war. There were simply too many elections. If Iraqis had voted and elected a government quickly, 2004 might not have been the turning point in the war, the year the violence really started.

This was the complicated, multi-step process that American and Iraqi officials eventually came up with to meet Sistani's strategy for Shiite empowerment:

STEP ONE: THE INTERIM GOVERNMENT

The Iraqi Governing Council in March 2004 would approve a temporary constitution, a blueprint for the political process.

American officials, after "extensive deliberations and consultations with cross-sections of the Iraqi people . . . and possibly in consultation with the United Nations," would choose an interim prime minister by June 2004. The interim prime minister's primary goal was to organize elections for an Iraqi parliament by December 2004.

STEP TWO: THE TRANSITIONAL GOVERNMENT

After nationwide elections in December 2004, the Iraqi parliament would convene and form a transitional government.

The transitional government's main objective would be to write the constitution. Once written, the constitution would be subject to a national referendum, a yes-or-no vote, by October 2005.

STEP THREE: THE CONSTITUTIONAL REFERENDUM

If the constitution passed the October 2005 referendum, Iraqis would advance to the next stage: final elections. If Iraqis rejected the constitution, there'd be new elections and the process would start over again.

STEP FOUR: FINAL ELECTIONS

Based on the constitution approved by the referendum, elections would be held for a fully sovereign parliament by December 2005. The elected government would serve a four-year term.

The process was not self-evident even for me, an American born and raised in a democracy. Iraqis had never voted in a free election before. Now they were supposed to have two elections and a referendum and write a binding constitution in twelve months.

After three days of consultations in Najaf, Iraq's Shiite leaders did eventually sign the temporary constitution, but refused to call it a constitution. Instead, they gave it the toothless name the Transitional Administrative Law, the TAL to acronym-loving American officials. It didn't sound binding. It didn't sound permanent like a constitution. The Shiites could live with it. It was just a temporary document to keep the Americans happy and allow the Shiites to start their slow march to power.

The failure to sign the TAL on the first try was a major embarrassment for the embassy in Baghdad. Reporters had been called in to record "the march of democracy." Instead, we filed stories about the Shiites' shuttle diplomacy in Najaf and their refusal to sign.

Bremer's smart, young, skinny American spokesman, Dan Senor, who later became a paid analyst for Fox News, said the setback and backroom negotiations were all part of a normal, healthy debate. "Democracy is messy," Senor said. "If you want neat and tidy, there's dictatorship."

Iraq was much more than "messy," and was just weeks away from a major outbreak in violence that would change the course of the war and how reporters covered it.

5

April 2004 was the turning point in the war. It happened fast. Before April 2004, reporters and Western contractors could move throughout Iraq almost at will. We had to be careful, but we could work and we found Iraqis excited to tell us their stories of oppression, often literally hiking up their shirts to show purple scars from where they'd been tortured in Saddam's gulags. After April, we were hunted down like prey in this country of excesses: heat in the summer like blasts from a furnace; cold and damp in the winter, when fine gray mud clumps like cement to your boots; suffocating in the spring when clouds of orange dust choke the air swarmed with biting black flies.

Even the caliphs reserved a unique contempt for their fabled city's unforgiving climate. An Abbasid court poet wrote:

> Baqirda and Bazabda for summer or for spring
> At Baqirda and Bazabda the sweet, cool fountains
>   sing
> And Baghdad, what is Bahgdad? Its dust
> Is shit, and its heat is appalling.

The change in April 2004 was abrupt. There was simply life in Iraq before April, and life after April. The time of exploration was over. The time for killing and torture and savagery had begun.

Obviously, there was some violence before the spring of 2004, but the tension had mostly been building under the surface like a volcano. In April, it erupted. Oddly, the explosion was triggered by what seemed to me to be the most trivial of provocations. American officials in Baghdad closed an Iraqi newspaper that regularly published incitement, rumors, and blatant lies. It was somewhat ironic because U.S. officials had long been bragging about the new free press they brought to Iraq. The closure was the spark the radical upstart cleric Moqtada al-Sadr was waiting to use to start his play for power.

The chubby, baby-faced Sadr, whose movement initially published the leaflets branding our first bureau "a nest of Jewish settlers," had graduated to newspapers. One of his papers, not surprisingly named *The Howza*, printed especially aggressive anti-American and anti-Sunni rhetoric.

At thirty years old, Moqtada al-Sadr was something of a brat in the Najaf hierarchy. His father, Mohammed Sadiq al-Sadr, assassinated by Saddam in 1999, had been profoundly respected, especially after he defied Saddam and ordered Shiites to pray in husseiniyas. Saddam had wanted Shiites to worship at home. He didn't want them congregating during the war with Iran, when they could be susceptible to Ayatollah Khomeini's calls for Shiite solidarity against Saddam's then pro-Western and secular military regime. Moqtada now lived in the shadow of his father's revered turban. Detractors sometimes called Moqtada the video game cleric, Sayid Atari, because fellow howza students claimed he spent more time playing Atari than contemplating religious texts.

U.S. officials were increasingly concerned that Moqtada had become a nuisance and was using the free press they made possible to work against the mission to plant democracy in the Fertile Crescent and spread it like wildflowers across what in January 1962 the *Evening Standard* called "The Simmering Arab World." I have a yellowed copy of the *Standard*'s weekly magazine in my Beirut apartment. The cover shows two Arab men with wizened faces in white dishdashas and egals, the white or red-checkered headscarf with a black band. Wooden-stocked rifles rest casually on their shoulders. Even then, the iconic image of Arabs was of men carrying guns.

The editorial on the back page of the magazine wisely wrote: "There is a saying in the Middle East that a foreign journalist who comes there and stays a week goes home to write a book, in which he presents a pat solution to all the Middle East's problems. If he stays a month, he writes a magazine article filled with 'ifs' and 'buts' and 'on the other hands.' If he stays a year, he writes nothing at all, for the complexities and paradoxes of this explosive area have left him bewildered and confused."

The issue, with a tragically ill-timed feature offering "an inside view of the intricate planning which assures [President] Kennedy's safety on his whirlwind trips," quotes an American official as saying, "If we can just keep [Arabs] from fighting, maybe in a few years, the old hatreds will begin to die down and some sort of stability will come. . . .

"But an old hand in that part of the world is dubious," the editorial continues, "for he remembers the story of the frog and the scorpion. The scorpion, wishing to cross the Nile, begged the frog to ferry him across on his back. The frog refused.

" 'No,' he said. 'When we are mid-stream you will sting me, and I will drown.'

" 'That is illogical,' the scorpion replied. 'If I sting you, we will both drown.'

"So the frog agreed and the scorpion climbed on his back. Halfway across, the scorpion stung him.

" 'I told you so,' screamed the dying frog. 'You've killed us both. What is the logic in that?'

" 'Who thinks of logic?' said the drowning scorpion. 'This is the Middle East.' "

U.S. officials in Baghdad were now trying to decipher the logic of this old Middle Eastern joke. Embassy public affairs experts and military intelligence agents formed a sixty-person team to produce a daily brief they called "The Mosquito." It was a summary of all the rumors, tabloids, and yellow journalism circulating in Iraq, reflecting the buzz on the streets. If there were reports of American soldiers raping women at checkpoints or indiscriminately killing civilians, the Americans wanted to know about it.

"The Mosquito," however, was only part of the information-monitoring campaign. I visited the American embassy's new "war room." It was a long, narrow hallway above the gold-leaf-and-marble-encrusted "green room" in Saddam's former Republican Palace. Four flat-screen televisions hung on a wall. Arabic-speaking translators sat by each television, writing summaries of correspondent reports, anchor introductions, and the analysis of commentators. In another room, more translators combed through Iraqi newspapers, searching for biased or anti-American articles. One of the war room's officials, Rob Tappan, showed me the fruit of all the translating. It was a large checkerboard spreadsheet taped to a wall. He called it "the truth matrix."

One column listed the dates of stories containing allegations against American soldiers and officials. The most common reports claimed American troops desecrated mosques or other Muslim holy sites, massacred Iraqi civilians, or raped women.

When I arrived, the war room had been up and running for only three weeks, but already Tappan's team had identified fifty-seven TV reports it classified as "false, biased, or inflammatory." Forty-six of them had been broadcast on al-Jazeera. Tappan didn't hide his disdain for the Qatar-based twenty-four-hour news channel. "It's costing coalition and American lives, and so that's why we are fighting the networks to make sure that they stick to Western-style journalistic standards," he said.

Al-Jazeera was particularly suspect because it received so many "exclusive" videos from Baath party members and other insurgent groups. Al-Jazeera and other Arab networks had been clearly against the war. Abu Dhabi television even gave the former Iraqi information minister Mohammed Sayid al-Sahaf, dubbed by the American press "Comical Ali" for his uncanny ability to claim victory in the face of overwhelming contrary evidence, his own television show during Ramadan, the most popular time of the year to watch TV as families across the Muslim world gather to break the day's fasting. It's like the Super Bowl every night, and Arab TV networks produce high-budget specials for the holy month.

On the roof of the Palestine hotel at the climax of the 2003 American invasion, Sahaf had told me, "There are no Americans in Baghdad." I was with about a dozen reporters and we could all see American Bradley Fighting Vehicles behind him.

"Are you considering surrender?" ITN reporter Johnny Irvine asked him.

"My opinion is, as usual, that we will slaughter them all. The Americans are so desperate, they are committing suicide on the banks of the Tigris, drowning themselves," Sahaf declared.

A day earlier, Sahaf had said there were "no American soldiers at the airport," even as Fox News reporters embedded with U.S. forces did live broadcasts from Baghdad's runways.

"But what about those vehicles?" I asked, pointing to the Bradleys belching smoke as they patrolled up and down the west bank of the Tigris.

Sahaf leaned in and whispered "a secret" in my ear. "It's a trap," he said, and walked down a staircase off the roof—and into hiding. He was not seen again until he reemerged as a TV star with his own prime-time show, *With Sahaf*.

When I asked al-Jazeera's editor in chief, Ahmed al-Sheikh, about allegations that his network was biased toward the Saddam regime and against American policy, he adamantly denied it. "We are not trying to incite anti-American emotions in the Arab streets. The Arabs already have what incites them," he said.

Over the years I have come to think of al-Jazeera coverage of the Iraq war, always fast and most-often accurate, to be like sports reporting. They don't add much context. They keep score.

"Insurgents killed five American soldiers in Baghdad," al-Jazeera often reports. "American troops bombed a suspected insurgent hideout in Falujah, killing ten people." But al-Jazeera does seem to favor "the underdog," the militants fighting American occupation.

Newspapers in Iraq were by far the worst rumor-mongers. The translators tracking print media reports in the embassy's war room told me they'd identified hundreds of dubious reports in just three weeks. The Bremer administration decided to act, ordering *The Howza*'s offices to be chained shut. Moqtada al-Sadr ordered his gunmen, the Mahdi Army, to the streets.

I drove to Baghdad's Shoala district to see the Mahdi Army's "deployment."

By now we were always traveling in convoys of at least two vehicles, in case one broke down or we needed an extra getaway car. I was in the front vehicle, a white armored Jeep Cherokee, as we pulled into Shoala, a poor Shiite district full of restaurants for truck drivers and construction workers serving shawarma—meat, most often lamb or chicken, cooked on a rotisserie—and rows of shops selling rusted auto parts, sheet metal, hammers, screwdrivers, and drills.

We didn't go far before I saw the Mahdi Army. A boy who looked about twelve years old was standing by two burning tires and blocks of wood piled in the center of the road. The boy was waving a pistol, telling us to stop at this checkpoint that looked more at home in Mogadishu than Baghdad.

We stopped and two men in black T-shirts carrying Kalashnikovs knocked on the Jeep's thick glass window. They looked confused by the deep thud their knuckles made against the bulletproof glass.

They wanted us to roll down the windows.

Bulletproof windows don't roll down.

One of our translator-fixers, Ashraf, opened the Jeep's door and tried to talk his way through. It was a mistake.

Another five or six gunmen gathered around the open door, poking their heads inside, peering in the car with an excited curiosity, as if there were naked women in the backseat. They made me get out of the car, but seemed more interested in the two-inch-thick, reinforced glass in the doors. One of the gunmen kept tapping the glass and kicking the tires like a prospective buyer.

"What kind of car is this?" he asked.

"It is a jeeb she-ROU-ki," I said.

"It's good," he said, nodding approvingly.

"Yes. It is."

"Who are you?"

"We are journalists."

"Let me see your *bataka*?"

I showed him my NBC press card. It was in English and he couldn't understand it. Ashraf, twenty, a smart, fast-talking fan of jeans, cigarettes, and cell phones, was busy negotiating our passage with another gunman.

"Richard," he told me, "they want to put one of their men in the car with us and take us inside the neighborhood."

Then we heard gunfire, loud bursts of AK fire. It was close, popping.

"Let's go," one of our "security consultants" ordered. NBC had hired a British company called Centurions Risk Assessment Services to be our chaperones. Their job was to make sure we were not in situations like this one.

The gunfire scattered the militiamen. They were holding their rifles at their chests, ready to fire. They were hopelessly disorganized and haphazardly pointed their guns at one another, and at us. If one had fired, we would have all been shot, the gunmen included.

"Richard, it is time to go!" a Centurion yelled.

I climbed back in the car, but a gunman grabbed my arm.

"*Shu?*" I asked him. What?

He was silent, but didn't let go of my arm.

"They are shooting. We are leaving," I said, and pulled my arm from his hand, slamming the Jeep's door shut. Thud.

The boy at the checkpoint had been watching me struggle with the gunman. Maybe it was his father. I don't know. The boy was now pointing his pistol at me through the glass. The bullet wouldn't

have penetrated, but if he'd fired, the shot would surely have excited the other gunmen and triggered what Iraqi soldiers call a
"death blossom," a bubble of intense gunfire at everyone and everything in the area. I stared at the boy and watched him lower his pistol and pull back the burning tires with a stick. We hit the gas and
drove around the barrier and back to our bureau.

The Centurions were angry at Ashraf.

Why did he open the door?

Why hadn't he checked out the neighborhood *before* we went?

How could he be so irresponsible?

They saw their million-dollar contract flash before their eyes.

It was still the early days and we didn't yet know how to work
with the security consultants. When I was in Somalia, I'd hired a car-
load of local gunmen to fend off bandits. A South African bush pilot
who dropped me off in Johar said if I were late, he'd leave me behind.
Bandits would steal his plane if he stayed too long. In Gaza, reporters
coordinated with local militant groups to be under their protection.
In Yemen, I bribed a police officer to be my guide and escort. He was
especially helpful because he had a badge and could pass through
checkpoints unbothered. Sometimes, he was even saluted, which
was a bonus. Before Iraq, I'd never had a professional bodyguard. I
didn't want one here either, but had no choice. It was now NBC policy that we were to travel with "security consultants." ABC, CBS, Fox,
CNN, and later the BBC had all made the same decision.

The consultants' mandate was "to keep us safe." Our job was to
go out and find stories in what were increasingly unsafe areas. We
were by definition at odds and it was unclear who was in charge. I
didn't want to take orders from them, but they had to answer to my
bosses in New York, who told them they should make sure we didn't
take "unnecessary" risks. Who determined what was unnecessary?
We didn't know. The Centurions threatened that if we didn't listen
to them and were injured, we would not be covered by insurance. It
was possible.

The Centurions were nearly all stocky, scarred, nicknamed, tattooed former British Royal Marines. Most had worked in Northern

Ireland, some undercover, and didn't cringe at the sound of gun-fire. The first major dilemma was what to do about weapons. Jour-nalists are supposed to be impartial observers, filing reports from the battlefield. We are supposed to be witnesses. In Baghdad in April, those rules no longer applied. We had become part of the conflict, like it or not. The Centurions believed they couldn't do their job without guns. Their goal was to avoid conflict, but if we were in a gunfight, they argued there wasn't much they could do without at least some firepower to blast their way out.

It was an ethical question for NBC and other news organiza-tions. We had budgets for uplinks, satellite phones, freelance crews, and translators, but not automatic rifles and grenades. NBC also wanted to be in compliance with the local laws, but had to decide how to operate in a country where there were no laws. After many debates at NBC and other news organizations at levels way above my pay grade, the Centurions' argument won out. They would be armed, but discreet. They would not brandish weapons and look like a band of hired mercenaries, but could have guns in our cars, and as the experts on the ground, they would decide when and how to use them. While I initially opposed having bodyguards, the Cen-turions would soon save my life.

Many newspapers never hired security consultants, I think be-cause they were too expensive. A team cost several thousand dollars a day. An armored car cost about $60,000. Instead, print reporters, with the exception of those from a few major, well-financed news-papers like *The New York Times, Los Angeles Times,* and *The Washing-ton Post,* generally decided to travel in unmarked, unarmored cars and rely on stealth. Their hope was that because print reporters move in small teams—often it would be just one reporter with a notebook—they could dart around Baghdad unnoticed. TV news crews, with our bulky cameras and tripods, don't have that option. We are spotted as soon as we start filming. The print reporters' reli-ance on moving below the insurgents' radar works well 99 percent of the time, but when it fails, it collapses completely. They have no last resort.

After our troubles in Shoala, I decided to set up a visit to one of
Sadr's offices in Kazimiya in east Baghdad. Sadr's forces were now
in open revolt across Iraq, overrunning Polish and Ukrainian forces
in the cities of Kut and Karbala.

Kut casts a long shadow over the failed British occupation of Mesopotamia in World War I. In his brilliant two-volume book, *The Long
Road to Baghdad*, Edmund Candler, the official British "eyewitness
in Mesopotamia," accompanied a force sent to rescue British troops
besieged in Kut.

Ottoman soldiers allied with the German kaiser had surrounded the British troops in Kut under the command of Major
General Sir Charles Townshend. Candler, in criticism remarkably
similar to that of the war ninety years later, described the Mesopotamia campaign as "ill considered," "adventurous," and not supported by enough troops. "There was no confidence in the higher
command. Mesopotamia became the grave of reputations," he
wrote.

"It was known that our reinforcements had not yet left France
and any serious opposition, a single stubbornly contested action,
would leave us too weak to hold the city even if we captured
it. . . . But we wanted Baghdad. The city was an irresistible lode-
star . . . and we were British and they were only Turks."

In almost chilling parallels to the Bush administration's oppor-
tunistic war, Candler describes how as soon as British forces pulled
out of Basra, "the place was given over to loot. The custom house
and warehouses were in flames."

I felt a connection with Candler. He witnessed horrors beyond
the modern war in Iraq: World War I trench battles and "hand to
hand fighting with bayonet." The casualties were staggering. "By
nightfall, the enemy were beaten; they evacuated their remaining
trenches in the dark; and they left behind them fourteen guns, 1,153
prisoners and nearly a thousand dead."

Candler watched 1,912 British and Indian conscripts killed in

Hannah. "Men who had last year been wheeling barrows, painting doors, singing in the choir, bringing round the milk, lay there a solid square of dead in the cursed alien mud. I shall never see a man asleep in a field again without thinking of them.

"Nearly every mail brought these sad letters from unhappy women at home. Sometimes they wrote asking for photographs of the graves."

But as Candler's war journal progressed, his sensitivities, like mine, dulled after witnessing too much pointless killing and brutality, and the crazy brave men in uniform dying far from home.

"The dead lie still and peaceful in their narrow graves, each with his dark blanket wound tightly round him like a mummy and his name written on a page of a notebook and fixed to the fold with a pin," Candler wrote.

"There is a baneful beauty in the shrapnel flashes, and one forgets that they are making more dead.

"Life is a gift that is rendered back to the Giver without a thought. Death is no more than a turn at the corner of the road we have been treading blindly."

Candler grew to both hate and love Iraq as it chewed through British forces, and the empire.

"There was malice in the sky and soil; malice of heat and drought; hunger and thirst and flies; damp and cold, fever and ague, flood, hurricane and rain; and malice interwoven in the web of circumstance. Allah was certainly with the Kaiser and Islam."

General Townshend's men couldn't hold out in Kut. On April 28, 1916, after a three-month siege, Townshend destroyed his remaining weapons, raised the white flag, and surrendered his surviving nine thousand men. For the last fourteen days, his troops had been living "on a daily ration of four ounces of flour and a slice of horseflesh or mule." They'd butchered their horses and mules for food. Townshend's holdout was heroic; his surrender was humiliating.

The rescue force Candler accompanied lost 22,000 men trying to relieve Townshend in Kut. They were just a few miles from the

city when Townshend surrendered. He didn't know how close
they'd come.

Townshend was flown to Istanbul as a trophy of the Sublime
Porte. His starving and exhausted men were put on a death march
from Samara to Aleppo in the June heat. Sixty-five percent of them
died in captivity.

Nearly a century later, the Poles and Ukrainians weren't up for
any last-stand battles. One Polish commander told me "our forces
are peacekeepers. They are not here to fight." The Ukrainians had
abandoned their base, surrendering it to the Mahdi Army.

The U.S. military called its war alliance of thirty nations to fight
in Iraq "The Coalition of the Willing." We started calling the group
of nations not known for their military prowess, including Latvia,
Moldova, Kazakhstan, Albania, and Armenia, "The Coalition of the
Unwilling." I called them "The Coalition of the Weak and Strong-
Armed." (We dubbed the security consultants "The Coalition of the
Billing.")

I went with Zohair to Kazimiya. He knew a leading Mahdi Army
commander in the area, Sheikh Raed al-Sabi. We parked our car at
the end of the long pedestrian street leading to the golden-domed
shrine and tomb of Musa al-Kazim, the seventh Shiite imam.

I walked with Zohair; our Iraqi cameraman, Saad Felahi, a tripod slung over his shoulder; and our British security consultant,
Dolly Gray. Dolly was a tough man, but the Centurions all seemed
to have these odd nicknames. We had another consultant called
"Bunny." He was stocky, bald, and tattooed. Dolly was traveling unarmed, or "clean fatigues." Since we were visiting the office with
the Mahdi Army's permission, Dolly, quick with a joke and a knife,
had decided a gun would only raise suspicions and be useless.
There were dozens of gunmen inside when we arrived at Sadr's
east Baghdad headquarters.

Sheikh Raed, in his late forties, sat in a corner room lined with
benches in the two-story building. He had a frayed white turban
and was flanked by five young gunmen in what had become the
Mahdi Army's impromptu uniform, black T-shirts with pictures of

Mohammed Sadiq al-Sadr on the chest. Below the image was written, *"Al-Kital lina aada, wa karamitina min Allah al-Shahada."* "Fighting is our way, and our honor comes from Allah and martyrdom."

Raed took me to a courtyard where fifty men were gathered for afternoon prayers. A cleric stood in front of the crowd. He was leading an impassioned sermon. The fifty men sang back: *"Allah, salli alla Mohammed . . . , Wa ahl Mohammed! Moqtada! Moqtada! Moqtada!"* "God, praise the Prophet Mohammed, and the family of Mohammed! Moqtada! Moqtada! Moqtada!"

The men sang the phrase to recognize and support the cleric's message. It was like Baptist Christians calling out "Hallelujah!" or "Praise the Lord!" during a sermon. But Sadr's men added three cheers of Moqtada's name like football players breaking their huddle.

"Moqtada! Moqtada! Moqtada!"

This cheer would be the last sound Saddam Hussein heard before he was hanged in a prison in Kazimiya by Mahdi Army guards.

"We are in control of holy Kazimiya," Sheikh Raed bragged as he guided me up a narrow set of chipped cement stairs onto the roof, where four snipers were lying on their bellies, guns trained on the street below.

As we walked back to the Jeep, Saad, a Sunni, asked me a question I still cannot answer.

"Are the Americans so smart that they have a plan for Iraq that's so complicated that I don't understand it, or are they so stupid and have no plan at all?"

I told Saad that an American officer complained to me that his prewar battle simulations in 2003—elaborate computer games in which he and other commanders pretended to be the "left hook" and "the tip of the spear"—ended once Iraq was defeated.

Saad refused to believe it, insisting that the United States must have a secret, genius plan to serve its long-term interests in the Middle East. "If America weren't clever, how could it be a great power?" he asked. But great powers have misunderstood Iraq before.

Moqtada al-Sadr was not the only one making a run for power. Sunni militants and al-Qaeda were about to explode onto the scene.

6

"Another reason not to speak about war is that it is so unspeakable."

KURT VONNEGUT

It took a year for most Sunnis to grasp the new reality in Iraq. The Americans had *really* toppled Saddam, and Shiites, long dismissed and derided by Sunnis as cowards, Iranian stooges, and half-Muslim infidels, were *really* making a successful run for power. The Sunnis had lost, and in April 2004 it was just sinking in.

After U.S. tanks stormed into Baghdad, most Sunnis had simply returned to villages in Anbar and Mosul, put on flowing dishdashas, and hoped the bad dream would end. After 1,300 years of state-sponsored privilege and power, Sunnis were now in danger of being marginalized and overrun. Army commanders, intelligence agents, and Baath members—the Sunni elite who lost the most from the war—were the first to awaken from their slumber of denial. By April 2004, they were panicking and had become dangerous.

Many of the senior army officers had looked for their old jobs immediately after the fall of Baghdad. They were shocked when the Americans treated them like criminals and, in a worse blow to Iraqis' overdeveloped sense of pride and masculinity, like peasants.

In the summer and fall of 2003, I saw hundreds of Iraqi army ma-
jors and colonels—the Iraqi army had a bloated officer corps—
lined up, appealing, in Arabic, to nineteen-year-old American
privates and specialists who couldn't understand them. The officers had been told in radio announcements that they would receive
"compensation" for Bremer's crazy decision to dissolve the Iraqi
armed forces.

The officers, mostly men in their upper forties with football
coach potbellies and thick mustaches blackened with dye, were addicted to state privilege and expensive gifts such as houses, cars,
and weekend trips to Saddam's palatial retreats with artificial lakes
stocked with fish. The U.S. military didn't know how to treat them.
The officers needed to be won over, perhaps even coddled, and
made part of the solution. After ancient Romans sacked a city, they
hosted weeks of free drunken festivals. Instead, the efficient American military machine processed the emasculated army commanders like prison inmates, leaving them standing on lines in dusty
fields for hours in the sun without water to wait for handouts
from American kids. I heard one former fighter pilot, the most respected of Iraq's military elite, ask a baffled American soldier, "We
backed the Americans and this is how you treat us?" The officers
were unceremoniously given a few hundred dollars and a message
to buzz off. It was humiliating. It would have been more dignified from an Iraqi perspective to lock the officers in jail. There is
no shame in Iraq for being punished, even unjustly. It can be a
source of pride. Insulting a man's honor and rank, however, demands retribution.

I returned with the pilot, who had been in charge of air force
logistics, to his five-bedroom villa in Mansour in west Baghdad.
The two-story villa, a gift from the state, was freshly painted white,
and we sat in the courtyard sipping black coffee and eating sesame
cookies topped with peanuts. He had pawned his limited-edition
Breitling air force watch for $600 and was now reduced to install-
ing satellite dishes for $30 a week. American officials in Baghdad
were very proud that Iraqis now could watch satellite TVs banned

under Saddam. It was a sign of progress, but not for the pilot. The U.S. Army had given him $300 in hardship pay and told him to go away.

"If they let me reassemble my unit, I could do many things," he pleaded. "We could rebuild the bases that were looted. I could have my unit together in a week, but we have been betrayed."

He was correct. Many officers had decided not to fight the American troops, crossing their cannons so they couldn't be fired, as instructed by tens of thousands of American leaflets dropped during the invasion. They felt the Americans owed them and had broken a promise. Their anger couldn't be contained any longer.

One day after Bremer ordered Sadr's *Howza* newspaper closed for incitement, triggering the first large-scale Shiite revolt since the invasion, Sunni militants in Falujah ambushed and killed four American security contractors from Blackwater USA, the leading American private-security company, which hires former members of the U.S. Special Operations Forces. But they didn't just kill the Americans. The murder at 9:30 in the morning quickly developed into an orgy of savagery, frustration, and mutilation. Crowds pulled the Americans from their SUVs, killed them, dragged their bodies through the streets, and then burned them, and their cars, with gasoline.

Our stringer in Falujah, Dr. Fadl Bedrani, a skinny former reporter for the Iraqi state news agency with a narrow face and a thin, pointed nose, brought us a shaky video from Falujah. On the tape, men and boys were whacking the Americans' charred and broken remains with iron pipes. One body was just a torso missing legs and arms. It looked like the men were clubbing a lump of burned meat. The crowd then hung the shattered bodies on a metal bridge. Passing cars honked their horns to celebrate, the same way Arabs across the region rejoice as brides and grooms drive through the streets in cars decorated with wreaths of flowers.

"Our heroic brothers slaughtered them like sheep!" one witness told Dr. Fadl.

I showed the tape to American soldiers stationed at Baghdad's airport, angering the army press office, which accused me of trying to "provoke the troops."

"I just don't understand," a soldier said. "You know, I just don't understand it. We're here to help these people, and, you know, I think we've got to start somewhere. But I just don't think they get it."

U.S. Marines had recently taken command in Falujah. At the arrival ceremony, I watched the marines unfurl their flags as a band played the Iraqi national anthem and Marine Corps fight songs. The new commander, Lieutenant General James T. Conway, had ambitious plans to win over the people of Falujah with the Marine motto: "No better friend, no worse enemy."

"My goal is to soon have soccer games between the people of Falujah and my marines," General Conway said after the ceremony.

But there would be no soccer games. A week after the lynching of the Blackwater contractors, the Marines launched Operation Vigilant Resolve, one of the biggest offensives since President Bush declared "Mission Accomplished" on an aircraft carrier in May 2003. But by the time the Marines declared war on Falujah, the Sunnis in the city were no longer fighting alone. In the weeks before the murder of the Blackwater contractors, dozens—some claim hundreds—of Sunni volunteers, freelance mujahideen (Arabic for those who pursue Jihad) from Saudi Arabia, Egypt, and Yemen had begun to flow into Iraq's Anbar province.

Anbar is about the size of South Carolina, Sunni, mostly desert, and ruled by tribal sheikhs, the descendants of desert Bedouins who, unlike urbanized Iraqis, still wear traditional white dishdashas and checkered headscarves, and raise camels and horses. They are also expert smugglers, a "profession" they have practiced with open pride for generations. The sheikhs—which in Arabic can refer to Muslim clerics, tribal leaders, or just old men—in western Iraq were the dominant men of large family clans that had long distrusted and resisted central authority. Even Saddam did not attempt to replace the sheikhs' authority in western Iraq, but instead used patronage to buy their loyalty. Saddam allowed the sheikhs to smug-gle guns, alcohol, and oil in exchange for calm. The system worked well. Saddam called Ramadi, the biggest city in Anbar, "the white city" because it never revolted against him.

Before the U.S. invasion, Saddam tried to use his capital with the tribes to fight the Americans. He knew his army was weak and needed all the help he could find. Saddam established a "tribal chiefs military committee" that operated independently from the army, the Fedayeen (a paramilitary force commanded by Saddam's cruel son Uday), and the Republican Guard. It didn't work. The tribes, like good smugglers, never fought the better-armed Americans. They hid and hibernated for a year, hoping the Americans would treat them as Saddam had done and stay out of their affairs.

But the Americans had a mission in Iraq. Saddam demanded only calm and loyalty. The Americans' goal was not only to stabilize Iraq but to actively import democracy, which by definition meant empowering the majority Shiites. The Sunni tribes felt threatened, angered, and most of all perplexed as to why Americans would travel across the world to empower "Shiite infidels." They assumed it must be an Iranian plot, and that America must be stealing oil to pay for this adventure. Why else would America bother? Why else fight a war in the hot desert to empower, in their opinion, Iranian stooges? They assumed the United States couldn't possibly be this stupid and must have another, secret goal, just as our Iraqi cameraman Saad Felahi had asked me. Otherwise how could America be a great power?

As foreign jihadists began arriving in droves in the spring of 2004 with money and promises of revenge and renewed independence, the tribes welcomed them. The army officers, Baath party members, and intelligence agents, bitter at the Americans' betrayal, went beyond that. They joined the foreign jihadists, giving them access to weapons (the officers knew where they'd been hidden after being looted from bases) and military expertise.

Most of the freelance jihadists—mainly young Sunni men determined to protect Muslims after hearing reports and rumors on TV and the Internet that American troops were committing atroci-

ties in Iraq—entered Anbar through Syria, which was more than
happy to keep American forces bogged down south of its border. In
the months after the much celebrated three-week desert blitz to
Baghdad in 2003, many White House officials, U.S. legislators,
military analysts, and journalists seemed to be itching for more
war, openly asking, "If it took us three weeks to reach Baghdad,
how long will it take to topple Damascus?"

NBC's expert on terrorism and national security, Bob Windrem,
whose tiny office is filled with books on terrorism, toy models of
Osama bin Laden made in Pakistan, and the business cards of former Iraqi nuclear scientists, told me, "Some people in Washington
are saying, 'Damascus next.' Others say, 'Let's go for the real hard
target, Iran.'" The message was diamond-clear in Damascus and
Tehran.

Windrem—who looks like a professor whose face might always
be covered in chalk, and who travels, even on vacation, with maps
of military bases and intelligence analysis—said U.S. security officials told him dozens of Iranian intelligence agents were operating
in the southern Iraqi city of Amara within three months of the fall
of Baghdad. It was no accident the Shiites were off to a running
start. They had help. The Americans were bringing democracy. Iran
sent in agents to make sure Iraqi Shiites took advantage of it.

Windrem told me a story I wish more people had heard before
the invasion. It sounded like a joke, and might have been funny
if the results were not so devastating for America's foreign policy in
the Middle East. "A few weeks before the invasion of Iraq, I saw an
Iranian representative to the U.N. He was smiling, clearly happy."

"Why are you smiling?" Windrem asked.

"The United States is about to topple Saddam Hussein, our
enemy who has killed tens of thousands of Iranians, and this makes
us happy."

"And?"

"And the United States says it is going to bring democracy to a
country that is 60 percent Shiite, and that makes us *very* happy. But
most of all, the U.S. is going to get stuck in Iraq and have to ask us
for help to get out of it, and that makes us *very, very* happy."

As far as I know, the official was not revealing a sinister Iranian plot. The simple fact was that Iran had the most to gain from the U.S. invasion, and Iranian intelligence was on the ground quickly to make sure Iraqi Shiites—many uneducated and unfamiliar with political power—didn't blow it.

The Sunnis were playing catch-up, and their help had just arrived from the worst place: al-Qaeda. But by 2004, al-Qaeda already had a history in this country of mysterious alliances. In April 2002, a year before the invasion, Abu Musab al-Zarqawi—the Jordanian petty criminal turned mujahid (the singular form in Arabic for mujahideen)—had set up a base in northern Iraq, joining a militant group called Ansar al-Sunna, which roughly translates to "Followers of the Prophet Mohammed's Teachings."

Ansar al-Sunna was based in the Kurdish areas in northern Iraq. The region was protected by a U.S.-patrolled "no fly zone," which meant Iraqi planes and army divisions weren't allowed to move in. The air cover gave the Kurds a degree of autonomy, although they were never fully in charge of northern Iraq. The Kurdish area was effectively a no-man's-land where the CIA, Israeli intelligence, Iraqi opposition groups, Kurdish fighters, the PKK (Kurdistan Workers Party, an anti-Turkish Kurdish separatist group), and Ansar al-Sunna all trained and gathered information about Saddam's regime. The Kurdish region was technically still part of Iraq and was awash with Iraqi intelligence agents, but it was also a safe haven for Saddam's enemies.

President Bush has tried to justify the war in Iraq by arguing that U.S. troops are fighting the same jihadists responsible for the 9/11 attacks. His argument has been criticized, particularly by Democrats, who say al-Qaeda came to Iraq only *after* the U.S. invasion. The truth is Zarqawi arrived in the Kurdish areas in 2002 with about a dozen fighters. Two al-Qaeda members who trained with Zarqawi in Afghanistan told me Zarqawi's goal was to set up an al-Qaeda cell in line with al-Qaeda's post-9/11 strategy to establish franchise operations across the Islamic world and, eventually, in the West.

In Jordan in 2007, one of Zarqawi's top lieutenants, a man

wanted by Jordanian authorities and sentenced in absentia to fifteen years in prison for sponsoring terrorism, explained Zarqawi's
precipitous rise to power. "Call me Abu Rabieya," he said during
our first of two meetings in his apartment near Zarqa, Abu Musab
al-Zarqawi's birthplace. Abu Rabieya had chosen the apartment because there were two exits, and the building was at an intersection
of four streets. There were many possible escape routes.

He was heavyset with baggy eyes and jowls. He was clean-
shaven and wore Western slacks and a button-down shirt. He didn't
rise from his couch to greet me when I walked in. He said Zarqawi
worked with bin Laden in Afghanistan, but was also an independent operator. Zarqawi had his own training camp near Herat. But
in 2001, Zarqawi left Afghanistan for Iraq with a plan.

In the run-up to the war, it was clear that Iraq was a land where
careers were going to be made. I sneaked into Iraq before the war
because I thought the conflict would be the turning point in the
Middle East, where I had already been living for seven years. As a
young freelancer, I believed some reporters would die covering the
Iraq war, and that others would make a name for themselves.
Zarqawi, another young and ambitious freelancer, had a similar
idea, albeit with a radically different goal. I wanted to be a great reporter. Zarqawi wanted to rival bin Laden.

My big break was being one of the few American journalists
who stayed in Iraq during the U.S. invasion. Zarqawi's break was
tapping into a stock of trained, frustrated army and intelligence officers spurned and betrayed by the United States, worried about
Shiite ascendancy, and looking for a new cause.

I bought a visa from a corrupt Iraqi official and stationed myself in Baghdad to wait for the American bombs to fall. Many of my
colleagues entered the Kurdish areas before the war, where they
could hide like the CIA, Mossad, and jihadist groups. Zarqawi
chose that route.

Saddam was an enemy of religious radicals, both Sunni and Shiite.
But as the U.S. invasion seemed inevitable, he changed his policy.

President Bush argued before launching the war that Iraq was supporting jihadist groups, including al-Qaeda. He was correct, if you
look at Iraq only in the months just before the war. As American
troops started to deploy to Turkey and Kuwait in 2002, Saddam
embraced al-Qaeda-style foreign fighters and even set up training camps for them near Baghdad. I know this because I saw the
fighters.

In the Palestine hotel before the invasion, I saw dozens of men
from Yemen and Syria who had been officially brought to Iraq by
the government for the specific purpose of fighting the Americans.
Knowing his army was bloated and rotten after more than a decade
of sanctions, Saddam armed the tribes in Anbar and hoped to add
suicide brigades to his arsenal. Some of Saddam's supporters have
said he knew Iraq would lose the war and that these jihadists would
become the core of a powerful anti-American insurgency. While it
is unclear what Saddam's ultimate vision might have been, by mid-
2002 he certainly was supporting al-Qaeda-style jihadists.

In the elevator of the Palestine hotel, I saw a jihadist who appeared to be from Southeast Asia wearing a green bandanna.

"What are you doing here?" I asked him as we rode up
together.

"I am here for the Jihad against the Americans," he told me.

"Oh, we missed my floor," I replied. I pushed a button and got
off on the next floor.

Another one of the jihadists, a midget from Zarqa, Jordan, later
told me the transfer of foreign fighters into Iraq was organized
through the Iraqi embassy in Syria.

Zarqawi—who traveled to Iraq through Iran to establish an
al-Qaeda cell and make a name for himself in the Jihad business—
suddenly had some state support, and from Iraq of all places. It
must have been quite a shock.

On the eve of the invasion, President Bush's war team specifically mentioned Zarqawi's presence in Iraq as proof that Saddam
was supporting al-Qaeda and was linked to 9/11. It was a stretch.

If I were a CIA analyst and asked to write a brief about Saddam
and al-Qaeda in 2002, I would likely have written that there *were*

connections, and some mutual benefit at the time. I would have added, however, that Saddam would not likely have supported the foreign mujahideen if he were not facing a war he suspected he'd lose. I further believe that if the U.S. invasion had not taken place, Saddam would have arrested, deported, or executed the jihadists he was helping in 2002, including Abu Musab al-Zarqawi. Saddam would have eliminated them not to help the U.S. war on terrorism. He simply would not have wanted those loose cannons running around his country. But facing an invasion—Shock and Awe—Saddam applied the simple logic of one of the oldest adages in the Middle East: my enemy's enemy is my friend. From Saddam's perspective, if the jihadists went on to form the backbone of a guerrilla war after the Americans pushed him from power, it would be a bonus.

But al-Qaeda, like the Bush administration, has chosen to skew the timeline. In 2007, Zarqawi's deputy told me the insurgency in Iraq was bin Laden's plan all along. "Bin Laden wanted the United States to attack Afghanistan," he said. "He knew that after 9/11 the United States would invade. But he also wanted the United States to invade Iraq and sent Zarqawi there before the war."

I am not sure, however, if this was merely convenient retrospect.

Did bin Laden provoke the American invasion of Iraq? I don't think so. Did al-Qaeda know it would benefit from the invasion and position itself to capitalize on it? You bet. It was obvious. I went to Iraq expecting an invasion. Zarqawi, with or without bin Laden's blessing, did the same. Did I expect that five years later I would be appointed the NBC Middle East bureau chief? No. I hoped it would work out, but a lot had to do with luck, circumstance, and some hard work. The same, I believe, applies to Zarqawi. He did travel to Iraq—the Kurdish regional areas—to establish an al-Qaeda cell. While he may have hoped it would happen, I don't think Zarqawi could have planned that he would be embraced by the Iraqi regime, then Syria; that the tribes and Iraqi army officers would be betrayed; and that he would become one of the world's most notorious terrorists. A lot had to do with luck, American mistakes, and his ruthless determination.

But Zarqawi's men like to tell a story that it was all planned and that he and bin Laden were strategic geniuses.

An al-Qaeda militant who served nearly five years in Guantánamo Bay, Cuba, gave me what I believe to be the most realistic picture of al-Qaeda and its plans for Iraq. He knew the players and their intentions. Khalid Suliman was personally recruited by bin Laden and fought in a bunker with him in Tora Bora in 2001. Khalid also knew Zarqawi and was surprised by his precipitous rise to power. We spoke at Khalid's apartment in Jeddah, Saudi Arabia, after his release.

"Zarqawi was a quiet guy. I was shocked when I heard about him in Iraq while I was in Guantánamo. You cannot imagine that this guy would do all this stuff, maybe become more famous than bin Laden. We never thought Zarqawi would be that guy," he said.

Like Zarqawi's deputy in Jordan, Khalid said bin Laden's strategy was to draw the United States into a bleeding war in Afghanistan. He wanted the United States to invade and thought fighting in Afghanistan—al-Qaeda's home court—would bankrupt and tire the United States, as had happened with the Soviet Union in the 1980s.

Khalid said bin Laden never expected the 9/11 attacks to be so successful. "Even bin Laden was shocked when the World Trade Center fell down. He thought that just the airplane would hit the building, you know, make damage, but not that the buildings would fall down. It wasn't the idea."

But Khalid said bin Laden miscalculated al-Qaeda's power in Afghanistan and assumed Pakistan and the Afghan people would continue to support him. "We found ourselves now hunted. Afghans were looking for us, the Americans were looking for us, it didn't go as planned."

After the war in Afghanistan, al-Qaeda was on the run, its chain of command broken and without state sponsors. The war in Iraq gave al-Qaeda a new life. The Americans were now suddenly involved in another bleeding war in a Muslim country. It was too good to be true. "Iraq was a gift to al-Qaeda," Khalid said. "And if the U.S. attacks Iran, I think it will be another gift.

"We never thought the Americans would invade Iraq. Even bin Laden, he never thought that."

But as the war approached, Zarqawi at least was preparing.

Zarqawi's deputy told me it was Zarqawi's plan all along to fight the Americans in Iraq, that he wouldn't have gone to Iraq if he didn't expect a war. By 2002, it was obvious. The American troops were already on their way to staging bases in Turkey and Kuwait. But did Zarqawi know that his presence in Kurdistan would be part of the U.S. justification for war? His supporters say he did. The argument supports both al-Qaeda and President Bush. President Bush can argue that he is fighting people connected to 9/11. Al-Qaeda can argue that the war in Iraq and American losses in the country were all part of a brilliant strategic plan.

Was al-Qaeda operating in Iraq with some state support before the war? Yes.

Was Saddam involved in any way in 9/11? No.

Was he supporting people with vague links to 9/11 after the attacks? Yes.

Would al-Qaeda militants have been in Iraq if Saddam didn't expect the United States to invade? I doubt it.

Did the invasion of Iraq make al-Qaeda stronger? Unquestionably.

By April 2004, Zarqawi—proud, vainglorious, and media-savvy—was itching to make a grand public announcement of his arrival in the big leagues.

––––––––

Like me, Nick Berg was another young, ambitious American looking for a break in Iraq. The twenty-six-year-old from suburban Philadelphia was a freelance contractor hoping to make his fortune from the billions of dollars the American government was spending on reconstruction projects. In December 2003, Berg packed a bag and shipped off to Iraq, looking for contracts for a small company he ran that rebuilt communications towers. Thinking he had secured work during the visit, he returned in March, but was detained by U.S. and Iraqi forces. In April, Berg decided to go home, but never made it. If he'd returned to Iraq just a few months earlier, he might have survived his gamble. But al-Qaeda was now infecting the Sunnis, turning their nascent rebellion into a sadistic killing machine that was hunting for victims.

Berg was only one of nine Americans kidnapped in mid-April, one year after U.S. troops pulled down Saddam's statue in Firdous Square in front of live TV cameras positioned on a balcony of the Palestine hotel.

Zarqawi used Berg to make his dramatic stage entrance. Berg was his grotesque premiere event.

On May 11, a video surfaced on the Internet. In Baghdad, we fed it over a satellite to our New York headquarters. We fed it only once. After that, NBC executives sent ethics and standards e-mails saying we should not feed videos of beheadings. They were disturbing to some of the control room technicians whose job was to receive and redirect transitions. The video was an abuse, designed to be an affront to our sensibilities.

Berg was kneeling in front of five men, two in ski masks and three with handkerchiefs over their faces. The man in a ski mask directly behind Berg was stocky, broad-shouldered, and had a low, grumbling voice. It was Zarqawi, the first time he had ever been seen on video. He reached into his shirt and unsheathed a butcher's knife. Berg couldn't see it. He kept staring straight ahead, peering lifelessly into the camera. Zarqawi grabbed him by the hair, turned his head to the side, pushed him over, and leaned in with the knife. The portion of the video we broadcast stopped there. But after that, Zarqawi cut through Berg's neck. Berg was screaming, a high-pitched whine. That is what struck me, the horrible screams. Zarqawi continued to slice until he'd cut off Berg's head and held it up to the camera like a trophy.

It was Zarqawi's way of saying, "I am here and I am in charge."

It was the same message al-Qaeda leader Khalid Sheikh Moham-med gave when he personally beheaded the American *Wall Street Journal* reporter Daniel Pearl in Pakistan in 2002. Both Moham-med and Zarqawi were establishing their credentials as leaders who don't just give orders from air-conditioned offices but are in the field, getting blood on their hands. After that, Zarqawi became known in Iraq as "Zarqawi the *debahh*," the butcher.

Berg's *debahh*—which is the root of the Arabic word for kitchen, harking back to days when animals were butchered at home— burned an image in my mind and left a scar. It was what I was think-ing about when one of our reporting teams was kidnapped in Falujah just a few weeks later. I feared our correspondent Ned Colt, cameraman Maurice Roper, soundman Robert Colvill, and Iraqi translator-fixer Ashraf al-Taie would also fall under Zarqawi's cruel blade.

Kidnappings had quickly become the Sunni insurgents' attack of choice. The reason is simple. They had a new movement and needed funding and publicity. The foreign fighters pouring into Anbar needed supplies and safe houses, and that cost money. In the four days after Berg was abducted, Sunni insurgents kidnapped another forty foreigners from thirteen nations. France, Russia, and the Czech Republic advised their citizens to leave Iraq. The FBI, CIA, and U.S. military set up a hostage working group at the embassy.

Nearly all of the kidnappings were taking place in and around Falujah. But Operation Vigilant Resolve was never permitted to stop it. The mission was cut short, and the Marines were angry. Bremer's civilian administration, "the goddamn embassy," as one marine described it, stopped the offensive. It was a political deci-sion. Bremer was facing one of many artificial deadlines the United States imposed to push Iraq forward on its limp toward indepen-dence and democracy.

In April 2004, Bremer was just two months away from the so-called transfer of authority and he needed the support of the Iraqi politicians to whom he was supposed to be handing power. The transfer of sovereignty was a key milestone on the political road-map. It would mean the end of the U.S.-appointed Governing Council and create an "interim government" that would organize national elections. It would be a concrete sign of progress in Iraq that the White House needed to fend off the increasing number of war critics. The Marine offensive was getting in the way.

As marines invaded Falujah, Governing Council members were up in arms and threatened to resign. They were being blamed for the fighting because of their association with the U.S. administration. Moqtada al-Sadr was also exploiting the fighting in Falujah to fuel his parallel Shiite rebellion, triggered when Bremer closed his newspaper. Anger was growing in Iraq, for the first time among both Sunnis and Shiites.

At the height of Vigilant Resolve, I went to a Baghdad police station in Dora where I knew the chief. I had just gone on a night patrol with his officers. They had driven like maniacs, speeding around corners, tossing me around in the backseat. They thought it was all very funny. One of the policemen, trying to show his bravery, was hanging out of the patrol car's window, firing his AK-47 in the air. He was drunk on arak (Arab Anisette) and laughing fiendishly.

When I arrived at the Dora police station that morning, the officers were crowded in the chief's office, throwing their badges at him, resigning en masse. "I am going to fight with the mujahideen!" one young policeman screamed in my face. They were surrounding our camera. Iraqis often yell and scream at the camera when trying to express their frustration. It can look hostile. This *was* hostile. "How can I work here and fight crime when the biggest crime is happening in my own country!" another policeman screamed at me.

Facing a revolt from Sunnis and Shiites, the ire of the Governing Council, and police walkouts, Bremer's message to the Marines was clear: cool it off. Vigilant Resolve didn't live up to its name.

General Conway told *The Washington Post* he was frustrated that he'd been ordered to invade Falujah when it seemed like revenge for the murders of the Blackwater contractors, and then been told to stop halfway through the mission. "When you order elements of a Marine division to attack a city, you really need to understand what the consequences of that are going to be and not perhaps vacillate in the middle of something like that. Once you commit, you got to stay committed," he said.

With their hands tied, the Marines' half-solution was to create a local militia in Falujah, the Falujah Brigade, made of former Baath party members and army officers. The United States mistakenly turned to the very men who had just joined al-Qaeda and asked them to root out the foreign fighters. They never even tried. But in the initial weeks after the fighting, the Falujah Brigade's mixed loyalties were not yet obvious. Ned Colt, a mild-mannered correspondent based in Hong Kong, planned to do a story about the new U.S.-allied militia. He says it was supposed to be a "good news" story about how the residents of Falujah were policing themselves. But Ned forgot Zohair's fundamental rule in Iraq: trust no one. His plan was to drive to Falujah and meet Dr. Fadl, the local stringer, at a gas station. Dr. Fadl would then escort the team to interview the Falujah Brigade's commanders. While risky, it was not by any means irresponsible. It is what journalists are supposed to do. Ned didn't get away with it. Ned and his team left a U.S. military base and drove in our armored Jeep Cherokee into Falujah to meet Dr. Fadl. As the Jeep pulled over, it was ambushed.

"A man in a green Saddam-era uniform came screaming up on a motorcycle," Ned said later. "He was followed by four men in a small foreign car. They started shouting at us, getting out of the vehicle, shooting off their AKs."

Ned opened the armored car's door, a mistake he still regrets.

"As they started to approach, I got out of the car. They grabbed me. I don't know Arabic, but I do know one word, and that's *Amriki*, American.

"They figured they had a good American, and they did. They put me in the back of their vehicle, covered me up with a coat, and drove me away amid, sort of, shouts of glee. They thought they had hit the lottery that day."

Ned, always cool and even-tempered, didn't resist. But now he was worried because he'd been separated from Ashraf, Maurice, and Rob.

"We'd been invited in. So our view was that this was some sort of minor hiccup that would be resolved once we got to chat with them.

"We drove a bit, I would say about ten minutes. . . . They made me keep my head down and took me into an empty warehouse. There were wooden pallets on the ground. I was doing my damnedest to avert my eyes because I didn't want to cause any trouble— more trouble than we were already in.

"I'd given them my wallet, and I told them who I was. But there were serious language barriers. They brought in a dishdasha, and through hand signs made me understand I should put it on. That was the first time that I got quite concerned."

A white dishdasha was, however, better than an orange jumpsuit. Zarqawi had dressed Berg in an orange jumpsuit similar to the ones worn by the prisoners at Guantánamo Bay. Orange was the color of al-Qaeda's death suit.

After Ned sat in the warehouse for fifteen minutes, the kidnappers moved him to a nearby farmhouse where he found Ashraf, Maurice, and Rob drinking tea.

"I said, what in the world's going on? They said, 'Well, there appears to be just a small problem. We want to make sure you are who you say you are. We're going to look over your papers, and talk to you. You'll be out of here tomorrow, or this afternoon. You'll be able to go and shoot your story.

"Being naive individuals, we said, 'You know, we want to tell your story, and provide you airtime so we can see what's happening here in your city.' "

After a few minutes, the kidnappers moved them again.

"They put us in the back of a car again and said, 'For your own safety, keep your heads down.' They were speaking a bit better English by this time and took us to a room next to the warehouse where I'd been held. They started to question us.

"They would take us out one by one into an adjoining room where someone who seemed to be more senior was asking questions, going over our passports, looking at papers in the vehicle. They were going through everything."

Ned said the kidnappers were polite, until they found something they found suspicious.

Maurice had traveled to Saudi Arabia to cover a visit by Defense Secretary Donald Rumsfeld. He had a visa in his passport that said, in Arabic, that he'd accompanied Rumsfeld. "He didn't even know he had that in his passport, and that's the kind of thing you're up against, little tiny things that made us even more suspect," Ned said.

The kidnappers nonetheless brought them lunch from Abu Tareq, the finest kebaab house in Falujah, which incidentally was Zarqawi's favorite. The chefs at Abu Tareq would grind huge chunks of fat from sheep tails in with the meat. As the kebaab cooked over charcoal, the fat melted away, making the meat tender.

After the meal, the kidnappers took one of Ned's cameras and forced them all to make video statements. Ned started to think about the Nick Berg video. "As journalists, we'd covered those stories. We'd seen these horrific tapes of people being beheaded in local clothing."

The next day, the kidnappers bundled Ned and the others into a car, and moved them again. "Our cameraman, Maurice, and I were put in the back of a car together, covered up, wearing our dishdashas. I just remember grabbing Maurice's wrist and saying, 'We gotta, we gotta hold on here.' We knew at this point that things were getting nasty. We were very worried.

"We drove for about twenty minutes. They weren't even talking to us now. It was a very, very cold relationship. We were taken to a house this time. The three Westerners [Ned, Maurice, and Rob] were put in one room, and our Iraqi interpreter [Ashraf] was put in another room.

"I noticed things, but I didn't say anything to my colleagues at the time. I saw a bloody handprint on the wall, and what looked like the top of someone's jaw that had been driven into the plaster of the wall."

It was a torture room.

The kidnappers then found something much more incriminating than the stamp in Maurice's passport. Ned's armored Jeep had Israeli registration papers. The kidnappers had just found them.

When the war began, TV networks corralled their armored vehicles from around the world, including Israel. There was a rush to bring the cars to Baghdad. Forgetting to strip down the Jeep had suddenly become a potentially fatal oversight. "These were all errors in hindsight. But our view was we were invited in. We did not expect this kind of scrutiny," Ned said.

"Your mind is racing in every direction. Adrenaline is surging through you. You're sitting there in foreign clothing. You've been videotaped. Your captors don't speak English. You don't speak Arabic. I kept being told that I'm taking water they gave me with the wrong hand because I'm a lefty."

The next morning took a dramatic turn for the worse.

"A Saudi came into the room and spoke English. He said, 'First off, I'm not going to speak English with you because it's the language of dogs. I despise you. You're the infidel.'"

Since the Saudi refused to speak English, the kidnappers brought Ashraf back into the room to translate for Ned, Maurice, and Rob.

"Within minutes the Saudi was saying, 'If I had my way I would be ripping the flesh off your neck.'

"This Saudi was clearly someone they treated with the utmost respect. They called him lord and the Iraqis were kowtowing to him. He then began to go off on what I would call political speeches about how we were the infidels here, all the foreigners should leave Iraq. I didn't want to bring it up then, but I thought he was a foreigner too.

"This was soon after Abu Ghraib. And he would say—our sisters, our mothers have been raped in Abu Ghraib, murdered in Abu Ghraib. 'How do you feel about that?' Of course, we said, 'We feel badly about that.' But when one of us responded that way, he immediately said, 'You have no idea!' "

Ned and the others decided to be silent. "Be polite. Be professional. State our case. But don't get involved in anything remotely political. . . . The Saudi continued to get more and more testy with us and would again say, 'I want to kill you. I want to rip the flesh off your neck.' Then he said, 'We want to Nicholas Berg you.'

"That's the way it was for the next two or three days. We were being constantly told we were evil. We were infidels. We should be killed. We would be killed.

"You'd grasp on to the tiniest bit of hope. They'd say, we think we're gonna be releasing you shortly. Then they would come back and say no. We found out that you're really a spy for the CIA.

"It was playing havoc with our minds. But throughout it all, it kept on being driven home: 'We are going to cut your head off as we did to Nicholas Berg.'

"We had three or four days to think about the good likelihood that we were going to be killed in a horrible way and that our families would see it on Web sites, videos of us being beheaded, our heads held up."

They saw a screwdriver the kidnappers had forgotten on a windowsill. Ned says they were considering using it to commit suicide. "I tried to put on a brave face, but deep down I was really, really worried that this was finally it. What had I done? I'd gotten three of my colleagues and myself into something and we were all quite likely going to be killed, or beheaded, and for a news story that wasn't going to change the world. We thought it was important. We had the best intentions.

"I started looking back on my life. Had I lived a good life? How was I going to approach death? Would I squeal like a stuck pig as they killed me? Would I be strong and just say, 'I've had a good life'? How's your family going to think about this? Your wife at home. Your parents. Your siblings. They're going to hurt a lot more than you.

"They treated us very coldly, but wanted to make sure that, in their view, they were treating us with some modicum of respect, better, they believed, than their people were treated in American-run jails in Iraq.

"They would keep bringing that up, saying, 'As you see, we treat you better than we treat ourselves. We're giving you fresh water. We're getting you food. You're eating before we are.' But at the same time, they kept saying, 'You deserve to die.' "

While Ned, Rob, Maurice, and Ashraf were being held, Dr. Fadl was pressuring the tribal sheikhs in Falujah to intervene. Dr. Fadl had recognized one of the kidnappers during the abduction at the gas station and was trying to convince the abductor's father to let them go. It ultimately worked. NBC paid nothing. The tribal elders managed to shame the kidnappers into releasing them.

Ned, Maurice, Rob, and Ashraf climbed back into the Cherokee and drove to an American checkpoint on the outskirts of Falujah. "We were still dressed in dishdashas, and the soldiers came racing up to us. We just said, 'You're a sight for sore eyes.' We realized then that this was over, and that we'd survived. You could physically feel the weight just pour off you."

Ned took a few months off, but continues to report from Iraq. He almost never talks about those five days. "As a journalist, I work overseas. This is part and parcel of what we do. I don't mean to make it sound more than it is. It's a job, and it's why I do what I do. So this is all part of it. I just feel an obligation to come here."

Ned doesn't often have nightmares, but sometimes "things will kick in.

"Someone might knock at the door, and for some reason I think it may be an unsavory character who's coming to take me away," he said.

The Falujah Brigade was eventually dissolved. Vigilant Resolve was quickly forgotten. At least six hundred Iraqis and nearly three dozen marines were killed in the offensive, which drove eighty thousand Iraqis from their homes. Kidnappings in and around Falujah only became more frequent.

In mid-April 2004, Sunni insurgents executed an Italian thirty-six-year-old security contractor, Fabrizio Quattrocchi. In his final moment—like Berg's, also videotaped—Quattrocchi faced the kidnappers. Struggling to his feet, he tried to tear off his hood as he yelled, "I'll show you how an Italian dies!" They shot him in the head. I have often wondered if I would be that brave.

7

Paul Bremer and "the goddamn embassy" had gotten their way. When Operation Vigilant Resolve was called off, the Marines grudgingly withdrew to their base and left Falujah in the untrustworthy hands of the Falujah Brigade, commanded by a former Iraqi general implicated in war crimes against the Kurds in 1996.

The kidnappers in Falujah were never brought to justice, and foreign fighters remained firmly entrenched in the city of 250,000, sheltered by the powerful tribal sheikhs. In fact, the al-Qaeda-inspired jihadists emerged stronger than ever. They had faced the Americans in battle and, from their perspective, won. It gave the foreign fighters, especially Zarqawi, street credibility with the tribes who had watched Saddam's army melt away during the three-week American invasion. This time, a few poorly armed Jordanians, Saudis, and Syrians eating dates and drinking sheep's milk (the Salafi jihadists prefer a simple diet that imitates the Prophet Mohammed's desert lifestyle) seemed able to repel the U.S. Marines.

Militarily, it was clearly a failure. But the mission to pacify Falujah was deliberately sacrificed for a goal the U.S. embassy and White House considered more important, "the political timetable"—the complicated and ill-conceived roadmap cooked up in Washington, and remodeled in Najaf, that was guiding and driving the Bush administration. It was supposed to be a blueprint for democracy and bring Iraq the stability of Western governments.

After Vigilant Resolve was ended, the Governing Council members *did* calm down, Iraq police stopped their minirevolt, and Moqtada al-Sadr's uprising lost some of its momentum. The four-step political roadmap—the democratic fairy dust the Americans thought they were sprinkling on Mesopotamia—could now proceed:

1. Approve a temporary constitution. (Done.)
2. Select an "interim government" to hold elections.
3. Elect a "transitional government" to write the constitution.
4. Approve the constitution in a referendum, and elect a "final" full-term government.

It was all supposed to take a year. By the end of 2004, Iraqis were to have an elected government, and the U.S. "mentoring" role—democracy tutors—would be over.

But first the Americans needed an interim prime minister to carry the torch of democracy over Iraq's next hurdle. The Americans had to have someone who was efficient and strong enough to rule for the six months that the U.S.-Sistani timeline (backed by the United Nations) allotted for an interim government to organize elections. The U.S. administration thought Iraq needed a leader who could hold the country together just long enough for the seeds of democracy to take root in the Fertile Crescent. After that, the interim prime minister would step aside and let the political process bloom. Many U.S. officials at the time were convinced that after free elections, Iraqis would be satisfied with their elected political leadership, "buy into the process," and peacefully sort out their differences, yelling and screaming in political debates instead of killing one another. On June 1, the Americans announced that they had selected Ayad Allawi to lead Iraq until voting day.

I had met Allawi several times when he was a member of the Governing Council and I called on him again after his appointment. We met in the Green Zone's convention center, a building with so much history it could be the subject of its own book.

Allawi was the kind of man Americans liked. He was tough, straightforward, ambitious, and secular. Quiet, calculating, pragmatic, and elusive, he was also fluent in English, and had the benefit of being physically imposing, over six feet tall, and weighing roughly 230 pounds, with broad shoulders, big hands, and a firm grip. Allawi looked you in the eye when he spoke. Journalist and author John Lee Anderson wrote in a profile of Allawi for *The New Yorker* that the interim prime minister had "the lumbering gait of an old prize fighter."

After Allawi was tapped to be interim prime minister, his advisors started spreading rumors that he had personally interrogated and executed at least four (some reports said as many as seven) captured foreign jihadists, shooting them dead with point-blank shots to the head with his pistol at a police station. Allawi never convincingly confirmed or denied it. Iraqis loved it. They were already sick of the mounting car bombings and assassinations and wanted a strongman. Allawi wanted to be that strongman.

Allawi also seemed to embody many of Iraq's various factions. While living in exile in London, he had worked for both U.S. and British intelligence, providing what turned out to be the false information that Iraq could deploy weapons of mass destruction with just forty-five minutes' notice, a report British officials cited as one of the reasons they supported the invasion. Allawi, like many others, was wrong, but the Americans still considered him an ally with a debt to Washington. While Ahmed Chalabi, another exile who provided false information before the war, was vilified in the United States as a liar who deliberately misled the U.S. administration to help him rise to power in Iraq, Allawi's mistakes were somehow forgotten. The Americans needed Allawi. He was one of the few Governing Council members they thought they could trust.

Allawi, who studied medicine in Baghdad and London, was also a Shiite, and a former high-ranking member of the Baath party. He joined the Baath party when he was only twelve years old in the

1950s, long before Saddam turned the pan-Arab socialist party into a murderous cult of personality. He rose in the Baath party's intelligence directorate until he left for the United Kingdom in 1971. While Allawi was in Britain, Saddam accused him of working for British intelligence. In 1978, Saddam dispatched two assassins—one wielding an ax—to Allawi's apartment on the outskirts of London. Allawi, alone with his wife at the time, Athour, was so badly injured in the attack he was hospitalized for nearly a year. After that, Allawi, known for his foul temper and ability to make quick decisions, dedicated his life to toppling Saddam's regime, forming the Iraqi National Accord, an exile group that worked to trigger a coup within the Baath party and Iraqi military. British intelligence passed him to the CIA in the early 1990s.

Within a week of his appointment as interim prime minister, Allawi made it clear he intended to use the often dubious but effective skills he'd honed from a life as an intelligence operative. He gave himself "emergency powers" to impose nationwide curfews and make arrests without warrants. He imposed a "militia law," formally outlawing armed groups with the notable exception of the Kurdish Peshmerga, the Kurds' regional army. Not surprisingly, Allawi quickly became the main enemy of both Abu Musab al-Zarqawi and Moqtada al-Sadr's Mahdi Army.

Allawi was a man willing to crack heads. Americans were calling him "Saddam Lite." At the time I thought that if the Americans weren't careful, Allawi had the potential to become another of the Middle East's thuggish, pro-American dictators. He could have easily developed into an Iraqi version of Egypt's Hosni Mubarak.

I think a strongman was what Iraq needed to get on its feet. Iraq never had a democracy, and, more to the point, Iraqis never asked for one. Iraqis wanted to be rid of Saddam Hussein and to get rich from oil they expected would gush from the desert after the tyrant was gone and sanctions were lifted. While in power, Saddam had constantly talked about Iraq's untapped oil riches. He dangled it in front of the Iraqis, saying, "You could be rich, but it's the Americans and their sanctions that are blocking Iraq's potential." Now that Saddam was in an American military prison near Baghdad's airport, Iraqis expected the cash they'd been dreaming about for years to start flowing in.

Immediately after the collapse of Saddam's regime, Iraqis in Baghdad excitedly told me they wanted their country to become like the Arabian Gulf. They wanted to be a ruling class of "kept men," like Arabs in Kuwait, Dubai, and Saudi Arabia who have Indian and Pakistani slavelike servants who build all the roads and airports and wait on them hand and foot. Iraqis felt they deserved it. Iraqis wanted air conditioners, new cars, and to travel to Europe to chase blondes as they did in the 1970s and early 1980s when a single Iraqi dinar was worth $1.50, compared to only a thirtieth of a penny by 2002—if anyone would accept the failed currency, which few would.

After the invasion, Iraqi friends proudly showed me yellowed photographs of thinner, younger versions of themselves in powder blue suits and tight pants, their arms lovingly wrapped around pale, chubby women from Hungary or Poland in panty hose, black leather skirts, and white boots with rhinestones. After Iraq was "liberated," the men wanted to find the women again, or better yet, younger ones. Iraqi Kurds wanted a state and to be left alone. The only people I heard praising "democracy" were members of the Shiite howza, the most undemocratic institution I can imagine.

Even before he was sworn in, Allawi found himself at war. Zarqawi wanted him dead. Since Allawi was protected by American bodyguards and rarely left the Green Zone except by helicopter, Zarqawi chose softer targets, including foreign contractors, oil pipelines, Allawi's deputies, and, with devastating long-term effects, Shiite religious leaders, mosques, and civilians. The civil war was starting.

On June 11, Sunni militants destroyed the key oil pipeline supplying power plants in Baghdad. Two days later, Zarqawi's militants assassinated two of Allawi's senior deputies. Four days after that, Sunni suicide bombers in Baghdad killed thirty-five Iraqi recruits signing up for jobs in the army. Every Friday, Zarqawi's jihadists bombed Shiite mosques during midday prayers. They assassinated at least two prominent Shiite clerics a week.

U.S. military intelligence predicted Zarqawi would continue with these frequent, unsophisticated attacks until June 30, when Allawi would formally take control from Bremer. But Zarqawi quickly proved to be more capable than U.S. intelligence expected. On June 24, Zarqawi's group, now called Tawhid wa Jihad, or Monotheism and Jihad, launched five nearly simultaneous car bombings at police stations in Mosul. To the south in Baquba, 150 of Zarqawi's fighters stormed another police station, paraded through the streets, and took over government buildings, hoisting the all-black flag of the Prophet Mohammed's army. Western intelligence analysts often dismiss the names of jihadist groups, which seem to appear on the Internet out of nowhere and change at random. But one of Zarqawi's fighters told me the group chose its name carefully.

I was eager to meet Zarqawi's followers, the Americans' main enemy, but setting up an interview was both complicated and risky. I didn't want to bring militants to our bureau, fearing they could memorize the layout and use the intelligence against us. I wanted to get close, but not that close. I also didn't want to go to a location of the militants' choosing. I trusted my contact who was setting up the meeting, but not entirely. He was a reporter-fixer in his early thirties from Haditha, a hard-line Sunni city north of Baghdad. He fully supported attacks on U.S. troops and thought it was a national duty to defend his country from occupation. Under Saddam's regime, he'd worked for Uday and had good connections with the intelligence service members who'd joined Zarqawi's foreign fighters in Falujah and other western Iraqi towns and villages. My contact had been arrested by the U.S. military for trafficking insurgent videos in late 2003 and served a year in U.S. military prisons at Abu Ghraib and Bucca in southern Iraq. While in captivity, he claimed American guards and their non-Iraqi, Arab translators had beaten and urinated on him.

"If you don't go into Abu Ghraib or Bucca a mujahid, you certainly come out one," he told me a few days after his release. "It is jihad school."

He'd met Zarqawi's fighter in Abu Ghraib and suggested we meet at a neutral location.

"The fewer people that know about it the better," he cautioned.

I decided to rent a room in a hotel a few blocks from our bureau and meet there. I never told NBC executives or my Western colleagues in the bureau about the meeting. In retrospect, it was irresponsible, but I didn't want our British security consultants to tag along. They would have insisted on frisking the fighter, scouting out the location, and having an escape-and-rescue plan in place in case the interview turned out to be a trap. I took my chances and went in clean, no security, no backup, no camera.

The militant swaggered into the hotel room about an hour late. In his early forties, he looked relaxed; he was clean-shaven and had a muscular build that was obvious in the jeans and tight buttondown shirt he wore. I assumed he'd been watching the hotel for the last hour to see if I'd set a trap for him. He came alone, but I was certain other militants were nearby, perhaps in a parked car, ready to move in if U.S. troops raided the hotel or if I pulled anything funny.

The fighter never smiled or shook my hand. He walked into the room, sat down on a couch, and launched into a tirade against U.S. troops, the Bush administration, Shiites, Allawi, and Iran. He had agreed to talk because he was angry that American officials insisted Zarqawi's movement was mainly composed of foreign fighters who had no support among Iraqis. "I am an Iraqi, and this is *Iraqi* resistance," he said. "Yes, Sheikh Abu Musab is from Jordan, but how can a Jordanian or an Egyptian operate in Iraq without Iraqis?

"It is impossible," he continued. "Foreigners don't know the roads, the villages, or how to move. There are many Iraqis with Abu Musab and most of the resistance is *Iraqi*."

He told me that Monotheism and Jihad was both the group's name and its credo. "By monotheism, we are stating our dedication is to Islam, the true Islam, of the Koran and the Sunna, only the Koran and Sunna. We are the group of 'There is no god but God, and Mohammed is the Prophet of God,' and not followers of what 'the refuters' call Islam." He said the word "refuters," what Sunni radicals call Shiites, with particular disdain, like he was spitting out a cherry pit.

Sunni purists like Wahabis and Salafists claim Shiites are not true monotheists because of their reverence of Ali and Hussein as saints. They call them "refuters" because they do not accept the Sunna, or the teachings and traditions of the Prophet Mohammed as described by his disciples. "The refuters are worse than the infidels and more dangerous because they corrupt Islam from within," he explained. "Jihad is an Islamic duty for all Muslims to defend their lands against occupation."

By calling themselves Monotheism and Jihad, Zarqawi's supporters were therefore defining their principal enemies as Shiites and the American occupiers. Tawheed was the battle for monotheism, and Jihad was the war against infidel occupation.

Osama bin Laden had a somewhat different goal. Before his organization became known as al-Qaeda, it was called the World Islamic Front Against Crusaders and Jews. Again, the name is important. Bin Laden was declaring that his movement was international in scope, and directed mainly against the United States (in bin Laden's view the leader of the modern crusaders) and Israel, the Jewish state. While bin Laden, a Salafi jihadist, clearly disdained Shiites, they did not seem to feature on his radar screen when he announced the formation of his militant network in February 1998.

I met with Zarqawi's henchman for about an hour. Most of our discussion was what you might call ideological. I hadn't realized the extent of the jihadists' paranoid lunacy. He told me stories of trees in Israel that will betray Jews on Judgment Day at the end of the world by calling out to the armies of the righteous, "There is a Jew hiding behind me, come and kill him!"

"The earth will flood with the Jews' blood and fill the Dead Sea. The Jews know this, and are trying to uproot these trees, but there are too many of them," the militant added with a satisfied grin. He told me giant spiders "empowered by the grace of God" were killing American soldiers by the dozens in Falujah.

To him, this was irrefutable truth.

American officials, worried that Zarqawi would try a spectacular attack on June 30, secretly moved up the handover date, officially transferring power to Allawi two days early in a brief, private, low-key ceremony in the Green Zone. Bremer left Iraq two hours later.

When President Bush was informed of the handover, he sent a written reply. "Let freedom reign," he wrote. I laughed when I read that. The only freedom reigning now was the freedom to yell fire in a crowded movie theater or kill your neighbor over an old grudge. Allawi was now formally in command, but I was about to realize that he was merely a figurehead with no real authority outside the Green Zone. Another power, much more influential than Allawi, Zarqawi, and perhaps even the Americans, was continuing its rapid advance onto Iraq's political landscape: Iran.

In early July 2004, just a few days after Allawi was sworn in, I drove with Zohair to the holy Shiite city of Karbala. After the April kidnapping spree, we now had to assume that all roads were unsafe, but we were still willing to take our chances. Zohair had arranged for a local sheikh to provide us with gunmen. I put my faith in Zohair's judgment and set off. I was confident we'd get away with taking the risk. After all, the Shiites were still on America's side. They were our friends, our partners in democracy.

Our first stop in Karbala was the Hassan mosque, a small, nondescript mosque about a mile from the city's ancient downtown. Like Najaf, Karbala radiates outward from the city's holy Shiite shrines. Najaf is home to Ali's tomb and the howza. Karbala boasts the tomb of Ali's martyred son Hussein, the Shiite hero and inspiration for their sacrifice. Najaf is the headquarters of the ayatollahs, the brain of the Shiite world. Karbala is its heart. Shiites study Ali's teachings and issue fatwas in Najaf. They go to war for Hussein and Karbala.

A few hundred yards from Hussein's golden-domed tomb

stands an almost identical mosque built for Hussein's slain companion Abass, the standard-bearer of his army. The two mosque/tombs, about three hundred yards apart, are supposedly constructed on the spots where Hussein and Abass were killed by the armies of the early Sunni caliph Yazid during the Shiites' failed attempt to avenge Ali's murder and reclaim the Islamic empire for the Ahl al-Bayt, the Prophet's perfect family. It was a failure, and Karbala is a permanent reminder to the Shiites of their loss of power to the Sunnis.

As in Najaf, the narrow streets and alleys surrounding the shrines in Karbala are packed with hotels for pilgrims, money-changers, bookshops, and stalls selling CDs of hypnotic *lutumiya* sermons, mournful lamentations set to the beat of men slapping their chests with their palms. Many of the tiny shops also sell *turba*, the flat gray stones made of compressed dust from Karbala. Pilgrims buy *turba* so that when they touch their foreheads to them during prayer back home, it *feels* like they are still praying on sacred ground. In the nineteenth century, Shiite princes from northern India brought huge caravans full of soil from Najaf. They constructed shrines on the Iraqi dirt, reducing the need to travel to pray on holy ground. Some Sunnis have a similar desire to be directly connected to holy sites. When Palestinian leader Yasser Arafat died in November 2004, Israel refused his request to be buried in Jerusalem. Never ones to give up easily, the Palestinians buried Arafat in Ramallah in the West Bank in soil from the al-Aqsa mosque compound in Jerusalem. For Shiites, the *turba* is a similar way of keeping a lasting connection to Iraq's holy cities.

Sheikh Abed Ali al-Hameri, our local contact who had promised Zohair protection, was waiting for us at the Hassan mosque when we pulled up. The mosque was on a modern, treeless, charmless paved street lined with parked cars.

"This wasn't really a mosque before," Sheikh Hameri told me, taking my hand and leading me inside. I was puzzled. To me, the building looked like every other mosque I'd visited, with a small dome, minaret, carpeted prayer room, washroom for ablutions, and administrative office in the back for the clerics.

"You see the minaret? See how high it is? It's much too high," the sheikh explained, pointing with long, straight fingers sparkling with silver rings and red semiprecious stones. "The building was made to look like a mosque, but it was a security outpost for Saddam's spies. When we arrived, we found binoculars and recording devices in the minaret. Saddam's officers would sit up there and watch Karbala. No one ever prayed here."

The minaret did look disproportionately tall, and from the top, there was a clear view of the pedestrian esplanade between the Hussein and Abass mosques, the area Iraqis call Bein al-Harameen, or Between the Shrines. Saddam was, with reason, deeply suspicious and fearful of Shiite power. In Najaf, he built a hotel directly in front of the Imam Ali mosque that was also a secret security headquarters.

Sheikh Hameri wasn't a religious cleric, but a tribal leader from a powerful clan in Karbala. He wore the Saudi-style egal and a crisp white dishdasha. He was tall, with a medium build, a dark complexion, a light beard, and a fine, handsome face.

Sheikh Hameri continued his tour of the small mosque. It was filled with boxes stacked to the ceiling. "You see all of this, this is for newlyweds," Sheikh Hameri proudly told me, pointing to the wooden crates packed with kitchen cooktops, blankets, dishes, tea sets, and wooden cupboards. "We have established a charity to help young couples get started in life. They get all of this for free," he said, estimating that each allotment was worth about $150. "We have already given out ten thousand household sets in just the past two months," he said.

If he was correct, Sheikh Hameri's little charity had already distributed $1.5 million worth of goods, which I found suspiciously impressive for a country at war and without a banking system.

"Where does all of this come from?" I asked.

Hameri was quiet for a second.

"It is from donations from rich families," the sheikh said.

But the facts were written on the crates in English. The boxes were stamped "Made in Iran."

"Yes, they are from Iran," Hameri admitted when I pointed out the labels. "They are donations from families in Iran. Many are Iraqis who were deported to Iran by Saddam. It all goes to newlyweds," he stressed.

As if on cue, a young man came in, signed a receipt, and packed his car with Iranian blankets, cups, and plates.

"See, it all goes to newlyweds. We have two more truckloads coming in tomorrow and will soon start distributing beds and cabinets, a full bedroom set, which can be so expensive for families to buy."

I remember finding it ironic that the Hassan mosque had been transformed from one of Saddam's security outposts into an Iranian outpost. How times had changed.

It was starting to get dark and I asked Sheikh Hameri if he knew a hotel where we could stay.

"You must stay at my home," he insisted. I told Zohair I preferred to stay in a hotel despite the sheikh's hospitality. After a compulsory visit to the sheikh's house, a huge villa, where he showed us swords and guns his family had used to fight the British in the 1920 revolt, Hameri agreed to help us find a hotel. It was not as easy as I expected. Karbala was booked solid.

Our first stop was at a hotel owned by one of Hameri's friends. The hotel was directly across from the Abass shrine, just a few feet from the city's famous fountain, which is filled during Ashura—when Shiites commemorate Hussein's martyrdom—with red water to symbolize the blood he shed in battle.

There were no vacancies that day at the hotel, or anytime in the foreseeable future. The hotel was packed, literally packed, with Iranian pilgrims, as many as ten to a room. Some Iranians were sleeping on mats in the hallways. They were standing in plastic slippers in a line to use the bathroom with a single sink and two squat toilets.

"I can give you a room, but there are four other people in it," the hotel owner told us. "The price is $75 a person. I suggest you take it."

The five of us included a female producer based in London, Yuka Tachibana, a Japanese-American woman who was reluctantly wearing a black chador. It kept falling off her head. She was annoyed that men kept pointing to her hair and telling her to tuck it in. The hotel owner wanted to put her in a room with ten Iranian women. I didn't even suggest it to her.

Zohair pleaded, telling the owner we were personal friends of Sheikh Hameri. The hotel owner eventually told us he was building a new hotel a few blocks away. It was still under construction, but a few rooms were ready. We could try there if we wanted. No guarantees.

The second hotel took up an entire block, but the receptionist didn't want to give us any rooms. "They are prebooked," he told us, explaining that the hotel had a deal with an Iranian tour operator. After a phone call from Sheikh Hameri, the receptionist eventually agreed to rent us three rooms for $200 a night on the condition that if any Iranians arrived, he would put them in with us. We had no choice. As we were checking in, the receptionist answered the phone in Farsi.

"That was the travel company in Tehran. We have a group coming in two days," he said, then took our money and quickly lost interest in us. He was busy with a group of workmen installing ceiling panels and polishing a new marble staircase.

The next morning, I was struck by the crowds in Karbala. There were thousands of Iranian pilgrims, many in tour groups, visiting the mosques, shopping, and eating in restaurants serving grilled lamb with Karbala's special vegetables pickled in a brine of vinegar and pomegranate juice.

In the Bein al-Harameen esplanade between the Hussein and Abass mosques, the Iranian government had paid to erect a tent city, where Iranian pilgrims who couldn't afford to stay in hotels were sleeping on thin foam mattresses. Men I didn't recognize patrolled the area with walkie-talkies. The black radios were not the Motorolas used by U.S. troops and supplied to the official Iraqi security forces.

Inside a large tent housing about two hundred pilgrims, Zohair, who speaks a little Farsi, found two brothers from Tehran.

"It is everyone in Iran's dream to come to Najaf and Karbala," one of the brothers said. "The government is encouraging people to come."

Outside the tent, men in green jumpsuits swept the streets. They were Iranians too, donated by the governor of Tehran to the city of Karbala to clean the holy sites.

While it was obvious that Iranian pilgrims had descended on Karbala, everyone we spoke to was secretive about Iran. No one liked to say the word "Iran" directly. "They are brothers from the east," Iraqis would say when I asked about the Iranian pilgrims or Iran's growing influence. "They are Iraqis who lived in Iran and have returned. It is normal."

It struck me as similar to the way Iraqis never uttered Saddam Hussein's name directly, but referred to him only as "*al-rais*," the president, or "*al-qa'ed*," the leader. Saddam had been omnipresent, but never mentioned. Iran had taken his place, and the people of Karbala were, for the first time, reaping huge benefits from their new patron.

Near the Hussein mosque, we met a real estate agent who was finalizing a deal with an Iraqi man who had lived in Iran for a decade. We followed the customer to the half-acre plot of land he had bought on the outskirts of Karbala for $100,000. Workmen had just broken ground on the two-story villa he was building for his son.

"Real estate prices have gone up forty times since the fall of Saddam. Four thousand percent!" the agent exclaimed, unable to contain himself. "Prices are going up every day. This man paid $100,000 for this land. He bought it last month. He could sell it today for $150,000."

Iran knew how to win hearts and minds, a tactic the United States never mastered in Iraq.

8

Allawi's rise to power was less than triumphant, and he knew it. The handover ceremony had been held early, in secret, and behind blast walls, the concrete teeth that ring the Green Zone. Allawi needed to publicly show that a new tough guy was in charge. The former Baath party operative and U.S. intelligence asset used a political trick as old as the Tigris. He wheeled out the former leader in chains.

On July 1, guards led Saddam Hussein, his feet and wrists in shackles, to a court on a U.S. military base near the Baghdad airport to hear that he was being charged with war crimes.

The day before the arraignment, Moufaq al-Rubaie, Iraq's national security advisor, told me he'd visited Saddam in his cell and seen him cower and tremble like a wet dog during a thunderstorm. Saddam was, al-Rubaie said, "a defeated man. He is really scared, you know. He was shaking. It feels great to the Iraqi people that at least once in his life, he's afraid that Iraqi justice is going to be implemented on him," Rubaie added in English, with a British accent picked up after years living as an exile in London. Rubaie, a Shiite historian and scholar with close ties to the howza, had mysteriously risen to power. Few understood why. He had no experience in security, but was suddenly placed in a senior position. "It's his English. That's the only reason why the Americans like him," one of Allawi's aides told me. "They imposed him on us."

Ironically, an American official said just the opposite. He told me he thought the Iraqis wanted Rubaie and had imposed him on the Americans. Rubaie's rise seems to have been something of an accident, but he was also shrewd and found ways to play the Iraqis off the Americans, slipping himself in the middle of frequent gaps in communication.

Whatever Rubaie saw in Saddam's cell, it didn't show in court. Unshackled at the door, Saddam walked into the courtroom like the CEO of a blue-chip company on casual dress Friday. He wore a charcoal gray suit with a faint pinstripe, a white button-down shirt open at the collar, and immaculately polished black dress shoes. He looked confident, fit, groomed, and in control. He'd been working out twice a day, running in circles and doing calisthenics in his cell during his seven months in captivity. He'd shaved the scraggly salt-and-pepper beard he'd grown while hiding in a hole and dyed his hair as black as his shoes. Saddam, never exactly vain but always conscious of his public image and weight, looked like he was still president, and everyone noticed.

The Turkish tailor who made Saddam's suit, Recep Cesur, the owner of a family-run business in Istanbul that had been supplying Saddam with forty suits a month for more than a decade, reported a 600 percent increase in sales after Saddam's first televised court appearance. Saddam was supposed to have been a trembling monster dragged into the Colosseum by Baghdad's new conquering emperor to be jeered by the masses in a public spectacle. Instead, he became the Middle East's newest fashion icon.

Saddam, then sixty-seven, was both polite and patronizing to the much younger judge. He did most of the talking. "Who are you?" he roared, pointing at the judge with the self-assurance only a dictator could know.

"A representative of the Iraqi people," the judge replied, and started his questioning. "What's your name?" the judge asked.

"Saddam Hussein, president of the Republic of Iraq."

The judge told his stenographer, "Write down the *former* president."

"No, still president," Saddam insisted, "by the will of the people."

"Where do you live?" the judge asked.

It was a stupid question. He obviously lived in American custody. Saddam didn't miss an opportunity.

"I live in every Iraqi home. Why don't I have a lawyer?" he asked.

"If you'd give me a moment," the judge said, getting testy, "I'd tell you, you have the right to one, according to our book of law."

"Yes, I know," Saddam said. "I signed it into law."

The judge accused Saddam of seven crimes, including killing tens of thousands of Kurds in the late 1980s, some with poison gas, assassinating political opponents and religious leaders, murdering thousands of Shiites after the 1991 Gulf War, and invading Kuwait.

"I hope you know this trial is all theater," Saddam said. "The real criminal is Bush."

Saddam's first day in court lasted only thirty minutes, but it was a disaster for Allawi and the Americans.

Allawi's aides tried to brush it off and, inadvertently, made it clear they had no intention of giving Saddam a real trial. For them, he was already guilty. The trial should be fair, they insisted, but there could be only one verdict: guilty.

"To be quite honest with you," Rubaie told me, "what is he going to defend? Defend the mass graves?"

An editor in New York asked me what I thought of Saddam's trial. "He's a dead man walking," I said. "They are just trying to figure out how and when to hang him. It is like an old Agatha Christie murder mystery. We know who died, and all the reasons why, we just don't know how it is going to piece together in the end."

The U.S. administration hoped the transfer of authority to Allawi and the start of Saddam's trial would be major public relations victories. After all, the Butcher of Baghdad was now facing justice, and Iraq was more sovereign than under Bremer. Instead, reporters were increasingly critical. We covered the handover and Saddam's hearing, but also Iran's spreading influence, the rising power of Moqtada al-Sadr, the growing Sunni insurgency, and mounting American casualties, which had just topped one thousand.

That's when we started to feel the pressure. Where were all the "good news" stories? NBC began to receive hundreds of e-mails complaining we were not reporting positive developments in Iraq.

The e-mails were clearly part of a campaign orchestrated by pro-war interest groups in the United States. I know it was organized because at almost exactly the same time, friends from *The Washington Post, Newsweek,* ABC, CNN, and other major news outlets started to complain that they too were facing pressure from their bosses to be more upbeat about Iraq.

I was in my office in Baghdad when I received a call from a very senior NBC executive who asked me if I could find some "good news" to report from Iraq. It was the first time he had called me in over a year in Iraq. I told him I wasn't looking for bad news or good news. I don't have an abacus, keeping track of positive or negative stories.

The morning I got the call, Ali, one of our best fixers and a cameraman, had been in the midst of fighting on Haifa Street in downtown Baghdad. Ali, in his early twenties, had been my driver during the invasion. His father, who was supposed to work with me, had fled the city with his wife. Ali chose to stay, in part out of curiosity, and saved my life several times. He sweet-talked Baath party members out of arresting me during the invasion, and helped me set up safe houses filled with water, crowbars (in case the door jammed, trapping us inside during the bombings), generators, diesel fuel, canned food, and bags of Iraqi dinars. I had trusted him with my life.

That morning, Ali had taken a small Sony PD-150 camera to Haifa Street and crept up on Sunni radicals firing on American soldiers. Ali has an uncanny ability to move without being noticed. He has an innocent baby face. Some people demand attention when they walk into a room and have a commanding presence. Ali is so unassuming he can stand in a corner and hardly be noticed.

Ali had simply parked his car on Haifa Street, walked up to the militants, and starting filming.

"What are you doing here?" an astonished Syrian fighter asked him. Ali could tell he was Syrian from his accent.

"I'm a journalist," he said.

"How did you get here? Who told you you could be here?"

"No one," Ali said, and kept filming.

"Stop that!" the insurgent yelled, and ripped the camera from Ali's hands.

"Wait! Don't take my camera. I need it."

"Get out of here," he said, and raised his rifle.

"Okay, but I need my camera."

"Who are you?"

"Can I have my camera?"

Amazingly, the militant took out the tape, crushed it under his foot, and returned the camera.

Ali walked back to his car—through the kill zone—found another tape, and went back to film more of the fighters, by then too busy shooting to bother with him. He stayed for another half hour filming the fighting just a few blocks from Allawi's office. Yet here I was getting phone calls from New York telling me to go look for flowers and rainbows.

ML Flynn told me there was "tremendous pressure" in the New York newsroom to lighten up our coverage of the war. "Kiddo, I don't tell you the half of it," she said. "I try to shield you from it, but there's a lot of pressure here."

ML, who had more than two decades of experience in the news business and was one of Tom Brokaw's senior producers, told me not to manufacture anything and "try to forget about the pressure." I trusted her judgment and ignored the calls and e-mails.

Secretly, it bothered me that executives and interest groups seven thousand miles away were trying to tell me what was going on outside my window. It really annoyed my colleague Larry Kaplow, an excellent reporter then working for the Cox Newspapers group. I'd known Larry since we'd covered the Palestinian al-Aqsa Intifada in the West Bank and Gaza Strip in 2000. Together we'd watched the daily bloody theater of protests, stone throwing, gun battles, and funerals, which inevitably led to more protests, stone throwing, gun battles, and funerals for both Palestinians and Israelis. We'd come to Iraq about the same time before the war and both stayed at the Palestine hotel during the bombardment. Larry briefly stopped reporting during the invasion to try to free his friend Matt McAllester, who'd been arrested by Saddam's intelligence service and locked in Abu Ghraib prison.

"This push for good news stories is everywhere," Larry said. "I was talking to a press spokesman at the embassy. She's been here all of two months and she is telling me Iraqis are happy and everything is working. I thought, 'It should be *illegal* for her to tell me what Iraqis think.' "

In Kaplow's typical dry wit he asked, "If it's raining outside and I tell you that you're getting wet, is that bad news?"

There was a growing impression in Washington and on the Internet that reporters in Iraq were a bunch of cynical "freedom haters" penned up in the Green Zone drinking gin and tonics and not brave enough to go out and report about the progress in Iraq. The Iraqis had written a temporary constitution. Authority had been transferred to Allawi. Saddam was in court. What was our problem? Were we blind, or just stupid? We didn't live in the Green Zone and I, like nearly all reporters, went out of the bureau every day. I believe most American journalists wanted the war to be a success. I personally didn't want to see American soldiers or Iraqis dying. I hate violence. I was delighted that Saddam had been removed from power. I wanted Iraqis to have a free society. The problem was that I just wasn't seeing good news stories when I visited cities like Samara.

The last time I'd visited Samara, it was under attack. In December 2003, the army's 4th Infantry Division launched Operation Ivy Blizzard with two thousand soldiers and two hundred Bradleys.

The goal was to clear the city of suspected Saddam loyalists in a single sweep. Saddam had just been captured and the army wanted to keep the momentum rolling. At 3 A.M. in a former airplane hangar outside Samara with a cold cement floor, the troops huddled for a pre-mission brief.

"The insurgency in Samara ends tonight!" an army captain told the men, their faces painted green and brown, their watches covered with black tape to block reflections off the glass.

The soldiers crept house to house, walking in gutters and staying away from walls. (Guerrilla fighters often pop around street corners and lean up against walls when they shoot. Staying a few feet off a wall can save your life.) The troops broke into homes, shooting solid shotgun slugs to knock off locks. They rigged medical IV bags with C-4 plastic explosives to push in metal gates. The water in the IV bag would spread the force of the blast across the surface of the gate, to rip the door from its hinges without damaging the rest of the building. In military-speak it's a "water-impulse charge." If the gates still didn't fall, Humvees smashed them in. It was the early days. There was no Iraqi government back then. It was still straight-up war: us versus them. The soldiers got it, and the people of Samara got it, or got out of the way.

After Allawi and the transfer of authority, the rules of the game changed. Confusion set in. The American civil administration ("the goddamn embassy") was operating under the illusion that there was now an Iraqi government in charge. They pretended Iraq was a normal state facing a few troubles and in need of some outside help from America. In his farewell speech, Bremer said the handover meant "the end of the occupation of Iraq," and that the interim government should "assume and exercise full sovereign authority on behalf of the Iraqi people."

It was delusional. Iraq was not anything like a sovereign nation. It had no effective troops. Bremer had dissolved them. Allawi wanted to be a strongman, but he had no forces. The Americans had handed Iraq to no one, but they were living the myth—with devastating results in places like Samara.

Samara had been mostly quiet after Operation Ivy Blizzard. The people of the city didn't want to be invaded again and stayed away from the Americans. But after Iraq became a "sovereign nation," the commanders in Baghdad ordered American forces out of Samara. It would now be up to Iraqi troops and Allawi's government to secure the city. It's now yours, run it.

Not surprisingly, the Iraqi security forces and government, existing mostly on paper, failed completely. Samara quickly fell into the hands of Zarqawi and foreign fighters who'd spread throughout western and northern Iraq after the aborted Marine offensive in Falujah in April. The military estimated that the number of hard-core fighters in Samara swelled from three hundred when the Americans left the city to two thousand just a few weeks later. It was a direct result of the handover myth.

We arrived just after American troops decided they had no choice but to reenter Samara. This time, however, they were trying an approach different from that of Ivy Blizzard. The new strategy was a mix of force and a hearts-and-minds campaign, tickling the city with a boxing glove. But even then, the idea was to reestablish order, and then quickly insert Iraqi troops and let them take charge. It's yours now, control it, damnit!

The U.S. hearts-and-minds campaign started with a simple mission. U.S. troops wanted to give a local sheikh $1,500. The money was to repair the minaret of a small mosque across town from Samara's golden-domed al-Askari shrine. "I'm going to make good on a promise to the sheikh and give him money. I am going to put it in his hand, look him in the eye, and tell him I expect to see results from this money," Captain Ben Marlin of Alpha Company, 1st Infantry Division, told us before heading into Samara for the first time in two months.

While I was embedded with the troops, we'd also dispatched an Iraqi team to Samara to report on the other half of the story. Saad the cameraman and Mohammed, one of our Sunni translators, drove from Baghdad to Samara. Their job was to talk to people in the city to see what they thought about the Americans and Allawi's new government. Our two teams were not in communication. The plan was to combine the two elements gathered independently into a single story.

Within minutes of arriving in Samara, insurgents forced Saad and Mohammed off the road. "I thought they were going to kill us," Mohammed later told me. "They took us to see their emir [prince]. We told him we were reporters and they forced us to follow them. They said they were going to attack American soldiers and wanted us to film it."

The American soldiers the insurgents planned to attack were Captain Marlin's men, along with our crew.

Marlin's convoy of Humvees rolled into Samara as planned. Marlin met the sheikh and gave him the $1,500. "The insurgents were watching the whole time," Mohammed said. "I saw our crew was with them, but we couldn't say anything. I had no way to communicate with you," Mohammed said apologetically.

Cell phones weren't working in the area, so our crew couldn't have gotten a message out even if the insurgents had let them. Mohammed and Saad feared they were about to record their own colleagues being ambushed. But the militants never attacked. After a short meeting with the sheikh, Captain Marlin left, satisfied he'd accomplished his mission. "The insurgents decided there were too many troops. They wanted to wait for a better time, but they kept following the patrol," Mohammed said.

After leaving the mosque, Marlin's soldiers stopped cars at a checkpoint and handed out battery-powered radios. It was more hearts and minds, but with a specific purpose. Marlin hoped Iraqis would use the radios to listen to American broadcasts that advertised the tip lines Iraqis could call if they had information about insurgent activity. "The radio station is pretty much used to get the American point across," Marlin said.

After the U.S. patrol left Samara to return to base, the insurgents moved in. They stopped cars and demanded the radios, which they smashed with stones.

I left Samara thinking the Americans had enough firepower to come in and out of the city as they pleased, but that they were not in control. No one was in clear control, but the insurgents were certainly organized.

A few days after our report, Condoleezza Rice, Bush's national security advisor, told Tom Brokaw in an interview that Samara was one of the success stories in Iraq that the media were ignoring. The sovereign Iraqi government was now in control of the city, she said. Brokaw told her we'd found a very different picture in Samara. Rice insisted we were mistaken. It seems she may have been given old information. Two weeks later, 1,500 marines and Iraqi national guards launched a major offensive to retake Samara. But again, they didn't stay long, thrusting responsibility back into the hands of an Iraqi army and government that didn't really exist.

9

The fall of 2004 was political crunch time for both Bush and Allawi. For Bush, zero hour was in November, when he would fight for a second term against Democrat John Kerry. "Isn't he the husband of that rich woman?" an Iraqi asked me when I asked him if he was following the American elections. Iraqis I interviewed didn't know much about Kerry, but generally thought he seemed effeminate. They preferred Bush's and Bremer's direct and macho demeanor.

Allawi's deadline was the end of December. By year's end, he would have to organize Iraq's first free election in decades and run his own political campaign. But Bush and Allawi faced a common immediate problem: the Sunnis of Anbar. Sunnis were threatening to boycott the vote, and Zarqawi was increasingly effective, carrying out thirty-eight car bombings in Baghdad in September alone. The Sunnis were fighting, not preparing for democracy.

In October, I signed up with the military press office—CPIC—to embed with marines in Ramadi, the capital of Anbar, to see what U.S. troops were doing to prepare for voting day in the hard-line Sunni city of 400,000.

I was lucky to have the right team. Producer Gene Choo: the irascible former Korean soldier who'd nearly been shot by an American soldier at a checkpoint in the Green Zone. Cameraman Kevin Burke: a classic type-A personality, an energetic perfectionist, and a former combat cameraman with the U.S. Navy. Soundman Martin Francis: a young, smart, and technically savvy engineer, and a former soldier in the British army. We gathered at midnight in the Green Zone, waiting at the LZ (landing zone) for "the bird."

The marines would travel by air from Baghdad to Ramadi only at night, worried their lumbering CH-46 Sea Knight transport helicopters could easily be shot down.

Midnight came and went. There was no sign of the bird. "If you've got time to spare, fly Marine Air," joked a marine leaning up against a concrete barrier and smoking a cigarette. He'd been waiting four hours for a flight. Our chances were worse than his.

As journalists, we flew "Space A," Space Available, and could be bumped if the marines needed to load more men or gear. Fair enough. But that night they had special cargo.

"It's an angel flight," a marine shouted at me as the tandem-rotor CH-46 touched down on the LZ, lit with red and blue lights. Colored lights can't be seen easily from a distance; they're "contained," unlike white light, which "splashes" like noise against rocks.

The chopper was still running, loud as hell, and I couldn't understand the marine on the LZ. I pulled out one of my foam earplugs. The marine leaned in, his lips almost touching my ears. He grabbed the back of my black Kevlar helmet like he was going to bite me.

"It's an angel flight! No filming!" he repeated into my ear.

"Okay," I yelled back, and gave a thumbs-up to show I understood.

The rear hatch of the chopper lowered like a ramp and we rolled our boxes of cameras, tapes, and lights inside.

The coffin was already on board, bound for an airbase in northern Iraq and then on to the States for yet another funeral for yet another young American. We weren't allowed to film funerals or angel flights. There weren't supposed to be dead Americans in Iraq. They didn't fit the picture, especially so close to the November presidential elections. If we filmed the coffin, the military would revoke our CPIC badges and blacklist us from embeds. Without a CPIC badge, you also can't go to the Green Zone, which houses the only trustworthy hospital in Baghdad. If you lose your CPIC badge, you can't even go to the U.S. embassy, which is also in the Green Zone. Without a CPIC badge, you're screwed, and the military knows it, holding the threat of pulling the credit-card-sized ID over the media like Damocles' sword.

Kevin and I sat at either end of the coffin, strapped onto the chopper's canvas benches by four-point straps with round metal buckles in the center of our chests.

We didn't talk. We couldn't. It was so noisy, we'd written our destination, Camp Blue Diamond, on the backs of our hands with a black Sharpie: "B.D." The chopper had to make several stops before landing at Blue Diamond, and at night all the LZs look the same, dusty and black. We didn't want to get off on the wrong one.

The chopper crew made sure the coffin was strapped in and gave the order to lift off. The rear hatch closed, but only halfway. The crew left it open so a gunner could point his .50 cal into the black night.

The chopper flew low and slow over Baghdad. I looked out the windows, big and round like the portals of an old submarine. My left leg was pressed against the coffin. I tried to pull it away out of respect.

Even though the motor was loud, I found myself drifting in and out of sleep. The CH-46 makes an oddly relaxing chukka-chukka-chukka sound like a steam train chugging along. The CH-46 has been in service since Vietnam. It's nothing like the slick, modulated, and computerized Apache attack helicopter. The CH-46's cabin is roomy and open and has exposed wires running along the walls. The Apache is like a high-end Mercedes, so computerized and packed with gadgets that it feels as foreign and intimidating as a spaceship. The CH-46 is as comfortable as an old Ford pickup. But Apaches rarely get shot down; CH-46s do.

Every time the bird landed, I held up my hand and showed the "B.D." to the crew, anonymous behind storm trooper face masks attached to their flight helmets. After about five stops a crewman yelled "Blue Diamond," and we rolled out our gear past the coffin.

Standing in dust up to my ankles, a powder so fine it penetrates every pore in your shoes and then mixes with sweat and turns to clay, I watched the chopper blades hit the sand in the air and turn it into yellow sparks. The sparks made a glowing halo over the dark green bird in the star-filled night. War and its machines can be so beautiful and seductive, until you remember what they do.

Blue Diamond was the main base in the Ramadi area. It was a giant, ugly mini-city with gravel roads, blast walls, rows of housing trailers (hooches), several chow halls, a PX (postal exchange), a Green Bean Café (the military's Starbucks), an Indian tailor, and a barbershop that gave military haircuts, "high and tight," for $3 apiece. Sometimes Blue Diamond was mortared, but it was so big most of the mortars fell as harmlessly as meteors.

Blue Diamond was an odd mix of military austerity and golf course comfort. In the MWR (morale, welfare, and recreation) there was a twenty-four-hour Internet connection, big-screen TVs, and signs advertising an upcoming Salsa Night. Some marines complained they'd been getting fat from the five kinds of cheesecake and four flavors of Baskin-Robbins ice cream served at the chow hall run by Halliburton's Kellogg, Brown & Root, KBR. A few marines called it "Kellogg, Burn & Loot."

There are two radically different military lives in Iraq. There are troops that live on the mega-FOBs (forward operating bases) like Blue Diamond. They are the military's "tail," the logisticians who handle payroll, transport, command and control, maintenance, and everything else that makes the military machine run. The other soldiers and marines are "the teeth," the fighters (they prefer to be called "warriors") "in theater" patrolling "outside the wire," kicking down doors on "cordon and knock" operations and searching for

IEDs (improvised explosive devices). These men, and a handful of women, live "in the shit" outside the FOB. They call the troops who serve on FOBs like Blue Diamond "Fobits." (Rhymes with "hobbits.")

"Fobits are the kind of people who will get on your case for not stopping at a stop sign, or being out of uniform," a soldier once told me. "They have no fucking idea of what's going on outside the wire. The generals are Fobits too. The Fobits run the war. Beware of the wrath of the Fobits."

The Green Zone is also an FOB. The American diplomats and contractors who live there are the worst Fobits of all.

I wasn't interested in the Fobits. I wanted to meet the marines who lived in downtown Ramadi, in the battle zone, twenty-four hours a day. I was heading to a small "firm base" simply and aptly named Combat Outpost. But getting to Combat Outpost meant stopping over at Blue Diamond. Combat Outpost was dependent on Blue Diamond for food, fuel, mail, toilet paper, and, most important, ammunition. After a night on cots in a visitors tent, we joined a convoy, a chuck wagon—the marines called it "Boxcar"—heading out to Combat Outpost. We were up early, before sunrise, at "o Dark 30."

Boxcar was a convoy of Humvees and "7-tons," which are little more than big stock trucks lined with sandbags. The Humvees were ratty too. The marines had welded plates of steel over the doors, "add-on armor." It was old-fashioned American ingenuity, but it came with a cost. The Humvees weren't built to handle the extra weight of the half-inch-thick plates. The metal put too much pressure on the doors' hinges. As a result, the Humvees were "harder," but you often couldn't open the doors from inside, which is a problem if the vehicle catches fire or the ammo starts to go up, or if you're injured, or in any of a thousand terrible but very possible scenarios. The Humvee I was in didn't even have full doors or windows at all. You had to hunch down in your seat to avoid sniper fire.

As Boxcar rolled out of Blue Diamond, crossing the wire, we passed a hand-painted sign that warned, "Complacency Kills." I shook my head in disbelief. "Complacency kills?" I thought. "How about these broken-down Humvees held together with glue and staples? It's the Fobits who never leave the base or ride in these pieces of shit who kill. It's the King Fobits, the commanders seven thousand miles away in Washington who kill. It's *their* complacency we should worry about." I was annoyed that so many politicians in the United States talked about supporting the troops but let them ride around Iraq like cowboys in busted jeeps with "hillbilly armor."

When Boxcar pulled into Combat Outpost, it was clear we were far away from the FOB, and its ice cream bars, Internet connections, and salsa nights. The first thing I saw was three marines stirring "burn toilets," oil drums cut in half and filled with shit, toilet paper, and diesel fuel. It's a primitive but effective latrine. When the oil drums fill up, unlucky marines drag them out from under outhouses, flood them with the diesel, and drop in a match. They have to stir the soup to keep it burning. I watched black fumes waft up into the marines' faces as they leaned over the pots with wooden paddles. You can't piss in a burn toilet. If you urinate in the outhouse, the marines get furious. Urine doesn't burn off with diesel. For urinals, the marines sank "piss tubes"—two feet of plastic pipe—into the ground and propped them up with rocks. Fortunately, the marines put us in a room upwind.

We bunked with eight visiting soldiers from a PsyOps team. Their job was to print leaflets, and ride around Ramadi in Humvees with loudspeakers on the roofs, taunting fighters in Arabic, calling them cowards and homosexuals. They wanted to enrage the militants and draw them into the open so the marines could shoot them. "It's not about hearts and minds out here," a marine said. "It's about finding the enemy and putting two [bullets] in his heart, and one in his mind."

Lieutenant Brian Iglesias, a muscular young officer with a shaved head, woke us the next morning at o Dark 30. Iglesias had a tattoo across his chest that read "*Teufelshunde,*" German for "Devil Dogs," the Marines' nickname. Marine lore says German soldiers during World War I gave the Marines the name after ferocious hand-to-hand combat at the battle of Belleau Wood. The Devil Dogs lost more than a thousand men, but drove the Germans from the wood. Iglesias was keeping up the Devil Dog tradition.

"Get up, I want to show you guys something," he said.

We followed Iglesias across a dusty motor pool to a shack on the far side of the base. Two Iraqi insurgents were on the floor. One was dead, shot in the chest near the heart. He was sprawled out on a cement floor. An RPG sat next to his dead hand. Marines had shot the other insurgent in the face. He was gurgling blood and feebly kicking his legs. As he moaned and tried to speak, he drooled blood and blew red foamy bubbles from his quivering lips.

"It's a good day," Iglesias said, congratulating the sniper team responsible for the "confirmed kills."

"These snipers snuck into an Iraqi house and waited for days. They moved in, entering through a window. The Iraqis in the house didn't even know they were there, that's how good they were," Iglesias told us proudly.

Our cameraman, Kevin, tried to take pictures of the dead insurgent in a way that would not be too disturbing to our audience. We don't run pictures of bleeding bodies, American or Iraqi. People die in war, but we don't show it. We're not allowed to show dead Americans. We don't run graphic pictures of dead Iraqis out of decorum. Kevin mostly shot close-ups of the dead man's hands and feet, the RPG, and blood on the floor. It was artistic, but the idea was clear enough.

"These guys," Iglesias said, pointing to the dead and dying insurgents, "have been ambushing us for weeks. They have been killing marines."

But they'd made a fatal mistake. The Iraqi militants had started to use the same road to stage their attacks. Patterns in Iraq will kill you. The Marine snipers had set up a counterambush, bunkering in a house overlooking the road, watching and waiting.

"As soon as this guy got out of the car with an RPG, they took him out. His friend tried to get away," Iglesias explained. "We say it's a good day not because we enjoy walking around and killing people, but these bad guys attack us on a daily basis and they slither through the town and they blend in with the people and put the civilians in jeopardy.

"This time we caught 'em. We caught 'em red-handed."

Several marines had started to gather around the shack. They were taking pictures of the dead and dying men. It was a rare treat. The marines hardly ever saw the militants who put bombs in the road or sniped from rooftops. One marine was carrying brass knuckles.

"What's that?" I asked him.

"It's an interrogation tool," was all he said.

Before the dying militant could be "interrogated," a medic gave him a lethal injection. He died quietly a few moments later. But the fighter had already been taught a lesson. As the marines brought the two insurgents back to Combat Outpost, they'd sat the injured man on top of his dead friend, giving him a final message: "Don't attack marines."

As I watched the marines take happy snaps, slap one another on the back, and poke at the now dead men with their boots, they seemed like hunters admiring a big elk they'd killed. I thought of them as urban hunters, camping on this horrible little base and stalking prey. They could have been in a duck blind in Arkansas shooting mallards. Instead, they were here at Combat Outpost, shooting Iraqi insurgents. But those were Ramadi's rules, and I was about to learn that a hunter one day could easily be prey the next.

On our fourth day at Combat Outpost, the marines were cursing under their breath. They were clearly annoyed and agitated. The army was about to arrive. U.S. Army soldiers based in Falujah were about to descend on Combat Outpost to stage an "op" (operation) nearby. They weren't asking the marines for help. They just wanted to use their real estate. The soldiers wanted the marines to stay out of their way.

The U.S. Army has soldiers. The Marine Corps has marines. Don't call a marine a soldier, especially at Combat Outpost.

Soldiers based near Falujah had turned up intelligence that the ill-fated Falujah Brigade had transferred huge stockpiles of rifles and ammunition to insurgent groups in Ramadi. The Falujah Brigade—the militia the United States created to control Falujah after calling off Vigilant Resolve—had taken American-purchased AK-47s and hundreds of thousands of rounds of ammunition and sold them to Baath party fighters in Ramadi. The Americans had inadvertently armed their own enemies. The army's intel indicated that the stolen weapons were being stored at an Iraqi army base near Combat Outpost. It was yet another betrayal. The United States was funding and training the new Iraqi army. But the new army was hiding weapons for insurgents in Ramadi.

The soldiers who discovered the duplicity could have asked the marines already in Ramadi to raid the base. It would have been safer, easier, and much cheaper. The marines knew the "AO" (area of operations) and were close by. But since the army had developed the intel, army commanders wanted to reap the glory and were willing to drive across western Iraq and into a city they didn't know to do it. The army wanted its soldiers to return the missing American weapons. It was a petty turf war. All the army asked was to use Combat Outpost as a staging area for a couple of hours before moving in to raid the Iraqi army base. The marines' answer was an unenthusiastic "Knock yourselves out."

The soldiers arrived at Combat Outpost in a huge convoy of APCs (armored personnel carriers), Bradleys, and up-armored Humvees. It seemed a bit much. They showed up with as much force as the marines had on the entire base. "They always go in heavy like that, but they never get out of the vehicles," I overheard one marine say. "It's a waste of time. You gotta have boots on the ground."

It was as if a neighbor had shown up to a dinner party with a fancy new car the host couldn't afford. The marines were critical and a bit jealous. The marines' worn-out Humvees and hillbilly trucks looked destined for the junk pile. The army's vehicles looked like they still had price tags on them. "The army always gets the best stuff," a marine told me. "We're a small corps, last on the list."

As the soldiers rolled out to raid the Iraqi base, another marine—by now all the marines had become armchair quarterbacks and military analysts—said, "Just wait, they're going to get hit as they leave. These bastards watch you when you go in, see how much force you got. Then hit you as you're leaving."

He was dead-on.

As the army finished loading the stolen weapons into their vehicles and pulling out, I heard the RPGs explode. We could see yellow flashes across Ramadi and hear the army's .50 cals and 30 mils chewing up the city. It was intense, but over quickly. After about five minutes, the night was silent again. The quiet didn't last long.

"QRF! QRF!" marines were yelling, scrabbling like firemen called to a seven-alarm.

A QRF, a quick reaction force, was being called into action.

I saw Lieutenant Iglesias loading his platoon into Humvees and a 7-ton.

"What's up?" I asked.

"They lost a guy," Brian said quickly, looking around to make sure all his men were in, "ready to roll."

"What?"

"They lost a guy, the army, they lost a guy. We gotta go."

"Can I come?"

"Climb in if you can find room."

I jumped in the back of the 7-ton. It started to move as Kevin climbed in and banged his knee into the side of the truck.

"What the fuck is going on?" I asked a marine next to me.

"Those fucking soldiers, after they got attacked, they left a guy in the fucking city. They didn't realize he was missing until they were back at their base, the fucking idiots," the marine said, his rifle raised, tracking buildings, doorways, parked cars, cats, shadows, and anything else that crossed his line of sight.

A soldier had been killed in the ambush outside the Iraqi army base. The other soldiers had dismounted, fired like crazy, and then mounted up again, accidentally leaving a man behind.

"It's so fucked up. It was a total cluster fuck," the marine said, not looking at me.

The QRF drove to the scene of the ambush, the last place the soldier had been seen, and started the manhunt.

"Let's stay together," I turned to say to Kevin, but he was already across the street filming and interviewing marines.

A marine cupped his hands by the sides of his mouth and called out the missing soldier's name like a lost dog. "Lux!" he yelled. "Lux!"

I could feel my heart pounding so hard I felt it throbbing in my fingers as I looked down empty alleys of shops gated shut for the night. I ran across the street to join Kevin. He was next to Iglesias.

"If you see anybody running around, make sure you make positive ID before you shoot because it could be him," Iglesias whispered to his men.

I could hear drones in the sky, and the marines had fired illumination flares to help in the search.

"You gotta move slow," Brian cautioned his men, "move stealthy 'cause you know those sons of bitches are out there. Stay in the shadows. Stay outta the light."

We all knew the search party was being hunted. Insurgents in Ramadi, most of them former soldiers themselves, studied the Americans' movements and watched the gates of the bases. They knew we were out there, hopelessly outnumbered. There were only about a dozen of us, on foot, in the center of Ramadi. There were no tracking devices implanted in the soldiers' uniforms, or high-tech satellite technology to help them like in Hollywood movies. They were on their own. A dozen men on foot—some carrying shotguns, others crowbars, "hooligan tools"—looking down streets and into Dumpsters for the missing soldier, or maybe his body.

Brian ordered his men to turn off the 7-ton's engine, then changed his mind.

"Turn it back on," he said, "maybe the kid can hear it and will come to it."

We walked for several hours, occasionally taking a knee, then running across alleys, searching.

We saw nothing, and heard nothing, until Iglesias got a call on his radio.

"I'll hug you and every other marine if we find this kid," he said. "He's not even a marine, but he's an American. I hope to God they found him.

"Roger—got him. We got him. Got the kid," Iglesias said. "It feels great 'cause I can only imagine what they woulda done to him if they did catch him."

Lux had stripped off his uniform and hidden behind a Dumpster. He ran out when he saw an American vehicle pass by and was rescued.

There were no cheers. We were still in the middle of Ramadi.

Iglesias and his marines made it back to Combat Outpost.

The base was mortared all night. The marines played poker. Twenty-dollar buy-in.

10

On November 3, 2004, George W. Bush won his reelection. Four more years. Four days later, the marines attacked Falujah. You do the math.

The White House, which had to authorize such a major offensive, didn't want marines dying as Americans went to the polls. By late 2004, America wasn't even supposed to be at war anymore, let alone invading entire renegade cities. After all, Bush had declared "major combat" over in May 2003. Now his spin doctors and spin nurses were busy chirping that Iraq was just swimming with "good news" stories that reporters like me refused to tell because we were no-good freedom haters, lazy Green Zone hacks, or just too obstinate or stupid to see the light at the end of the tunnel of democratic bliss.

The marines had been itching to fight Sunni insurgents in Falujah since Bremer and his "goddamn embassy" halted Operation Vigilant Resolve in April 2004 to allow the "transfer of sovereignty" to take place according to yet another White House–driven timeline. After that aborted mission, marines complained that Zarqawi's suicide brigades had become emboldened and intensified their car bombings. Sunni insurgents bragged on their Web sites that they'd won.

This time, the marines planned to be decisive. They planned to kick ass.

A frustrated army officer based in Taji, north of Baghdad, once told me, "The Bush administration always says, 'Decisions in Iraq are *conditions-based*, and that timing is strictly based on *conditions on the ground*.' But they don't say that the ground is in D.C."

About three weeks before the U.S. elections, commanders started to corral more than ten thousand marines and soldiers from across Iraq to ring Falujah, the "city of mosques." But that was only part of the offensive. They also called in the press. The marines wanted a big show. Operation Vigilant Resolve had been a public embarrassment. It was as if the marines didn't have it in them to take one little upstart city; and there's nothing more dangerous than an embarrassed marine.

Media liaison officers and CPIC coordinated with American TV networks and major newspapers to embed camera crews and re- porters for the fight. They wanted us in position about a week be- fore "the big push." We began to squabble right away. The marines' plan was to embed journalists with units we would follow though- out the battle; the plan was simple and fair. Every network would get one crew. Every crew would be assigned to one unit. There would be no switiching from unit to unit. It was as if we were being assigned to teams before a big game of Capture the Flag. The prob- lem was, journalists don't think that way. We all want to be the ex- ception, every time. We all wanted to be with front-line units, the best teams, seeing the most action. If ABC or CNN was going to be at the tip of the spear, pushing into Falujah, we at NBC were damned if we were going to be stuck with rear-echelon troops firing artillery from a distance. It was supposed to be luck of the draw, but we were jostling for the best seats for the performance, front row center. War makes great TV. It's the sexiest ugly fucking thing in the world. Don't let anyone tell you different.

To prevent us from elbowing to get to the front of the line, we thankfully decided to pool our coverage. If one unit happened to get into a major firefight, which is what we were all fishing for, all the networks would be allowed to broadcast the footage. This way, we wouldn't have to fight over the best images and push ourselves deeper into battle. Otherwise, we would have killed one another.

By Election Day, the stage was set. The marines were in place, the reporters were ready, and our cameras were rolling. When Bush won, the marines went wild.

The major offensive in Falujah lasted only about ten days. I was stuck in Baghdad covering the big-picture story, reporting on what the offensive meant for Iraq and American policy. I was furious. Another of our correspondents, Kevin Sites, had moved in on me and taken my place. He had embedded with the marines a few weeks before the U.S. elections. I was supposed to swap out with him before the action kicked off, but Sites refused to leave. "The marines don't want to swap me out," he told our editors. It was bullshit. He didn't want to leave, and the marines didn't care. One media body was as good as the next for them. Ours is a cutthroat business. Sites caught me napping. He screwed me, but ultimately did a superb job. I was angry with myself for having let my guard down and missing the big fight.

Over too many drinks in my room at the Hamra before the Falujah offensive, veteran cameraman Seb Rich advised me that "only fools rush in." He'd know. Seb was shot in the chest in Bosnia (he was wearing a flak jacket, but the force of the bullet knocked his heart out of rhythm) and hit by shrapnel in his face. Seb's face no longer springs back in place when he rubs it. Instead, his skin moves like putty. If he pushes down his cheek, it stays there, locked in a frown, until he pushes it back up again.

Seb is right, only fools rush in, but when you're caught up in the moment and your blood is hot and the battle is so close you can almost smell the munitions, it's easy to be that fool.

I finally arrived in Falujah on Thanksgiving Day. As usual with the military, the day began at 0 Dark 30. I was with with my usual "combat team," cameraman Kevin Burke and soundman Martin Francis. We gathered at Camp Falujah—one of the Wal-Mart-like Super-FOBs on the outskirts of the city—and watched marines load up their hulking "War Pigs" with insulated brown plastic tubs of sliced turkey, roast beef, mashed potatoes, canned corn, cranberry sauce, and, yes, even pumpkin pie, all supplied by KBR.

The War Pig is the marines' version of the army's Bradley. It's a big, boxy troop carrier with a pointed front that looks, at least to some marines, like a pig's snout. It's a piece of junk and makes a hell of a racket when it rolls on its tracks. The War Pig was designed to be deployed from a landing craft to make a beach landing, which, needless to say, is pretty useless in Iraq. It was built to be light and float, which also means that its armor is too thin to protect against most IEDs. The army—the military's giant—and the air force—its pampered elite—get the best toys. The marines—the military's tough guys—slug it out with War Pigs and 7-tons.

Gunnery Sergeant Eduardo Ramos, a stocky man with a big, toothy smile and a low boiling point, was in charge of the meal run. His mission was to bring holiday chow to a company of marines living on a tiny firm base in south Falujah's Golan neighborhood, one of the most damaged areas where al-Qaeda fighters had been holed up. The chow run was a chance for me to see Falujah. After the offensive, the marines made it difficult for reporters to go to the city. The CPIC and the military's PR bureaucracy brought us in for the sound-and-light show, but then kept us away when the performance was over. I was about to see why.

The firm base in Golan was nothing more than an unremarkable two-story tan cement house surrounded by other equally unremarkable two-story tan cement houses. The marines of Alpha Company were packed in every room, sleeping on the floor, shaving, or reading *FHM* and *Men's Health* magazines. The house smelled like urine and rotting feet. I expected the marines to be excited when the chuck wagon pulled in. Instead, they were silent and barely seemed to notice. They'd lost two men in the last two weeks and were too tired to care about us, chow, cleaning up, or anything else. They hadn't showered or eaten a hot meal in two weeks. The dust was so thick on the floor I left boot prints as if I'd been walking in snow.

In a yard behind the house, I watched a marine piss into a water bottle and then toss it over his head like a grenade into the garden of a house next door. Bombs away. The marines never bothered much with hearts and minds. Another marine in the yard was reading *Lord of the Flies*. The FOB, KBR, and the Fobits seemed hundreds of miles away. This was "the suck."

Gunnery Sergeant Ramos immediately started to yell. He had no time for Alpha Company's apathy, exhaustion, and depression. He needed to unload the chow, eat, and get the hell out of there in less than two hours. "Everybody, organize a line!" he yelled, moving through the house, shaking sleeping marines, and kicking them with his boots.

"Get up. Organize a line! Help unload the trucks!"

Corporal Ron Underdahl of Albany, Georgia, slowly climbed out of his sleeping bag and stretched. Then he reached back into the bag and pulled out two puppies. They squirmed in his hands, swimming in the air. The dogs couldn't have been more than six weeks old. Underdahl said he'd found them abandoned during the fighting. Now they slept on his chest, keeping each other warm. "It'd be nice to be back with my family for Thanksgiving, but, out here, I'm with my buddies," he told me as he petted one of the dogs. He never looked at me. He just stared at the puppy. "We've been going through all this stuff, so I don't mind it, as long as I get to eat with my friends."

Outside, the marines had arranged the foil-covered tubs into a single-file line. The orderly chow line seemed to relax Ramos, an eighteen-year marine veteran.

"I ain't a tough guy. Am I a tough guy?" Ramos jokingly asked a marine. "I'm a sweetheart."

The marines moved down the line dressed in "full battle rattle"—body armor and Kevlar—as they served themselves turkey, corn, and pumpkin pie.

But then a marine served himself both turkey *and* roast beef. Ramos exploded.

"Hey, it's one or one! You know what I'm saying? Until, hey, it looks like there's going to be enough. You know what I'm saying? Everyone gets one or the other. Who's got the potatoes? Okay. One scoop. Gravy? One scoop."

While we ate, word came over the radio that two other marines were killed a few blocks away. Ten marines put down their plates and set off on foot to see if they could help.

It was too late. Half an hour later, they came back and finished their meals. No one talked about what they had seen. I didn't want to ask.

We left the firm base with Ramos and returned to Camp Falujah. We headed to the medical station, Bravo Surgical Company— "The Cheaters of Death"—to find out more about the two dead marines. Doctors and navy corpsmen were running through the OR, carrying needles, IV bags, and blood. Although the offensive was supposed to be over, Bravo Surgical was still receiving twenty-five casualties a day.

"Let's go. Let's see what we got here," a corpsman yelled as he wheeled in a gurney piled with three bleeding Iraqi soldiers. They'd been ambushed, shot, and hit with a "frag" grenade.

"What have we got?" called out another corpsman.

"Multiple shrapnel wounds!"

"Which one's your most serious injured?"

"This one."

Dr. Eric Lovell, head of Bravo Surgical, moved in to see for himself.

"Abdominal wounds," he said.

Lovell, a handsome, athletic man, was fast and efficient. His team worked like a NASCAR pit crew. Bravo Surgical had only three operating rooms, fifty beds, and five surgeons. At the peak of the offensive, they'd treated seventy-five casualties a day. Even now, they barely slept.

But Lovell was calm and quietly called out instructions. "You just listen to his lungs," he told a corpsman. "Good."

"Heart rate, 94. Let's keep him warm. With a wool blanket, if we can get one."

They couldn't find a blanket. The Iraqi soldier, naked and bleeding, shivered on the operating table.

I interviewed Dr. Lovell as he sewed up the soldier. It was so routine, Lovell would sew, turn to look up at the camera for a few seconds, look back at the wounds, and keep talking. "The wounded came in waves, some were brought right to the door in tanks," he said. "I treated gunshots to the head. I watched wounded marines carry in wounded marines."

He sewed a bit more in silence, concentrating, then resumed the interview. "Many asked to go straight back to the front to fight alongside their buddies. 'Doc,' they'd say, 'I need to get back out there.' "

Lovell was silent for a few more minutes as he closed the wound and wiped his hands. He stared at me for a minute before speaking again, with a 1,000-yard stare. I doubt he saw me. He never blinked.

Then Lovell told me about a marine he'd treated. The young man had been brought in with an unexploded RPG embedded in his abdomen. RPGs (mostly Russian-made) are designed to be shot at tanks or armored troop carriers. They explode on impact. But this round had hit the marine directly and didn't go off. His chest was too soft. The rocket just bored in like a big spear.

Still staring through me, Lovell said he operated on the marine for an hour and gave him a blood transfusion, but couldn't save him. "When it became apparent that our efforts would not succeed, the chaplain was in the operating room with him and began— began to give him last rites," Lovell said. His voice was cracking. "And he—he could see a tear from the patient's eyes as—as he gave him last rites. And it was—it was very moving for everyone in the room. And then the patient passed on."

I swallowed hard and I pictured that marine, dying but still awake, crying as he heard the chaplain reading him last rites. I could see the man—they are all so damn young—on the operating table, the priest over him, sending him off. I looked up and saw Lovell was quietly crying to himself. He said everyone in the

OR had broken down as they watched the marine realize that he was listening to his final words and that they could do nothing to help him.

We filed one of our little two-minute movies for the 6:30 *Nightly News* about Dr. Lovell and the Bravo Surgical Company. Everybody loved it. The editors sent us "hero grams." The e-mails said:

"Very moving!"

"Great stuff."

"Wow!!!"

"What do you have next?"

We'd become war pornographers.

Two days later, we went with a "cleanup" team of engineers to the center of Falujah. A bulldozer was knocking down what was left of a bombed-out building when we arrived.

Downtown Falujah looked frozen in a moment of horror, as if the life had been sucked out of the city at once. I walked through a barbershop. The windows were shattered, but shaving brushes still sat undisturbed in chipped teacups full of dried-out cream. There was still hair on the floor. Next door, a candy shop looked like it had been looted. Bags of chewing gum in green and pink wrappers were scattered on the ground along with crushed packets of cigarettes. It reminded me of Pompeii, the city buried in ash so quickly its last tragic moments were locked in place for centuries like a photograph of a dying man.

The only sign of life I saw in Falujah was a stray dog. I saw it out of the corner of my eye as it ran behind me and darted down an alley. I followed the dog up the narrow street. There was so much broken concrete and debris, I had to climb over it, balancing myself against a wall with my hands. My flak jacket and helmet were heavy. I looked for flat stones where I could put my feet. There were signs of the battle everywhere. I saw an unexploded RPG round tangled among downed power lines like a mangled spiderweb. Empty shell casings glittered from under the chunks of broken concrete like seashells.

When the dog reached the end of the alley, another stray quickly crossed its path. That dog was carrying a severed human head in its teeth. The head lolled back and forth, dangling, swinging, as the dog scampered over the rubble on its nimble paws, before disappearing into a hole in a wall. I looked down at my boots and saw a cluster of wires leading into a hole. Suspecting it might be a booby trap left for U.S. soldiers, I turned back, trying to retrace my steps.

After a few hours, the unit of engineers moved on to check on a local mosque where some of the five thousand people still in the city were living without power, food, or water.

"My family is gone. I stayed to protect my house. Now my house is gone. Why should I stay now?" a man asked me.

"How will we greet the Americans in Falujah?" asked another man rhetorically. "With guns and rockets."

We stayed for only a few minutes at the mosque before heading to the CMOC, the Civil Military Operations Center, in a former youth center.

I was supposed to interview a colonel at the CMOC about the marines' reconstruction plans. I waited in an office, watching a young female soldier hang a poster of marines carrying boxes of food aid on their shoulders and giving out meals to Iraqi families. Her supervisor told me they had taken the original poster down the day before. "They delivered thousands of boxes of Kosher meals to us," she complained.

A Star of David and the words "Kosher Meals" had been printed on the boxes the marines were carrying in the poster. "She didn't even realize it was a problem," the supervisor said of her young assistant, who had spent the day erasing the Star of David and "Kosher Meals" label from the posters with Photoshop.

Outside, Iraqi soldiers were eating pretzels and granola bars from the Kosher meal kits. Since they don't contain pork, kosher meals adhere to Muslim dietary restrictions. Some Fobit obviously thought it would be a good idea to give them out as food aid, not realizing that most Iraqis already believed the war was an Israeli-Zionist-Jewish plot to steal Iraq's oil and gradually take over the Middle East.

The colonel arrived with a female aide, who took me aside and asked about "my line of questioning." After I explained to her that I planned to talk about the reconstruction of Falujah, she brought over the colonel. He told me the people of Falujah were now "free from the grip of terrorists" and that the military would soon start to distribute up to $2,500 per family to compensate for damaged property or deaths.

"Do you really think the people of Falujah, mostly now living as refugees outside the city, will return here and thank you when they find their homes destroyed?" I asked.

"The people now have the opportunity to rebuild," the colonel said, and explained how the Marines had a plan to implement a type of martial law in Falujah with ID cards, checkpoints, curfews, and a traffic ban "to prevent the terrorists from sneaking back in and once again turning this into a safe haven for terrorism."

"An opportunity?" I asked. "Do you really think you have freed them? Don't you worry that you are creating more militants? You have just destroyed—"

The colonel's aide stopped the interview, stepping in between us like a referee in a boxing ring. "I think that's enough," she said.

After the colonel left, she accused me of using "mind games" to trick the colonel into saying something political and getting himself in trouble.

"I know you are trained to ask questions like that, to use these mind games. It's not fair. It's not ethical. When I spoke to you, you said you were just going to talk about reconstruction. You attacked him."

After that, we were treated like pariahs and spies until the unit that had brought us into the city was ready to take us back to Camp Falujah. We were no longer allowed to go into the main building, and could only stand in a hallway until our ride was ready. We waited a few hours. While I was outside relieving myself, a marine told me he'd been out all day and seen rotting bodies. He didn't introduce himself. He just walked up to me, asked me where we were from, and said he'd seen bodies.

"I saw a dog carrying a human head in its teeth," he said.

I wondered if he'd seen the same dog I'd seen, but he'd been in another part of the city.

11

The end of 2004 was Allawi's last chance to become a tough national hero. Elections were just a month away. But Allawi had been dealt a losing hand. The White House had waited to invade Falujah so the offensive and the inevitable dead marines (a Rumsfeldian "known unknown" in a battle this size) wouldn't impact American voters. Allawi didn't have that option. By December 2004, there was no way to hide from Iraqis that the Sunni city of mosques was destroyed, and nearly all of its quarter-million ferociously independent and historically xenophobic inhabitants were homeless, kicked out by infidel outsiders. Allawi was the "traitor" who ordered this disaster. In Iraq, there were just three job titles: traitor, martyr, and profiteer, and all usually died loathsome, lonely deaths. With Falujah, Allawi lost the Sunnis. He never had the Shiites. They belonged to the howza.

Sunnis from across Iraq were livid and confused. After thirteen centuries, they'd been thrown from power and now found themselves being hunted by marines, the Devil Dogs, which in Arabic translates to *klaab al-sheitaan*, which may be the most evil-sounding phrase I can imagine in the Arabic language and culture. Not surprisingly, Sunni Arabs—20 percent of the population—decided to boycott the vote. They wanted the elections to be flawed, and if possible canceled or at least delayed. But pushing back the date was out of the question. The White House apparently had a bus to catch, and a schedule to keep.

Poor old Adnan al-Pachachi, the Sunni elder statesman edged out of power and relevance, suggested postponing the elections, saying there was no way to have a representative vote in a country that was still smoldering from the Falujah offensive. Nobody listened.

Shiites certainly didn't want to hear it. With the Sunnis boycotting, this was their moment to strike. Their fatwa-powered campaign was uncontested. The mullahs were as delighted as mullahs can be. For many, it was another sign of divine intervention. As in the Jewish identity, Shiites believe they are a chosen and victimized people, the true followers of Mohammed's flawless family. Also like many Jews, Shiites believe that since they are beloved above others, they must suffer above others. It's the ticket price for being part of God's inner circle. Now, they thought, God was finally cutting them some slack. *Al Hamdu Illah.*

In our bureau at the Hamra, Mohammed, our Sunni translator who reported from Samara, couldn't understand this American push for democracy. "Why should I vote?" he asked. "The elections are not fair or legitimate. Do the Americans know that the Shiites will win? They must know that. I don't think they really want that. The ayatollahs will tell the Shiites how to vote, and all of the Shiites will go vote. They follow orders."

Mohammed was convinced the elections wouldn't take place, or that when the ballot boxes were cracked open, the Americans would sort things out. Sunnis wouldn't be excluded. That would be crazy, a stupid historical anomaly. Mohammed didn't think America, the world's superpower filled with universities, laboratories, and movies that cost $100 million, would let that happen.

"Mohammed, if you don't want the Shiites to win you should vote," I encouraged him.

"The Americans won't let the Shiites win," he assured himself.

But Mohammed was starting to realize how much Baghdad had changed. A few days earlier he'd walked into my office looking pale and frightened. Mohammed was normally so polite he would wait outside until I called him in. This time he walked right in to tell me he'd had the worst cab ride of his life on his way home from work. I could sympathize. I reserve a special disdain for cab drivers in Baghdad, who race their beat-up wrecks like maniacs; it is never a good idea to have a cab driver who believes too much in fate. God may be omnipotent, but seatbelts help.

Mohammed told me he was in Karadah, waiting on a corner as barbershops and electronics stores were closing their gates for the day. He hailed the taxi and, in accordance with one of many fraternal Arab customs, sat in the front seat, so as not to make the driver feel too much like a driver. "Where are you going?" the cabbie wanted to know.

"Dora," said Mohammed, who looks remarkably like Saddam Hussein when he was in his forties, with thick black hair, a bristly mustache, a muscular build, and deep-set, brooding eyes.

But their conversation was interrupted by a convoy of Humvees that cut them off. An American gunner in the turret pointed a machine gun at the car, a warning to the driver to stay back.

"Where I'm from they can't do that," the driver grumbled.

The driver said he was from Mahmoudiya, a dangerous Sunni town south of Baghdad. "If we see a Humvee, we destroy it. The Americans can't come into our city," said the driver, also in his early forties, with an unkempt salt-and-pepper beard and the solidly plump physique of an old construction foreman.

"How do you manage that?" Mohammed asked.

"Why do you ask?" the driver shot back, which in an Arabic conversation—often amply sprinkled with saccharine platitudes—translates to something like, "What's it to you, smart guy?"

To assuage the driver, the two men played the Iraqi "tribal game."

The rules are simple. Mohammed listed his family's credentials, ticking off names of prominent relatives, some alive, most distant and long dead. The two men were not from the same tribe, but were both descendants of giant extended families known to be friendly to each other, powerful, and, most important in Iraq, "honorable."

So now the two acted like reunited cousins. The driver explained that he lived in Mahmoudiya, but came to Baghdad every day to work the cab, which he used for his "real job."

"And what's that?"

"I specialize in killing women," he said.

Mohammed said the mood in the car suddenly turned stifling and tense, as if an inconsonant note had been played on an unseen piano.

"I kill whores, women who go to the Green Zone to have sex with the Americans," the driver added as justification.

Mohammed eyeballed the road for a place to get out.

"I use this," continued the driver, taking a nearly foot-long folding knife from under his seat. He opened the long blade. The handle was encrusted with blood.

"I pick up women as they leave the Green Zone, drive them to a quiet area, and kill them," he said, waving the big knife like a violin bow.

Like most Iraqis who lived under Saddam's Orwellian state, Mohammed was an expert at saving his own skin. He feigned sympathy for those who kill "whores" and other transgressors and soon had the murderer laughing and relaxed.

Mohammed got out of the cab well short of his home.

"I didn't want this man to know where I lived," he told me.

Baghdad had become a place where taxi drivers could butcher women like joints of meat and show their freshly used tools to strangers, confident there would be no repercussions.

"It's not a good sign of the times," I said.

"No, it isn't."

This was the backdrop for Iraq's first free elections.

———

Election posters were by now all over Baghdad. In one, Ahmed Chalabi claimed he'd personally liberated Iraq. It was pure Chalabi, a manipulator with a baby face. Some neocons, including Paul Wolfowitz, deputy secretary of defense, wanted him to be prime minister. Now Chalabi claimed to have led the invasion. Nobody bought it. *Newsweek* didn't like Chalabi much either. When the magazine printed a cover story about false intelligence Chalabi had given about Iraq's weapons of mass destruction program, the cover read, "OUR CON MAN IN IRAQ." The words "CON MAN" were in bright red next to a picture of Chalabi.

But at least Chalabi was smart—very smart—and a survivor. Moqtada al-Sadr, the Atari mullah, didn't know what to do. The vote was a mystery to him. He didn't call on supporters to boycott the elections, but didn't encourage them to participate either. He was noncommittal and confused. Sistani and Abdul Aziz al-Hakim, the official howza, were left alone to charge ahead at full speed; so was the U.S. military. The military's plan was "to keep the momentum going" after Falujah. Commanders believed they had Zarqawi and his followers on the run. They wanted to keep the pressure on.

I joined troops for a pre-election "shaping mission" in Latifiya, one of three cities south of Baghdad that formed the "Triangle of Death."

Of course, we rolled out at o Dark 30.

I slept in the back of a Humvee behind Lieutenant Colonel Tim Ryan from Glenville, North Carolina, a twenty-year veteran, an army ranger, amateur guitar player, hunter, carpenter, and father of three daughters. Ryan was pushing his troops south to a new forward operating base in the Euphrates valley. His mission was to bring extra forces into the Triangle of Death and prepare the AO for elections.

The convoy suddenly came to a screeching halt, jolting me awake. As I opened my eyes, I looked out the Humvee's thick bulletproof glass window and saw a body dumped on the road. It was an Iraqi man, killed execution style. His wrists were bound behind his back with wire. Another piece of wire was twisted around his neck. I thought the man had been strangled to death with the wire, until I saw that he'd been shot in the face. His murderers had apparently used the wire around his neck as a handle to drag the body onto the road. They often left bodies of traitors—anyone working with U.S. troops—on the main roads as a public warning and proof that "justice" had been carried out.

But not everyone had seen the body. In the darkness of the previous night, a passing U.S. tank had run over the man's legs, crushing them against the pavement and tearing off his pants. There were tank treads in the pulverized flesh, and a bloody pattern on the road. The pressure of the ninety-ton tank had also squeezed the man's organs, and part of his intestines hung out of his anus. It looked like a section of bright yellow tube. A stray dog was pulling on it, thrashing his head back and forth like a shark as it tried to tear off a piece.

"What is it about dogs in this country?" I wondered as I tried to shoo it away.

"Go on, get!" I said, waving my boot.

The dog took a few steps back, snarled at me, and then walked away.

Lieutenant Colonel Ryan and I returned to the Humvee while an EOD (explosive ordnance disposal) team checked the body for booby traps. As I watched a robot poke the remains, Ryan was appreciating the wildlife in the dense reeds and palm groves that lined the road. He pointed out cormorants, which he said he could identify from "the length of the tail" and "how they fly in formations."

Out the Humvee's left window, I saw the mutilated body of an Iraqi man who'd been bound, executed, run over by a tank, and picked at by a dog chewing organs out of his anus. If I looked out the other side of the Humvee, I could see cormorants, storks, and ducks in an area that was once the heart of Mesopotamia's Fertile Crescent, the Cradle of Civilization. From inside the Humvee, it didn't seem that we'd progressed very far as a civilization in the past five thousand years.

The body wasn't booby trapped, but the soldiers didn't want to take it with them.

What would they do with it?

Throw it in the trunk?

Then what?

The soldiers dragged the body off the road and left it in the reeds. Ryan promised to alert tribal sheikhs in the area to pick it up. The dogs probably got it first.

The convoy pushed on to a new outpost that had just been built by American contractors. They hadn't done much. The outpost had been a former Iraqi military base, which, like most, was abandoned and looted after the 2003 invasion. The contractors had renovated some of the old buildings, brought in chemical toilets, spread gravel on several roads, erected a prefab metal dining hall, and lined up a few rows of cement T-walls and HESCO barriers, canvas and wire boxes filled with sand. Voilà! Instant base. One of Ryan's aides told me in disgust that the contractors had charged $30 million for the project.

"Thirty million for what? What the hell did they do?" I asked.

"This is it," he said, spreading his arms in disbelief. "And we had to pull security for them. They are making a killing. There is so much overbilling going on it makes me sick."

It was war profiteering at its finest. The invasion of Iraq was always a war of opportunity, a preemptive strike that was possible only because the American people were so angry and scared by the atrocities of 9/11 that they gave President Bush carte blanche to punish anyone remotely responsible. The problem was that the United States invaded the wrong country, destroying an odious government that was not responsible for 9/11. I don't know how you recover from invading the wrong country, no matter how you spin it. The conflict has also been a war of opportunism with ample chances to pad bills and inflate hidden "security costs."

Of course, KBR provided plenty of snacks to the new outpost. The soldiers were covered in dust. The showers barely worked. The buildings weren't reinforced. The troops were in the Triangle of

Death selling democracy to people who wanted security and prosperity. But in the tiny chow hall there were enough peanut butter cookies, chocolate chip muffins, glazed breakfast bars, and Froot Loops to make an American teenager split his jeans. The room was stocked like a cafeteria in a public middle school in Texas. Off plastic trays, we ate hash brown sticks, bacon, and French toast with artificial maple-flavored syrup in single-serve tubs like on airplanes. There was also an express to-go line where the soldiers grabbed bacon, egg, and cheese sandwiches on English muffins. This was just breakfast. God bless KBR.

It's hard to complain about waste in Iraq because American officials don't want to deny the troops a few comforts. They certainly deserve them. Why shouldn't "the boys" have Otis Spunkmeyer's Banana Nut premium muffins and juice boxes with every meal? But these little luxuries aren't where the big money goes missing. It's on $30 million outposts, built to last just a few months. They rip you off in transport, gas, shipping, and maintenance costs, money that disappears like smoke in the air.

I spent the next week with Ryan and his men, hiking through the palm groves along the Euphrates. On one of the patrols, the soldiers saw a black BMW parked behind a poor farmhouse. It looked out of place. Sometimes that's all it takes. A feeling that something doesn't look right. The soldiers jimmied the trunk and saw it had been enlarged to carry mortar tubes. In the glove box, they found a hit list with names—some crossed off—of local officials and other "traitors."

In the farmhouse, they found a makeshift clinic with needles, painkillers, and IV bags. Insurgents generally are afraid to go to public hospitals, fearing arrest. Here they'd built an ER for themselves. There were mattresses, books, and CDs about Jihad on the floor. There was even a black cloth sign that militants use as a background when they behead hostages on camera. They might as well have put a neon sign out front announcing, "Zarqawi's Men Welcome! Vacancy!"

Some of the insurgents are dumb. But the ones at this safe

house were at least smart enough not to be home. The farmhouse was empty except for a fat old woman dressed all in black who claimed not to know anything, or to have ever known anything, ever. She said she didn't know how old she was, her full name, who lived in the house, or who owned it.

As the troops grew frustrated with the old and toothless woman—her wet, spraying speech was almost impossible to understand—a boy about five years old stood crying in the doorway. "How you doing, little man?" asked a soldier, kneeling down. He took off his helmet and blast goggles to look less intimidating. "You guys got any candy?" he called out.

"I know you are sad," he told the boy, "but we are looking for bad men, bad men who do bad things. I hope one day you will understand that."

The boy, his face red and striped with trails of tears, crossed his chubby arms and turned his back to the soldier.

A soldier found some candy in one of the Humvees.

"Hey, I got something for you. Here. Look," the soldier said, showing the boy a handful of bright green and red Jolly Rancher sucking candies.

The boy took the candy and stopped crying. It was time to move on.

"That kid is going to grow up to be an insurgent," the soldier told me as we walked away. "I wonder where his dad is. Would love to find that fucking guy."

Iraqi soldiers drove the black BMW back to the base. One of their officers eventually took it home. War booty.

My editors in New York weren't too excited about my material from Latifiya. Not much happened, they complained. There was no drama. There were no "great characters" like Dr. Lovell. No heroes and no villains. It was just soldiers patrolling, doing their thing, and that doesn't make great television. The only person who died was the mangled Iraqi "traitor" on the road, and nobody cared about him.

I returned to Baghdad exhausted and slightly depressed. We'd been out a week, walked miles, and didn't file a single spot. But we didn't stay down for long. As soon as our crew landed in Baghdad, we were told an embed request for Mosul had just come through. I took it, hoping our next fishing trip would be more productive. "Happy hunting," I often say when colleagues go out on embeds. "I hope you get away with it."

Mosul was the complete opposite of Latifiya. The city was falling apart. It was alive with action. Sunni jihadists had overrun the police stations, leaving Iraq's second largest city in anarchy. U.S. troops were attacked every day. Zarqawi's men declared that they'd taken over Mosul, which, like Falujah, was home to many former Baath party members and former military officers.

We landed at FOB Marez, the super-FOB on the edge of Mosul, and were greeted by our illustrious host, Lieutenant Colonel Erik Kurilla, a tall man with bright eyes, a tiny, mischievous smile, and a bluntness that would stop a train. Before he took me inside his TOC—tactical operations center—the classified command center where he directed and tracked missions, Kurilla wanted to establish some ground rules.

"Let's get this straight right away. I'll take you where you want to go. I'll show you secret stuff. I'll be straight up with you. But if you fuck me, I'll wrap you in an American flag and leave you on Main Street in downtown Mosul. You got it?"

"Yes sir. We got it."

Kurilla's "Annihilators" had been having a rough time. Two weeks earlier, a suicide bomber wearing an Iraqi army uniform penetrated the FOB and attacked the mess hall. Another insurgent filmed from a distance. The blast—military investigators said it was carried out by someone who knew the base, perhaps even a local employee—killed twenty-two soldiers and injured more than sixty. It made everyone on the base uncomfortable. Dying outside the wire is one thing. Getting blown up waiting for buffalo wings is another.

Kurilla showed us the data from all the recent attacks, and pictures of vehicles destroyed by IEDs. One big IED had actually split open a giant Abrams tank, the hardest vehicle in Iraq. It looked like a cracked lobster splayed out on a plate.

Around ten that night, Kurilla poked his head into the trailer where we were staying. There was no "Hello" or "Are you guys sleeping?"

Instead, he said, "You guys want to see something? But you can't film it."

"What is it?" I asked.

"You'll see when you come. We're rolling in a few minutes. You're gonna like it."

"But if I am going to like it, I'll want to film it," I said. "I don't do radio."

"That's your problem. No filming. We're leaving in a few minutes."

Of course we went. How could we pass it up? There seemed to be so much hidden behind Kurilla's smile.

We loaded in Kurilla's Stryker and left the FOB. Kurilla never told us where we were going.

The Stryker is the army's Cadillac. It's tough, roomy, and quiet, a smooth ride. It's the only vehicle actually built for the kind of urban fighting done in Iraq. It is unlike the War Pig, designed for beach landings, or the Bradley, a clumsy, noisy, cramped behemoth with so much firepower it's useless in most urban settings. If soldiers fire the Bradley's cannon on a crowded street, people will die, which is a problem in what is basically a police and peacekeeping mission. The Stryker rolls on eight huge tires, which makes it nearly as quiet as a car (so you can sneak up on a target) and much faster than a Bradley or a War Pig. It can also hold up to twelve "dismounts," even with their bulky flak jackets, grenades, medical kits, assault rifles, and ammo punches—the full battle rattle. The Bradley can take only six dismounts, but soldiers often pack them with seven or eight. They joke, "How many soldiers can fit in a Bradley? One more."

Kurilla parked the Stryker at the edge of a hill overlooking Mosul. It was dark. Most of the power was out in the city. There was nothing pretty about the skyline except the bright stars.

"Look over there," Kurilla said, pointing to the sky.

"Where?"

"Over there."

Suddenly, the sky opened up. Huge beams of red and blue tracer fire tore through the darkness. I could hear a Gatling gun grinding overhead. Rockets slammed into the hillside.

"What the fuck are they doing?" I asked.

"Show of force. Denial of terrain," Kurilla said.

They were shooting at empty ground. Insurgents had been firing mortars at the FOB from these fields. Kurilla wanted them to know what would happen if they kept doing it. He'd brought us out to watch the fireworks.

Lieutenant Colonel Kurilla was filming it all on a small DV camera.

"Hey, that's not fair," I said.

"I never promised it would be."

We stayed with Kurilla and his men for two weeks. The trip changed on what was supposed to be a simple assignment. On January 10, a civil affairs team was leaving the FOB to deliver kerosene heaters to a girls' school. It was around 10 A.M. and the day was cold and damp. The schools in Mosul had no heat. The state simply didn't exist in Mosul. Nobody picked up trash, repaired the streets, or worked the power plants. Hospitals functioned only because doctors and nurses, often unpaid, felt morally obliged to go to work.

"You guys want to come along?" a soldier asked while packing the Strykers with heaters. He wanted some attention. Nobody pays much attention to the guys handing out heaters to schools. We'd show them some love. Why not?

"Sure, what the hell," I said, and looked over to Kevin and Martin. They were happy to go.

Kevin and Martin found room in the first Stryker in the convoy, the one that would be in front in the "order of march." I was in the third vehicle. Nestled between us was a pickup truck full of Iraqi soldiers. The civil affairs teams liked to bring Iraqi troops along when they did hearts and minds missions. They wanted the Iraqis to get some of the credit. We'd been driving only about fifteen minutes when I heard the bomb explode. At first, I didn't think it was serious. The blast barely shook the Stryker. It was as if someone outside was rocking the big car back and forth. Even the bang wasn't that loud. It was just a pop. Then I smelled a waft of smoke that drifted into the Stryker. It had the bitter taste of munitions, the kind of smell that lingers in the back of your throat and burns your nostrils. Some smells stick on you. For me, they're munitions and bodies. You can't wash them off. I've tried putting water up my nose. It doesn't work. Bodies and munitions stick in your nostrils like caramel on your teeth. But unlike the rot of bodies—a dank, sugary smell like mulled wine—the taste of military-grade explosive is clean, acrid, and pure. When I swallow now I can still taste it going down the back of my throat. There's a hint of ammonia in it. But mostly, it tastes like the smell of a match right after you strike it.

"Drop the hatch!" a soldier yelled.

It was game on.

I was just another pair of hands and expected to pull my weight.

"Grab the fire blanket," a soldier ordered as the Stryker's rear door dropped onto the asphalt with the deep thud of thick metal.

The fire blanket was in a plastic tube about the size of a fire extinguisher. I grabbed it and jumped out of the smoke-filled Stryker onto Route Tampa, as this stretch of road was known.

The sky seemed so bright.

My adrenaline was up.

I could hear my helmet sliding on my head and feel the strap on my chin.

I could hear myself swallow saliva that tasted like pennies.

Adrenaline is a mean drug. It makes you twitchy. The world snaps into focus and time slows down. It's how I imagine prey see the world when lions are close, their ears perked, eyes wide, watching every blade of grass. It's addictive as hell.

The soldiers hated Route Tampa. They'd been attacked here many times before. The road looked like any freeway in the United

States. It was big, modern, open, long, and straight. It could have been between any two little towns in America. It was the kind of road in the States where you'd see signs announcing gas stations 5.5 miles away. Route Tampa's openness gave insurgents a broad, clear view. There was no cover. It was perfect ambush country.

The bomb had hit the Iraqi pickup in front of my Stryker. I could now see that the white unarmored truck was on fire, coughing puffs of black smoke. I ran with the soldiers to the pickup. They had their guns at their shoulders as they moved. I was unarmed and wearing a bright blue flak jacket. I felt obvious and vulnerable.

The blast had thrown three of the six Iraqi soldiers in the pickup onto the road. One of the soldiers was mangled and lifeless. I didn't find his body disgusting or even particularly sad. It was like looking at roadkill. But I couldn't stand the screams of the three Iraqi soldiers burning to death in the cab, trapped behind the truck's twisted doors.

I popped open the fire blanket tube. The blanket was about the size of a small beach towel and coated in a fire-retardant jelly that spilled down my leg. A soldier wrenched the blanket from my hands and wrapped it around one of the Iraqi soldiers injured on the road. His uniform was on fire. I helped the soldiers drag him away from the burning truck and rushed back to see if I could help free the three screaming and burning men. But we had to leave them.

The fire was now setting off ammunition in the truck. It began crackling slowly, a few pops at a time, but within seconds it became a roar like popcorn on a stovetop.

"Get back, get back!" a soldier yelled. "The ammo's going up! Take cover!"

For a second, I stood paralyzed. I looked one of the Iraqi soldiers in the eye. He was bleeding from his head and pinned in the burning vehicle. He was pleading with his eyes for me to help. But the ammunition kept going up. A soldier grabbed me and tried to pull me away. But before I dove onto my stomach, I watched that soldier die in the truck, me powerless to help.

On my belly, I looked up and saw Kevin and Martin running down the highway toward me. Kevin, the ex-sailor with short silver hair, was filming the whole thing. Martin was behind him, plugging cables into a mixer in a fanny pack that bounced against his legs as he ran. They were running toward the gunfire.

"Take this," Martin said, and handed me a wireless microphone covered in a fluffy wind guard that looked like a poodle on a stick.

Then Martin, a six-foot-three former soldier, heard a different kind of gunfire.

"They're shooting at us," he said. His military experience taught him to distinguish between the randomness of exploding ammo and the single directed shots that were now pinging off the pavement beside us.

It was a secondary ambush. Gunmen were shooting down at us from the windows of a huge mosque under construction across the highway. Martin was the first one to notice. The soldiers were busy treating the wounded Iraqis.

"Let's get in here," Kevin said, pointing to a grassy center divider between the lanes of the highway. Kevin never stopped rolling.

But Martin didn't take cover. "Hey," he told an American soldier hunched over a wounded Iraqi, bandaging his bleeding thigh. "They're shooting at us. I just saw a muzzle flash from one of those windows. You mind if I take that?" Martin asked, pointing to the soldier's rifle lying on the road. The soldier's hands were covered in blood. If he stopped giving first aid, the Iraqi might have bled to death. The soldier couldn't return fire. He needed Martin's help.

"Go for it," the soldier told him.

Martin picked up the rifle, flipped off the safety with his thumb, and fired ten or fifteen rounds toward the mosque construction site, the insurgents' sniper post.

"Martin, get the fuck down here," I yelled.

Martin fired a few more rounds. "It's on safe," he finally said as he put the rifle back on the road next to the soldier and scrambled to join us in the grass.

"I think I got him," Martin said. "I think I got him."

I have no idea if he did. The building site of the mosque was several hundred yards away and the windows were small. It would have been a very difficult shot.

But the shooting didn't stop. We were now pinned down. In the grass, I recorded several stand-ups describing the ambush. I was practically screaming into the microphone to try to talk over all the gunfire.

"There is still a lot of fire coming at us; some of it's exploding in the car that was hit by an improvised explosive device," I yelled. "There are—U.S. troops are retaliating, trying to fight off what they think could be an intense ambush."

When the shooting slowed, I climbed to my feet and looked for better cover. It was a mistake. As soon as I was on my feet, the shots resumed. I could hear the bullets fly past my head, cracking like a whip. When you are shot at, you usually hear the bang of the round going off. When the bullets are close, you also hear the crack as the bullet flies by.

I heard other rounds bounce off the road.

I was standing up, dressed like a blue target, too far from the center divider to get back to it. I thought it was curtains, until a soldier I hadn't seen before stepped in front of me, raised his rifle, and returned fire.

"I got you," he said as he stood between me and the mosque, the source of fire, protecting me with his body. He emptied a full magazine.

But as quickly as he'd come, the soldier was gone. I scrambled for cover behind one of the Strykers.

I never had a chance to thank that soldier. I never saw him again. I want to buy him a beer.

We were stuck on that road in the ambush for what seemed to be about an hour until reinforcements, led, not surprisingly, by Lieutenant Colonel Kurilla, stopped the attack by pouring so much firepower at the mosque site that the insurgents either were killed or fled.

Kurilla inspected the burned-out pickup and managed to pry

open the door. We looked at the charred bodies of the Iraqi soldiers inside. Kurilla grabbed one of them by the arm. It was so burned the arm broke off at the elbow. It looked like Kurilla was holding a club.

That night our story led the *Nightly News*. We had "great" pictures. I wrote the entire script in the first person.

It had become *our* convoy, and *we* had been attacked. I didn't feel like an observer. I felt like I was part of it. I felt jazzed and tough. But I was quickly humbled. After the show, I sat with Staff Sergeant Jeremy Brown. Since the mess hall had been bombed, Brown was eating off a tray in his lap next to a small campfire. He sat in silence. There was no backslapping or storytelling. He didn't talk about the IED attack we'd been in. After all, it was his seventeenth IED attack. Brown had been in Iraq for only four months, and he knew he'd be back on Route Tampa the next morning. There was nothing to say.

THE INSURGENCY

12

Baghdad was alive when Election Day, January 30, finally came. The normally drab city of two-story cement buildings was vibrant, expectant, and nervous all at once, like a new father pacing outside a maternity ward. There had been a lot of hype. American officials and Allawi had sold the vote as if a savior were about to be born. Just drop a ballot into a box and all the misery would be over. The Americans had promised Iraqis that their liberation was a gift of freedom from Uncle Sam. It was now time to collect.

The U.S.-funded Iraqi state television station, al-Iraqiya, was in overdrive, running ads explaining how to vote and appealing to Iraqi pride. "Voting is a national duty," the ads said. Shiite-run channels interrupted their normal programming of stern-faced clerics in turbans discussing the intricacies of marriage, prayer, fasting, and premarital sex to broadcast call-in shows discussing the joys and benefits of voting. Everyone was talking about the elections. Kids were excited about the vote.

The mood was contagious. I was wired all night and couldn't sleep. I wanted to see what would happen. At dawn, I listened to the muezzin's lyrical call to prayer, which Sir Richard Burton described as "beautiful" and "human," preferring it to Christianity's "brazen clang of the bell."

Whenever I could hear the muezzin at night, I knew the city was at ease. There were no cars or shelling, none of the Baghdad noise to drown out the imploring "Come to pray! Come to salvation!" The silence was mainly a result of a vehicle traffic ban Allawi had imposed. He'd also ordered all the main highways shut. Allawi was particularly anxious. His reputation was riding on the vote. It was also personal. Zarqawi had just tried to kill Allawi, again. A week before the election, Zarqawi dispatched a suicide bomber to Allawi's headquarters. Allawi wasn't there, but ten people were killed.

The curfew left us in a bind. How were we supposed to move around Baghdad and film the elections with the traffic ban? It was a major story, *the* major story, but you can only get so far on foot. Luckily, an elementary school just three blocks from the Hamra had been designated as a polling station. So we walked.

With a tripod over my shoulder like a hunting rifle, I walked past children playing soccer and riding their bikes down the empty streets near the Hamra. A man was carrying his son on his shoulders. The boy smiled and waved at me as I walked by. It felt good to be on the streets, walking, looking, taking it all in. I had bought into the hype. I was jazzed.

I was also excited to see Iraqi soldiers in their own armored vehicles for the first time since the invasion. They were blocking intersections and shooing away the odd car violating the traffic ban. When Saddam was in power, I often saw Iraqi tanks and APCs parked under bridges or dug into the embankments beside highways like spiders waiting to pounce. The rusty old war machines had been part of the cityscape like squeegee men in New York City in the 1980s. You came to expect them. They were part of the background. During the 2003 invasion, however, American tanks and planes chewed through much of Iraq's armored fleet. Most of the dead tanks were piled in a giant field in Mahmoudiya, south of Baghdad, flipped on their sides and missing turrets. They looked like beetles dried out in the sun, legs curled in the air.

But now Iraqi tanks and APCs were back on the streets, cleaned up, repaired, and polished. Two tanks were parked on the corner outside the Hamra. There were just clunky old Russian T-series, but somebody obviously loved them. The soldiers had painted Iraqi flags on the sides and hung garlands of flowers around the cannons. Tanks, by design, are meant to look intimidating, but these seemed almost happy. If they'd been yellow dogs, they would have been wagging their tails. The Iraqi soldiers were so proud of them, smiling in spotless and starched uniforms.

"Hello! Hello! Welcome!" a soldier in the turret said as I passed.

"Hello," I shouted back.

Ashraf was waiting by the school's main gate when we arrived. He'd gone ahead to sweet-talk the local police. I always sent him ahead to make sure we wouldn't be turned away when we showed up with cameras. Iraqi police like to turn away journalists with cameras. They always have. It must be something in the Tigris. The Interior Ministry had tried to issue special passes to journalists that were supposed to give us access to a limited number of pre-assigned polling stations. It was all going to be so organized. An American advisor in the Interior Ministry wanted everything to run as smoothly as a press conference at the L.A. County Sheriff's Office. The advisor was an energetic young woman who'd come to Iraq after her boyfriend shot his wife. So many of the American officials in the Green Zone were running away from crazy pasts. They were all running, or saving money, or both. I met one woman who worked in the Green Zone advising the Iraqi media. I have no idea how she thought she could help, speaking no Arabic and never leaving the Green Zone. She told me she'd volunteered to come to Iraq mainly to lose weight. "I've already lost forty pounds," she said with a little twirl.

Not surprisingly, the advisor at the Interior Ministry (who also enjoyed playing commando and loved the fact that she carried guns and badges and flew in helicopters) didn't get her way. She'd once wanted to be a soldier, but hadn't pursued it because the military doesn't generally allow women into front-line combat units. Now she got to play Rambo *and* order around a ministryful of Iraqi officials. It beat sitting in a cubicle back home in the States.

By the time the polls opened, almost no one had the correct passes. We'd spent days going back and forth to the Interior Ministry, signing documents in triplicate and submitting passport photographs so we would be issued these all-powerful ID cards. In the end, all we needed was Ashraf, who with his good looks, confident saunter, and smarts could charm his way into anywhere. Ashraf was smooth. Ladies loved him, and he loved them back.

When we arrived at the school, not only did the police at the gate let us in without permission, they helped carry our equipment and called me *saydi*, an honorific somewhere between "sir" and "lord" on the politeness scale. Ashraf was wired that way. At Baghdad's airport—a den of thieving bureaucrats who spend their miserable days in nicotine-stained back offices plotting how to most effectively skim and steal—Ashraf always breezed us through. We could show up with twenty cases of television equipment—a pot of gold that airport customs officials tell bedtime stories about to their corrupt little children—and Ashraf would know how to discreetly slip a few dollars in the pockets of the right people and make them wait for other prey. He had become a great grease man, and everybody needs a grease man in Baghdad.

I had assembled a formidable little team: gray-haired Zohair, the wise fixer—sly as a fox—who always smiled but trusted no one. Ali had learned to slip in and out of Baghdad's most dangerous neighborhoods and take pictures before anyone seemed to notice he was there. He was my inside man. Ashraf was the smooth-talking grease man, and Kevin and Martin were my tough, ex-military crew. I was the front man, the face, and I got all the credit. TV news is unfair like that.

As we walked past the police guarding the entrance of the school, however, it soon became obvious that the cops were not in charge of the polling station. They checked bags, nothing more. The real power players were the six men with clipboards and video cameras who stood outside each classroom where the ballot boxes

were set up on tables under posters of ducks and cartoon characters. After all, it was still an elementary school. The principal, an el-
egant, strict woman, had been up all night with her staff scrubbing
the floors, straightening the posters, cleaning the blackboards, and
sweeping the little garden outside. She didn't let anyone smoke inside (a miracle in Baghdad) and said she planned to spend the night
at the school after the voting was finished to personally supervise
the first counting of the ballots. I was confident she wouldn't have
accepted any funny business. If anyone tried to fake the count,
she'd send them straight to detention. The men with the clipboards
didn't speak, but just stood filming and taking notes like football
coaches scouting for the best talent during a preseason game.

The men were election observers from 169, the bloc of Shiite
parties that had been preparing for this day for months. The observers all wore dark, badly cut suits with big shoulder pads, white
or light blue shirts without neckties, and scuffless, snub-nosed
black shoes that looked like they'd been bought that morning. Their
hair was cut short, or gelled back. They looked like they meant business.

The 169 had run a superb campaign powered by the Grand
Ayatollah Ali al-Sistani and the howza's network of mosques and
husseiniyas. In the final days before the election, campaign workers from 169 went door-to-door, stressing that voting was a religious duty. While al-Iraqiya television appealed to national pride,
169 drew on faith and religious obedience. Sistani had even issued
a fatwa granting a woman the right to divorce her husband if he
prevented her from voting. According to the Shiite hierarchy, Sistani spoke for God, and God evidently wanted all Shiites to vote,
and to vote for 169.

While Sistani was the grand ayatollah in Najaf, he was not the
only leader of the howza. But under the force of Sistani's vision, all
of the howza and Shiite parties (except the confused bully Moqtada
al-Sadr) had agreed to put their differences aside and run on a single list. It was a brilliant decision. It was *the* decision.

Unlike in elections in the States, here Iraqis were not voting for individuals but for lists of candidates. Iraq's new government was modeled on a parliamentary system similar to those in Western Europe and in Israel. They are very democratic, but have one key problem—they collapse easily. Political parties constantly have to form blocs and shift alliances to maintain a majority. Italy had eight different governments in the 1980s. Israel had five in the 1990s.

Although the election was the most important day for what American officials called "Iraq's transition to democracy," I don't think most Americans actually understood how the voting was supposed to work. I don't think all of my editors in New York ever quite understood it either, or much cared. Iraqis were voting. Democracy was under way. The fetters of Saddam's regime were removed. That was the important thing. They were wrong. The system was critical, and it was flawed and manipulated.

According to Iraq's interim constitution—the document that wasn't signed until Sistani approved it—the purpose of the election was to select 275 members of parliament.

It was up to each party, or bloc of parties, to compose a list of up to 275 candidates. Each list was randomly assigned a number. The Shiite bloc—called the United Iraqi Alliance—was given 169. Allawi's list, simply named the Iraqi List, was 285.

If Allawi, for example, won 100 percent of the vote, then every one of the 275 candidates on his list would win a seat in parliament. He'd sweep the vote. If Allawi's list won only half the vote—about what he was expecting—then half of the names on his list would become members of parliament. The lists were also prioritized. If Allawi's bloc won only two seats, the first two names on his list would be selected and the rest would be dropped.

But Allawi never stood a chance. The Shiites stacked the deck. Their 169 list incorporated all the candidates endorsed by the howza and Sistani. It was the official howza list. No other group in Iraq could muster the support of the howza, and now the howza— the amorphous web of seminaries and clerics—was united. The Shiites were coming to power. There was no way around it. The question was how much of a majority would they win, and would they even need the Sunnis at all to help them rule Iraq?

The electoral system was undeniably complicated. Most Iraqis understood it even less than my editors. Not surprisingly, the system had been devised by the United Nations, a bureaucracy never known for clarity or efficiency. For religious Shiites, however, voting was simple. They were ordered by Sistani to vote 169. End of story. It was a divine command.

Iraqis made jokes about it, especially Shiites. Shiites are known, somewhat infamously, for a tradition known as pleasure marriage, *jawaz al-mutaa*. It's a way of allowing premarital sex. If a man and woman want to have sex, they can arrange a *jawaz al-mutaa*, which gives them full rights to consummate their relationship but lasts only a few weeks, or even a single day. Sunnis have a similar system, *jawaz al-orfi*, but it's the Shiites who made these convenient little trysts famous, legal, and morally acceptable.

By a linguistic coincidence, Arabic for 1-6-9 (*meya sitta tisaa*) rhymes with pleasure marriage (*jawaz al-mutaa*). Iraqis joked, "*Man turid jawaz al-mutaa, ikhtar meya, sita, tisaa,*" "If you want pleasure marriages, vote for 1-6-9." Of course, that wasn't the slogan printed on the thousands of election posters and giant banners 169 plastered on almost every wall in Baghdad. Instead, the posters showed a picture of Sistani and a candle, a symbol of light and hope.

The Sunnis had no posters. They were grim, sullen, frustrated, abandoned, confused, embittered, and betrayed. They were sulking, having decided not to play this complicated American-imposed game. They didn't understand the system of voting lists cooked up by some Europeans at the United Nations. They knew Americans were killing Sunnis and hunting them down in Falujah and throughout Anbar province. So the Sunnis had decided to boycott the vote. In most countries, a boycott of 20 percent of the population—and all members of a single religious group—would be problematic to say the least. But the American administration didn't seem to care. These elections were going to take place on time. As the political philosopher and maxim craftsman Donald Rumsfeld often said, "Democracy is messy."

In Iraq, the American attitude sent a clear message: "If the Sunnis don't want to vote, screw them! They're attacking our boys anyway." There was understandably not a lot of sympathy for the Sunnis among the U.S. military, Shiites, and Kurds. The Sunnis had been the rulers of one of the worst dictatorships in the twentieth century. They were driven from power, only to form an alliance with radical al-Qaeda types like Zarqawi. They were attacking American soldiers and Shiites with ever-increasing ferocity. Screw them.

The Shiites meanwhile were absorbing an enormous amount of punishment. Although Shiite clerics were assassinated and their husseiniyas bombed every day, Sistani preached restraint. He refused to permit revenge and even reined in Moqtada al-Sadr. As far as the Americans were concerned, the Shiites "got it." They were "on board, building the new Iraq." The Kurds were so pro-American that when I went to Kurdistan and told people I was from the United States, they would take me to lunch. I saw American flags in shop windows. The Sunnis were Rumsfeldian "dead-enders." We were still Shiites.

The American decision to ignore repeated requests by Sunni leaders to postpone the vote played into Zarqawi's hands. Sunnis didn't believe the Americans were acting out of arrogance, ignorance, or on a Washington timeline. They assumed the U.S. administration was deliberately trying to undermine Sunnis. "How could a superpower remain a superpower and be ignorant?" Sunnis wondered. They suspected a plot.

Zarqawi's infamy was already on the rise, and in Iraq infamy can be better than fame and respect. After all, fear and order were what Allawi always wanted. Machiavelli would have loved Baghdad. Zarqawi was the new rising star in the pantheon of international jihadists. His battles in Falujah—which led the news across the world—had been noticed by the chairman of the international Jihad movement, Osama bin Laden. Falujah was Zarqawi's big break.

A month before the January 2005 elections, al-Qaeda officially adopted Zarqawi's group, Tawhid wa Jihad, Monotheism and Jihad.

In Mafia terms, bin Laden had opened up the books and sorted Zarqawi out. Zarqawi—the freelancer who'd run his own training camps near Herat, escaped Afghanistan through Iran, and moved to Iraq to make a name in the jihad business—had finally become a made man. Bin Laden called Zarqawi the "emir of Iraq." It was the jihadist version of the *baci di tutti i baci*.

With the promotion, Zarqawi renamed his organization al-Qaeda in Iraq. A week before the elections, Zarqawi spelled out his vision in a forty-five minute Internet broadcast, attacking democracy as an anti-Islamic "wicked trap" to empower the Shiite refuters, a derogatory term for Shiites who refute the traditional succession of Sunni power. "Democracy is also based on the right to choose your religion, and this is against the rule of God," Zarqawi said.

"You have to be careful of the enemy's plots that involve applying democracy in your country and confront these plots, because they only want to give the refuters the rule of Iraq.

"After fighting the Baathists ... and the Sunnis, they will spread their insidious beliefs, and Baghdad and all the Sunni areas will become refutist domains.

"Oh, people of Iraq, where is your honor? Have you accepted oppression of the crusader harlots and the refutist pigs?

"Four million refuters have been brought in from Iran to take part in the elections so that they realize their aim of taking most seats in the atheist assembly [parliament]. . . . For these and other reasons, we have declared all-out war on this wicked course."

Zarqawi also predicted that the Shiites would sweep the vote and "form a majority government that would control the strategic, economic, and security infrastructure of the state."

While Zarqawi was never a popular man—the vast majority of Iraqis cringes at his savagery—many Sunnis conceded that the new al-Qaeda in Iraq leader at least had a point. Sunnis knew the elections were inevitably going to isolate them and further empower Iran. In many ways they were correct. Iran helped 169's campaign, bankrolling Shiite television stations promoting the vote, and supporting hundreds of get-out-the-vote charities from Basra to Baghdad.

About a month before the elections I visited a man named Hajj Raed, a charismatic Dawa party member who escaped Iraq in the 1980s and bounced between Scandinavia and Iran, working for the opposition. He had come back after the American invasion and opened a charity near the Hamra promoting women's education. The center was on the second floor of an apartment building above a money-changer. Inside the center, I saw about fifty women in black abayas sitting behind new desktop computers, learning basic accounting and how to use Microsoft spreadsheets.

Hajj Raed didn't want to talk about his Iran connection. But one of his assistants said that he'd been going back and forth to Iran to collect funds. "It's easy," the assistant said. "They are promoting so much development here. All you need to do is go, present a business plan, and within a few weeks, they'll give you money."

Hajj Raed wouldn't say who gave him the money or exactly how much he'd taken from Iran, but judging from the size of the center, the new equipment, and the villa he was renting nearby, he must have received a few hundred thousand dollars.

After the computer lessons, the women prayed and held a democracy seminar. Then the women went house-to-house in the neighborhood, visiting housewives, handing out 169 flyers and pamphlets of Sistani's fatwa endorsing the vote.

While I was at Raed's center, another man came in, also from the Dawa party. He ran another Iranian-funded charity helping the families of Shiite martyrs killed by Saddam's regime. His center was also holding democracy seminars and get-out-the-vote campaigns. Iran funded the grassroots campaign. Iran made sure the Shiites didn't miss their opportunity. It was all perfectly legal. Iran was just promoting democracy like the United States. They just promoted it more among Shiites. The Sunni boycott was the best thing Iran could have hoped for.

But the most serious Iranian intervention came behind the scenes. Iran allegedly helped choose the 169 list, approving the candidates and the order in which they appeared on the ballot. I didn't know this at the time.

———

In his office on the Tigris in early 2007, Mithal Allusi, a well-known Sunni politician, first told me about the ballot rigging. "Several members of the 169 list told me that the head of the [Iranian] Revolutionary Guards Quds Brigade personally approved the ballot list," Allusi said. "Many of the Shiites on the list were opposed to it, mostly because Iran pushed its favorite candidates to make sure they were elected."

It was a bold claim. It would be the equivalent of Iran picking the Republican or Democratic ticket before elections in the United States. It would be like Iran deciding who ran and with which running mates. It would mean the democratic experiment in Iraq was a con. President Bush often offered the vote as proof that the war in Iraq was worth the sacrifice. Allusi told me the vote was a sham. The actual ballot casting was free, but the candidates were pre-screened by Tehran.

I suspected Allusi might be exaggerating. He was a Sunni, albeit extremely secular. I also wondered why he would talk. Such a bold claim could easily get you killed in Iraq. But by the time I spoke to Allusi, he didn't care anymore. Sunni insurgents had murdered his two sons. In his office, he sat under portraits of the two boys, both under fifteen when they died. Allusi had a pistol tucked into the pants of his suit and expected to be killed himself.

I needed more evidence and turned to my best source in the howza, Sayid Emad Kalanter. Sayid Emad and I have been friends for several years. It was he who arranged my visit to Najaf and my interview with Hojat al Islam Mohammed Sayid al-Hakim, the man who first explained to me the Shiites' vision for empowerment through the ballot box.

Sayid Emad is a quiet man in his late forties. His power comes from his superb diplomatic skills, smarts, and family connections. He is the son of a revered Najaf family. He is the only person I know who receives phone calls from Moqtada and who lectures the tyrannical cleric as if he were an undisciplined child. Sayid Emad is also profoundly pro-American, believing that Washington empowered Shiites in Iraq. He's a pragmatist and has the ability to remove himself from emotional debates, a rare quality in Iraq, where most discussions quickly degenerate into overblown sermons on pride, honor, hate, vendetta, and history.

Sayid Emad had been offered several posts in the Iraqi government, but turned them down. He prefers to be a behind-the-scenes man, a deal-maker. When Sadr and Abdul Aziz al-Hakim, leader of the Supreme Council for Islamic Revolution in Iraq and the Badr Brigade, have a problem, they come to Sayid Emad to resolve it. "It would be an exaggeration to say that the head of the Quds Force personally approved every name on the ballots, but Iran did have a lot of influence," he said.

Two other independent Shiite politicians involved in the elections also told me that Iran helped select the names and the order in which they were listed on the ballot.

Even with Iran's influence, it would be inaccurate to say that Iraq's first elections were not democratic. Although Sistani encouraged his supporters to vote, he and his army of election monitors didn't force anyone to cast ballots in a particular way. At the school near the Hamra, I didn't see any pressure or intimidation. The election monitors never said a word. People were free to vote as they wished. But several credible Iraqis told me the voting lists were fixed ahead of time, and Iran supported its candidates in the way the United States never did. The United States built the system and worked incredibly hard to make sure the elections took place. Iran spent its time and money making sure its friends won. It seems the elections were free, but not fair.

But the elections nonetheless made great television. On voting day the world saw thousands of Iraqis, doctors, teachers, farmers, crippled men in wheelchairs, and entire families packed into polling stations to drop ballots into plastic boxes and dip their fingers into purple ink, the mark designed to prevent them from voting more than once. Kurds from mountain villages dressed in traditional jewel-colored jackets and black baggy pants and walked miles to vote, many for the first time in their lives. At the school near the Hamra I watched an old woman dance and cheer after she cast her ballot, twirling and raising her hand in the air triumphantly as she sang poetry about the greatness and glory of Iraq. We took pictures of it all. Snap, snap, snap.

But in Ramadi another of our correspondents, Jim Maceda, saw a completely different picture. Almost no one showed up to vote in the Sunni heartland. He broadcast images of empty voting stations and reported that, at least in Ramadi, "the vote was a failure." Maceda was embedded with the marines at the time. The marines were furious at Maceda's report. They took it personally.

When Maceda said the election in Ramadi was a failure, the marines felt he was suggesting their mission was a failure too. The United States had too much riding on it. But the media, NBC included, didn't focus much on the fact that the Sunnis didn't vote. It was mentioned in our newscast and in the newspapers, but "the real story," we said, was that millions of Iraqis had turned out despite Zarqawi's threats, "defying the terrorists" and embracing democracy. It was mainly true. Millions did in fact turn out, but many weren't embracing democracy. They were just following orders, and an entire segment of society wasn't playing the game at all, a game Iran skewed in its favor.

13

About two years into the war, I was starting to get nervous and show signs of stress. I was getting beat down.

I'd come to Iraq, to the war, gung ho, feeling bulletproof. But the constant gunshots, explosions, fear of kidnapping, and all the bodies—all the roadkill—were taking a toll. Too much adrenaline had passed through my blood, which like acid was slowly burning it sour. I'd had too many bad mornings.

At 7 A.M. two weeks before the elections, a giant explosion jolted me awake in my room in the Hamra. It was a deep rumbling crash, much bigger than the mortars I usually heard at daybreak. Insurgents often fired mortars just after sunrise and at dusk, when it was light enough for them to aim, and while traffic was flowing quickly so they could make a fast escape. Stop and drop, shoot and run. But this sounded different. It was a truck bomb.

I first saw the blast before I opened my eyes. The bright orange light from the ball of fire shone through my closed eyelids. I saw my room glow red for a split second before my eyes snapped open. I was instantly in the zone, adrenaline pumping. The muscles in my back and legs tightened, bracing for another explosion, "a secondary." It never came.

When I opened my eyes, the room was full of dust and smoke. I could barely see. I rolled off the bed and crawled toward the door, elbowing past shards of shattered glass. Several of the ceiling panels had come crashing in. The sliding glass door leading to the balcony was pushed in, ripped off the frame. The concrete wall around it was cracked. Ducking down, I crept to the balcony, stepped over the broken door, and peered outside. I wanted to see what had exploded. It was a stupid move. Curiosity killed the cat. But I wanted to see.

Several cars were burning across the street. I saw the twisted remains of the truck bomb, which had driven into the Australian embassy a few hundred yards away. My room was a straight line from the explosion.

I had a small video camera in my room. Since I arrived in Iraq, I'd been keeping a video journal, turning the camera on myself at pivotal and emotional moments, trying to capture what I saw and how I was feeling. This was one of those moments.

My voice was shaky. I was unshaven, tired and wild-eyed.

"When the explosion happened, I thought . . . finally this was it, that they'd blown up a bomb right in the basement," I said into the camera.

"I thought when it exploded that—that they'd done what they had been threatening to do."

I thought it was curtains.

It was my third hotel room that had been destroyed. At the Palestine hotel during the 2003 invasion, a bullet had come through my balcony door, missing my head and digging into the ceiling. Less than a year later, a madman inspired by Moqtada al-Sadr had exploded a bomb at our first bureau, thinking we were Jewish settlers moving in to steal Iraq's oil and occupy the country. Now this truck bomb had trashed my room at the Hamra.

I saw a piece of shrapnel on the floor, a sharp, heavy chunk of metal about the size of an egg. It had come flying through my window, bounced off my bed, and landed on the carpet. It was still hot, and melted the synthetic fibers of the cheap industrial wall-to-wall.

I was lucky, but started to ask myself, "How often can you get lucky? How many times can you push it?" I looked into the camera again.

"It makes you wonder, how much more can you do of this? How much more is worth it? Obviously today I am not traumatized, we've had these types of explosions in the past . . . but you wonder all the time, is the next one going to be the one that gets you?

"It has a toll on you. It has an impact—a weight—that I don't know how long is going to take to wear off. I've absorbed so much violence, so many scenes, so many ugly things since when I first came to Iraq . . . I am more jumpy than normal. I'm more skittish.

"Am I just lucky so far, and how far can you push your luck? When do you decide that this is just not worth it? This is not my country, not my conflict, not my problem . . . but I do feel attached to it to a certain degree. I've been covering it for so long.

"On a morning like this, you wonder if we've gotten anywhere since I first arrived.

"Iraqis were living under the terror of Saddam. Now they are living under the terror of militant groups, Islamic fundamentalist groups.

"Obviously things have changed, but I am still cheating death. That's what it feels like. I'm not trying to overstate, but it really feels that way. I have a toast that I sometimes say to people. I say, 'Here is to getting away with it.' That is what it feels like every time you are here. It feels like you are trying to pull a fast one on history, that you are trying to get away with it, get out, sneak out, get information, and get back without being kidnapped or losing an eye or a limb. It feels like you are trying to get away with it.

"Today with this explosion, I got away with another little bit . . . but how many more times can you get away with it? I don't know."

I was slowly becoming paranoid. I saw danger everywhere, and had tied an escape rope to a drainage pipe off the balcony. If trouble came, I would scale down the building. I started to dream—

sometimes at night, but mostly while awake—about how I would be remembered if I died. I wondered if anyone would notice, or care, and if so, for how long? I assumed my life and death would be reduced to a mention on the *Nightly News*. I gave myself half a news cycle. I'd be a three-day story, if it was a slow week.

I have a theory that all reporters go through four stages while covering war zones.

Stage One: I'm invincible. Nothing can hurt me. I'm Superman.

Stage Two: What I'm doing is dangerous. I might get hurt over here. I'd better be careful.

Stage Three: What I'm doing is really dangerous. I am *probably* going to get hurt over here no matter how careful I am. Math and probability and time are working against me.

Stage Four: I have been here too long. I am going to die over here. It is just a matter of time. I've played the game too long.

I was changing stages. I arrived in Baghdad in Stage One, twenty-nine years old and cocky as hell. I moved to Stage Two once the bombs started to fall during Shock and Awe. I surfed that for about two years. Now I was creeping into Stage Three, and it was affecting me and my relationships. I couldn't relate to friends and family in the States anymore. I couldn't relate to my wife. Our relationship had been on the rocks for over a year. She was my college girlfriend, and my best friend. Now we were getting a divorce.

She couldn't understand what I was doing, or why. She kept telling me that I didn't understand that life is for living and creating a family. I told her life is about exploring, a giant road trip, and that I was lucky enough to have a front seat as the train of history crashed through the Middle East. I was able to see raw human nature, unpolished and unrestrained by laws. I was fascinated and addicted. We couldn't resolve our marriage. The paperwork was being finalized.

I felt alone, but I was able to bury myself in work. Iraq was popping. The Sunnis were going crazy. I was busy, up from 9 A.M. to 3 A.M. filing stories.

It took two weeks for all the votes to be counted and, as expected, 169 won the most seats in parliament. But the Shiite bloc didn't do as well as it expected. The Shiite list won only about 40 percent of the vote, and therefore 40 percent of the 275 seats in parliament. Allawi bombed completely. His list took only 16 percent of the vote, less than half of what he'd hoped. The big unexpected winners were the Kurds. The Kurdish parties—the two long-warring clans led by Jalal Talabani and Masoud Barzani—took 26 percent. The Sunnis were out, and even more frustrated and isolated than before.

One of my best sources in Haditha—a Sunni village on the Euphrates northwest of Baghdad—said Sunni radicals had decided to form their own state in response to the elections. Zarqawi was its president. "Since the Shiites decided to take Iraq through the American elections," the stringer said, "the Sunnis decided to form a parallel government, an Islamic state with sharia [Islamic law] as their law and the Koran as the constitution." He said insurgents were already implementing their ferociously intolerant version of an Islamic state days after the elections.

Iraq was still one country, but now there were three nations, which I started to call Shiastan, Kurdistan, and Jihadistan. The culture of Jihadistan—a huge swath of land stretching from the border with Syria, to Jordan, to west Baghdad—was as extreme as the Taliban's regime in Afghanistan.

Men were forbidden to wear shorts. Barbers were ordered to stop shaving beards. Goatees were seen as especially sinful. Insurgents in Haditha had even banned grocers from mixing cucumbers and tomatoes in the same bag. The two vegetables had to be kept separate. The intermingling was seen as overtly sexual because of the cucumber's phallic shape and the tomato's red color, evocative (at least to them) of a woman's vagina. Arabic divides nouns into masculine and feminine forms. A cucumber (*khiar*) is a male noun, while a tomato (*banadora*) is female. It was all too sexual for the jihadists to tolerate. They could behead people in public, but got squeamish at the thought of raw mixed vegetables. There was an element of sexual repression in their extremism. Martyrs in heaven would be rewarded with seventy-two houris, sweet-smelling dark-eyed virgins with pale skin. But in life, women had to cover up and remain sexually anonymous. The jihadists dreamt of God-given sexual ecstasy, but outlawed it on religious grounds. One Saudi friend of mine, an exquisitely beautiful woman fed up with the hypocrisy in her country, said sarcastically, "Why should I save my virginity? So I can give it to some suicide bomber in paradise?"

The stringer from Haditha brought me a poem that had been pinned on the door of a mosque. The title of the poem was "Jihad Has Told Me That Islam Is a Tree That Lives on Nothing but Blood."

> *Come to the Garden to Eden,*
> *It is your first place, and there you will stay.*
> *He who vows to live for his religion, his life will*
> *   be extinguished, but he will live and die a*
> *   great man.*
>
> *Honest men are they who make themselves vessels*
> *   through which they save the Islamic nation*
> *   from losing its way . . .*
>
> *We are coming.*
> *Those who flout the dignity for Muslims await an*
> *   angry flow and storming danger.*

He also brought a photocopy of a poster describing the punishments reserved for those who defied the jihadists' laws:

Those who fight God and His messenger and try to
corrupt life must be killed or crucified or have their
hands and feet cut off on opposite sides. They will
be shamed in life as well as death.

The poster listed the names of eight people already punished.

Before the elections, Sunnis had mostly attacked American and Iraqi troops, politicians, and Shiite religious leaders. Now Shiite civilians were also targets. The Shiites had voted. They had participated in the political process. They were responsible for having elected the howza. They were fair game—men, women, children, all of them.

But as powerful as the howza, Sistani, and Iran had been to mobilize voters, the Shiite coalition struggled to hold together once the results were announced. The politicians fought over who would rule. They bickered over ministries and portfolios.

The work kept me busy, but didn't make me forget the danger. After the bombing at the Australian embassy, I started to sleep on the floor. I wanted to stay low and away from the window. I'd flipped my bed on its side like a shield and slept next to it. If more shrapnel flew in, I hoped the mattress would provide at least some protection. I slept that way for the next six months.

But life in the Hamra wasn't always dreary and frightening. In March, while we were waiting for the newly elected Iraqi politicians to form a government, we had a party. We held it in the Chinese restaurant in the Hamra's lobby, which hadn't seen any customers in months. Parties had also become rare. The freelancers—generally the greenest, keenest, youngest, and most fun of the reporting community—were nearly all gone. In the beginning of the war, there'd been filmmakers, entrepreneurs, and freelancers at the Hamra pool, stringers in string bikinis. But I could hardly remember those days anymore. Iraq had become too dangerous and, more important, too expensive for anyone but the big American TV networks, newspapers, and magazines. The European journalists had nearly all left too. The war wasn't a big story in Europe anymore, not big enough to carry the huge cost—$100,000 to $200,000 a month—of a full Baghdad bureau with armored cars, bodyguards, satellite phones, and local staff.

Iraq had become a very antisocial war. We were having a party for the leftovers, the hangers-on, and of them, only the ones willing to risk their lives to trek across Baghdad to have a few cocktails with people they already knew. It was a lot to ask, but parties were our only social outlet. We weren't going out to dinner or shopping anymore. It wasn't worth it. There was no reporters' bar where we swapped stories and smoked hash all night like at the Commodore Hotel during the Lebanese civil war in the 1980s.

Still, we were not the type of crowd that liked to be penned in. We were all social, young, and single, or soon to be single. The war was wrecking so many marriages and relationships. That night, about thirty of us got a bit unhinged in the Hamra's Chinese restaurant. The music was loud. We drank a lot, and danced a lot. Everyone was a little tipsy, some more than that.

Marla Ruzicka stood out. While the gaggle of reporters tended to be grumpy, cynical, and generally unwashed, she was a twenty-six-year-old with bright blond hair, dazzling eyes, and a giant smile. Everybody knew Marla, and she floated through the room, hugging everyone. That was her style: warm, affectionate, and giving. Marla was one of the only humanitarian workers left in Iraq. She ran a small charity she'd founded to help civilian casualties of war, the often ignored collateral damage.

The United Nations was locked down in the Green Zone. The Red Cross was gone. Even Doctors Without Borders, which won the 1999 Nobel Peace Prize for bringing medical aid to some of the most dangerous, godforsaken corners of the globe, had left. But Marla stayed, a one-woman charity, relying on her friends in the media to help her. She lived with us, bouncing from bureau to bureau, using the Internet and telephones when we weren't busy. She often stayed at the *Washington Post* bureau, just across the street from the Hamra.

Marla's goal was to convince the U.S. military to take more re-

sponsibility for Iraqi civilian casualties and pay compensation. She
didn't spend a dime on herself, keeping all the money she raised
for the families of victims and to lobby the military. Baghdad can be
lonely and sometimes people found each other. That night we
found each other.

Marla was the opposite of all that was ugly and brutal about
Baghdad. She was sensitive, cried a lot, sometimes drank too much,
and always wore her heart on her sleeve. Marla was the closest thing
to an angel I have ever met, the kindest person I knew. I was attracted to that goodness. It seemed, and she seemed, just beautiful.

We ended up leaving together and going up to my room. It was
one of the last times I saw her alive. A few weeks later, Marla was
killed on the airport road. She was returning from a meeting at
Camp Victory, the main U.S. base at Baghdad's airport. She'd been
making progress, and had just convinced several commanders to
review policy on Iraqi civilian deaths. She was excited, but she never
made it back.

In the Green Zone, I saw Brigadier General Karl Horst from
the 3rd ID. General Horst was a good man, active, dynamic, and always in the field. He cooperated with journalists, seemed to understand what we were doing, and gave out his cell phone number. I
asked him what he knew about Marla's death.

He had the full report. A suicide car bomb had attacked a
two-car convoy of contractors working on "democracy development." They were in armored vehicles, hard cars. Marla had been
driving in an unarmored sedan nearby when the convoy was attacked. She wasn't the target, but the blast mostly bounced off the
armored cars and splashed onto Marla's car, setting it on fire. Her
driver was killed instantly. Marla was badly burned, so badly that
Horst said the soldiers who arrived on the scene could barely tell if
she was alive. There was just a little tuft of her blond hair left, Horst
said. The rest was burned away.

Marla apparently knew how bad she looked. "I'm still alive,"
Horst said Marla told the soldiers. "I'm an American, and I'm still
alive."

That statement hit me hard. I pictured Marla asking the American soldiers to save her. Don't leave me, she was saying in her dying breath, I'm still alive, and I'm an American. The U.S. troops didn't leave Marla. They tried to medevac her to Camp Victory, just a few miles away. But she died on the way.

I was numb. Her death hit home. She'd left my hotel room, where we'd been drinking cheap Lebanese red wine and talking about life, Iraq, relationships, and all the other little things that make conversation, and now she'd burned to death on the airport road. Marla wanted to help Iraqis. She'd dedicated her life to it. But Iraq had killed her. No one deserves to die, but Marla deserved to live. It seemed unfair. It seemed pointless.

I didn't want to cover her story. I didn't want to reduce her life to a two-minute news package and search for ten-second sound bites that would be her final words to the world. It would have been easy, a formula. A pretty American girl goes to Iraq to help the locals, but is killed by more of the daily violence, a tragedy . . . and in other news tonight . . . I couldn't do it. Another correspondent filed the report.

Back in my room, I cried for the first time in Baghdad.

At a memorial service on the lawn of the *Washington Post* bureau, reporters read poems and played songs they thought Marla would have liked. I sat in a plastic chair in silence. Jill Carroll, one of the only remaining freelancers in Baghdad, who worked for *The Christian Science Monitor*, gave what I thought was the most moving tribute. The two women—both around the same age—were close friends. "Marla said 'I love you' a lot," Jill remembered, "and she meant it every time."

I again buried myself in work. At least that was easy. There was a lot going on. On May 4, 2005, more than three months after the vote, Iraq's parliament had finally convened to swear in Ibrahim al-Jaafari as Iraq's first freely elected prime minister. How times had changed. Allawi had at least shared some similarities to Saddam Hussein. He wasn't a murderous dictator, but was a strongman, was secular, and appealed to nationalism more than faith. Jaafari was a totally different type of leader. I interviewed him after he was tapped to be prime minister.

Unlike Allawi, Jaafari was a small, soft-spoken man with a tiny, delicate frame. As we clipped a microphone to his suit, he was exceptionally polite, apologizing unnecessarily for shifting in his chair or accidentally stepping on our cables. He had thin gray hair, a short gray beard, and a kindly face, lit up by bright, friendly eyes. He seemed like he would have been a wonderful uncle. Jaafari had been a family doctor while living in exile for ten years in Iran before moving to London. I imagine he had a very reassuring bedside manner.

Jaafari was also an intellectual, a Shiite scholar, and a sayid. But he preferred business suits to the black turban, his right as a descendant of the Prophet Mohammed. He told me he didn't want an Islamic state like in Iran, but supported Islamic values. He thought sharia should govern family law and morals, making things like homosexuality illegal. But that was nothing new in the Islamic world. What was different about Jaafari was his past.

Jaafari was the leader of the Dawa party—Arabic for Islamic call. If a non-Muslim converts to Islam, he is said to have answered the *Dawa*. The Dawa party was a Shiite opposition group that Saddam (and many other world leaders) considered a terrorist group. While there was no evidence that Jaafari was personally involved in violence, Dawa party operatives carried out several attacks in Iraq and across the Middle East to undermine the Iraqi regime and its supporters, including the United States.

In 1980, Dawa militants, and their Iranian backers, launched a grenade attack at Baghdad's Mustansariya University. In March the same year, Saddam made belonging to the Dawa party a crime punishable by death. Many of their members were hanged in a dungeon-like prison in Kazimiya, the holiest Shiite area in east Baghdad.

In December 1983, the Dawa party was held responsible for bombing the U.S. and French embassies in Kuwait, along with a power station, a flight control tower, and the compound of a U.S. defense contractor. The Dawa party later said the attacks were carried out by "rogue" members working with Iranian Revolutionary Guards.

But the Dawa party's most famous attack was the 1982 assassination attempt on Saddam in the Shiite village of Dujail, forty miles north of Baghdad. The Iran-Iraq War was in full swing, and Saddam was on an official visit to the village. As Saddam's convoy entered Dujail, a woman rushed to greet the Iraqi president. The visit was during Eid al-Adha—Islam's Feast of the Sacrifice—when Muslims who can afford to do so sacrifice a sheep to commemorate God's test of faith when he commanded Abraham to slaughter his son.

The woman's hands were covered in sheep's blood, and she stamped handprints on the car's door. Bloody handprints are a traditional good-luck charm in much of the Middle East, especially in rural communities like Dujail. Villagers put the handprints on their tractors or the walls of their homes to keep away bad omens. This time, it was a trick. The woman had marked Saddam's vehicle so that Dawa party gunmen hiding in nearby orchards would know which vehicle to attack. When Saddam's convoy pulled away, the gunmen opened fire.

Saddam survived and ordered a brutal crackdown. Hundreds of villagers were arrested and deported to concentration camps. One hundred forty-eight men and boys were sentenced to death. Bulldozers razed the orchards where the gunmen staged the ambush. The gunmen who survived escaped to Iran.

Now Ibrahim al-Jaafari, the leader of the party that had tried to kill Saddam, a group Saddam considered an Iranian-backed terrorist organization, was Iraq's prime minister, brought to power by elections backed by Washington, Saddam's enemy. It was too bizarre for words.

Personally, Jaafari was a gentleman and a charming host. He held a dinner for a small group of journalists after being sworn in. I sat next to CNN's Christiane Amanpour at a table covered with lamb, rice, and chicken soup. She chatted with Jaafari in fluent Farsi. Surprisingly, Jaafari spoke little about Iraqi politics, but seemed fascinated by American history. He quoted from the *Federalist Papers* and referred to debates held by the founding fathers. He embarrassed us all with his memory for dates and the intricacies of the creation of American democracy. Jaafari barely touched his food. He was too engaged in the discussion. After the plates were cleared away, Jaafari read us love poems he'd written for his wife, a gynecologist. But he wouldn't read the most intimate ones. "They are just for my wife," he said with a little smile.

Jaafari also denied that Iran was directly interfering in Iraq. "There is no evidence of it, but I can't prevent a country from exporting ideas," he said.

Jaafari seemed perplexed by the American embassy's growing concern about the Saddam trial. The embassy wanted a fair and open trial. Saddam, as far as Jaafari was concerned, was as guilty as Hitler. He said he was reading books about the Nazi war crimes tribunal at Nuremberg. "I don't think there are clearer crimes in the world than those of Saddam Hussein," he said. "His trial has been delayed too long. It should have been much earlier. To do a complete study of Saddam's crimes would take a century." Jaafari said five of his relatives had been killed by Saddam's regime, several of them tortured to find out information about him. Jaafari said he felt personally responsible.

Jaafari was a complex character, a poet, a theologian, a romantic even. A Kurdish politician told me about his frustration working with Jaafari. "You can't get answers from him. All he does is talk philosophy." Iraq didn't need a philosopher. It needed a leader.

I saw Allawi a few days later. He was depressed and felt betrayed by the Americans. He sincerely believed the Americans would have helped him win, even by cheating. Iran was backing its favorite candidates. "Why shouldn't the U.S. do the same?" he wondered. Until the end, Allawi, who all his life worked for the Baath party and foreign intelligence agencies, believed that when the ballots were counted his name would have mysteriously come out as the winner.

The elections profoundly changed Iraq. It was the biggest turning point since Hussein was martyred in Karbala and the Shiites lost their struggle to regain power in the seventh century. And I was changing along with it.

14

The elections had made great TV. We lived on them for months, recycling the same five or six pictures of Iraqis holding up their purple ink-stained fingers for the cameras. The viewers seemed to lap it up. We loved it too. Together, we were as happy as thirsty horses at a trough, drinking in all the good news. We'd been under pressure to find a reason why thousands of boys and girls from faraway places like Texas, Florida, and Louisiana were coming home burned, blind, and with chronic headaches, or in inky black bags we couldn't film. Now at least we had something to show for their sacrifice, progress through purple fingers. But the reality was that the elections laid the foundation for civil war in Iraq. As soon as the curfews were lifted, security collapsed and hunting season began.

I left the Hamra for a background briefing on the new government with an admiral in the Green Zone. The military had closed a nearby checkpoint into the Zone to civilian traffic. We had to go the long way round, a forty-minute drive to another entrance. The military never made it easy for us to go to the Green Zone. The commanders always held briefings behind the blast walls, but closed most of the gates. The rule was, "Come at your own risk." Since the briefing was off-camera, I didn't take a crew or producer. There was no need to risk taking a full team, better to keep the numbers small.

I suited up, pulled my blue flak jacket over my shoulders, grabbed a notebook, and met our security team in front of the hotel. Our British security consultants, the Centurions, checked the cars, tires, gas, guns, and radios, and we rolled out in a defensive little convoy. I was in the backseat of the lead car, our armored Jeep Cherokee. A "chase car" followed about twenty feet back. It was routine.

We were picked up almost immediately. The driver of my Jeep— the unfortunately nicknamed "Bunny"—was the first to notice the BMW behind us. It was acting up, weaving in traffic, moving fast and then slowing down, approaching us and then pulling back. "Somebody's playing with us," Bunny called out, putting us on alert.

His gunner, riding shotgun, locked and loaded his AK-47, putting it in his lap, finger on the trigger, keeping it low and out of sight. It was a last resort.

I perked up in the backseat. "What's going on?" I asked.

"The car behind us," Bunny said, adjusting the two rearview mirrors he'd installed to give him a better view of the road. It was only one of many modifications to our vehicles. The consultants repainted the cars every few weeks to make them harder to track, routinely changed the license plates, and installed "run-flat tires," which have a solid inner core and roll even when shot out. It all gave us at least a fighting chance of escaping an "engagement."

Then I saw the dark metallic blue 1990s model BMW pull up alongside us. There were four men in the car. They were looking over at us, necks craned, seeing if we were worth kidnapping. They were testing us, driving fast and slow to see how many cars were in our convoy, and how we'd react to an ambush. Were we armed? Would we immediately open fire? Did we know how to drive? The BMW was probing to find out. They knew what they were doing. Many of the insurgents had been special agents in Saddam's security services, trained in surveillance, counterintelligence, and covert operations. Saddam had his own assassination squads that helped him repress 25 million people for nearly three decades. They were pros.

My stomach felt like it was on the floor in the backseat. It was full of adrenaline and fear. It was heavy and sour and it hurt. I had a metallic taste in my mouth. Superaware, I could almost feel the hair on the back of my head going gray. It was game on, yet again.

Bunny swerved unexpectedly, turning into the BMW, trying to ram him off us. He was also sending a message. "I see you. I know you're there. I know what I'm doing. Don't fuck with us!"

But the BMW was much more powerful than our heavy bulletproof Jeep, never meant to handle the weight of all the armor. The Jeep was top-heavy and accelerated like an old tank. The BMW easily swerved out of our path, sped past us, and cut us off. The BMW seemed to move with an animal quickness and agility. It may have been modified with a souped-up engine. It also had new tires and no license plate. It was an ambushmobile.

Now in front of us, the driver of the BMW slammed on his brakes. He was trying to get us to ram him from behind, to slow us down. Bunny smashed the brakes, but our sluggish Jeep didn't stop in time. We nearly rear-ended the BMW.

That's when a second car, a white Toyota, moved in from behind. It was a trap. They were sandwiching us in: Carjacking 101. "Another car, behind us!" I yelled. "Coming in fast."

"Eyes on it," the gunner called back.

The Toyota moved in tighter. It was just a few inches from our back bumper. Both cars started to steer right, trying to guide us to the side of the road. They'd trapped us. Now they were hauling in the net.

Bunny saw an exit ramp, and took a hard right. He looked like he was making a run for the off ramp, trying to escape. It was a bluff, and the BMW bought it. The BMW followed our lead and also steered right, trying to keep us penned in. It was a mistake. The BMW's turn made an opening. Bunny had a split second to take advantage of it. He hit the brakes, jolting us forward, and made a severe left, almost a 90-degree turn. Like a boxer, he'd faked right and now was slipping left. The tires screamed and the Jeep leaned over to the left, nearly bottoming out on the road. Bunny kept going, jumping a center divider and barreling into traffic on the other side of the road. He was driving about 80 miles an hour, weaving between cars.

But the carjackers didn't give up. Our gunner spotted a third car moving in behind us, gaining ground. We were being hunted. In the savannas of East Africa, elephants will circle to protect their young from attacking lions. But herds of wildebeest just step aside or run away and let the lions take their meal. That's what was happening to us. The other cars peeled off to the side of the road, getting out of the way and letting nature take its course. They didn't want to see the kill. It would be over quickly.

Bunny kept moving. He whipped around a traffic circle and headed back toward the bureau. We pulled in just as the third car was on our tail. It slowed down as we drove into the hotel's gate, lingered for a few seconds, and then left, ready to hunt another day.

As I walked through the lobby, I scanned the hotel staff. I was furious and suspicious. We'd been picked up as we left the Hamra. Someone had tipped them off. Someone in the lobby had used a cell phone as we left and said, "A convoy is leaving with a foreigner inside, go get him." I looked to see if anyone in the lobby was on a cell phone. I was ready to pounce. If I'd seen anyone acting suspiciously, secretly talking into a phone or averting his eyes, I would have attacked him. My fists and teeth were clenched as I looked around the hotel. I hated everyone I saw. But the receptionists and cleaners in the lobby were just milling around, seemingly oblivious to what had happened. Someone had set us up. I couldn't figure out who it was.

Upstairs in the bureau, I told Zohair and Ali what had happened. "They were probably criminals," Zohair said.

Ali told me Sunni radicals at his university had put up posters offering $5,000 for any foreigner. We were a commodity, prey for big-game hunters who would sell us to the highest bidder.

I wrote an e-mail to my editors about the failed kidnapping attempt and praising Bunny for his "damn good driving." Within minutes I heard back from a senior executive.

"Call me, urgently," the e-mail said.

When I called the executive, he immediately started to yell. "What are you trying to do?" he asked accusingly.

"What do you mean?" I asked.

"Obviously, you don't understand how things work here. Why did you send that note?" he demanded to know.

"I thought my editors, the people I work with every day, the people who assign and approve my stories, should know what happened. They should know what the environment is like here, so they understand what is and what isn't possible to do."

The executive kept yelling, saying that security concerns were "only to be brought up" with a small group of "senior executives," and that I should not have informed the editors. I'd violated protocol. I'd CC'd the wrong people on the e-mail. It was unacceptable.

"I thought you understood how things work here. Obviously, you don't," he barked.

He actually expected me to apologize. I did not.

"Okay, I understand," I said, and hung up the phone.

"Fuck you!" I screamed at the dead phone on my desk. I wished I'd told the executive what I really felt, but I didn't want to lose my job. I felt like a coward.

It seemed that we were on our own. Undoubtedly, the executives wanted us to survive, but equally important, it seemed from where I sat in Baghdad, they didn't want to get in trouble themselves. They didn't want lawsuits. They were covering their backs, worried that if I told too many people at the network that something had happened, it could jeopardize their careers. Perhaps they'd be fired. Perhaps someone would question their security plans. The message to me was diamond-clear.

The Centurions got a similar message. There were no congratulatory notes even though they'd saved my life.

In Baghdad, we made a pact. If there were another kidnapping attempt, we would try to fight out of it. Better to die shot in the back, running away, than to be executed on your knees, begging for your life in an orange suit while some maniac films it and posts the video on Ogrish.

I told a soldier about the attempted kidnapping and the pact we'd made to try to escape at any cost. He immediately understood. The troops had the same attitude. "I'd rather face twelve than be carried by six," he said.

A few days later, I found out my divorce papers were nearly complete. It was a rough few weeks, but the stories after the formation of the new government were fascinating, more complex than ever. Iraq had become a puzzle that took all my time and attention to try to unravel.

The new government that took office in May 2005 realized the Sunnis' worst conspiracy theories. It seemed Zarqawi's predictions had been correct. The government was now led by a grab bag of Iraq's former enemies, allies of Washington, Iran, and/or the howza, often playing one side against the other. The political lineup made patriotic Sunni nationalists like our translator Mohammed, fed for years a diet of propaganda about Iraqi national pride and honor, shake his head in amazement.

Jalal Talabani, a rotund gray-haired former Kurdish rebel who had cooperated with both Iran and the CIA to topple Saddam, was the new president. Ibrahim al-Jaafari, the leader of the Iranian-backed Dawa party and a Shiite sayid, was prime minister. Hussein Tahan, a former military commander from the Badr Brigade, the Iranian-backed military wing of the Supreme Council for Islamic Revolution in Iraq (SCIRI), was the governor of Baghdad. Tahan bragged that he'd memorized the Koran, and that he'd personally fired rockets at Saddam's units in the 1990s.

But it was the new interior minister, Beyan Jabr, who really outraged the Sunnis. The Americans were nervous about "Haji Beyan" too, and with good reason.

During the Iran-Iraq War, Iran's Revolutionary Guards trained thousands of Iraqi exiles to fight against Saddam. They were called the Badr Brigade, named after a battle led by the Prophet Mohammed in the Hijaz in 624. Throughout the Iran-Iraq War, the Badr Brigade ambushed Iraqi soldiers in the southern marshes. Not surprisingly, Saddam considered the group a terrorist organization.

But Saddam had his own militia of Iranians loyal to him, the Mujahideen Khalq. They were Iranian dissidents Saddam's government trained on a base in Falujah later occupied by U.S. troops. Both Iran and Iraq armed themselves with insiders who knew the enemy. But now the American-sponsored elections had given the Badr Brigade control of the strategic Interior Ministry. It was a huge coup for Iran.

I interviewed Jabr—a short, slender man with a closely cropped beard—in a villa in Kazimiya shortly after his appointment. He was the son of one of Iraq's biggest textile merchants, but had escaped Iraq under Saddam and moved to Iran and Syria, where he was the SCIRI representative in Damascus and worked at the party's newspaper.

I was amazed that he didn't attempt to hide his connections to the Badr Brigade, bragging that he used the group as a personal intelligence agency. "We get very important knowledge from them through the telephone, direct to my office," he said.

Then Jabr leaned in and made a threat to anyone plotting to unseat him, especially former army officers and members of the Baath party. "The Badr Brigade has given me many files, secret files, intelligence, that I can use at my discretion," he said with smug satisfaction.

The American embassy was pushing for Shiites to reach out to Sunnis and include them in the new government, even though they'd boycotted the vote. Jabr was saying to the Sunnis, "I have files on you, don't challenge me" and to the Americans, "If you push me, I'll use them." But while Jabr claimed to have files and an intelligence agency, he needed muscle. His first step was to create a loyal armed force.

The new Iraqi army was out of the question. It was mainly run by the Americans, and many of the senior officers were Sunnis. U.S. military advisors, led by Lieutenant General David Petraeus, were deeply involved in training and equipping the army to replace the one Bremer dissolved six weeks after the fall of Baghdad. Jabr couldn't get near them, and the army wasn't technically even under his ministry's authority. The army belonged to the Ministry of Defense.

But within the Interior Ministry, Jabr found another force that would do the job, al-Maghaweer, the Commandos. The Commandos were first established under Allawi and his interior minister, Fallah al-Nakib. The group was born out of necessity, and on shaky moral and ethical ground. Allawi created the Commandos to make sure the elections took place on time, accomplishing the White House's almost sacred goal. But as attacks intensified leading up to the vote, it was clear Iraq didn't have the right forces to secure the country.

Petraeus, leader of Multi-National Security Transition Command—Iraq (MNSTC-I), was methodically rebuilding Iraq's army along conventional lines. The new force was being designed to protect Iraq's borders and defend against a ground invasion by Syria or Iran. The U.S. military was building an army to do what armed forces generally do, protect Iraq's sovereignty. But Iraq didn't need a conventional army in late 2004 and early 2005. The Syrians and Iranians weren't likely to invade, especially with more than 100,000 American soldiers in Iraq. An army of tanks and troop formations couldn't stop car bombers and kidnappers. In theory, it was the police—the Interior Ministry—that was supposed to patrol the cities. But beat cops are trained to arrest rapists and thieves, not fight well-funded suicide bombers armed with military-grade weapons. Allawi determined that Iraq needed a light, aggressive paramilitary police force, a counterterrorism unit that could operate in urban areas. Iraq needed the Commandos, and the Americans had just the right men on hand to build it.

Jim Steele, Steve Casteel, and Colonel James Coffman were all security experts stationed in Iraq with ample experience working in the shadows, and with dubious, often unscrupulous, forces that could make problems, and their enemies, disappear. Each man could be the subject of his own book or Hollywood blockbuster.

Jim Steele started his career during the Vietnam War and was shot twice in battle. Steele's commander, General George S. Patton Jr., son of the legendary World War II general, called Steele "the best small unit combat leader" he had witnessed during two wars. After Vietnam, Steele led Special Operations Forces advisors in El Salvador, according to a brilliant article on the Commandos by Peter Maass in *The New York Times Magazine*. El Salvador was one of the Cold War's dirty conflicts. The Reagan administration backed the anticommunist Salvadoran army against leftist rebels in a vicious civil war. Seventy thousand people died in twelve years of fighting. Most of the victims were killed by the army and its allied death squads, widely accused of torture and kidnapping. It was in El Salvador that Steele honed his skills. The Reagan administration funneled hundreds of millions of dollars to back El Salvador. Some of it may have gone through Steele.

In 1986, Steele was questioned by investigators about his suspected involvement in the Iran-contra scandal, the secret U.S. program to sell weapons to Iran, an enemy state, and use the money to aid anti-communist contra rebels in Nicaragua. Steele was specifically asked about allegations that weapons were transported through El Salvador's Ilopango Air Base while he was stationed in the country. He denied any involvement in the arms deals. In his 1997 book *Firewall*, independent counsel Lawrence Walsh, who investigated the Iran-contra scandal, reported that a lie detector test showed Steele "was not being truthful."

In Iraq, Bremer appointed Steele as a security advisor. In 2004, Steele led a group of U.S. and Iraqi Special Operations Forces to recover the bodies of the Blackwater contractors massacred in Falujah before the first U.S. invasion of the city. Steele certainly had the qualifications to create a paramilitary force in Iraq that could deal with insurgents, using tactics that would make conventional armies squirm.

Steve Casteel also worked in Latin America, mainly for the U.S. Drug Enforcement Agency. He rose to be the DEA's director of intelligence, leading special operations and investigations.

Casteel became one of the key players in the drug wars in Peru, Bolivia, and Colombia, and was personally involved in the hunt for cocaine cartel kingpin Pablo Escobar. Maass reported that Casteel was the primary founder of Iraq's Commandos while serving as a personal advisor to Interior Minister Fallah al-Nakib.

I met Casteel regularly in his office in the Adnan palace in the Green Zone. He compared the Bush administration's war on terrorism to Reagan's war on drugs. "There's no victory, no day when the enemy surrenders," he said. "But is there as much cocaine on American streets today as there was before the war on drugs? If the answer is no, we won." He said the United States would know if it won the war on terrorism when it can answer the same question about the number of terrorist attacks.

Colonel Coffman was a brave, perhaps even fearless, commander.

In November 2004, Coffman led a small unit of Commandos and held off a five-hour ambush on a police station in Mosul. After most of the Commandos were killed by RPG and small-arms fire, Coffman rallied the survivors and held the police station. Although he was fifty years old, out of ammunition, and shot in the hand, Coffman picked up loose rounds from the ground, wedged his rifle between his knees, and fed in bullets with his good hand. According to a statement by the U.S. military, the besieged Commandos under Coffman's command killed twenty-four of the attackers before reinforcements arrived.

Steele, Casteel, and Coffman together created a ferocious force, drawing mainly from Sunni members of Saddam's elite units. From the start the Commandos were a monster, but Allawi, Nakib, Casteel, Steele, and Coffman kept them in check, at least most of the time. The Commandos still beat and occasionally killed unarmed prisoners. Nonetheless, most Iraqis considered the Commandos a necessary evil. The Commandos were proud of their zeal for catching and killing insurgents, and many Iraqis were happy to have them do so.

One of the most unusual stories I covered was the launch of the Commandos' own television show, modeled on the violent American true crime program *Cops.* The Commandos called it *Terrorists in the Grip of Justice.* The show, which ran every night on al-Iraqiya TV, was simple. There were no special effects or graphics. Instead, viewers watched in amazement as a Commando commander interrogated insurgents who confessed to unspeakable horrors.

"I stalked ten college girls, translators for the U.S. Army, then raped and murdered them," confessed one man sitting in a chair in front of a wall emblazoned with the Commandos' logo.

The man didn't look like a brave freedom fighter. He was staring sheepishly at the floor as he spoke. He looked defeated and terrified. Both of his eyes were black, apparently from having been beaten during interrogation.

Terrorists in the Grip of Justice aired twenty confessions a week. I saw another man confess to having beheaded ten people, first practicing on animals. Like many, he claimed to have been sent to carry out atrocities in Iraq by Syrian intelligence.

Iraqis loved it. The show was a hit. The program gave the insurgents a face, and conveniently blamed the violence on outsiders. The militants were a foreign problem. They were Arab mercenaries sent by Syria. During their confessions, the captives didn't talk about Sunnis or Shiites. They made Iraq's problems seem manageable and criminal, not a civil war. But critics said *Terrorists in the Grip of Justice* was nothing more than televised show trials. Many of the confessions appeared to have been forced.

When our stringer visited the police station in Mosul where the Commandos filmed the show, a relative of a murdered policeman bragged that he'd personally interrogated and beaten one of the suspects.

I was amazed the Americans were helping to sponsor the show. U.S. taxpayer dollars paid for al-Iraqiya, which broadcast the program.

Once Jabr took over the Interior Ministry, the Commandos, always on the edge of morality, took a dramatic turn for the worse. Jabr created new, decidedly Shiite units like the Hussein Brigade that hunted down Baath party members.

In August 2005, Coffman was awarded the Distinguished Service Cross, second only to the Congressional Medal of Honor, for his bravery at the police station in Mosul.

Ironically, Jabr—the man who turned commando units into a personal death squad—attended the ceremony. I sat in the back row of the ceremony in the Green Zone. "Colonel Coffman, the blood you shed will never be forgotten," Jabr said. "We, the forces of the Ministry of the Interior and the Ministry of Defense, will continue to fight until we defeat terrorism. Right will always defeat wrong."

Jabr had good reason to thank Coffman. The colonel had armed him with an effective weapon.

Iraq was rapidly becoming a complicated mix of militias and insurgents. For U.S. troops, it was increasingly difficult to distinguish their allies from their enemies.

Ali found a story that captured the confusion of Iraq's new dirty battlefields. Sitting in my office under an original poster of the classic *The Thief of Baghdad,* which I bought from an old man who lived in a one-room apartment above the Sinbad Theater on the once bustling Saadoon Street, Ali told me what locals had seen in Dora, a working-class, mixed Sunni-Shiite neighborhood a few miles south of the Hamra.

"Last week, insurgents came at 9:30 at night with two 'coaster' buses. [Iraqis call a bus that holds about thirty people a "coaster."] They were going house-to-house in Dora. They were stopping at houses they knew belonged to Shiites," Ali said. He always spoke so quietly I had to almost close my eyes to hear him.

"They were wearing Iraqi army uniforms, so people didn't know there was a problem. The insurgents were very polite. They'd go into a house, and were working off a list of names. They'd tell the families they just needed to take the men in for questioning. 'It's just questioning. They'll be back in a few minutes,' they promised."

Ali said some people started to argue. One man refused to get on the bus.

"But then American soldiers came," Ali said.

I looked up from my notes.

"The Americans were there?"

"Yes, a unit of American soldiers arrived in Humvees. They surrounded the area, blocking the streets."

"The Americans were helping the insurgents? They set up roadblocks? Why?" I asked.

"Maybe they didn't know what was going on? The insurgents were wearing army uniforms. Since the Americans were on the scene, the locals thought everything must be all right. They stopped arguing and got on the buses."

Ali said the bodies of everyone who got on the buses, twenty-two men and boys, were found dumped in an orchard outside Baghdad. "They'd been tortured and then executed. Their hands were tied behind their backs. Some were strangled with those plastic handcuffs the Americans use," he said. "One man was stabbed twenty-two times. Some were beheaded."

Ali spoke without emotion or emphasis. He could have been telling me what he'd had for lunch. His voice was flat, straightforward, and lifeless.

I was shocked and suspected it might be a rumor. I had heard mass executions were starting to take place, but found it hard to believe American troops had been on the scene. But it was plausible.

I asked Colonel Ed Cardon, assistant division commander (support) of the 3rd Infantry Division. I knew him to be honest and pragmatic. Cardon worked with General Horst. The two men didn't speak in talking points. They understood the Shiite-Sunni tensions and the undeclared power struggle between allies of Washington and Tehran. They were not the kind of commanders who would tell their troops to close their eyes and imagine a suicide bomber killing their families while Christmas shopping. They understood that a civil war was starting, and that it was brutal.

Cardon confirmed what Ali had been told. He said the American unit thought that Iraqi soldiers were making arrests in Dora and set up a cordon to support them. After all, the Americans had been demanding that Iraqi forces shoulder more of the burden.

Iraqis were supposed to be taking the lead after they formed their government. The American soldiers had assumed that that was what they were seeing. They thought they were watching Iraqi soldiers take charge. Instead, they were watching ethnic cleansing.

Cardon told me the men taken away on buses in Dora were likely executed in some sort of factory.

"How do you know that?" I asked.

"They were beheaded with what appears to have been a band saw. The cuts were so clean," he said.

Insurgents had gone house-to-house, rounding up Shiites, who cooperated only because they thought the U.S. military had sanctioned it. Then they took their victims, laid them flat on a slab, and cut off their heads with an industrial saw.

I couldn't believe the mess we were in. I was starting to hate the war.

15

The spring and summer of 2005 raced by in a blur of murders, bombings, shootings, and kidnappings. There were mortars at dawn every morning, car bombs by 11 A.M., drive-by shootings for tea, and mortars again at dusk to kiss the Green Zone good night. Kidnappers and death squads were mostly nocturnal, hunting invisibly in the darkness. It was hard to tell the days apart. If it rained every day for six months, how could you distinguish if one day was wetter than another?

The "aftermath pix," as we called them, all looked the same. A burned-out car or Humvee. Kids climbing on the debris. Women in loose black dresses wailing on a curbside. A shirtless injured man in his thirties with a mustache on a bloody hospital bed. If only they spoke English, perhaps the viewers would have cared. To many of our viewers, and many of the American soldiers in Iraq, it all looked like "Arab savages" killing one another for no good reason. American news broadcasts, including ours, often summed up the chaos with tired, generic throwaway lines like, "Good evening, more senseless violence today in Iraq" or "More random violence in Baghdad." Then I'd have one minute and fifty seconds to moan about attacks in towns no one had ever heard of that killed people nobody wanted to know about.

But there was little senseless or random about the violence. It was a civil war, although it was still mostly one-sided. Sunnis wanted power, blamed the Shiites for having won the elections, and were determined to punish them. In the spring, summer, and fall of 2005, Sunni radicals and Zarqawi's paradise-obsessed martyrs ferociously attacked Shiites in markets, mosques, and movie theaters, and even at their funerals.

Restaurants were especially popular targets, particularly cheap, greasy kebaab houses—Baghdad's version of donut shops popular with Iraqi cops and soldiers. I arrived at one on Abu Nawaz Street along the Tigris about a half hour after it was attacked. Nearly thirty police and other customers were killed as they ate breakfast.

I saw pools of blood on the white tile floor when I arrived. Metal tables were overturned and the walls were pockmarked with shrapnel. Blah-blah-blah. It looked like more of the same, more aftermath pix. But on the ceiling, I saw something different: a perfectly intact face. It had been ripped off someone's skull (witnesses suspected it was the bomber's face), thrown in the air like a pizza, and glued to the plaster ceiling. It was staring down at me like some macabre modern art installation.

As I approached it with a certain degree of scientific curiosity (I hadn't imagined that a face could peel off like a mask), I accidentally stepped into a soupy pool of blood and chunks of flesh. I instinctively raised my hands in the universal "I surrender" position and flashed an apologetic and completely inappropriate nervous smile. It was how I would have reacted if I'd walked over a floor in a hotel lobby without realizing that a workman was still waxing it. "Whoops, sorry about that." I tiptoed out of the blood, jumped to a dry spot, and joined my crew outside. I started to wipe my shoes, smearing the blood on the curb, but again became embarrassed and self-conscious. What I was doing seemed incredibly disrespectful. This was the blood of someone's son or father, and I was scraping it off my shoes like dog shit.

But there were just so many attacks.

In the middle of April, Sunni militants kidnapped and executed 150 Shiites in Ma'dein, a mixed town twenty miles south of Baghdad. Shiite families paid skindivers $35 a day to search the Tigris for their often headless remains.

A senior U.S. diplomat said tensions had been building in Ma'dein as Shiites started to move into traditionally Sunni neighborhoods. "But I don't see signs of a civil war," he said.

I certainly did. There were fourteen car bombs, forty-two roadside bombs, and twenty-two shootings in Baghdad the same week. At least fifty-eight Iraqi security forces, eighteen Western contractors, ten U.S. troops, and one journalist (AP cameraman Salah Ibrahim) were killed the following week. U.S. military officials said there were now seventy attacks a day. They were just numbers, adding up, and I was there, with my death abacus, keeping track. I didn't think I cared about the carnage. It just seemed like white noise. I didn't feel affected, but friends said I didn't look them in the eyes as much anymore. I was jittery, cold, wired, hungry, and most of all detached. I was always scrambling for stories, and then moving on, revved hot.

But the seemingly senseless violence always became more real, more immediate, when I spent time with the troops. To our viewers, the soldiers and marines weren't nameless, Arabic-speaking killers, or victims fighting for religions and ethnic groups most Americans really didn't want to know about. Americans had never asked to know about Sunnis, Shiites, and Kurds and lions and tigers and bears, oh my. But the troops were mostly churchgoing young men, former high school athletes, husbands, and fathers from the small towns and inner cities of America. Everyone could relate to them.

In late June, I learned the Marines were about to launch yet another offensive. I signed up to go and assembled Kevin and Martin. We were heading back to Anbar, the Sunni badlands, the home of the Devil Dogs, the U.S. Marine Corps.

After a few chopper rides, our first meeting was with the com-

mander of Marine Regimental Combat Team 2, Colonel Stephen
Davis. For "op sec" (operational security) reasons, we were never
told exactly where or when an offensive would take place. Those details always came once we were on the ground. I had come to know
several Marine PAOs—public affairs officers—and they would call
or e-mail with cryptic messages like "There's an opportunity to
embed in Anbar. I strongly suggest you take it."

Naturally suspicious of PAOs, when we arrived in Anbar for
the offensive I worried we'd been suckered into a dog-and-pony
show. I didn't want to watch some Marine commander and his PSD
(personal security detail) visit the one school that was working. I
asked Davis what he had in store for us. "I hope we're not out here
to watch marines hand out soccer balls and lollipops," I said.

Davis didn't seem to have any time or tolerance for fluff either. I
wasn't there to make PR movies for the Marines, and neither was
Davis. He was trying to, as he put it, "out-guerrilla the guerrillas"
and fight an interwoven network of organized criminals, tribal
sheikhs, and Zarqawi's jihadists.

"Hearts and minds?" Davis asked rhetorically. "Out here, it's
about power, respect, keeping your word, and backing up what you
say. The alpha male left standing on the block after the fight will
win the hearts. It's not about love. The leader is loved."

Colonel Davis described his mission as a "primal fight." "We're
not here to hold terrorists, but kill the enemy. People understand
survival," he said.

In Anbar there was no need to pretend that Iraq had a legitimate government. There was no government out in western Iraq
yet. There were only men like Davis and his enemies. Davis told me
militants in his OA were "daisy-chaining" dozens of IEDs together
like strings of Chinese firecrackers so they could take out an entire
convoy at once. He showed me pictures (many of the marines carried digital cameras and flash drives) of twisted wrecks. It was as if
he were an obsessed surgeon, showing off photographs of unusu-
ally large tumors he'd extracted or a particularly rotted liver. These
were his specimens. But I was also enjoying it. I liked the jargon,

cursing, bad coffee in the TOC, and all the macho brotherhood. I was happy to be back out with the marines. There was no spin, bullshit, or talking points, just business.

Davis said a main front of the offensive would be in Heet, a rural city of 130,000 northwest of Ramadi. "It's a nasty little place," he said, and told me how Sunni radicals had killed or scared away all of the local police and government troops. As part of the intimidation campaign, militants from Ansar al-Sunna, Zarqawi's first group, killed fifteen contractors working with Americans, stacked their bodies in a pile, and booby-trapped them with C-4. The insurgents had then turned Heet into one of Anbar's main transit routes for foreign fighters coming to Iraq through Syria. We'd be joining marines as they moved in to take back Heet and install Iraqi forces. The marines would first have to drive out the insurgents, who'd taken over the city's hospital and were dug into a hilltop neighborhood of abandoned ruins. It would be dangerous.

Davis was trying a diversionary tactic. He had moved men and equipment north toward Haditha to try to fool the insurgents, while secretly sending other troops to Heet. He was tired of playing Whack-a-Mole, moving into a village only to find the militants had been tipped off and left. This time, Davis was faking north in Haditha and striking in Heet. "Sooner or later the marines are coming to a town near you with a rock-and-roll show," he said.

Before daybreak, we climbed in the back of a 7-ton, the marines' hulking workhorse of a truck. The 7-ton was full of supplies. Kevin, Martin, and I sat on top of piles of cots and boxes of water and MREs (meals ready to eat) in the open air, exposed as hell. Marines were posted on each corner of the 7-ton, their rifles pointing out into the darkness as we rolled to a forward operating base near Heet. We'd move out into the city from there.

The convoy drove in total darkness. There were no lights for miles and the sky was brilliant with stars. It was a spectacular desert night and I drank in the cool, clean air like a glass of dry white wine.

But Davis's diversionary tactic didn't fool the militants. They were waiting for us. They ambushed the convoy just a few miles from the FOB. I first saw the glowing red tracer fire coming toward us, and then heard the crack, crack, crack of the insurgents' AKs. We didn't have much cover. The 7-ton was nearly full and we were perched on top of it like cherries on ice cream, easy, tempting targets. I got on my stomach, trying to stay as flat as possible, cramming myself between the boxes and cots. Kevin was crouched in a corner next to a marine, holding up his small camera over the edge, filming the ambush.

Then we heard a deep rumbling explosion, an IED detonating next to one of the 7-tons at the back of the convoy. The marines in our vehicle were aiming their shots, popping off bursts whenever they saw tracer fire or muzzle flashes. I think they killed a few of the attackers, but it was hard to tell. They were shooting into the dark.

It was over quickly. After just ten or fifteen minutes, the convoy rolled out again. The IED had been small. None of the marines was hurt. But the insurgents weren't done yet. As soon as we arrived at the base, there was another attack. Mortars! Incoming! Whoomp, splash. Whoomp, splash.

We ran into a concrete "duck and cover" shelter until the rain of metal and high explosive stopped. Then we rushed into a building, pushing open a plywood door rigged with a water bottle on a string that pulled it shut behind us. The door had to stay closed. There were white lights in the room. Mortar teams can use them to target. In the little room, I drank an orange Gatorade and ate a packet of peanut butter cookies.

Situations like this always make me laugh. We'd been mortared just a few minutes earlier, but here I was wearing a flak jacket covered in so much sweat that salt had stained it white around my armpits, snacking on cookies like I was at a campfire with a troop of Boy Scouts.

The next morning we met the marines of Kilo Company (Marine lingo for "K" company), who would be leading the offensive in Heet. I was surprised, and somewhat nervous, to learn that they were Marine reserves. At home, these men were plumbers, electricians, and highway patrolmen. I wondered if they were as well trained as active-duty troops. Were these just yahoos and weekend warriors?

I also didn't expect we'd be walking every day. We set out into Heet on foot. We walked about five miles the first morning, searching homes, shops, and palm groves. We went down narrow footpaths in a long single-file line. These men may have been Marine reserves, but they had quickly become pros. They never bunched up as they marched (making a concentrated target for mortars and IEDS) and were in damn good physical shape. It was up to 120 degrees in the sun and each marine carried nearly one hundred pounds of ammunition, grenades, tools, radios, and clothing.

We walked from 6:30 in the morning until noon. When it got too hot to patrol, the marines searched for a place to "go firm." They found an abandoned construction site, the shell of a half-built private home. It looked like a good spot for a rest. It was isolated, had a clear view of the area from the roof, and was built of reinforced concrete. Here we would rest for a few hours before patrolling again until dark. In the house, the men collapsed on the floor. It was covered with rocks, dirt, and blocks of concrete. Each man took out an MRE.

"Anybody want Skittles?" a marine called out.

They swapped vanilla dairy shakes for apple cider beverages, pasta primavera for Country Captain chicken, jalapeño cheese spread for peanut butter and crackers. But nobody wanted the Charms. The hard sucking candy is considered bad luck. Just throw them away. Never eat the Charms. I'm not superstitious by nature, but I'll never eat Charms on an embed.

The trades were much more than just social bonding. Each man had only one MRE per day and had to suck out every bit of energy from the 1,200-calorie meal. Swapping was efficient. Nothing was thrown away. Except the Charms.

What seemed so unique to me was that these were normal men who'd been transformed by the war and their unit. Sitting on the floor eating an MRE with a brown plastic spoon was Lance Corporal Anton Uzoni, a baby-faced teddy bear of a man with glasses and a big smile. In Pittsburgh, he was a "Prada retail specialist" at Saks Fifth Avenue. "I sell shoes, purses, dresses, everything. No matter. The whole store," he said, laughing, his 34.2-pound rifle between his feet.

Uzoni was now a machine gunner and had a bandolier of bullets draped across his shoulders. He had recently survived an RPG attack that killed his buddy. Uzoni still had shrapnel in his back. The former Prada salesman now talked tough and had lost fifty pounds. "It's the best diet program since Auschwitz," he joked.

It wasn't funny, but Uzoni, just twenty years old, was trying to live up to his nickname, "Animal Mother," the crazy tough killer in Stanley Kubrick's Vietnam movie *Full Metal Jacket*. "I like to kill people," Uzoni said. "My business is killing and right now business is slow." There was tons of macho bullshit. Uzoni was showing off, trying to sound cool.

Platoon Commander Captain Sean O'Neill was older and wiser. His personal kit consisted of nothing more than a dozen pairs of socks, extra underwear, and ten pouches of chewing tobacco. He'd run out of tobacco once and clearly didn't want that to happen again. He was one of the platoon's "mothers." "In the end, you share socks, you share baby powder, you share baby wipes, you share everything. It makes for a tight platoon," he said.

As soon as Staff Sergeant Michael Valenti finished eating, he started to write in his little journal. "I have a deal with my daughter, she's sixteen," Valenti told me. "I promised to write an entry in this journal every day telling her what I'm doing. She's promised to do the same. When I get back, we are going to swap journals so we know what we've been doing all the time I'm away. That way we can catch up."

While Valenti wrote in his journal, other marines played "What's your favorite?"

"What's your favorite color?"

"Blue."

"Favorite car?"

"Corvette."

"Favorite sexual position?"

"Woman on top."

"Favorite beer?"

"Michelob."

"Favorite number?"

"Five."

"Favorite football team?"

"Patriots."

When the temperature dropped to about 100 degrees, the men set off on more patrols. At dusk, they looked for a place to spend the night. They didn't have tents. Instead, they stayed in Iraqi homes. The marines knocked on the door of one of the bigger houses in the area. The Iraqi owner immediately agreed to let them stay, not that he had much choice. When sixty-five fully armed marines show up at the door and ask to spend the night, the answer tends to be yes.

Poor guy. The marines didn't trash his house, but they were not good guests. The men piled in, took off their sweaty boots and "blouses," and crashed out on every couch and blanket they could find. The whole house immediately smelled like a damp locker room. The pungent funk in the air made the quiet thirty-year-old medic Alvin Ocampo nervous. The father of a three-year-old daughter and five-year-old son back in Dallas wanted to check the men's feet for blisters, pus, warts, and fungus. He smelled something funny in the room. He smelled "foot rot."

The marines sat in a circle as Ocampo looked between their toes.

"I don't know what's going on here. I got some cracks, a little bleeding going on," he said. Many of their feet were alive with stinking fungus. Ocampo sprinkled on foot powder, wrapped Band-Aids around toes, and advised the marines to change their socks more often.

The smell was too much for me. I slept the night in the backseat of a car parked in the yard.

When the marines left in the morning, they paid the owner of the house about $25. He accepted it with a smile. He was happy we were moving on.

I stayed with the marines for the next week, patrolling, sleeping, eating, and talking about the war, but more about whiskey and women. The men didn't give a damn about Shiites, Sunnis, or Kurds. They cared about their platoon. They'd become tighter than brothers. They had had every possible conversation, talked about every sexual encounter they'd ever had, and imagined countless more.

When I returned to Baghdad, I called Valenti's home in Ohio. "Hi, this is Richard Engel from NBC News. I'm calling from Baghdad," I said when a woman answered the phone.

It was Valenti's wife, Kathleen. She nearly had a heart attack.

"What? What is it?" she asked.

"No, no, everything is fine," I said. "Your husband is fine. I was just with him. That's why I am calling."

She still didn't seem to believe me.

"You can see him tonight in fact. I am calling to let you know that the story we did about your husband's unit is airing tonight at 6:30 P.M., if you have a chance to watch it."

That seemed to calm her down.

"Oh yes, thank you for calling," she said.

I told her about the unit and what her husband was doing in Heet.

"One more thing," I said. "Is your daughter keeping up her journal? I hope she is because your husband is doing his very diligently. He's taking it very seriously."

She said she'd make sure her daughter stayed on top of her entries, then she hung up.

It felt good to call Valenti's family. I'd been with his unit for only a week, but I felt connected. Increasingly, though, I didn't understand what they hoped to accomplish in godforsaken places like Heet, seven thousand miles from anything they knew. Their sacrifices didn't seem worth it.

16

On August 31, 2005, America wasn't watching Iraq. We were off the news radar. Hurricane Katrina had just flooded 80 percent of New Orleans, and nearly all of southeast Louisiana and southern Mississippi had been evacuated. Thousands of Louisianans who were too poor, old, sick, or stubborn to leave the city were holed up in the Superdome. It was the biggest domestic story since 9/11.

August 31 was also the deadliest day in Baghdad since the start of the war, although almost nobody outside of Iraq seemed to notice it. That morning, several hundred thousand Shiites gathered in Baghdad's Kazimiya neighborhood, an ancient quarter in a bend in the Tigris filled with mosques, shops for Shiite pilgrims, and, recently, the offices of militia leader Moqtada al-Sadr. Sadr's office called it "Medinit al-Kazimiya," the City of Kazimiya, and claimed to control the area.

The crowds that morning were taking part in an annual pilgrimage to commemorate the eighth-century Shiite martyr Musa al-Kazim, the seventh of the "Twelver" Shiite imams. Kazim is like the Shiite patron saint of Baghdad. Most Iraqi, Iranian, and Leba-

nese Shiites are Twelvers and, as the name implies, recognize
twelve imams they believe were the rightful descendants of Ali. According to the Twelver interpretation, the final or twelfth imam was
the Mahdi al-Montazar, the "awaited savior" who disappeared so he
could return and redeem the earth. The promise of the Mahdi is
particularly important to hard-line Shiite groups like Lebanon's
Hezbollah, Moqtada al-Sadr's militia (which derived its name, the
Mahdi Army, from the name of the Imam), and Iranian president
Mahmoud Ahmadinejad. Hezbollah officially says it needs weapons to fight Israel. But Hezbollah members have also told me their
rockets and guns are to defend the Mahdi. President Ahmadinejad
reportedly even drew up plans to construct a special highway to
ease the Mahdi's travel during his return. It would be like fundamentalist Christians building a landing strip for the Second Coming of Jesus.

The tomb of Musa al-Kazim is covered by a giant mosque with
two golden domes and new gold doors. Pilgrims kiss and press
their foreheads against the doors as they enter the mosque. The
doors were a gift from Iran after the fall of Baghdad.

Many of the pilgrims that morning were coming from Sadr City
further to the east and had to walk through the nearby Sunni neighborhood of Adhamiya. As they marched, many supporters of the
Mahdi Army chanted anti-Sunni slogans and declared themselves
to be from "the Islamic State of Sadr City." The Sunnis didn't like
it, but let the pilgrims pass and cross the Imma bridge over the
Tigris.

The Imma is a wide, sturdy, three-hundred-yard bridge about
thirty feet above the water. It is also highly symbolic, the physical
link between the holiest Shiite and Sunni neighborhoods in Baghdad. While Shiites revere Kazimiya for Musa al-Kazim, Sunnis
across the Tigris in Adhamiya worship at the Abu Hanifa mosque
built over the tomb of the eighth-century Sunni jurist Abu Hanifa
al-Nu'man, one of the architects of the Sunni Hanafi school of
sharia law. The Abu Hanifa mosque had also become a symbol of
the anti-American, anti-Shiite insurgency. After the fall of Bagh-

dad, Saddam Hussein gave his final speech in front of the mosque before going into hiding. It was one of the birthplaces of Sunni resistance. The Imma bridge divides not only Kazimiya and Adhamiya but also two different worlds.

On the morning of August 31, the Imma bridge looked like the Verrazano at the start of the New York City Marathon. Shiite pilgrims, including hundreds of entire families, were packed so tightly together that they could only inch their way forward. Many of the pilgrims were also lost in religious ecstasy, crying and beating their chests to ritually mourn and honor the Imam al-Kazim, executed by early Sunnis.

Then, someone deep in the crowd yelled "suicide bomber!" Panic broke out. A stampede erupted. Thousands rushed to escape, running toward the Kazimiya end of the bridge. But thousands more charged in the opposite direction toward Adhamiya. The waves of terrified pilgrims collided in the middle of the bridge. The weight of the pressing, swelling mass of people collapsed the side railing. Hundreds fell to the ground and were trampled. Others were pushed or jumped in the water. Iraqis kicked off their sandals to run faster or, out of some inexplicable instinct, took them off before leaping into the river. But many couldn't swim, or were knocked unconscious when they hit debris and other victims in the water.

There were no U.S. troops in the area. They stayed away from religious processions. The Iraqi government didn't have any forces to send or the communications equipment to coordinate a rescue. Only one Iraqi river patrol unit and a few Sunnis from Adhamiya responded on their own initiative. The police and local heroes dove into the Tigris, filled with several thousand frenzied pilgrims clamoring to stay afloat, some drowning others to survive. The divers saved dozens of lives, but were overwhelmed.

More than a thousand people died in the stampede or drowned in the Tigris. The most haunting image was of the hundreds of pairs of sandals they left on the bridge before jumping or being pushed to their deaths. Bodies were still found floating downriver several weeks later. It was the deadliest single event in Iraq since the American invasion, but it wasn't caused by a single bomb. Fear was the killer. Iraqi Shiites had become so terrified by the relentless bombings that just the idea of an attack had driven them to hysteria.

It was a major story, but it was hard to get my editors' attention. They gave me one minute, fifteen seconds to tell the story on the evening broadcast. There's only so much you can say in seventy-five seconds. Good evening. There was a procession. Someone yelled "suicide bomber." A bridge collapsed. Many people died. Look at all their shoes. Tragic. Thank you and good night.

The poet, doctor, and unlikely prime minister, Ibrahim al-Jaafari, called the Imma bridge disaster both a national tragedy and a terrorist attack. He said Sunni radicals had deliberately provoked and panicked the crowds. I can't imagine how he could have known who triggered the stampede or if it was premeditated, but at least now Iraqi Shiites had a familiar enemy to blame. "It is like al-Kazim, like the imam," one Shiite man cried when I asked him his reaction to the government's claim that the bridge collapse was an act of terrorism.

During the eighth century, Musa al-Kazim was imprisoned and poised by Haroun al-Rashid, the caliph who became a legend in the *Arabian Nights*. Rashid was an Abbasid caliph, one of the Sunni lords of Baghdad. Sunnis had killed Shiite saints then, and were killing Shiites again today.

The historical parallel was not lost on Jaafari, a Shiite scholar and historian. I saw him shortly after the Imma bridge collapse. While he'd always been frail and thin (unlike Allawi, a thick ox of a man who'd survived nearly being chopped to pieces by Saddam's goons), Jaafari had lost weight and was pale. His hands were clammy. He looked sick and nervous. He was deeply upset by the Imma bridge disaster, but also said the political pressure was getting to him. Jaafari's government had just written the constitution after several all-night sessions. He was exhausted.

The White House had made it clear to Jaafari that he must have the constitution written by the end of August 2005, in time for a national referendum on the document on October 15. They were dead-lines not to be missed. In May, Secretary of State Condoleezza Rice, warned Jaafari that Iraq needed "decisive leadership" and to "stick to the deadlines." Word in Washington was that Jaafari was "wishy-washy" and might not be up to the task. There was a degree of Al-lawi nostalgia. At least Allawi took decisions quickly. Jaafari was a worrier.

But the difficulties Iraqis faced in drafting the final constitution were understandable. They were trying to answer the most funda-mental questions about their society on a U.S.-imposed timeline. What role would Islam play in government? Would Iraq be an Arab state? How much power would be given to the traditional tribal chiefs, long accustomed to running their own affairs? How would oil and water be distributed?

But the thorniest dispute was about how much power the cen-tral government would exercise over Iraq's eighteen provinces. Would the regions be self-governing? Could the regional govern-ments manage their own natural resources? Could they bond to-gether to form regional blocs? Who would ultimately be in charge, the states or the central government?

Sunnis were pushing for a strong central government with a powerful army and for Iraq to be specifically called an Arab state. They wanted Iraq to reassume its role before the 1991 Gulf War, when the country was a leader of the Arab world, and for the gov-ernment to look similar to the days of Saddam Hussein, but with-out a dictator in charge. Shiites were divided. Jaafari's Dawa party also wanted to keep power centralized in Baghdad—after all, the Dawa party ran the government—but opposed the idea that Iraq would be specifically designated as an Arab state. The Shiites had suffered enough under Saddam's pan-Arab regime. They didn't want another one.

The other powerful Shiite bloc, led by Abdul Aziz al-Hakim and his unlikely ally Ahmed Chalabi, favored giving more authority to the regional governments. Hakim and Chalabi were pushing for the creation of a federal state in southern Iraq. They wanted to combine the oil-rich province of Basra with the adjoining governorates of Maysan and Thi Qar into a single administrative unit. They wanted to create "Shiastan," a mini-state on the border with Iran, rich in oil and with control over access to the Persian Gulf. It would be powerful, wealthy, strategically located, and pro-Iranian. As far as Hakim and Chalabi were concerned, the Sunnis could have the deserts of central Iraq, the worst part of the country, without any known oil reserves or control over sources of fresh water.

The Kurds were united behind a single goal. They wanted maximum autonomy in the north and to gain undisputed control of the city of Kirkuk and its oilfields. The Kurds needed Kirkuk's oil to make their autonomy in Kurdistan viable and economically sustainable. But Kirkuk was divided between Arabs, Kurds, and ethnic Turks, or Turkomen. The Kurds were prepared to lend their political support to anyone willing to give them Kirkuk and turn Kurdistan into a wealthy homeland. The Kurds also wanted the right to secede from Iraq.

These were real issues, questions that had never been adequately resolved since Western powers cobbled Iraq together from the ruins of the Ottoman Empire after World War I.

In his 1969 book *The Emergence of the Middle East, 1914–1924,* historian Howard Sachar described how the British uncomfortably tried to answer the same questions as they searched for a way to end their costly and ruinous occupation of Iraq:

> *As the British tightened their grip on Mesopotamia in the last year of the war, they found themselves in occupation of a ruinously neglected semi-desert, semi-swamp of 171,599 square miles.*
>
> *Its population of some three million inhabitants was a festering agglomeration of sectarian and social rivalries.*
>
> *The Arab Muslim majority was divided almost equally between the Sunni and Shi'a sects, the one oriented toward Mecca, the other toward Persia,*

> *and then infinitely fractured into tribes and clans,*
> *each nurturing its private fealties and blood*
> *feuds.*

How little Iraq had changed in nine decades.

It was the newly arrived U.S. ambassador, Zalmay Khalilzad, who helped Sunnis, Shiites, and Kurds reach a compromise on the constitution. Unlike his almost invisible predecessor, John Negroponte, who rarely spoke to the press or developed personal connections with many Iraqi politicians, Khalilzad was a hands-on diplomat.

The son of a civil servant and an illiterate mother, Khalilzad was born in the Afghan city of Mazar-i-Sharif in 1951. As a teenager, he won a scholarship to study in California, and then another to attend the American University in Beirut, where he earned a degree in political science. Khalilzad began his career as an academic, developing relationships with neocons, including Richard Perle and former deputy secretary of defense Paul Wolfowitz. Khalilzad was himself a hawk and had been pushing for "regime change" in Iraq for more than a decade before the U.S. invasion.

By 2001, Khalilzad had secured a relatively low-profile job in Washington at the National Security Council. But after 9/11 propelled Afghanistan to the top of the White House's agenda, Khalilzad's specialty in the region was suddenly in demand. He became one of the White House's point men for the war on terrorism, focusing on both Afghanistan and Iraq. After the fall of Kabul, Khalilzad helped assemble Hamid Karzai's transitional government. In 2003, he became the U.S. ambassador to Afghanistan. Khalilzad arrived as ambassador in Baghdad in June 2005. His first mission was to make sure the Iraqis wrote the constitution by the end of August. He had just three months, but he did it.

Khalilzad spoke fluent Farsi and understood Arabic well enough that he didn't need a translator. He was also a Sunni Muslim, and had the temperament and cultural awareness of an Eastern diplomat and intellectual. He would sit for hours drinking tea with Iraqi politicians, conspicuously thumbing his worry beads, reminding everyone in the room of his Muslim credentials. Khalilzad, "Zal" to his friends, was proactive and dynamic like Bremer, but infinitely more qualified.

In moments of frustration, American officials have often said Iraqis don't understand modern politics. They are wrong. Try buying a carpet in Iraq. It takes hours of negotiations, walkouts, tea, cigarettes, telephone calls to superiors, bluffing, subterfuge, and ultimately cash, the ability to close the deal on the spot. Credit and promises are meaningless. Iraqis are highly skilled political negotiators. They've been doing it for thousands of years. Khalilzad understood the rituals. He knew how to buy a carpet. Bremer, a catastrophe as civil administrator, would have ordered the carpet store closed down, forced it to modernize, restructured its workforce, and ended up offending the workers, as well as the owner and his entire family. Negroponte wouldn't have bothered shopping for carpets at all. They were three very different men. Khalilzad was the best suited for Baghdad.

On August 22, Iraqi negotiators finally announced that they'd reached a deal. The constitution was ready for the referendum on October 15. It seemed that Khalilzad had saved the day. He had proposed a compromise and the Iraqis had accepted it.

But the problem with Khalilzad's compromise was that it didn't resolve the radically different Sunni, Shiite, and Kurdish visions for Iraq. Khalilzad had simply postponed the most difficult issues. The constitution Iraqis were about to vote on was purposely left vague and flexible. The constitution said Iraq was to be a "federal democratic state," but there was no explanation of what "federalism" meant. It was also unclear how much power the central, federal government would exercise over the provinces. The proposed constitution guaranteed autonomy to the Kurds, but postponed the dispute over Kirkuk. Khalilzad's compromise made the constitution subject to future referendums and amendments. He'd allowed the Iraqis to agree to disagree.

It may have been the only way to prevent the constitution from collapsing and keep the political process moving. At least now, the Iraqis had a basic document, a bill of rights, and the parameters for future negotiations. They had something to vote on in October, and the White House could again claim progress. The constitution was flawed but flexible, more than most could have hoped.

But a senior Kurdish official I spoke to was nervous about the constitution the Iraqis had agreed to submit for a referendum. He told me Jaafari had shown a draft to the Iranian ambassador for approval. "Jaafari wanted Iranian sign-off before he agreed to it," said the official, who was directly involved in the negotiations.

"Is that surprising?" I asked. "Aren't the Americans already writing the constitution? How can you worry about foreign influence when Zal wrote most of it?"

"Yes, but he's an American. This is *Iran*," the Kurdish official said.

It was yet another battle for influence between Washington and Tehran. Washington's pressure was overt. Iraqi politicians accused Khalilzad of being "pushy" and "rushing" them. Tehran worked the back door.

On October 15, Iraqis freely went to the polls for the second time in modern history. Again, roads were closed, curfews were imposed, and the pots of purple ink were dusted off. This time, it was a simple yes-no vote. Yes, we accept the constitution, or no we do not.

Iraqis I saw at the polling stations were generally upbeat. They liked the idea of having a new constitution, even though many didn't know what the document actually said. Yet again the howza drove voters to the poll, faith before reason. But this time the Sunnis were voting too. They'd joined the political process. It was a major development.

While some Sunnis voted against the constitution, most of them voted for it. They were betting on Khalilzad's compromise that the constitution was to be modified in future amendments. The Sunnis realized they were in a weak position after having boycotted the first election and cutting themselves out of the political process. Now on board, they were waiting for the next elections just two months away at the end of December. The Sunni plan was to approve the constitution, participate in December's general election, win it, and then use their new power to modify the constitution to suit their interests.

One senior U.S. diplomat told me, "The Sunnis have decided it's better to be on the train than off it."

Democracy seemed to be working. Successfully writing and passing the constitution was a tremendous accomplishment. Iraqis, Americans, and even the Iranians had all agreed on the constitution, which was also one of the most dynamic, modern, and progressive in the Middle East. The constitution included a bill of rights that guaranteed equal civil liberties for women. It prohibited the return of a dictator. The constitution reserved a role for Islam in government, but it was not as strict as in many Arab and Islamic countries. Instead of making Islam the "sole basis for all laws," a clause in several Middle Eastern constitutions, Iraq's constitution simply said "no law could violate Islam." Islam was the "official religion," but Iraq was not an Islamic state, at least on paper.

As a reward for approving the constitution, Jaafari and the Americans decided to give Iraqis a present. The constitutional debates and referendum had gone smoothly, but brought up difficult, divisive issues. Jaafari and the Americans wanted to give Iraqis something they would all enjoy: Saddam Hussein in chains.

Saddam hadn't been seen in public for a year, kept locked away after he embarrassed the government during his brief arraignment in July 2004, when he'd impressed so many Iraqis and other Arabs with his defiance, dominance, and stylish Turkish suits. Back then, Saddam had overpowered and outshone the much younger judge, Raed Jouhi, who struggled to extract even basic biographic information from the former dictator and to formally tell him he was being charged with war crimes.

Now, the long-awaited trial itself was about to begin. Iraqis were excited. Many bought new generators and extra fuel to make sure they'd be able to watch the proceedings on television even with

Baghdad's frequent power cuts. The U.S. and Iraqi governments knew they'd be in the spotlight, so they changed the legal team. They didn't want a repeat of July. They didn't want to make Saddam a hero again.

The U.S.-funded Iraqi High Tribunal appointed a new chief judge, Rizgar Mohammed Amin, an ethnic Kurd and law professor at Sulimaniya University. I visited Sulimaniya, the artistic and intellectual capital of Kurdistan, to meet Amin before the trial. I wanted to see if he could stand up to Saddam. Amin was remarkably self-deprecating and humble. He agreed to meet me in his modest home and answered the door himself. I was surprised there weren't any guards outside. "This guy is going to die," was the first thing I thought.

The fifty-five-year-old Amin looked more like a professor than a judge. He wore a tweed jacket without a necktie and had a long, narrow face and a thin nose. His handshake was light. His children sat by his side as we spoke.

Over bottles of 7-Up, which he brought out himself on a metal tray, Amin said he was treating Saddam's case like any other. "I am a judge and he is a defendant. That is the extent of our relationship," he said.

Amin never raised his voice or bragged about his credentials. There was nothing flashy about him. He didn't wear a big watch or any rings. He quietly showed me photographs from a training course he'd attended in the United States. One of the tribunal's American legal advisors told me Amin had been a top student.

I found Amin to be an odd choice for the Iraqi government. He seemed professional, qualified, and unbiased. He didn't seem to have any agenda, or a vendetta to settle. I frankly hadn't expected the government to make what seemed to be such an enlightened choice. Amin said he wasn't enthusiastic about the death penalty and refused to speculate if he'd sentence Saddam to the gallows. I wondered if he'd last as chief judge. Iraqi officials I knew wanted to see Saddam swing on a rope, nothing more. They wanted an executioner, not a judge. Amin didn't seem like their man.

Despite his humility, Amin was already a hero in Kurdistan. I accompanied him to one of his lectures at Sulimaniya University. Professors and students stopped him on campus to shake his hand and take his photograph. His lecture was packed. There were many young women in the front row. I imagined quite a few of them left apples for Amin at the end of class.

While I waited for Amin to finish his lecture, one of his colleagues told me, "With Rizgar as the judge, the trial will be fair. But it will take a long time. He's good, but very slow."

"The Iraqi government is going to dump him," I said. "They don't have the patience for that. They want this over quickly and for Saddam to be executed."

"You're probably right," his colleague said. "But it must be fair. Otherwise, we are no better than Saddam."

After class, Amin insisted on taking us to lunch and drove his own car to a nearby hilltop restaurant. The maître d' greeted him grandly and showed us to the best table by the window. Amin waved him away with a simple thank-you. He didn't like the attention.

On October 19, 2005, reporters were ordered to assemble in the Green Zone to attend the opening session of Saddam's trial. U.S. marshals were in charge of security. They were rude, pushy, and insistent. They made us feel like we were all being processed for arrest. There were so many rules. They allowed only one representative from each major news agency to attend the trial. We were retina-scanned, and told, repeatedly and in writing, that we were not allowed to bring cell phones, cameras, or even notebooks and pens into the courtroom.

"You will be given pencils inside," one of the marshals said as we were frisked for what must have been the sixth time and loaded onto shuttle buses that would take us to the court's "secret location." It was no secret. We all knew where we were going. The courtroom was in the Baath party's massive central headquarters in the Green Zone. Saddam had built it to be the United Nations of the Baath party, the central address of the party's international branches.

It was one of those pompous vanity palaces dictators build to impress other dictators. A triumphal arch more than three meters thick guarded the building's entrance. Inside, the halls dripped with marble, onyx, and fake crystal chandeliers. It looked like a cheap wedding hall in Vegas, grand and chintzy. Size mattered. Taste did not.

As we were waiting by the door to be checked by security yet again, Ahmed Chalabi pushed passed us, cutting the line. What a guy. It was like he was rushing to the theater. The marshals then herded us again through more metal detectors and X-ray scanners that examined our bodies for foreign objects. The machines could see if we were carrying a plastic knife or a coil of rope invisible to metal detectors. The scanners had been tested at airports in the United States, but drew complaints because they show the body's naked outline.

The marshals finally locked us in the observation room, a glass-enclosed box at the back of the courtroom. It was like a fish tank, similar to an observation gallery overlooking an operating room at a medical school, or an execution chamber.

The courtroom was empty when we arrived. Cleaners were still sweeping the floor. I overheard one of them arguing with his supervisor.

"I don't want to go in there," he said, lingering by the door.

"Why not?"

"Saddam is going to be in there."

"So what? He's a prisoner."

The cleaner refused to go in, scared of Saddam's presence. Saddam hadn't just been Iraq's dictator. He'd been a god-king. Many Iraqis were still terrified of him, as if he were a demon with supernatural powers.

The defense attorneys, dressed in black robes with green sashes, were the first to enter the room. They marched in like a basketball team from a side door and took their places on wooden benches. Saddam had just rejected 1,500 lawyers from Europe and the Arab world who'd volunteered to defend him. Most of them were ambulance chasers trying to be part of a big trial.

The prosecutors, dressed in black robes with red sashes, filed in on the other side of the courtroom and sat opposite the defense team.

Finally, Chief Judge Amin and his four assistants took their seats at the bench in the center of the trial chamber. A statue of the scales of justice hung on the wall behind the judges. Above it was a quote from the Koran, *Iza hokomtu ben i-nas, ihkum b-adel,* "If you judge among people, judge them with justice."

Almost hidden behind an Iraqi flag in the corner of the room was an American soldier, a combat cameraman from AFN, the American Forces Network. He was operating the official courtroom camera. But the soldier wasn't in any of the footage being broadcast to the world with a twenty-minute delay. He was behind the camera. The Americans claimed this was "an entirely Iraqi court." The U.S. marshals and soldiers were supposed to be ghosts, present but not seen.

It was a farce. The trial was an American proceeding. The U.S. government had paid more then $138 million to train the judges, fly in legal advisors, and build the courtroom. Americans ran the simultaneous translation booth and the media company that coordinated the satellite uplink. The Americans held Saddam in custody. The Iraqis were actors on an American stage. "The Americans seem to have set the table for all this," I wrote in a yellow legal pad that the U.S. marshals had given me as I waited for the trial to begin.

When the cleaners left, the court's speaker called out the defendants' names one at a time. Saddam was being tried with seven other men accused of helping him carry out the brutal crackdown on the villagers of Dujail after Dawa party gunmen tried to assassinate the Iraqi dictator during a state visit to the village in 1982. Saddam and his co-defendants, including his half brother and intelligence chief, Barzan Ibrahim, and former vice president Taha Yassin Ramadan, were charged with deporting several thousand villagers to concentration camps where forty-six of them died from torture and where women were raped, with bulldozing Dujail's orchards, and with sentencing 148 men and boys to death.

Saddam was the last defendant to be called into the courtroom.

"Saddam Hussein al-Majid!" the court speaker screamed.

All of the journalists in the fish tank leaned forward in our seats. The room was silent. The guards, judges, lawyers, and prosecutors were all looking at the door.

Saddam walked in slowly, flanked by Iraqi guards in blue flak jackets. They were holding him by his arms. Saddam looked like a tired old man. There were deep bags under his eyes. His beard was flecked with gray. He moved sluggishly. But then, suddenly, as he noticed the camera and the press watching him, he perked up and broke into a confident stride. I was in the front row, leaning forward, my face less than an inch from the glass. Saddam walked right in front of me and smiled a toothy grin. I have to admit, it was frightening.

Iraqis say you couldn't look Saddam in the eye, that his very gaze prevented you from talking. Others say Saddam had the power to tell if someone were lying. There were so many myths, but they were based on something. Saddam's gaze *was* powerful.

"The first time I saw Saddam I was frightened," another reporter told me. I was relieved it wasn't just me.

Saddam was carrying a Koran, and wearing a pressed white shirt and charcoal gray suit similar to the one that had set Arab fashion trends a year before.

There was a standoff right away.

Amin ordered Saddam to sit down.

Saddam refused.

Amin repeated the demand six times, but Saddam kept standing.

Saddam immediately started to address the court, but we couldn't hear him. The microphones didn't work!

I put my ear to the glass and managed to hear Saddam say, "I am not a collaborator."

Christiane Amanpour started banging on the door. "Let us out! We can't hear!"

The marshals were furious. They threatened to throw her out,

but a few minutes later they switched on the microphones. Amin
was asking Saddam to state his name.

"You know me. If you're an Iraqi, and I can tell you are Iraqi
from your accent, then you know me. I demand to know who *you*
are," Saddam said, waving his finger accusingly. "I reserve my constitutional rights as president, including immunity from prosecution. I do not recognize this so-called court."

Amin wasn't flustered. He must have expected this.

"Please, just state your name."

"I'm president of Iraq and I do not recognize the body that au-
thorized you and I do not recognize the aggression," Saddam said.

"Write that the defendant has identified himself as the former
president Saddam Hussein," Amin told the stenographer.

"I said I am the president of Iraq. I didn't say deposed president," Saddam said, and then quoted a common Arab expression.
"What is founded on injustice, is itself unjust. I do not recognize
this court, with all due respect." Saddam seemed satisfied with his
answer. He finally sat down in a chair in the front row of a metal
holding pen in the center of the courtroom. He leaned back in the
chair and looked down his nose at Amin. If Saddam had a cigar, he
looked like he would have lit it and puffed away.

Amin told Saddam he was being tried for the Dujail case, a
crime against humanity, and could receive the death penalty.

The prosecutors then attempted to play a recording of a
witness's testimony.

"I do not even have a pencil and paper? How can I be expected
to take notes when I don't have even a pencil and paper?" Saddam
complained.

Amin ordered a bailiff to bring him a pencil and paper.

Saddam put on his thick, black-rimmed glasses and started to
take notes on a yellow legal pad. But he quickly grew frustrated
watching the video, which played without sound, and then stopped.
The prosecutors couldn't get the DVD player to work. They were
visibly embarrassed. Saddam was annoyed by their incompetence
and didn't miss the opportunity to rub it in. "I speak for all Iraqis

who oppose this fraudulence. The court should not take into account these *recordings*. They are not legally permissible as evidence in court."

The defense lawyers followed Saddam's lead and chimed in with a litany of complaints of their own. They hadn't been given enough time to prepare, they said, and claimed thousands of pages of photocopied documents provided by the prosecution were too blurry to read.

Amin finally asked Saddam for a plea. "The defendant shall now rise and enter his plea."

Saddam, who first refused to sit, now wouldn't stand.

Amin didn't press the subject. He didn't want to pick a fight.

"Okay, remain seated. But what is your plea, guilty or innocent?"

"I've said what I mean. I'm innocent, innocent."

Amin's politeness had worked. He'd managed to get Saddam to enter a plea. The trial was moving forward. Saddam had unwittingly cooperated. It was a victory for Amin. He ordered a brief recess.

During the break, the cameras stopped rolling. It was the most interesting time of the day.

Saddam and his former aides, now fellow defendants, had the rare opportunity to speak together. They didn't act like old friends. His lawyers saluted him. His former aides called him "sir" and remained silent when he spoke. Saddam looked like he still believed he was running Iraq, and that this was just another meeting of his politburo.

Then two bailiffs moved in to break up the reunion. But Saddam wasn't finished. He ignored their orders to "come with us."

Saddam kept talking.

"Come with us," one of the guards repeated.

Saddam gestured for him to calm down and leave him alone. He flicked his hand dismissively at the guard, giving him the Iraqi gesture to "buzz off."

It irritated the guard. "Come with us!" he suddenly shouted.

This was the guard's big moment. He was going to stand up to Saddam Hussein.

"Just wait," Saddam barked back, trying to put the guard in his place. Iraqis never spoke to Saddam like this, especially ones he considered traitors. They were executed.

The two guards grabbed Saddam by the arms, gripping his elbows. Saddam boiled with rage. His eyes flashed more hate than I have ever seen on anyone's face.

"Don't you put your hands on me!" he threatened, and jerked his arms, trying to break the guards' grip.

The guards didn't let go.

Saddam pulled harder, and then stopped in his tracks. He refused to walk toward the door. He looked down at his arms, and then into the guards' eyes. He held his gaze. The guards let go, and Saddam was able to walk out of the courtroom with his head held high. He'd scored a victory as well.

17

The U.S.-sponsored, and Sistani-approved, political roadmap for Iraq was almost complete. There was just one more step, final elections on December 15, 2005. There had been rapid political development. In less than twelve months, Iraqis, with some help from Iran, had chosen Jaafari's government in their first free election, and written and ratified a constitution. All that was left now was to hold one final vote based on the constitution for a new government that would serve a four-year term. Two elections down, one to go.

On paper, the goal line for American involvement in Iraq appeared close. American troops were supposedly in Iraq to overthrow a dangerous dictator (who seemed to have been, at some point, pursuing nuclear weapons, and supporting al-Qaeda types at another) and create a democratic state. Iraq, we were told, was at the dawn of full democracy, so American troops could soon start to go home in large numbers and allow the "New Iraq" to be accepted into the community of nations as a free, unoccupied country. Mission accomplished, eventually, sort of. It had been messier than the White House had hoped, but still, a job fairly well done. It had been tough, but our "Iraqi brothers" and "coalition partners" were "getting the job done." That was the message in Washington and echoed by U.S. embassy and military officials at Baghdad press conferences that few of us believed or even bothered to attend anymore. We called them the "Baghdad Follies," after the Vietnam War's "Five O'Clock Follies."

The reality was much different. To see how far Iraq had descended into anarchy, all you needed to do was take a walk around Baghdad, if you could survive it. While the political track had moved quickly, Baghdad had become a safe haven for kidnappers, gangsters, car bombers, and state-sponsored (sometimes U.S.-trained) death squads. The Iraqi security forces that American generals claimed were "stepping up" were corrupt and infiltrated by killers and sectarian militias and insurgents. Many of the Iraqi soldiers didn't even show up for work. U.S. commanders said they couldn't account for a quarter of all Iraqi troops on the payroll.

The director of Yarmouk hospital told me he'd noticed an odd phenomenon. All the injured and dead the Iraqi police brought to his emergency room had empty wallets. "It seems the car bombs not only kill, but have learned to pick pockets too," he said.

Iraq was spiraling deeper into civil war, and the violence was circling closer to the Hamra. At 7:45 A.M. on October 10, a car bomb jarred me awake. I looked at my alarm clock and thought it was a little early for a car bomb. It was mortar time, but no matter. It was still the morning wake-up call. Four Iraqi policemen were dead. As I stretched (my back was always a little stiff from sleeping on the floor next to my bed), I found myself smiling. I wasn't happy that anyone had been killed, but the rumble of the car bomb was somehow comforting, soothing like thunder on a warm summer night. The explosions had become familiar sounds of home, the way the screeching of police cars and whining of ambulances do for New Yorkers when they leave Gotham. They often don't realize they miss the noise while they're away, but are happy to hear it when they return. Similarly, the car bombs reminded me of where I was. Baghdad was now my only home. Since my divorce I had no place to go on breaks. I had taken up scuba diving as my respite and refuge. I loved the silence and solitude of being under sixty feet of water. There's nothing more relaxing than staring a fish in the face and watching it stare back at you. I'd fallen into a pattern. I would do six to eight weeks in Baghdad, and then chase fish. But I always returned to Iraq. It was where I had my friends, and Zohair and Ali, my new family.

After the morning bomb, I decided not to take a shower. I went up to the bureau to read, check e-mails, and make coffee. It may have saved my life. When I returned to my room about an hour later, I saw that the bathroom window was shattered. A bullet had crashed through the glass, bored a hole in the medicine cabinet over my sink (detonating a bottle of shaving cream), hit the tiled bathroom wall, and dropped dead on the floor. I picked up the cold brass-colored slug. It was about the size of a tooth, but much heavier. It was an AK-47 round. I assumed it was a stray. Iraqi police were always firing in the air to disperse traffic as they screamed through the streets like bandits. They were always shooting off their guns. Pop. Pop. Pop. If I'd been taking a shower or brushing my teeth when the bullet came through, it could have easily killed me. I scooped up the glass on the floor, took a shower, dressed, put the slug in my pocket, and went to work. It was as normal and natural as if I'd seen a big spider.

Two weeks later, our bureau chief, Karl Bostic, was on a mundane errand, driving to the Palestine hotel to pay bills at the AP office. He almost didn't make it back. Karl was just a few hundred yards from the first car bomb. The blast was so close that it blew out the tires in his car and stalled the engine. He was suddenly trapped, helpless in an immobile car, waiting to die in the backseat.

After the first car bomb, Iraqi police started to fire wildly in the air, a death blossom. It only added to the pandemonium. The attackers had been counting on it. The first bomb was a diversion. The insurgents wanted to distract the police. There were two more bombs waiting. The next car bomb exploded up against the Palestine's outer wall of concrete blast barriers. It obliterated two of the twelve-foot-high, steel-reinforced concrete slabs, punching a hole in the Palestine's defensive perimeter.

Then, a third bomb, a huge cement mixer filled with high explosives, moved in for the kill. The truck drove through the breach in the Palestine's blast barriers and headed straight for the hotel's main entrance. But the truck got stuck. There was too much debris on the ground, too many pieces of concrete and twisted coils of concertina wire. The truck's tires were caught in the wire.

An American soldier posted on one of the Palestine's balconies was the first to notice. He saw the cement mixer driving back and forth, trying to shake off the wire. The soldier opened fire on the truck. He must have hit something because within seconds the truck bomb detonated into a fireball that could be seen across downtown Baghdad. Even the windows at the Hamra shook four miles away. Twelve people were killed by the bombs at the Palestine hotel, but the attack could have been much worse. If the cement mixer had gotten even a hundred yards closer to the Palestine's entrance, the entire building might have collapsed and killed several hundred people, including everyone in the AP and Fox News bureaus.

When Karl finally came back to the Hamra he was shaking, and staring through me. He had the full 1,000-yard stare. "Everything went orange around us!" he said. "We felt the car rock and then lifted! It felt as though the car was lifted off the ground and landed with a thump! It was like the bomb was right underneath the car!"

Karl was so excited he didn't realize he was yelling. He also couldn't hear much. The explosions and gunshots were still ringing in his ears.

"Then another kaboom was right there in front of us, waiting for us! If we had driven into that, forget it! Forget it! I can tell you that!

"I shouldn't say it, but I almost felt like, 'Well, what part of me could I afford to lose and still be alive?' Can I afford to lose an arm, a leg?

"It's not worth it! No story is worth any of this! No story is worth any of this!"

A few weeks later, it was our turn to be attacked.

At 8:12 on the morning of November 18, a white minivan pulled up alongside the Hamra's blast barriers. It didn't park for long. Seconds later, the minivan exploded, filling the sky with fire and smoke and dust. Again, that was just the first bomb. The attackers were trying the same tactic that had nearly worked at the Palestine. The bomb in the minivan blew a hole in our blast wall, creating a path for a water truck filled with enough explosive to collapse the Hamra and kill us all.

Luckily, the attackers were not demolition experts. They had filled the minivan with far too much explosive. The first bomb not only turned a section of our blast wall to dust, but dug a ten-foot-deep crater in the street. Twenty-one seconds after the first blast, the second suicide bomber in the water truck drove straight into the crater, falling in as if it were a giant pothole. The bomber detonated the second explosive at the bottom of the pit. There were six hundred pounds of explosive in the water truck. The bomb killed seven people, including an entire family living in a nearby apartment. But it was too far from the Hamra to knock it down. Our bureau was trashed. Computers, desks, televisions, and almost everything else was smashed. The hotel's walls were cracked. All the windows, doors, and ceiling panels were torn out. People in the Hamra were thrown to the ground, but everyone in the hotel survived. It was a goddamn miracle.

I was out of Baghdad when the Hamra was attacked, off chasing sea turtles and leopard sharks in Thailand. I immediately headed back. The bureau was in a crisis. After the bombing, we had staffing problems. Producers and correspondents didn't want to come to Baghdad anymore. There was a mini-revolt in our London office, which generally staffs the Baghdad operation. Many of the London-based journalists decided it was no longer worth it to go to Baghdad, that it was just too dangerous. They wanted other bureaus to share the burden of doing Baghdad rotations. Would we have to shut down? NBC needed to keep the Baghdad bureau running. Iraq was still the top foreign story.

But the executives had to walk a thin line. They couldn't force people to go. ABC was facing a lawsuit by one of its former London-based correspondents, Richard Gizbert. He claimed he'd been fired from the network for refusing to go to war zones in Afghanistan and Iraq. Gizbert, who'd covered the conflicts in Bosnia-Herzegovina and Chechnya, had two children and told the network this time he wanted to give it a pass. ABC said his refusal to go to Iraq had no bearing on his dismissal. A London court didn't agree, and eventually awarded Gizbert a $100,000 settlement.

NBC didn't want any of the same mess. I provided an easy solution. I actually liked the Baghdad bureau. It was home. I felt comfortable there, perhaps in a way that some battered wives can't leave the men abusing them. I now believed Baghdad would eventually hurt or kill me, but I wanted to stay. I had moved into Stage Four and now assumed I was going to die in Iraq. It was cold math, and just a matter of time until death came pounding on my door.

When I arrived back at the Hamra, most of the debris had been cleaned up, but not all of it. I was standing under a tree outside the lobby moving my suitcases and listening to birds chirping and flapping above my head when, suddenly, I heard a thud. The birds had knocked something out of the tree. It landed next to my foot. It was the face of one of the suicide bombers who'd attacked the hotel. I turned it over with my shoe. It was dried out, and curled up at the edges like an old leather scroll. It was mostly intact, and I could easily identify a nose, lips, eye sockets, and half a mouth.

I was face-to-face with the man who'd tried to kill everyone in our bureau a few days earlier. I was speechless. The hotel guards gathered around the face. They picked it up, wrapped it in a cloth, and buried it the next morning in a flower bed. It's considered bad luck in Iraq to bury a body, or even body parts, at night.

I told our security team about the face in the tree. They said they'd fished a leg out of the pool. I later found a finger on a fifth-floor balcony. Welcome fucking home.

But there was no time to wallow in self-exploration. War is not a petri dish to examine and analyze our emotions. Iraq was going through historic times. America was spending billions of dollars a month on this project, and the U.S. military death toll had just topped two thousand. A revolution was under way in Iraq and across the Middle East, and the most important election in Iraq's modern history was just weeks away.

We spent too much time in Baghdad. Before the December vote, I wanted to see how other parts of the country were shaping up. Basra was supposedly stable, a success story. There were rarely car bombings, and few attacks on the British troops in the city. The perception was that the Brits were better occupiers than the Americans, having learned from Northern Ireland. British troops did have a keen understanding of hearts and minds: they did foot patrols without wearing flak jackets to show the locals how much they trusted them.

But when I arrived in Basra I quickly discovered that it wasn't the British trust-building tactics that were keeping their forces safe. It was that the Brits hardly ever left their bases anymore. They'd surrendered the city of three million to Shiite militias.

The main British base was at Basra's airport. It was a beautiful base and the commanders who gave us a background brief were superbly well informed, erudite, and schooled in Britain's rich heritage of intelligence gathering. Many of the commanders spoke Arabic. They knew the history of the region, were soldiers and scholars. We talked about the shortcomings of the treaties that established Iraq under British authority after World War I. Over a breakfast of baked beans, bacon, and poached eggs (the classic English breakfast they'd imported in true colonial tradition), we discussed the old Ottoman boundaries and even my book collection of eighteenth- and nineteenth-century travelers' accounts of the Middle East. The British commanders were impeccably informed, but their equipment was terrible, even laughable.

I went on a patrol in the British version of the Humvee, a white lightly armored Land Rover. It looked like an ice cream truck. The armor was so thin I could have jammed a screwdriver through the side of it. The Brits called it a "Snatch." A few miles off base it broke down. The lead vehicle in our convoy had to tie a rope to the bumper and tow us back. The soldiers apologized with excruciating politeness, explaining that they rarely went out. "We're only doing this patrol today because you are here," one of them told me. "Sorry about this. I bet you don't have this problem with the Americans."

We didn't. I'd never been in a Humvee that had to be towed back to base. I'd been attacked, but the vehicles at least worked. The soldier said there were so few British troops in southern Iraq—just seven thousand in charge of an area bigger than the state of New York—that they husbanded their resources and launched only a few big operations a year.

Once our Snatch was repaired, the patrol set off again to visit a local police station. It was a Mahdi Army stronghold. There were posters of Moqtada al-Sadr on nearly every wall. I asked one of the policemen about the posters. He said he wasn't a member of the Mahdi Army, but praised the group. "The militias and the police work closely together to protect the people, and the militias have better intelligence than we do," he said. "We want to develop. We want to use our oil, and become like Dubai, even better than Dubai," he added. "So far, how many investment projects do you see here? None. Just leave us alone and let us develop. You'll see in a few years we'll be better off than Dubai."

It didn't seem likely. Dubai is the Las Vegas of the Gulf, a boomtown where foreigners, real estate developers, money launderers, and even prostitutes are left alone. In Basra, the Mahdi Army had closed all the liquor stores, hurling the bottles into the harbor. They were also forcing women to veil, and killing journalists. The police chief of Basra told me he didn't trust 60 percent of his force. This was not the success story it seemed. Basra was quiet, but you wouldn't want to live there.

We stayed in Basra for five days. I left thinking the British troops didn't have control of the city. "There's no point in them even being here," I wrote in my notebook.

We returned to Baghdad, a few days before the December election.

The howza was in overdrive, more active than I'd ever seen it before. The Shiite religious parties—Dawa and SCIRI (Supreme Council for Islamic Revolution in Iraq)—were worried, and with reason. Ayad Allawi, the ardent secularist, was gaining in popularity. Jaafari's government was deeply unpopular, almost universally considered a failure. With American and Iranian help, it had written the constitution, but had accomplished nothing for the people. Gas lines were longer than ever in Baghdad, the police were openly corrupt, and the violence kept getting worse. The Shiite religious parties, given a chance to rule Iraq, had failed. Allawi was remembered with increasing fondness. The Shiite religious parties also worried about splinter groups. Several Shiite politicians had broken away from the mother alliance and were running as independents.

But the biggest threat came from the Sunnis. This time they were running. The Shiite religious bloc knew it was going to have a difficult time at the polls, so they naturally reached for their trump card, the Grand Ayatollah Ali al-Sistani. The time had come to dust off—and reinterpret—Sistani's old fatwa on voting. At Shiite husseiniyas in Baghdad, Abdul Aziz al-Hakim and Jaafari's coalition handed out flyers saying, "Sistani issued a fatwa to vote, to oppose secularism [a dig at Allawi], and not to vote for small parties."

Sistani had done no such thing. All he had ever decreed was that Shiites should go out and vote. But the Shiite religious coalition was counting on Sistani's sense of decorum, order, and his absolute solitude. They assumed he would never come out and correct them and break Shiite ranks. They were right. Sistani remained silent as Jaafari and Hakim changed his fatwa. Allawi tried to correct it himself. His supporters launched a counter-fatwa campaign, handing out flyers that said, "The Grand Ayatollah Ali al-Sistani never said what people are saying he said."

Eventually, Sistani's office did issue a statement. In a feeble attempt at clarity it said, "I, the Grand Ayatollah Ali al-Sistani, didn't say what people said I said. I only said what I said I said." So now everything was as clear as tomato soup.

But the Shiite religious coalition did have one new ace in the hole. Moqtada al-Sadr had decided to take part in the December election. In part, he'd regretted his decision to be ambivalent about participating in the first election. It had made him look indecisive and foolish. But mainly, Sadr wanted to destroy Allawi. In fact, he wanted to kill him.

I saw Allawi the day after Sadr's followers tried to murder him in Najaf. Allawi had gone to the holy Shiite city on a campaign trip. He wanted to press the flesh. He was attacked in the Imam Ali shrine by men armed with knives and swords. Allawi returned with a big red contusion on his neck from where someone had smacked him. The brawler looked like he'd been in a bar fight. He was proud of the welt, and pulled down the collar of his shirt to show it to me more clearly.

In December, everyone was campaigning ahead of the election, including the U.S. military. The 3rd Infantry Division, which was in command of Baghdad, had evidently gotten tired of American journalists writing nasty articles and failing to find all those "good news" stories. They were paying Iraqis to write them instead.

The 3rd ID founded the unfortunately named "Baghdad Press Club." There was no bar at the Baghdad Press Club nor smoke-filled rooms. In fact, there was no clubhouse. The Baghdad Press Club was a semisecret (it wasn't technically classified, but no one talked about it) association of Iraqi reporters who specialized in covering, not surprisingly, the 3rd ID. It was their job. A U.S. Army officer familiar with the program told me Iraqi reporters were paid $35 for every story they managed to print in their newspapers, and $10 more if it ran with a picture.

Iraqi journalists said U.S. commanders took Baghdad Press Club members to events that made the 3rd ID look good. They reported on soldiers opening schools or giving out toys and medicine. Anytime the 3rd ID had a dog-and-pony show, they called in the Baghdad Press Club. A spokesman for the 3rd ID, Lieutenant Colonel Robert Whetstone, told me he didn't see any "ethical conflicts" with the program. "We don't tell the reporters that they only have to print positive stories," he said. "In fact, we don't tell them

what to write at all, and we do not look at stories before they go out."
He said Iraqi reporters were taken to events "that involve their communities."

An Iraqi newspaper editor, who had also been approached by
the Lincoln Group, a company with a Defense Department contract
to place favorable stories about the military in the Iraqi media, said
members of the Baghdad Press Club had become pariahs among
their colleagues. "We told them, we warned them, but Iraqi newspapers don't have much money to pay their reporters, so they were
tempted," he said. "And many Iraqi reporters don't want to be seen
covering American events, so I guess the Americans decided they
needed an incentive to get them to go."

A U.S. military spokesman told me he didn't know how many
articles Baghdad Press Club members had printed since the group
was founded in 2004, but that they recently averaged fifty-three a
month.

It was a shame. The Americans had praised the creation of a
free press in Iraq as one of the few tangible successes after the fall
of Saddam. But the Americans and the Iraqi press had given in to
temptation. Iraqi reporters were more than willing to do flattery
journalism. In fact, it was the only type of reporting they'd done
under Saddam.

Many of the mistakes in Iraq were made simply because people
could get away with them scot-free. The guards at Abu Ghraib
forced detainees to play naked Twister because they could, and because their commanders wanted to see the prisoners behave more
cooperatively during interrogations. Foreign security contractors
like Blackwater USA and South African mercenaries killed Iraqis
on the roads because they could. It was easy, maybe even fun, and
there were no consequences. In the end, the road was cleared, a few
Iraqis died, and the contractors drove on with happy, safe clients. It
was the same with the military buying "good news" stories. They
wanted positive coverage, and Iraqis were more than willing to do
it. There were no ethics in Baghdad, and the absence of a moral
compass tempted and infected many.

On December 15, the election came and went. It was anticli-
mactic. There was more purple ink, and more plastic ballot boxes.
The American audience had seen it all before. The first election
was a novelty. Voting had now become routine and increasingly
complicated. In December's election there were more than seven
thousand candidates from 250 political parties and coalitions.
There were alliances between Sadr, SCIRI, and Dawa. Allawi was
doing better, but faced fatwa problems. The Kurds were united, but
wanted Kirkuk. The winners of the election would be in a strong
position to make amendments to the constitution. My editors called
it "broccoli," news you have to eat because it's good for you, but
which is fundamentally unappealing.

U.S. ambassador Zalmay Khalilzad didn't see it that way. If anything, he overstated the importance of the vote. "What's at stake
here is the future of the world," he said. Khalilzad stressed that
voter participation had increased with each vote. He was right.

In January 2005, 58 percent of eligible Iraqis cast ballots. In October, 63 percent turned out for the constitutional referendum.
Now in December, 68 to 72 percent of Iraqis participated in the
election. The process was working, but it did not produce democracy. The election was democratic, but it brought people to power
who fundamentally didn't believe in democracy, at least not in a
way Americans understand it.

The election results were a disaster for Allawi. Sadr's participation drowned him out. Allawi won only 8 percent of the vote. The
Shiite religious parties and the Kurds again did well, winning 41
and 22 percent respectively. The Sunnis, despite a huge turnout in
cities like Ramadi and Falujah, walked away with only 19 percent of
the vote. It was a bitter pill for them. Sunnis had expected to win 40
to 60 percent of the votes. Many Sunnis firmly believed they were
the majority in Iraq, but the election results proved they weren't. In
typical Iraqi style, the Sunnis claimed there had been a conspiracy
against them. They said the election had been a fraud and blamed
their historic enemy, Iran, which they said had rigged the vote.

Sunnis held demonstrations against the election results

throughout Anbar and Baghdad. When I arrived at one protest, I heard Sunnis shouting, *"Iran bara, bara! Baghdad tibka horra,"* "Iran out, out, so Baghdad can stay free!"

"Do the Americans want the Iranians to rule Iraq?" asked one man.

Others told me trucks filled with ballots already marked in favor of Shiite candidates were secretly shipped across the border from Iran before the vote. U.S. military officials dismissed the reports as rumors. But the Sunnis now were more frustrated than ever. They'd taken a gamble and lost. They felt cheated by the Americans, yet again. Zarqawi and other Sunni radicals were quick to capitalize on the frustration.

On January 5, 2006, 134 people were killed by bombs and mortars across Iraq. Nearly all of the victims were Shiites and Iraqi police and soldiers, who were targeted because they worked for the Shiite-led government and its American backers. Five U.S. soldiers in Baghdad were also killed.

That night I wrote an e-mail to Major General William Webster, commander of the 3rd ID and Task Force Baghdad. Webster was the overall commander of U.S. and coalition troops in the Baghdad area. He had also been deputy commanding general of all ground forces during the 2003 invasion.

Webster was not a big, burly, good ole boy like so many American generals. He studied chaos theory, and spent as much time trying to understand his enemy as he did thinking of ways to kill him. Webster spoke slowly and calmly in a way that reminded me of Jordan's late King Hussein, who always carried himself with tremendous dignity and humility. General Webster and the 3rd ID were about to rotate out of Iraq. I asked Webster for his analysis of the surge in violence: "What a day," I wrote. "These your guys killed today? The five by an IED? I'd hate to think they were on their last patrol before heading home. Why do you think this is going on? 200 dead in 48 hours. Any reason, or just because they can?"

Webster wrote back right away, clearly frustrated: "Because they can. And because the Shiites won the election. And because the Shiites are consolidating their power by firing many of the Sunni leaders of the Army and Police. Because of vengeance, hatred, fear, money, and to show the world that this democratic thing is not good for Iraq, and the occupiers must go, and crime, and because some insurgent/terrorist leaders said the right thing to do now is to attack the Shia/US/government coalition. They have no other choice, some believe. Many voted, but did not win by a majority. Isn't that what we promised? All said, remember we predicted this would happen. A huge spike as the results are about to be released, as the only tool left to possibly get their way. And because they can. Some IEDs can be pre-made and dropped in about 30 seconds now. Webster"

I appreciated his frankness. According to Webster's analysis, American troops were now fighting at least five enemies:

1. Zarqawi and his lieutenants, who had easy access to money and were skilled at Internet propaganda
2. Former Baath party members
3. Religious, anti-Shiite, anti-Kurdish Sunni tribal leaders
4. Iranian-backed Shiite militias and Moqtada al-Sadr
5. Criminal gangs

For most Iraqis, criminals were the most terrifying of Webster's five. Baghdad was overrun by gangs of kidnappers. Any five men with a few guns, ski masks, a fast car, and a safe house had the opportunity to make a fortune with little risk of being caught. The breakdown of society brought out the worst of Iraq's tribalism, chauvinism, and cruelty. It brought out the worst in our human nature.

I met a grocer I'd known since the days of Saddam's regime. He was famous in his neighborhood for having a beautiful daughter. He was an ugly man with a bent back and snaggled teeth and his wife was a squat old toad, but somehow they'd produced a daughter who was fairy-tale beautiful, with thick dark hair, round eyes, and pale skin. I'd seen her only once. Her beauty worried her father. He kept her hidden. In Baghdad, it's considered dangerous to possess such beauty. The grocer kept his daughter like a jewel that had mysteriously come into his possession, and which everyone wanted to steal.

The grocer's daughter had just been kidnapped. She was seventeen years old. Obviously her father wasn't a rich man. Anyone could see that. His grocery was tiny and sold onions, tomatoes, and potatoes by the kilo. The kidnappers had grabbed his daughter off the street simply because she was tempting, and taking her was cheap and easy. The grocer didn't tell me what happened to his daughter. Instead, his nephew told me the story. He was furious at his uncle.

"A few days after she was abducted, the kidnappers called her father," he said.

"We have your daughter and want ten dafar or we'll kill her."

Iraqis call a packet of $10,000 from the bank a dafar, Arabic for notebook. They were asking for ten notebooks, $100,000.

"Where do you think I can get that money? I am a poor grocer," he told them.

"Sell your house, sell your store. I don't care where you get the money, just get it, or your daughter dies."

"Is she there, with you?" the grocer asked.

"Yes."

"Put her on the phone."

She was sobbing when the kidnappers put her on the cell phone.

"Daddy?"

"Yes, my treasure."

"Daddy?"

"Yes, I'm here, my treasure. Don't cry. Everything is going to be okay."

"I'm scared."

"It's okay. Tell me, did those bad men hurt you? Did they aggress you? You know, violate your honor?"

The girl just wept.

"Don't worry. But tell me, did those men, you know, rape you?"

"Yes," she finally said.

"Okay, put them back on the phone."

The main kidnapper got back on the line.

"Fuck you, keep her," the grocer told him. "I don't want her anymore."

The girl was killed. Her body was found a few days later. Her throat had been cut.

The story made me furious. I walked out of the grocer's store. I couldn't look him in the eye. I wanted to spit in his face. In a normal country I would have called the police. But here the police were kidnappers themselves, and American troops didn't get involved in investigating crimes.

"How could he abandon his own daughter?" I wondered. "How can our nature be so weak and evil?"

An Iraqi politician told me, "After the invasion, Iraq was supposed to inspire the world. Instead, we are horrifying the world."

2006

THE CIVIL WAR

18

After the December elections, the reporters at the Hamra needed to let off some steam. We'd been going nonstop. The hotel had just been bombed. Some of the rooms were still missing doors. There'd been a damn leg in the swimming pool.

On New Year's Eve we had a party and everyone got drunk. The music was loud. We were dancing like fools. We knocked over tables and lamps. Two reporters from a major American newspaper started kissing at midnight and didn't stop until morning.

I was dancing with Jill Carroll, a young freelance reporter who worked mostly for *The Christian Science Monitor*. She was one of the only freelancers left in Baghdad. She immediately reminded me of Marla Ruzicka. Jill was young, attractive, and idealistic. She was also pushing her luck. Many of us had armored cars and big bureaus that tracked our movements twenty-four hours a day. The TV networks and major newspapers had armed security teams. Jill had nothing. She traveled alone with her translator. Many of us warned her she was going to be kidnapped, but Jill was determined. She told me she was going to write a book about Iraq, *the* book about the war. To her, journalism was a public service. It's a quest to tell the truth, she said. Jill was kidnapped a week later.

It was a final straw. Our bureau was bombed twice. Ned was kidnapped in Falujah. I'd nearly been taken hostage. Jill was a hostage. Marla was dead. Karl had nearly been blown up. A face fell out of a tree in front of the bureau. At least eighty-six reporters and assistants had been killed so far covering the war in Iraq, more than in any conflict since World War II. Another thirty-eight journalists were taken hostage. It was clear that we had to seriously reconsider how we gathered news in Iraq.

For almost three years, reporters had enjoyed unprecedented access to Iraq. The country had never been so well explored and documented. Saddam Hussein had never allowed nearly as much press freedom. But now it was simply too dangerous for Western reporters to roam the streets, casting our nets for news. Iraq had been dangerous since April 2004. But now it had turned yet another corner and we had to adapt. I gathered my three trusted Iraqi fixers, Zohair, Ali, and Ashraf, and devised a new emergency reporting system. I told them I would have to rely on them more than ever to be my eyes and ears.

We devised a beat structure. Zohair took the political, police, and hospital beats. It was to be a total immersion plan. He'd be responsible for finding out everything that went on in police stations, hospitals, and government ministries. It was a good match. Zohair already had contacts at the hospitals, a cousin who was deputy police chief of Baghdad, and strong inroads into the howza, and therefore into the Shiite-dominated government.

Ashraf tracked Sunni insurgents and their statements and videos on the Web. He was Sunni. His father had been a senior Baath party member, and Ashraf already spent several hours a day trolling jihadi Web sites. He had passwords to their closed chat rooms and forums. He and Ned had been kidnapped by Sunni radicals in Falujah. Ashraf knew them well.

Zarqawi had taken Internet propaganda to a new level. Insurgents were now broadcasting their own newscasts on the Web, anchored by a masked man sitting at a desk in front of a black flag. They even had roving reporters, who would travel to cities like Ramadi and interview Iraqis who said they loved the insurgents, which wasn't a surprising reaction considering that the "reporter" was accompanied by armed men in ski masks.

Ali took Sadr City and the Mahdi Army. He was a Shiite and lived nearby. He was also young and could blend in. Most of the Mahdi Army fighters were his age.

All three assignments were dangerous, and Zohair, Ali, and Ashraf knew they would have to work mainly in secret.

Ali had the best personality for stealth. He rarely spoke or exposed his emotions. He was a born observer. He quickly infiltrated the Mahdi Army. He told them he was a journalist and carried a camera. They knew he was taking notes and pictures. But they trusted Ali. He'd managed to secure a recommendation from a Mahdi Army cleric. He'd been vouched for. We started to call him "Ali Sadr City." After just a few weeks, Ali started to use the nickname himself. He was lost in his new role. He'd quickly become Ali Sadr City.

I'd known Ali longer than any of the other fixers. He had been my driver during the 2003 invasion. When I sneaked into Iraq with $20,000 strapped to my leg waiting for the war to start, it was Ali who kept me alive and hidden from Saddam's security forces. While I moved from house to house before Shock and Awe, Ali brought me bread, juice, and gas for the generators he helped me stockpile in safe houses. I'd trusted him with my life. I didn't have a proper visa at the time and Ali could have turned me over to Saddam's agents a hundred times.

While Ali had the best natural inclination, Zohair, the elder statesman of the group, was already a master at secrecy. He had years of practice under Saddam, dodging the army, evading execution, and keeping his head down.

Zohair told me he'd already been operating like a thief, moving around Baghdad, stealing stories and trying to escape with the goods. "Trust is very hard to gain nowadays. I always believed that

God is the protector, and I feel that every man has his destiny. It is something that is written. We all have our day, but I protect myself," he once told me. "In the morning before I leave for the streets, before I come to the office, before I open the doors, I check to see what's going on outside. Maybe someone left something on my doorstep? Maybe someone left a threatening note for me? I check beneath my car every day, then I open the door and I drive off with my life in God's hands. I keep my eyes on the mirror and I take different routes every day. Sometimes I use the back streets, other times I take the side streets."

Zohair didn't even tell his wife where he went in the morning. He told friends he was a taxi driver, a used car dealer, or unemployed. It didn't matter. On the streets, Zohair's answer to every question from a stranger was "Yes."

"What do you do? Do you work for the government?"

"Yes."

"Or are you a journalist?"

"Yes."

"Are you from Baghdad?"

"Yes."

"Are you doing a story about traffic police?"

"Yes."

"Is that your car?"

"Yes."

"I thought you had a different car?"

"Yes."

Then he'd disappear, leaving people to scratch their heads. Zohair answered their questions, but told them nothing.

Zohair dove into his new role and quickly earned the trust of several key Iraqi politicians. He worked for them twenty-four hours a day. He even ran errands for them. He helped one senior government official decorate his villa. He helped another buy suits. He brought whiskey to clerics who didn't want their staff to know they drank. If an official needed a ride to the airport, Zohair would take him. Everybody loved Zohair, even if they didn't know much about him. Zohair worked hard and seemed to love what he was doing. He was discovering his country. The man who'd been persecuted for having an Iranian mother was now an insider.

Ashraf was also enthusiastic about his assignment. He was a natural hunter, and truly seemed to enjoy going to meetings in mosques and dark apartments to talk about jihad with "the mooj," as he called them, the mujahideen.

"Don't screw with these people," I warned him. "Get what you need and get the hell out of there."

I didn't trust the Sunni insurgents. They talked a big game about honor and national resistance, until they didn't get their way. Then they reverted to threats and violence. We had once interviewed an insurgent who insisted he was followed after our meeting. If he was, it had nothing to do with us. He claimed we'd set him up and said he wanted to kill us. It took a series of tense phone calls to convince him he was wrong.

I had rules. No story was worth any of our lives. Ali and Zohair would call me before going anywhere. I spoke to them at least ten times a day. Ashraf's movements were less predictable. He made me the most nervous, but assured me he was taking precautions.

Zohair's contacts in the police started to tip him off each time there was a bombing. I'd get five or six calls a day from Zohair saying "there has just been a car bomb" in Khadra, New Baghdad, Adel, or any one of a dozen *manatek sukhena*, "hot neighborhoods." "Do you want me to go and film?" he'd ask.

My answer was usually the same. "Wait a few minutes, and then see how close you can get. If there's shooting, get the hell out of there. Don't take too many risks."

I didn't want Zohair to rush to any bomb site with his camera. The militants loved come-ons. They'd set off a bomb, wait for the police to arrive, and then detonate another. By waiting, Zohair would be a little late and his pictures somewhat less dramatic, but who cared? I certainly didn't.

I had mixed feelings about my new role. I felt terribly responsible. I was asking them to go where I could no longer go myself. I was asking them to take risks I could no longer take. While they wanted to do it, they were also my brothers.

I still went out every day, but I limited my movements. If Zohair operated like a thief, I moved like an outlaw hunted by the FBI. I went on crash outings, banging off interviews and stand-ups, and then rushed back to the bureau. If I had to interview a doctor, lawyer, or politician, we would first send an advance team of Iraqis, tough guys in black leather jackets, to take GPS coordinates of the location and map out possible escape routes. Our security advisors wanted to know what floor the interview was on, if we could park our cars inside, and how many people knew we were coming. Zohair and Ali could move more quickly.

I also had a half dozen other stringers from Mosul to Basra. They worked on day rates, and since there was no cell phone coverage where most of them lived, they had to operate on their own. They would often come into the bureau unannounced with tapes and amazing stories of cunning and survival.

I remember when one of the stringers from Baqouba brought in a tape from Heet. I'd asked him to interview Sunnis in the city about their reaction to the elections. I wanted to see if Ocampo, Uzoni, and the other marines had made a difference.

It didn't sound like it.

"I finished the interviews in Heet and was driving out of town when a car pulled in front of me and cut me off," the stringer said. "Gunmen got out of the car with headscarves over their faces.

"I talked to the gunmen and they said they had seen me in Heet."

He said the militants didn't believe he was a journalist.

"No reporters come out here," the gunmen argued, and asked what he was *really* doing.

"And did you tell them?" I asked.

"I told them I was doing a story on Sunni reaction to the election."

"Is it positive or negative?" the gunmen asked, and demanded to see his tape.

I could picture our reporter by the side of the road in a huddle of gunmen looking at the screen of his mini–DV camera. I was nervous just picturing it. The militants could be so erratic. If they hadn't liked what was on the tape they would have killed him.

Luckily, the gunmen were satisfied that our stringer was telling the truth. Then they turned remarkably polite and cooperative.

"Do you need any help from us?" one of the militants asked the stringer.

"Actually," he said, "I'm low on gas."

The masked men went to the trunk of their car, took out two jerry cans, and filled up his tank. As he left, the gunmen said that if he'd been from al-Iraqiya television they would have "cut him up."

Life had become so cheap. One slip of the tongue, one miscalculation, and you could be killed and left by the side of the road.

But the new news-gathering system was working remarkably well. Ali was able to move in places I'd never seen. In Sadr City, Ali uncovered how Jaafari's government had been giving out plots of state land to commanders from the Badr Brigade and the Mahdi Army, in addition to "hundreds" of senior positions in the army and police. He'd seen it happen.

I asked George Casey, the commanding general in Iraq, to confirm what Ali had told me.

Since he had assumed command of all coalition forces in Iraq in June 2004, I met General Casey every few months for coffee and a sandwich. He was a quiet, almost shy man, who generally avoided the media. Casey told me he was "very concerned" about the purging of the ministries and that he'd made it clear to Interior Minister Beyan Jabr. "I don't want to see the Ministry of the Interior politicized. This is not going to be a ministry for your militia," Casey said he told the minister.

Ali's information seemed spot-on.

Zohair also helped break what became a major story about secret prisons and torture dungeons run by the police Commandos. U.S. forces later found hundreds of malnourished Sunni detainees and the whips and blocks of wood the Commandos used to beat them.

Iraqi journalist Kamal Samaraie told me that after he criticized the police Commandos in his newspaper, he was arrested, hung upside down, and clubbed with a metal pipe.

"The police whispered to me, 'There's no freedom. You can't write what you want,' " he said, and showed me bruises on his legs.

Zohair was getting great access.

At 6:55 A.M. on February 22, 2006, something happened we hadn't expected. Zarqawi's jihadists destroyed the al-Askari mosque in Samara.

Sunni insurgents had destroyed many Shiite husseiniyas and mosques before, but none as important as Samara's al-Askari shrine. It was a strike directly at the promise of salvation.

Twelver Shiites believe the Mahdi al-Montazer, the hidden twelfth imam and their savior, disappeared in a basement just a few feet from the al-Askari shrine in the ninth century, and it is here he is expected to return. Samara was the Shiites' gateway to the divine, and now Sunnis had attacked it.

Sistani's calls for tolerance became meaningless. He was suddenly yesterday's man. Sadr wanted to be tomorrow's leader, the man who defended Samara and the Mahdi.

The Mahdi Army quickly mobilized for war. Until the destruction of the golden-domed al-Askari mosque, the Shiite death squads were mainly run by the Badr Brigade, working through Jabr's Interior Ministry and using its Commandos. They were professional paramilitary assassination teams and didn't bother most Sunnis. Their targets were former Baath party members, hard-line Sunni clerics, and anyone who stood in their way. The situation radically changed when Sadr's Mahdi Army entered the battle. The Mahdi Army had fought the Americans before, but then went quiet. It was a reserve force. When members were called, they fought. After that, they went back to work. The Mahdi Army was far less organized than the Badr Brigade. Most of the Mahdi Army's fighters were untrained, undisciplined, and uneducated. Some of them had been drug addicts who found religion and purpose in what was more a gang-on-demand than an army.

The Badr Brigade was also relatively small, elite, and well funded by the Iranian Revolutionary Guards. The Mahdi Army was huge. It had tens of thousands of members, many of them the poorest of Iraq's urban poor. Now that the Mahdi Army had decided to fight Sunnis, it needed cash to keep its members loyal. Just as the Sunnis had done when their insurgency began in April 2004, the Mahdi Army turned to kidnapping to raise funds after the Samara bombing. They did it on a massive scale. Any Sunni doctor, dentist, or homeowner was fair game. The standard asking price for a hostage was $100,000. After negotiations, most ransoms were settled for $30,000.

I'd been following the Mahdi Army since it was created in the summer of 2003. Moqtada al-Sadr had taken out a newspaper ad calling on young men to defend Shiite holy sites and the howza. I drove to Najaf to see the Mahdi Army's first enrollment day.

It was over 100 degrees as our crew walked up a narrow alley behind the Imam Ali mosque. The air was thick with sweat. There looked like there were more than three thousand people crammed into the alley, less than eight feet wide. Clerics stood in shaded doorways, fanned by assistants waving pieces of cardboard.

The main hall in Sadr's office was packed with a swarm of young men circling and beating their chests under a spinning ceiling fan that did nothing to cool the air. A cleric, who couldn't have been more than twenty-five years old, stood in the center of the crowd, screaming and pointing to the heavens. In a room upstairs, a midget with big bulging eyes, a hunched back, and a wispy beard sat cross-legged on the floor surrounded by howza students in dirty white robes. Down the hall, young men lined up to sign their names in a logbook, put their hands on the Koran, and swear an oath of allegiance to the Mahdi Army.

By early 2006, the Mahdi Army had grown, fought two battles against U.S. troops, and secured a steady supply of weapons from both Iraq's black market and Iran. Ali saw short-range rockets from Iran in a warehouse in Sadr City.

After the Samara bombing, Ali was suddenly in the middle of one of the most violent militias in Iraq. His position instantly became more important, and infinitely more dangerous. He'd gained the Mahdi Army's trust and lived among its fighters. A few days after the al-Askari mosque bombing, Ali was waiting to donate blood at a clinic in Sadr City. "I was on line. You know, there have been a lot of attacks in Sadr City and people were crowded at the hospital to give blood. I saw this man. We were all crowded at the door and he said he wanted to go inside and join his brother giving blood. But people must have suspected him. Suddenly, two men grabbed him by the arms, one holding each arm."

Ali held out his arms to show me how the man was restrained.

"The militiamen took off his jacket and found he was wearing an explosive belt. It was crowded outside, but this man had to go *inside* to kill even more people. He could have done it outside, but no, he wanted to kill *more*."

"Then what?" I asked.

"They took him and put a blindfold around his head."

"And the man, the would-be bomber, what was he doing?"

"He kept saying, 'Just kill me. I want to die. Kill me!'"

"And after that?"

"The Mahdi Army put him on his knees and shot him twice in the head. I felt sorry for him, even though he was a terrorist. He was put on this earth by God."

I asked Ali if he'd ever seen a man executed before, and how he felt.

"No, it was the first time. Of course it affects you."

Then he said something so sacrilegious in Iraqi culture that I was shocked to hear it: "You know, and I shouldn't say this, but all this makes me hate Islam. It seems that the more you kill the more you go to heaven."

After that Ali was silent, stunned at what he had said. Ali was from a devout family. He'd never questioned his faith before.

We let the moment hang in the air.

Ali said he watched the Mahdi Army fighters hang up the executed man for public display. He said he didn't sleep well for two days after that. "This is the worst it has been in Baghdad, Richard," he said.

By March, it seemed that every Iraqi was in hiding. Zohair set up a safe room in his home, stocked with dried dates, candles, and water. He put a ladder by a back window. If anyone, including Iraqi security forces, came to the door, he planned to climb onto the roof and escape with his wife. It was almost the same plan he'd had when he tried to avoid Saddam's draft two decades earlier.

Many Iraqis were living double lives. I met one of Ayad Allawi's political advisors, a man in his late thirties. In Washington, he would have been the equivalent of a senior White House staffer and would wear a blue blazer and chinos. But in Baghdad he was dressed in a shabby polyester suit. It was part of his disguise. He was pretending to be a taxi driver.

"You know what, I just had my first fare," he told me. He thought it was funny. He'd been one of the former prime minister's closest aides. Now he was pretending to be a cabbie, and had just been caught in his own bluff.

"A neighbor came and asked me if I would take her across town," he said.

"So did you take her?"

"What could I do?" He laughed. "I tell everyone I am a taxi driver, so I took her. I even haggled about the price."

"What did you charge her?"

"Three thousand dinars [about $2]. She was going to pick up her food rations in another neighborhood."

All of Baghdad's elite felt threatened. But Ahmed Rikabi, the owner of Iraq's most popular radio station, told me the violence now reached every level of society. "Anyone could be a target. A hairdresser is a target in Iraq today. The garbage collector in the street is a target. The butchers are targets," he said.

Mixed Sunni/Shiite neighborhoods were being purged. Iraq's middle class was leaving the country. A hundred civilians a day were being killed by rival Sunni and Shiite militias, according to U.N. estimates.

In Sunni neighborhoods in west Baghdad, residents were cutting down palm trees in their gardens to barricade their streets. They formed neighborhood watch groups that would shoot strangers on sight.

The blogs I wrote about life in Baghdad for MSNBC.com had become so graphic the editors decided to attach "advisory content" warnings on many of the posts.

I think the *Los Angeles Times* Baghdad bureau chief, Borzou Daragahi, may have put it best. In his room in the Hamra he told me, "This is not war reporting, it's science fiction reporting. This is like some futuristic nightmare, a *Blade Runner* world of concrete checkpoints, barbed wire, bread riots, killings in the streets, and people trapped behind walls to escape it all. It is science fiction."

But the White House didn't see it that way. The day after I interviewed Rikabi and reported that Sunnis were desperately using palm trees to protect their neighborhoods, President Bush gave a speech in Washington criticizing journalists in Iraq for playing into the terrorists' media strategy. "They're capable of blowing up innocent life so it ends up on your TV show," Bush said.

The Baghdad press corps' inability, or unwillingness, to find "good news" in Iraq quickly became the cause du jour of conservative American talk show hosts yet again.

Rush Limbaugh said reporters in Baghdad "go out and find a video of a burning, smoldering vehicle that was blown up by an IED and that's the news of the day." On the *Today* show, radio host Laura Ingraham criticized NBC for spending too much money on vanity anchor projects instead of covering Iraq.

"To do a show from Iraq means to talk to the Iraqi military, to go out with the Iraqi military, to actually have a conversation with the people instead of reporting from hotel balconies about the latest IEDs going off," she said.

While I never wanted to engage in these types of debates, this time the criticism was particularly out of touch. While I couldn't control how much of the network's coverage was dedicated to Iraq, journalists in Baghdad certainly weren't just reporting from hotel balconies. We were dying and being kidnapped in record numbers.

David Gregory, filling in as host of the *Today* show, asked me if I thought the media focused too much on negative stories. I told him, "Most Iraqis I speak to say most reporters get it wrong. The situation on the ground is worse than the images we project on television. Reporting on everyday life is increasingly dangerous because life here is getting more dangerous."

I'd finally said it. Iraq was not as bad as it looked on TV, it was worse. Ali agreed completely. He said our news reports were far too sanitized. He took his cell phone out of his pocket. It was a new computerized phone with a two-inch screen and the capability to play video. He showed me his home movies. He showed me what Baghdad had become. The first video clip was of the severed head of a suicide bomber. Ali filmed it while out with the Mahdi Army. The head was intact, although missing a few front teeth. It was on the street, surrounded by Iraqi soldiers. Ali said most of them were also from the Mahdi Army. They had their cell phones out, and took pictures as they stomped on the head. When the head slipped from under their feet, the soldiers laughed and kicked it like a soccer ball, batting it back and forth. Then they picked it up and tossed it into a Dumpster.

The second video on Ali's phone showed a suicide bomber's severed torso. The bomber had been wearing an explosives belt that sliced him in half. His head and shoulders were intact and sat upright on the ground. It looked as if the bomber had been buried in the pavement up to his ribs. The Iraqi soldiers kicked over the bloody stump, which fell like a piano bust.

"Why do you have this on your phone?" I asked Ali.

He just shrugged and gave me a look that said, "I dunno."

Ali was becoming addicted to violence. It had become a fascination. In addition to the videos, he had dozens of pictures of attacks and bodies on his phone. He was collecting war porn. Baghdad was starting to destroy my friend Ali, robbing him of his humanity.

19

At 5:21 P.M. on March 27, 2006, I received one of the worst phone calls of my life.

"Is that you, Ashraf?"

"*Salam allekum*"—Peace be with you—was all I heard back.

"Ashraf?"

"Ashraf is our guest," said a man with a deep, steady voice. "He will be our guest for a day, or perhaps a few days."

Ashraf had been kidnapped.

My hands were trembling, but mostly I was angry with myself. Why did I let Ashraf go to all those dangerous meetings with dubious people? He was just a kid and thought it was cool to hang out with the mooj. I should have known better and reined him in. Jill Carroll was still a hostage, missing for nearly three months. Now Ashraf was gone again, having already survived being kidnapped with Ned in Falujah.

"What the hell is wrong with this place!" I thought. I wanted the chaos to stop, just for a few days. It was chewing through my friends.

I immediately called our New York headquarters. The management, for all the grief I'd given them, acted fantastically. They instantly took the threat seriously and gave me access to experts, psychologists, and hostage negotiators. They pulled out the stops and wanted updates every few hours. I felt lucky to be part of a big organization with the resources to deal with a life-or-death crisis. I stopped filing so I could focus entirely on trying to secure Ashraf's release. But I knew I was out of my depth. I'd never done this before. I'd be negotiating with the kidnappers in Arabic. There would be no second chances.

I tried to learn as much as possible from the professional hostage negotiators before the kidnappers called back. They told me to sleep whenever I could because kidnappers tend to call at unpredictable hours, or in rapid succession, anything to put one off balance. Demand proof of life. They taught me how to listen for background noises. Is Ashraf being kept outside or indoors? In a large room? Could I hear traffic? Birds? Anything could help.

They told me to keep detailed notes after each conversation so I could identify patterns or inconsistencies. "This is going to be tough," the negotiator warned. "They are going to try to push you to the limit and exploit your friendship. But in the end, it's a business transaction. You each have something the other wants."

That evening the kidnapper called back to tell me he'd abandoned Ashraf's car in front of a restaurant in west Baghdad. I listened closely to his voice. He seemed to be a heavy smoker and didn't sound like an Islamist. He wasn't using all the flowery Islamic phrases and pleasantries like "may God keep you" and "if God wills it" that make up half of everything Islamists tend to say. He spoke with a decisiveness that gave me the impression he'd been in the military. Maybe he was an auto mechanic? His voice had a thuggish drawl. I imagined him to be a thick, heavy man in his forties or early fifties who worked with his hands for a living. I could have been completely off base, but I was starting to build a profile.

The next day the kidnapper called back again, demanding a ransom. Now I knew what he wanted. I was glad he'd asked for cash.

Everybody understands money. It would have been more difficult if he was motivated by politics, religion, or revenge. This was just business.

"We want twenty-five dafar. Do you know what a dafar is?"

"Yes," I said. He wanted twenty-five "notebooks," a quarter million dollars.

I'd been told repeatedly we were "not to pay ransoms to terrorists and kidnappers." NBC wasn't going to do it. It was policy, and I agreed. An American expert from the U.S. embassy's Hostage Working Group, a joint task force of American military, FBI, Special Operations Forces, and intelligence agents, told me that paying emboldens kidnappers. I didn't want to give these bastards a dime. They'd just come hunting for more of our staff. But I wanted Ashraf free.

I got the best advice from an Iraqi policeman. He'd dealt with dozens of kidnappings in the past few months. "There were seventy kidnappings in Baghdad this week," he said.

The policeman never told me his name, but he knew the rules. He said that it was important to keep the negotiations going for as long as possible. "If you pay, especially as much as they are asking, which is way too much, he'll be killed. You'll be buying a body. Offer to let them keep the car they stole. Say they can keep it and sell it."

"That's it? They're asking for a quarter million dollars."

"Offer them five thousand, tell them you'll sell the car for them and give them the money. Nothing more."

I knew it would not go over.

The kidnapper called at 1:33 P.M. the next day.

"Did you do what we asked?"

"I want to speak to Ashraf. I want to hear his voice."

"Now you will hear it."

They put Ashraf on the phone.

"Hello? Ashraf?"

"Yes, who is this?"

"It's Richard."

"Hello, Richard."

"How is your health?"

"Bad, very bad," he said. He didn't sound stressed. He seemed tired, but he wasn't crying or hysterical. He was calm.

Then they took the phone away.

"So did you do what we asked?"

"I do have some money, a lot. The car is worth five thousand."

"What?"

"You can keep the car, or sell it."

"What! That is too far off. What is this? We will sell him to the mujahideen and that's it."

"Let's keep talking, keep negotiating. I am working hard. It is not my money. I consider Ashraf like a brother."

"So why don't you help your brother and help him to be back with his family. Don't you think that would make them happy?"

"Of course, it would make us all happy."

"So?"

"So what?"

"So what about the money?"

"You only gave me a day. I can keep trying."

"Keep trying. I will call you in two hours, and if we don't hear what we want, we will sell him to the mujahideen and that will be the end of Ashraf. Based on the documents he has, they will kill him."

"We don't want that," I said. "I'll wait for your call in two hours."

Ashraf, like other reporters working for Western networks, carried a CPIC badge, an ID card issued by the U.S. military press office. I assumed this was the "document" the kidnapper had referred to. The Iraqi policeman advising me didn't buy their argument. "If they could have sold him to the mujahideen, they would have already done it. The mujahideen don't want to buy Iraqis," he said. "Don't offer them any more money."

He said the strategy was to tire them out. "Time is on your side. They don't want to hold him for long. It's risky and expensive. They have to feed him and hide him," he said. "Stay strong."

The next day the kidnapper had a new tactic. He started threatening to kill me.

When I told him I didn't have any more money, he raised his voice for the first time. "We will give Ashraf to the mujahideen as a gift! And they will send a car bomb to you! A bomb that even your armored cars won't stop! Ashraf has suffered a lot. If you don't believe us, we can cut off a hand, or even a leg. No more of these small amounts of money. We know your company. We know what they are capable of. No more of these small amounts. If I hear more of the same when I call you tomorrow, it's over. On the spot, consider him dead. I will hand him over to the mujahideen or kill him. Consider it over."

Ashraf had evidently been talking. The kidnappers knew about our armored cars. I had to assume they knew everything that Ashraf knew, our names, the layout of the bureau, the strength of our security team. The stakes were suddenly higher. Everyone in the bureau was at risk. I wanted to find these bastards. I wanted them dead. I was starting to think in Baghdad rules, jungle rules.

Our security team was on high alert, ready for an attack. We were nearly in lockdown. I told Zohair and Ali to leave town. They hid out with relatives outside Baghdad. This was not journalism anymore.

It had now been four days since Ashraf went missing. I'd barely slept. I was taking meals in my room, waiting for the phone to ring. I hadn't shaved. I had a cold sore on my lip from the stress and lack of sleep. The entire bureau was on edge.

But the Iraqi negotiator's strategy was working. We were tiring them out too. They were furious at me. They'd assumed I'd be an easy mark, but I was being difficult. I've bought a few carpets in the Middle East too.

"We are sick of this, we want our money," the kidnapper said. "Forget it. It is all off. We are selling Ashraf and we are through with him, but we are not finished with you. We will attack you and make you suffer!"

"Why us?"

"Because you didn't meet our demands. So this is it. We are through. He is dead. You killed him, but we are not through."

"You have to understand I am just a link. It is not up to me. The decisions are not in my hands. I can ask."

"So we are going to get our money?"

"I can ask, but the decision is not up to me."

I asked to speak to Ashraf again.

"Abu Abdullah, get him," the kidnapper called out. He was starting to make mistakes, using names. He was losing discipline.

The kidnapper put Ashraf on the phone again.

"Hello," he said.

"Hello, Ashraf. How are you?"

"Terrible. I am suffering very much."

"Are they mistreating you?"

"Yes, every so often they come and hurt me. How are you?" he asked. It seemed an odd question.

"Fine."

"How is my family?"

"Okay. I have been in touch with them."

"Where are they?"

"I don't know. Are they beating you?"

"Yes."

"Do you have food?"

They took the phone away.

"Do what you need to do. Talk to your bosses. You have two hours," the kidnapper said. He kept extending the deadlines. But he seemed in a rush. One hour later, he called back. "So what have you done?" he asked.

"Nothing," I said. "What can I do in one hour?"

"We even gave you more than an hour, isn't that right?" he said, apparently asking someone in the room to look at a watch. "Yes, about an hour, whatever."

"It is not enough time," I said. I was starting to think they were amateurs. They were calling constantly, always using the same phone. They seemed confused. I felt I was starting to win.

"Look," I said, "I have spoken with my company. They are not willing to pay kidnappers. What can I do?"

"Are you deaf? Are you stupid? Do you know what we will do to Ashraf?"

"I am sorry for that. It doesn't matter. They have a policy, lawyers, money, and accountants. They are not going to pay. I am still trying to find the family to help you. Perhaps they have some more money."

It was a bluff. I was trying to redirect responsibility, lower expectations, and make it seem that holding Ashraf was useless.

"I am sure the family has more money," he said.

"I am not so sure. If they had more money, they would have left the country."

I'd prepared that line in advance.

"You are not listening. We will kill him or sell him to the mujahideen."

"What can I do?"

"How would you like it if we kidnapped you? We would beat you in ways you cannot even imagine."

"I would not like that at all."

"So?"

"Yes, I would not like it. But that does not change things."

"How about when we kill everyone in your company? Would that change things? If you can even set a foot outside your office, even go outside, I will give you twenty-five dafar."

"You'd give it to me, like a gift?" I said, and laughed.

"Yes, a gift."

"You must be very rich."

"I want you to hear Ashraf suffer so you know we are serious."

"Listen, we have done all this talking, but you have not told me your name. What's your name?"

"Abu Zohair."

"Okay, Abu Zohair. What's the solution here? We are not getting anywhere. I am against a wall. You want something that I can't give you. But I am trying to help."

"No! I want you to hear Ashraf suffer."

"Why? He's an innocent kid. He didn't do anything."

"I want you to hear what you are doing to Ashraf. I want you to hear him scream."

"That's not necessary. I understand you already."

Then the kidnapper put down the phone. I could hear the sound of flesh pounding flesh. I heard the slap of a punch, followed by a groan.

Punch . . . ughhh!

Punch . . . ughhh!

But it didn't sound real. It was like a bad sound effect in a low-budget movie. I didn't believe it.

"You hear that? I won't tell you what it is, but he is suffering."

I'd been having doubts about the entire situation. It seemed amateurish. Ashraf didn't seem nervous over the phone, and now this phony beating. They'd lost me.

As I was talking with the "kidnapper" and listening to "the beating," news broke that Jill Carroll had been released.

The kidnapper kept talking, making more threats, but I wasn't listening anymore. I was watching CNN's breaking news coverage about Jill's release. Even though I had known her for only a few days, I'd taken Jill's kidnapping personally. I'd worked with the U.S. military to distribute her photograph and helped maintain a media blackout in the first days after she went missing. Jill had been kidnapped and faced a horrible threat. This was bullshit. Ashraf was not a hostage. It was a put-on. He was wasting my time.

When the kidnappers called back a few hours later, I took a different tone with them. I was now the aggressor. I was through playing with them. "I told you, we will not negotiate with terrorists. That's it. Don't call back," I said, and hung up.

Ashraf was "released" a few hours later, unharmed. He came into the bureau, claiming to have injuries. But there were no marks on his body, except for a tiny cut on his shoulder that looked self-inflicted. He had blood on the collar of his shirt, but he wasn't bleeding from his face. He said the kidnappers had thrown him out of a moving car, but his pants weren't stained. I looked more tired than he did. I was disillusioned. I'd been betrayed. Zohair had been right. Trust no one. Ashraf denied that he'd faked his kidnapping, but our security advisors, including a former professional interrogator, didn't believe him.

But as always, there was no time to spend lingering on emotions or betrayals. I had to get back to work. There were so many stories to do. Iraq had a new prime minister, Nouri al-Maliki, and Ali's father had just been kidnapped. It was immediately clear that Ali was telling the truth. He never asked for money or help. He was an emotional wreck and barely spoke. On his own, Ali started to go to hospital morgues every day to search for his father's body.

Officials at the morgues told Ali the police were now dropping off as many as seventy unidentified bodies in Baghdad a day. They let Ali search through the refrigerators, the white-tiled rooms where they kept all the bodies. But the refrigerators, meat lockers for bodies, weren't always cold, as there were constant power cuts. Ali said most of the bodies he saw were rotting and covered in maggots. He told me how he turned them over so he could look at their faces. "I go without having breakfast to look at the piled-up bodies," he said. "My mother told me, 'Enough, stop looking. If you keep digging like this you will follow your father and be kidnapped yourself.' I told her I didn't care."

Ali said the worst morgue was at Baghdad's Tib al-Adly hospital. He said the refrigerator there was filled with several hundred bodies a week.

Every Friday, a Shiite man from Sadr City would collect the bodies at Tib al-Adly and bury them in Najaf. It didn't matter if they were Shiites or Sunnis. He buried them all. "He's a religious man. He believes that everyone deserves a proper burial," Ali said.

Ali accompanied the man from Sadr City on his next trip to Najaf and recorded the entire journey. The images he took were the most disturbing I'd seen yet during the war.

His first stop was Tib al-Adly. The bodies in the refrigerator— about the size of a standard hotel room—were stacked three deep, piled haphazardly on top of one another. They were a golden brown color and looked oily and wet. They were tangled like crabs in a cage, with their arms, legs, heads, and feet all twisted together. It was hard to tell where one body stopped and another began. Some were still clothed. Others were naked. More bodies were lined up on the street outside. They were all covered in maggots. Many of the corpses were bloated, puffed up like balloons. These had been found in the river and had floated to the surface as they rotted and filled with gas. They'd exploded out of their clothing, bursting through shirts and pants. Their faces were distorted beyond recognition. Most of the corpses had wire around their wrists. They'd been bound before execution.

Ali spent the day wrapping bodies in plastic sheets, loading them into a truck, and digging graves in Najaf. He said limbs would sometimes come off in his hands as he lifted the bodies. He never found his father. "I thought to myself, my father could be any one of them and I may not even recognize him because the bodies are so mutilated."

When Ali returned from Najaf he changed his name. He bought false identity papers. Ali was too recognizable as a Shiite name. Militant gangs had started to set up checkpoints across the country, killing people solely because of their names. He chose Ahmed, a name common among both Sunnis and Shiites.

After his trip to Najaf, Ali said he had trouble sleeping. He started to lose his hair.

Zohair told me he was drinking more whiskey than before. He said he needed it to sleep. He'd filmed so many car bombings. A neighbor was kidnapped. A bullet had just smashed a window in his car while he was driving. "I used to have a drink or two, but now I drink almost a quarter or half a liter of whiskey a day," he said. "I have to drink. I used to drink for fun, but now I drink to forget and for a few hours I don't think about anything."

But Zohair's wife didn't drink. By June, she was starting to go stir-crazy. She hadn't left their small apartment since the Samara bombing in February. To keep herself sane, she started pretending to go out, changing her clothing several times a day as if she were going to dinner or a movie. In the morning, she'd put on a housedress. In the afternoon, she was sporty and wore a track suit. At night, she'd linger for hours in front of the mirror, putting on lipstick, eyeliner, and all her jewelry, and then watch a DVD.

"I live in a five-star prison," she said. "I have a TV, a DVD player, and a generator. Yes, I do go out. I go from one room to the other. I change like I am leaving the house and going to the cinema. If I didn't do that, I would collapse."

Everyone felt like prisoners, but it was the children who seemed to be the most affected. I went to the Alwiya orphanage near the Hamra. I wanted to try to show how everyone had become a prisoner of fear.

The Alwiya orphanage was home to fifty-six girls, ages six to thirteen. The state-run facility was surprisingly clean and well managed. There was no abuse as far as we could tell, and the staff truly seemed to care about the girls. In fact, the director of the orphanage—a woman with glasses and the sense of humor of a high school librarian—was very suspicious of outsiders. She wanted to protect her girls at all costs. I respected her for it. It took us three visits for coffee and written permission from the minister of social affairs himself (one of Zohair's contacts, of course) before she finally allowed us in with cameras. The girls we saw were all traumatized.

In the dining room, where they were eating chicken, rice, and plain yogurt off shiny metal plates, we met the three Hessein sisters, Marwa, Aliya, and Sora. Gunmen had broken into their home at night and killed their parents. The girls had been asleep at the time. They awoke to find their mother shot dead, and watched their father die as the gunmen robbed the house. It was a typical combination of sectarian violence and crime, a marriage of hate and war profiteering. Marwa, thirteen, was tall and mature for her age. She had dark eyes and a long, slender neck, and carried herself like an adult, keeping her shoulders back and head up straight as she sat eating lunch. She looked like she was dining in a fine, white-tablecloth restaurant. Marwa was the new mother of the group. She combed her sisters' hair, and washed the sheets when they wet the bed from the nightmares they often had. Sora, six, was much more mischievous. As we tried to film her, she giggled and hid behind other girls, peeking back playfully at the camera with a crooked smile. Aliya, ten, was shy and hardly ever spoke. Her eyes looked dead. It was as if the little girl in the rainbow-colored blouse and with the cropped chocolate brown hair was in a trance.

Marwa showed me the room she shared with ten other girls. The beds, in two rows against the walls, were all neatly made. At night, Marwa said she dreamed her mother was still alive. "I remember she would take us to the market for the holidays and buy us fabric for new clothing."

She imagined having conversations with her mother. "I just tell her I love her," Marwa said.

Marwa had almost nothing of her own anymore. Her only possessions were a few blouses, one doll, a hairbrush, and a couple of creams. But the only thing she said she missed was a photograph. "I really wish I had a photograph of my parents," she said.

Sora came up behind her. She needed help tying her shoe. She called Marwa "Mommy."

We heard gunshots outside. The girls didn't flinch, but said they hardly ever went outside. "When I hear gunfire in the streets, I feel like I'm the one they're shooting at," Aliya said.

Their lives were regimented:

7:30 A.M.	Wake-up; breakfast of bread and cheese
8:30 A.M.	School
12:30 P.M.	Lunch
1:00 P.M.	Half-hour playtime or rest
1:30 P.M.	Two hours of study
3:30 P.M.	Break; shower or do laundry
4:00 P.M.	Two more hours of study
6:00 P.M.	Free time; play or, when the electricity works, watch TV
9:00 P.M.	Chores, then bedtime

It was the same every day, but our visit was at least a diversion. The girls were all over us. They loved our cameras. Every girl wanted to have her picture taken. We took hundreds of photographs, group shots, the girls with me, the girls with our cameraman, the girls with the teachers.

It was clear they needed attention. All day, the orphans would come up and hold my hand. I would be talking to one girl and suddenly find another sneak up behind me and slip her hand into my palm, or take hold of my elbow. I couldn't walk without dragging four or five girls behind me. It was the same for our cameraman, Steve O'Neil, and his soundman, Steve LoMonaco. We were surrounded, and all the children wanted to do was hold our hands or be picked up.

"They need attention and there is no love here in Baghdad," a social worker at the orphanage said. "We can't give them what they really want, their mothers' touch."

They needed affection as much as food and water and air. They were starving for it. The girls started to call Steve the cameraman "Daddy," and asked me if I had any children and would I adopt them. I was nearly in tears and wanted to bundle them all up and take them home. I had never been as affected by a story.

As we left, we lent one of the girls named Dunya a cell phone. Dunya had a mother who had "dropped her off" at the Alwiya orphanage a few months earlier. I turned around to see Dunya crying hysterically. A woman had answered the phone, but it wasn't her mother. The woman told Dunya her mother had moved to Syria. Dunya had just learned she was abandoned.

Marwa, who was shy and skeptical at first, started to warm up to us after a few hours. She told me she wanted to be a doctor when she grew up. Aliya said she wanted to be an engineer, like her father. But a social worker told us their future was likely to be much more bleak. "The stigma of being an orphan will stay with them forever, and they'll end up living on the streets, or working in the orphanages themselves," he said.

When the girls were too old to live in the orphanage, the social worker said, some would be forced to make a living as prostitutes.

There was a massive viewer response to the orphanage story. We received thousands of e-mails. Many viewers offered to adopt the girls. Some said they'd be willing to take in all three sisters. Unfortunately, I had to write a blog explaining that under Iraqi law it's illegal for foreigners to adopt Iraqis. We directed them to several charities working with Iraqi children.

On the evening of June 7, U.S. Special Operations Forces killed Abu Musab al-Zarqawi in a small cinder block farmhouse in a village called Hibhib forty miles north of Baghdad. The military locked down the area for forty-eight hours to comb it for evidence. They found a treasure trove, including computer memory sticks, phone books, and Zarqawi's personal diary.

After they completed the forensic investigations, the military brought a handful of reporters to see Zarqawi's final hideout. As we circled Hibhib from the air in a Black Hawk, it was hard to see where the farmhouse had been. There was not a single wall standing. All I could see was a deep crater surrounded by palm groves and wildflowers.

U.S. Special Operations Forces had been tracking Zarqawi's deputy, Abu Abdel Rahman, and had followed him to the safe house. An informant, a member of Zarqawi's inner circle, then went outside and called American troops, confirming that the al-Qaeda in Iraq leader was in the building. Within minutes, U.S. forces diverted two F-16 jets to the target. The fighters dropped two five-hundred-pound bombs, shattering the farmhouse and digging a twenty-foot crater in the soft black soil beneath it.

Amazingly, Zarqawi survived the initial air strike. "He was like a cockroach," a soldier said. "You just can't kill this guy."

The bombs threw Zarqawi against a wall, breaking his leg, and then tossed him in the air and out into a field next to the farmhouse. He was still breathing when U.S. troops arrived. Army medics tried to revive him. "A coalition medic treated Zarqawi while he did lapse in and out of consciousness," explained U.S. military spokesman Major General William Caldwell. "The medic secured his airway, at which point Zarqawi expelled blood."

An Iraqi intelligence agent told me Zarqawi had been living in the farmhouse for about a week. He moved frequently between safe houses, avoiding highways, traveling mainly on unmarked desert and country roads, often putting women at the front of his convoy. In Baghdad, he sometimes traveled on fishing boats on the Tigris. One time, Zarqawi disguised himself as a pregnant woman. But more often, he avoided checkpoints by using corrupt Iraqi soldiers and police to wave him through. Funding was never a problem. Iraqi intelligence agents said Zarqawi used a network of money-transfer centers and foreign exchange offices. Most of the money came from Islamic charities in Saudi Arabia and the United Arab Emirates.

Finding Zarqawi had been top-class detective work. Again, the U.S. military proved to the world that American soldiers were good hunters and fighters, even if they were failing as occupiers and nation builders.

After reporting the death of Zarqawi, I moved to Lebanon. I'd convinced NBC to open a Middle East bureau in the Arab world, arguing that the war in Iraq had clearly spilled beyond the country's borders.

Beirut is also a wonderful place to live, with a busy nightlife, French bistros, boardwalks on the Mediterranean, and enough high life and low life to keep it interesting. I wanted a home, a place where I could escape from Baghdad. I knew Lebanon was unstable, but I didn't expect that war would break out between Israel and Lebanon-based Hezbollah two weeks after I arrived. I spent the rest of the summer reporting from destroyed villages in southern Lebanon and covering refugees in my new home.

NBC's Washington bureau chief, Tim Russert, told me I was bad luck. "Engel, don't come to Washington," he said.

As I covered the fighting in Lebanon, there was no way to escape Baghdad. While I was in Lebanon's ancient Phoenician city of Tyre, pounded by Israeli jets and naval gunships trying to stop Hezbollah from launching rockets into northern Israel, I learned that Ali had been kidnapped. He was released after a single day, but he'd been interrogated and tortured. When the war in Lebanon ended, with more than a thousand dead, most of them Lebanese civilians, and nearly every road and bridge in south Lebanon destroyed, I returned to Baghdad.

The Mahdi Army, Ali told me, turned on him. He'd been filming a demonstration in Sadr City in support of Hezbollah. As Ali left, he saw he was being followed. "Three cars with tinted glass blocked my way. Men got out and asked me who I was and what business I had in Sadr City. I wanted to call my friends in the Mahdi Army, but then someone hit the back of my head with a gun and I passed out."

Ali awoke in the back of a car. The first thing he thought of was his father. "I opened my eyes and I told them, 'I have just one request. Please call my family and tell them where to find my body. Don't make them go around looking for it, not knowing if I am alive or dead. I have suffered the same thing with my father, so I do not want the same to happen to them.' "

The militants said they had other plans. "Do you think it is going to be that easy?" they said. "Do you think we will have mercy on you and kill you? Killing is very easy."

They drove him to a safe house for interrogation. "They accused me of being a collaborator with the Americans. I told them I am not and to check the numbers on my phone and see all the contacts I had, all the names of Shiite clerics. They did, and recognized the names and were surprised. They asked me, 'Is it possible that you know all those people?' "

"Call any one of them and ask about me. You will see how they trust me," Ali told them.

But they never called.

"They took me into a room and started beating me with a bat and I started shouting. They said that they would make me confess. I told them, 'I have nothing else to add. If you want me to start making stuff up, I can do that, but my story is not changing.' Then they hung me upside down on a hook in the ceiling and started to beat me with a metal rod.

"I could not even scream. They put tissue in my mouth and

taped it closed. I was shocked how much cotton they put down my throat. I was choking on it. They beat me from that afternoon until early the next morning. They hit me everywhere, then would stop, empty my mouth, and ask me again, 'Tell us who you really are?'

"I told them I was a journalist, but they saw my CPIC badge. They said I was a collaborator."

Ali was rescued when a Mahdi Army cleric finally called to vouch for him. "They apologized to me and demanded that I forgive them and relieve them of all responsibility. They brought me water and let me wash up. One of them said, 'It's good we did not do anything to you.'

"What do you mean, you didn't do anything?" Ali shot back. He could barely stand. "All this, and you did nothing?" he asked.

The man pointed to some large screws on the floor and said, "We were about to drive those screws into your body."

It was the Mahdi Army's newest tactic. They'd become infamous for using power drills on their victims' knees, chests, and skulls. They used hammers and screws too. It was medieval.

Baghdad had finally become too dangerous even for locals to go out reporting. It was now almost impossible to work in Iraq.

20

By the spring of 2006 America's mission in Iraq had changed yet again. First, U.S. troops were told they were "liberators," fighting way back in 2003 to topple a tyrant armed with weapons of mass destruction and al-Qaeda allies. It was a lie, or a mistake, or both, and eventually the world caught on. The troops then became "warriors for democracy," defending a nation of "freedom lovers" who held elections and wrote a constitution just like Americans. The third mission was to defend Iraqis from terrorists, who, conveniently, also called themselves al-Qaeda something or other. Our Sunni militant enemies in Iraq even formed an open alliance with Osama bin Laden.

For the Bush administration, it was manna from Jihad heaven. Americans hated al-Qaeda and now al-Qaeda was flourishing in Iraq. Perfect! It made the critical link to 9/11. But by 2006, stressing a link to 9/11 was scandalously misleading. American troops were never fighting militants in Iraq who had attacked America on 9/11. They were fighting the same *type* of violent Salafi jihadists in Iraq, who, after America declared war on Baghdad, made an alliance with our enemies. Zarqawi and other militants who trained with bin Laden in Afghanistan ended up fighting in Iraq, but they came after 9/11. The chronology is important, and actually quite clear.

2001: 9/11 attacks

2001–2002: The United States launches a war in Afghanistan against the 9/11 plotters and their Taliban hosts. Militants scatter. Many cross the Afghan border to Pakistan. Zarqawi escapes to northern Iraq.

2002–2003: The United States starts to openly prepare for war on Iraq. Saddam first thinks it's a bluff, but finally accepts that the war is coming. He expects to lose, releases criminals from prison, and forms alliances with anybody he can find, including jihadists. In the months before the invasion, Saddam even starts to bus them in from Syria. His message to America: You want Iraq? Choke on it. You'll be sorry, and need me later.

2006: The White House blurs the chronology and continues to suggest that jihadists in Iraq were responsible for 9/11, or at least cut from the same cloth; even if they weren't involved in 9/11, they'd probably be behind the next attack on America.

Most of the soldiers seemed to accept the new rationale. They were happy to be "hunting bad guys," and al-Qaeda in Iraq certainly fit that description. Over the years, many young soldiers in Iraq have told me they joined the army after 9/11 specifically to go kick Arab jihadist ass and "take the fight to the enemy." While I admire their patriotic desire to respond to an assault on American soil, the problem has always been they were kicking the wrong jihadist ass in the wrong country.

Still, the first three missions were clear enough and seemed to have a direct impact on American lives at home. They were good

stories, and most soldiers were happy to live them. But after the attack on the al-Askari mosque in Samara, the war changed into a
murky fight between sects, militias, and thieves. No rationale could
explain why the soldiers were playing referee in an ugly, 1,300-year-
old religious war. Who's the enemy? Does America back Sunnis or
Shiites? Are the Iraqi security forces on our side, or against us? Is
the Iraqi government part of the problem or the solution? Do Iraqis
really want democracy? There were no clear answers. Everything
was fluid and gray, and the soldiers were getting frustrated. A few
were losing control.

On July 8, 2006, the military charged five soldiers with stalking, raping, and killing a fourteen-year-old girl in Mahmoudiya,
south of Baghdad. According to a military investigation and witness testimony, the soldiers followed the girl to her home, broke in,
pinned her down, gang-raped her, shot her dead, poured kerosene
on her body, and set her on fire to destroy the evidence. They also
allegedly killed the girl's mother, father, and five-year-old sister.

It was one of the most shocking war crimes documented in Iraq.
The abuse of prisoners at Abu Ghraib had been a worldwide scandal. The images of hooded men smeared with their own excrement
and stacked naked in cheerleading formations outraged Muslims
from Morocco to Indonesia, and shamed the American public.

But the rape and massacre in Mahmoudiya, a military spokesman told me, was much worse. "This is really bad. It's one of those
'what the fuck?' moments," he said.

In March 2006, just a few days after the rape and murders in
Mahmoudiya, Iraqi police claimed American troops in the village
of Ishaqi killed eleven Iraqis, including women and children. U.S.
forces said they were responding to an insurgent attack. A month
later, military investigators said American soldiers in Hamdaniya
kidnapped and killed a disabled fifty-four-year-old man, and then
placed an AK-47 by his side to make him look like an insurgent. By
July, a senior military official told me there were more than a dozen
criminal investigations under way.

Something had obviously changed. Some soldiers, still just a tiny percentage, were snapping. "They're frustrated," the senior officer told me. He was visibly upset. He wanted to talk, but didn't want his commanders to know he was meeting a reporter. We met in secret in his jeep in a parking lot near Baghdad airport.

"But why now?" I asked. "What's changed now?"

"Some of it has to do with better accountability," he said. "You are hearing more about it because we are looking more closely into the issue of abuse. But I think it's mainly frustration. Some of the soldiers and marines are now back on their second, third, and even fourth rotations. Often they're finding that Iraq is not better off than it was when they left. Actually, it's worse in many cases, and that makes them feel like all the work they did on their last deployments was for nothing, and their fellow soldiers died for no reason."

The soldiers also knew most Americans weren't behind the war anymore. The public had turned on Iraq and wasn't buying the rationale anymore. By the fall of 2006, the Democrats seemed poised to win U.S. congressional midterm elections in November. Iraq was *the* campaign issue. It dominated the debates and talk shows. From Baghdad, it looked like the Democrats were turning failure in Iraq into their success. The worse it got in Baghdad, the more the Democrats attacked President Bush and the Iraq war. It added even more confusion for the soldiers. Here they were fighting dangerous enemies for increasingly unclear reasons and their own compatriots didn't even support the war anymore.

I decided to spend most of the fall of 2006 with the troops, jumping from base to base, embed to embed. I wanted to understand what they thought about the new mission. The new mission: stuck in an Iraqi civil war. I also had a practical motivation. It was the only way left to move. Baghdad had become so dangerous that I could no longer ask Ali and Zohair to go to unfamiliar neighborhoods. Zohair couldn't chase a story in a Sunni area anymore. He'd never come back. Not surprisingly, Ali lost his taste for Sadr City after his kidnapping and torture. And I didn't want him to go back. It had come to a point that I assumed I would have more access to battlefield neighborhoods by traveling with armed U.S. soldiers who go anywhere they please. The troops may have been misled, and were even at times happy to be told what they wanted to hear, but they were always brave. I never saw a single soldier try to refuse a mission.

The first stop was Camp Falcon in Dora, the mixed neighborhood in south Baghdad where Sunni insurgents in Iraqi army uniforms had kidnapped Shiites from their homes in front of unsuspecting American troops.

On one of the first patrols, soldiers from the 1-14 Cavalry found a body thrown by the side of a main road. More fucking bodies. The city seemed to be paved with them. The back hatch of the Stryker slapped the pavement, *ka-chunk*, and we scampered out and surrounded the body. It was a clear blue sunny fall morning. The dead man had just been shot. He was still fresh, on the ground, the troops estimated, for less than twenty minutes. The blood around him was still wet. Blood dries quickly and forms a crispy, filmy crust on top like pond scum. His blood was fanning out red from where he'd been shot, execution style, in the temple. I assumed the body was still warm, although the soldiers didn't touch it. He was roadkill, and you don't check roadkill for its vitals. You just drive by, or, if you have to, scrape it in a pizza box and toss it in the woods.

But the soldiers from 1-14, 3rd Platoon ("Crazy Horse") couldn't do that. They had to follow procedure, even though it didn't mean a damn thing. They had to take photographs, collect evidence, and write a report. Nobody was going to track down this man's killers. He was just another dead guy named Omar. His name was on an ID card in his wallet, along with a photograph of his daughter. She looked about five years old and had dark curly hair and fat cheeks. Omar's name probably killed him. It was a bad name to have. Sunnis were killing Shiites named Ali and Hussein. Shiites were killing Sunnis named Omar and Abu Bakr, names of early caliphs revered by Sunnis. Mohammed and Ahmed were safe names because they were commonly used by both Sunnis and Shiites. Hospital officials said Mohammed and Ahmed were the most common baby names in Iraq in 2006.

The tide had shifted since our last report from Dora. Sunnis were now the targets, and the Shiites, backed up by the Iraqi security forces and their allies in the Mahdi Army, were taking revenge.

An Iraqi police patrol arrived as the soldiers stood around snapping more pictures of Omar and writing down the "likely cause of death," in case the hole in his head wasn't obvious enough. The Iraqi lieutenant commanding the patrol told me he thought police from his station killed Omar.

"What?" I asked, taken aback by his frankness. It was a rare admission. Normally all the Iraqi police ever did when they saw reporters was complain about not having enough equipment, pay, food, or clean uniforms. It was all true, but annoying to hear over and over again. I usually wanted to grab them by the shoulders and yell, "It's your goddamn country! Go sew some uniforms or have your mothers cook if you need to. It's your inept and corrupt government that you were stupid enough to elect that can't provide even the most basic supplies. Enough with the whining for more handouts!"

But this police commander wasn't moaning about low pay or dirty uniforms. He thought the entire police force was broken and wanted the Americans to know it. "Yes, I believe *my* men did *this*," he said, emphatically pointing down at the body, which by now had stopped bleeding and was starting to stick to the road. "*My* men are infiltrated by Shiite militias, and I can't get rid of them," the lieutenant said. "If I report them, they'll kill me."

It was a striking admission and a powerful image. Here was a police officer, a patrol commander, saying, on camera and in front of a body, that his men were overrun by militias. Next to him were American soldiers trying to clean it up and filing reports no one would read.

"What are we doing out here?" I wondered. "How do you tell these soldiers that any of this is making their families safer in Las Vegas, New York, Puerto Rico, or El Paso? It's game over."

Our patrol moved on, now on foot. The soldiers walked through a slum of shacks with plastic sheets for windows. Between the

houses, chickens pecked in mud littered with trash, clumps of toilet paper, and piles of human feces covered in flies. I gagged and almost vomited as I followed them down a cement alley with a groove
cut down the center of the pavement. It was an open sewer, full but
not flowing. Shit and piss and maxi pads and chicken bones just sat
there in rotting little pools, feeding flies that kept landing on my
face and lips.

"Do the soldiers here ever ask themselves, 'Why are we here? Is
this our war anymore?' " I asked a soldier, waving my hand in front
of my mouth so I wouldn't end up swallowing any of the fast little
black flies.

"Oh, yes, all the time," he said. "I ask myself that a lot. We've
been here for so long, and we've done so much, but there's just so
far we can go." As we spoke, the soldier—just a kid of twenty with
clunky military-issue glasses—wasn't looking at me or where he
walked. His eyes scanned windows and rooftops for snipers. He
was so focused, he seemed not to notice as his boots sloshed
through the filth and sent flies swarming up into our faces. One
flew up my nostril and got stuck, nearly in my sinus. I could feel it
squirming and scampering, burrowing toward my brain. I had to
plug my other nostril and blow him out.

We patrolled for several more hours and didn't accomplish a
goddamn thing.

Back at Camp Falcon, the squadron commander, Lieutenant
Colonel Jeff Peterson, 1–14 Cavalry, said he was happy our patrol had
found a body. He didn't want our embed to be sanitized, or censored.
I appreciated that. He wanted us to see what Dora had become.

The next morning, Peterson took us to a place his men called
the "Killing Fields." It was worse than the fly-infested, sewage-
covered slum behind the road where we'd found Omar. The Killing
Fields was a trash dump on the edge of Dora where Shiite militias
dropped the bodies of their victims. It's considered particularly insulting to be dumped in trash to be picked over by dogs. Omar was
thrown from a car and shot. Goodbye Omar. The Killing Fields was
the final stop for real acts of sadism and revenge.

"It's a horrible place to die. It's also a horrible way to die," Peterson said as we walked over piles of tin cans, plastic bags, and what seemed to be ubiquitous clumps of used toilet paper. Peterson explained that most of the victims they found in the Killing Fields were first tortured in a safe house, and then brought here barely alive to be finished off with a coup de grâce.

"We find them sometimes with marks on their back or broken bones," Peterson said. "They are beaten. They drill into all parts of the body, usually the extremities of the body. The legs and arms have been the most common." Peterson said that most of the bodies his men found were blindfolded, and bound at the hands and feet with wire or rubber tubing.

"Some were shot in the groin, had broken arms, and burns on their hands."

Just a year earlier, the brutality would have seemed beyond what I previously thought human beings were capable of doing to one another. Now, it was par for the course.

I wrote in my notes:

> *Shot in groin,*
> *drilled into bodies,*
> *hands burned,*
> *usual stuff.*

I'd heard worse. According to a senior police officer, not far from Dora, Sunni insurgents had recently kidnapped a toddler from a Shiite family that refused to leave the neighborhood. The militants killed the boy, sliced him open, stuffed him with rice, baked him in a restaurant oven, and then served him on a platter on his family's doorstep. He was cooked golden brown. The police officer told me it wasn't the first time militants seemed to enjoy turning their victims into national dishes. His men had pulled one body from the Tigris with a metal rod driven through his rib cage. "They put tomatoes on each side of the metal spike," the officer said. "They turned him into a shish kebaab."

Sheep and goats were grazing amid the trash in the Dora Kill-ing Fields, and children were playing soccer. "We find dead bodies mostly over there," said eleven-year-old Allawi Abdul-Munaem, pointing to a distant trash hill. "I don't know who dumps them. When you are patrolling the area, there are not as many. Before, we found them every day."

Allawi spoke to me like I was a soldier. He assumed I was part of the unit. Iraqis always did that. I often ended up playing translator.

Allawi's friend Mohammed, who had a blue T-shirt pulled over his head, had seen bodies too. "When we came to play soccer, I saw one of them. He was shot three times. Here," he said, pointing to his forehead, "another here that took his eye out, and one in his mouth. His hands were so oily!

"Another guy had his hands tied together like this," Moham-med added, and clapped his wrists together. "One guy was drilled in his head, and then his head was tied with a rope."

"Why do you come here to play if there are bodies?" I asked.

"We come here to see them, 'cause some of them might be re-lated to us. I am an Iraqi," Allawi said. He pointed to an Iraqi flag printed on his shirt. "I'm an Iraqi," he repeated, thumping his chest to make sure I understood.

I turned to Peterson and told him what the children had said in Arabic. "Did you ever think when you came over to Iraq that you would be fighting this kind of war?" I asked.

"I didn't expect that it would materialize in this kind of dump-ing grounds," he said. "There is intimidation and threats, and an attempt to homogenize neighborhoods and force people out of their homes."

"Is it ethnic cleansing?" I asked.

"I don't know if it has reached the level of ethnic cleansing, but it is certainly ethnic conflict. And the dimension of the fight is a lit-tle under the radar and it's hard to stop."

One of Peterson's men, Sergeant Christopher Mills, said he'd found a body stuffed in a sewer pipe. "They'd cut off his knees and cut off half his head. He was pretty rotten when we found him. It was pretty disgusting. It was one of the worst things I have ever seen in my life."

Mills was on his second tour in Iraq. "I didn't really see any bad dead bodies last time I was here," he said. "If I can make this little part of Iraq better at the end of my year here, then I had a good year."

One of the reasons Baghdad had become so brutal was that the Mahdi Army had a new death squad commander every bit as evil as the Sunnis' al-Qaeda–inspired insurgents. The Shiites had their own Zarqawi. They called him Abu Durra. Ali had seen his gruesome work.

Abu Durra started out as a field commander in Moqtada al-Sadr's Mahdi Army in Sadr City. He was a low-level operator with experience in Saddam's special forces. He didn't look like much. He was ugly, squat, and a poor speaker. He inspired no one. But he made up for his shortcomings with ruthless tactics. Abu Durra had risen through the Mahdi Army's disorganized ranks, but broke away when Sadr joined the political process. Abu Durra took the hard line. After the second election, Sadr at least paid lip service to the principle of national dialogue and sharing power with Sunnis. Abu Durra's only mission was to take revenge for the three years of attacks on Shiite mosques and markets.

Ali first saw Abu Durra at a funeral for one of his many relatives in the Iraqi security forces in Sadr City. He was surrounded by about a dozen bodyguards, some wearing Iraqi army uniforms and driving government-issued vehicles with mounted machine guns. The militias were always hand in glove with the government. After the funeral, Abu Durra's men asked Ali, knowing he was a journalist, if he wanted to see "their work." If Ali had asked me for permission, I would have told him not to go.

The next morning Ali told me where he'd been. Unlike Zohair, who smoked, waved his hands, and would jump to his feet while telling stories, Ali was always emotionless. "They said they were going on a mission to Azamiya and Dora," Ali said. "They said, 'We pick up Sunnis in the morning, interrogate them during the day, and kill them at night.'

"We met at midnight on a corner in Sadr City. Four cars pulled up, filled with Abu Durra's men. They drove in a convoy to an open market that was already closed for the night. There was trash in the streets and the fruit and vegetable stands were all shut.

"We stopped the cars and Abu Durra's men took a man out of one of the cars. He was blindfolded and his hands were tied behind his back. They sat him down on the curb and shot him three or four times in the head."

"Then what?" I asked, with the morbid curiosity that draws people to public executions.

"Then they just left his body in the market amid the garbage. After that, the cars drove a few blocks away to another part of the market. They took another man out of the cars. He was like the first man, bound and blindfolded. They shot him in the head a few times and left his body there."

"How many people did they execute while you were with them?" I asked.

"Six or seven."

"And each time, they drove to a new place? Why? Were they worried the police or soldiers would come after hearing the gunshots?" I asked.

"No, they *are* the police and soldiers. They weren't worried about that at all. They were proud of what they were doing. They went from place to place so they would spread out the bodies. They wanted as many people as possible to see what they had done."

"Were they trying to send a message—a warning or threat to Sunnis? Were they trying to say, 'Don't come here, or else?' "

"No, it's not about intimidation. It was their way of saying 'Look at what we have done.' They were proud. It was a way for them to show the people that they were the defenders of justice, that they don't just arrest people and release them like the security services. No, these people make arrests and then carry out the executions. They wanted people to know that."

"Then what happened? The bodies just stayed in the market until it opened?" I asked.

"The police came and collected them in the morning. That is all the police do. They collect bodies," he said, laughing.

I was struck by his laughter. It seemed out of character, and out of place. I was sad to see my friend's emotions so badly skewed that this seemed somehow comical.

"How did all this make you feel?" I asked.

"It made it all seem so easy, that life can be extinguished so easily. One of the men they shot that night was a big man. He was a big, burly guy, but in one second he was dead. I was like, 'That's it? It's over?' He was probably a father and has children, but he can be killed so easily. A dog wouldn't be killed like this."

I put my hand on Ali's shoulder. "You are all going crazy. You are all losing your minds," I said.

"We already have," Ali said.

From what Ali had told me, I wasn't surprised when the patrol left Dora's Killing Fields for an upscale residential street that was now mostly abandoned. A Sunni man told us 60 percent of his neighbors had left the country. Thousands of Iraqis were now leaving every week. The upper class—the doctors, engineers, and businessmen—had escaped to Jordan in 2003 to find higher-paying jobs. Now, anyone who could scrape together $4,000 or $5,000 was escaping to Syria, which had a more relaxed immigration policy and where the cost of living was lower.

Jordan wanted only the elite. Syria, officially a pan-Arab Baathist state, would take in anyone from the Arab world. Iraqis the Americans "liberated" from Saddam were choosing to live in Syria, another Baath party dictatorship.

Iraq's Ministry of Migration said that by October 2006, ethnic fighting had caused 300,000 Iraqis to leave their neighborhoods, and more than one million to escape the country.

The Sunni man in Dora showed me a printed letter from the

Mahdi Army that had been slipped under his door. "Leave your home in seventy-two hours, or you'll end up in the morgue," it said. "They put it in an envelope with a bullet," he explained.

Captain Rowland, the leader of our patrol, tried to reassure the Sunni man. "If you see these gangs of thugs running through the neighborhood, you let me know. Give me a call and we will be here immediately."

Rowland gave him a "tip card" with a phone number to a TOC, tactical operation center, at Camp Falcon and explained they were putting in extra checkpoints throughout Dora. "We are isolating your area to prevent the thugs from coming here," he promised.

But the Sunni man had another plan. "The militias are not afraid of the checkpoints because the police work with them. I have seen gunmen drive through checkpoints, stop, and joke with the police. The American troops are now popular here. It has changed 100 percent. It is the Iranians who are behind this, and now it is the American forces, the occupying forces, who must stop them."

Sunnis started to surround Captain Rowland, pleading to be deputized. "Why don't you give us badges and let us use our guns to protect our own neighborhoods?

"We will stand on the corner with our guns and protect the area from any stranger. That's what we want. We are scared of the forces here operating with the Interior Ministry." They were especially afraid of the Commandos. "When they come with the Americans, we don't have a problem. But when they come by themselves, we don't trust them and don't know if it is a real mission or not. The American forces are not on the streets all the time."

Rowland said U.S. forces were pulling the Commandos out of Dora. It was the opposite of what was supposed to be happening. U.S. generals told reporters Iraqis were taking charge and replacing American troops, but in Dora American troops were replacing Iraqis because they couldn't be trusted.

Back at Camp Falcon, Peterson explained that the ties between the Shiite militias and Iraqi security forces put him in an uncomfortable position. He drew me a diagram on a piece of paper like a football coach explaining a complicated play. "Here's a Sunni mosque," he said, drawing a circle in the center of the paper. "Let's say insurgents are inside and they're being attacked by a Shiite militia. There's a gunfight."

He drew another circle to represent the Shiite militia attacking the Sunni mosque, with lines between them showing how the bullets would be flying back and forth. "The militia then either calls in the Iraqi forces, or the Iraqi forces come on their own. So now, the militias and the Iraqi police are both shooting at the Sunnis in the mosque."

Peterson added a third circle to his diagram to represent the Iraqi forces. Both the militia and the Iraqi security forces were shooting at the Sunnis in the mosque. "Then the Iraqi security forces, who have an official relationship with American troops, call us in for support. We arrive, see gunmen shooting at Iraqi security forces, and intervene."

He added a fourth circle showing the position of U.S. troops. All three groups—the militia, the Iraqi forces, and U.S. soldiers—were now shooting at the Sunnis in the mosque. "If you are a Sunni in the mosque, it looks like the militias, the Iraqi police, and U.S. troops are all working together against you. We obviously don't have a relationship with the militias, but from where they are sitting in the mosque, it looks like we are fighting with them."

"So what do you do?" I asked.

"We pull back."

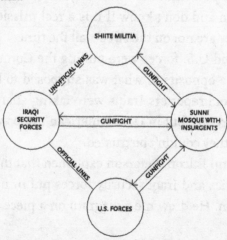

After Dora, we moved to Camp Stryker, one of the giant FOBs at the Baghdad airport. It was a full-service FOB with a big MWR, KBR chow halls, and Poetry Night on Thursdays.

The base also had a Combat Stress Center, a mini–psychiatric ward for soldiers dealing with PTSD, post-traumatic stress disorder. I was shocked that the public affairs officers agreed to let us in with our cameras. They knew we would talk to soldiers about their depression and fears. It was amazing. Soldiers weren't supposed to be depressed. They were always supposed to be "on message." This was going to be completely different. We'd be talking to still-deployed soldiers suffering from PTSD about their intimate feelings. It was a rare opportunity.

The Combat Stress Center didn't look like a medical facility. I half-expected that it would have been painted in soothing pastel colors and filled with stuffed animals, signs with cartoon letters philosophizing "Don't Worry, Be Happy!" and black-and-white posters of babies dressed like adults and kissing on bridges in Paris. Thankfully, the center was as drab and institutional as the rest of the FOB. It was just a few metal trailers linked together with a small gravel smoking area in the back.

In one of the rooms, half a dozen soldiers were gathering for a group therapy session. They sat in chairs in a circle as the counselor dimmed the lights.

Private Russell Kemery looked like he'd been up all night. The skinny twenty-one-year-old from Pittsburgh had tousled, dirty blond hair, bloodshot eyes, and an expression of devastating depression. Kemery sat hunched in his chair, shoulders slouched forward, his feet crossed at the ankles, his hands folded in his lap.

"I hardly eat. If I am okay, one meal a day. Sleep, you know? I either hardly sleep, or I sleep all the time," Kemery told the group. "Sometimes I get a really bad headache that won't go away for five or eight days no matter what I do. You know, heartburn all the time."

There were two other combat soldiers in the circle, men like Kemery who went outside the wire. Next to them were two female soldiers who worked logistics and payroll and never left the FOB. One of the female soldiers was quiet and withdrawn. She looked as if she wanted to hide, didn't make eye contact, and kept fidgeting in her chair. The other woman was agitated and aggressive, snapping at everyone.

The counselor looked stiff and uncomfortable. He didn't like it that our cameras were in the room. The soldiers didn't seem to mind, part of a generation used to watching television shows where people inexplicably feel compelled to tell their most intimate secrets to the nation.

But this was far more serious than Dr. Phil. PTSD can be crippling. The director of the Combat Stress Center said soldiers who failed to cope with their PTSD could have trouble holding down jobs, nightmares, difficulty concentrating, and severe anger. It could ruin their lives. All of the soldiers in the group complained they were having marriage and relationship problems.

The woman who kept fidgeting told the group that the long deployments had ended her marriage. "He would call me, and he wasn't the same person. I didn't know who I was talking to anymore. I couldn't hang with it, and we did have a strong marriage, we did."

The other female soldier tore into her. "So when people say that 'I got divorced 'cause I was deployed, stressed out, whatever,' no! If you have a strong marriage in the beginning, when you get back to the States that marriage should still be intact. It has nothing to do with the fact that you are deployed 'cause I could be on a trip to Jamaica for an entire year and then, what you gonna tell me, that 'I got a divorce 'cause I was in Jamaica'? No. I hate that. I just hate when people say that 'I got a divorce 'cause I was deployed.' Whoever says 'I got divorced 'cause I was deployed,' wrong answer, ain't no way."

The two women had come to the stress management center voluntarily. They wanted therapy to cope with their relationships. Kemery had to be here. He'd been committed. Kemery had been demoted and docked pay for falling asleep on patrol. He had been in the turret of a Bradley and was supposed to have been watching the road. He'd endangered his unit. The other soldiers wanted him out.

"I fell asleep," Kemery confessed to the group. "I was not doing my job, you know? Thank God it was my Bradley commander, my BC, and you know the gunner, they woke me up. They're like, 'You gotta wake up. You gotta stay awake, you know? There's these guys out there planting IEDs on this route. You gotta stay awake.'

"It's because I'm stressed," Kemery said. "I was getting a good eight, ten hours of sleep. That's ample enough sleep, you know? I was getting sleep, but it wasn't the restful sleep."

Kemery said he had other symptoms of PTSD too. He could no longer tolerate listening to his unit constantly talk about the possibility of getting blown up. "We can joke about it, but for some of us, you know, like myself, I don't really wanna hear it. 'Am I gonna get blown up today?' or 'Today is my day to get blown up or get shot.' I don't wanna hear that."

Kemery told me he was also disturbed by what his unit had done. On one of their patrols, his unit had found a suspected insurgent. They arrested the man and strapped him to the front hood of a Humvee, lashing him down on top of a coil of barbed wire. They tied him up like a deer they'd just killed. But the man was still alive, and strapped to razor wire as the Humvee made the bumpy journey back to the base. When the patrol finally arrived, Kemery said the detainee was covered in cuts and gashes.

"There was like, no need to do that," Kemery said.

The therapist offered lame advice for Kemery's sleeping problems. "Keep caffeine intake to a minimum," he said. "Eat fewer sugary foods. Increase fibers, B-complex vitamins, and vitamin C.

"It is pretty much important to eat very healthy," he advised the group, reading from notes. "We have to take care of ourselves and one of the ways of doing this is by eating healthy. We don't need junk food or stuff like that because that might mean gaining weight.

"It is better to do different things such as exercise. Instead of smoking, go out and walk for two miles," he suggested.

Diet and fresh air weren't going to solve Kemery's problems.

His wife already had one foot out the door. "She almost left me because she thought I was doing this for myself to, you know, get kicked out of the army so I could go back to being a civilian."

But Kemery said the hardest part of being in Iraq was losing a friend on patrol. It almost made him snap. "I can't go out there with all this anger built up in me. It could end up with me doing something stupid. I could end up killing someone innocent. They could put me in jail for the rest of my life if I did that. You've gotta learn to let it go."

A PAO (public affairs officer) was sitting in on the meeting. He quietly came up to me, tapped me on the shoulder, and asked in my ear that we not use Kemery's last quote. "I don't want him talking about killing people on the news."

During a break, Kemery went outside for a smoke. It was the first time we were able to speak in private, away from the PAO. Kemery said he no longer believed in the war. "I mean we've done a lot. We've caught a lot of guys on the blacklist. We've done a lot, but now more or less it seems more like a religious war than any type of war to me. I think it's the wrong fight. At the beginning, I thought it was an actual war, you know? When I was in basic, you know, they were like, 'This is what's happening in Iraq right now' and I was like, 'Wow, I need to hurry up and graduate basic so I can get over there' and, you know, be an aid to the cause. Now we don't really know who we're fighting. It's just, we're fighting terrorists. Well, who are these terrorists, you know, these insurgents? Who are they?"

I was stunned by his candor. The soldiers were normally so on message, told that dissent is cowardly and unpatriotic. Kemery clearly didn't care anymore what his unit thought of him. He said they'd been bullying and ostracizing him for months. "People just look at me like I'm worthless, you know? They've looked at me that way pretty much since I got in here, I mean, 'cause I've had problems since I came in. They all look at me: 'Oh, he's worthless, he ain't no good.' Their term for it, you know, is 'a shitbag,' that's the term they use."

While I was interviewing Kemery, a PAO from the FOB's main press office came rushing over. She was out of breath and almost in a state of a panic. She said the commander of Kemery's unit had found out we were filming at the Combat Stress Center and had exploded at her. She was nearly in tears. She had gone out on a limb by agreeing to let us in and film. Now that limb was crashing down. The commander had ordered her to stop us, to seize our tapes, to do whatever it took to kill the story. She said he had gone "totally ballistic" when he found out we were interviewing Kemery, who was damaged goods.

The military generally embedded reporters with the best units, full of gung ho warriors. But here was NBC News trolling the bottom of the barrel, digging for bad news! It seemed to confirm the commander's disdain for the liberal, antiwar media. The PAO didn't know what to do.

She was aware I would never surrender the tapes. Kemery had a genuine, seldom heard, and valid perspective. But I also understood the commander's concerns. It would have been easy for me to string together a few of Kemery's strongest sound bites, find a few other disgruntled soldiers, and make it seem like all the troops in Iraq were depressed, dysfunctional basket cases. It would have been both unfair and untrue. The vast majority of the troops were coping amazingly well.

To balance our report, we went out on patrol with the EOD team (explosive ordnance disposal) from 172th Stryker Brigade. It was one of the best ride-alongs I'd ever done. We bonded immediately with the unit and stayed with them for an entire week. By the end of the embed, we were posing for pictures together and exchanging e-mails. We're not all manipulative bastards searching for a headline at any cost, despite what you might have heard.

The EOD team had one of the most stressful jobs in the military. The men drove around Baghdad in Strykers specifically looking for IEDs. They sought out the most dangerous routes so they could find and disable roadside bombs before they killed other soldiers or Iraqis. It's a dangerous and generally thankless job. Making matters much worse, the soldiers, based out of Fort Wainwright, Alaska, home of America's "Arctic Warriors," had just been extended in Iraq. They had been due to go home after twelve months in theater. But in July, Defense Secretary Donald Rumsfeld gave the order that would keep them in Iraq for another four months.

One soldier told me he had to cancel his wedding. They had all been dreaming about vacations, fishing, hunting, and most of all, tons of "catch-up sex." The troops loved the social networking site MySpace. For months, they'd been setting up hook-ups with young women, starting the moment they landed back in the States. All the romantic plans and fantasies had to be scrapped. Three hundred soldiers were already home with their families, thinking they were done with the deployment, when they were unexpectedly called back to Baghdad for four more months. These men had every reason in the world to hate the world, but they didn't. They found ways to manage their stress within the platoon.

In the back of the Stryker was Christian Wolter, platoon sergeant, 1st Platoon, 562nd Engineer Company. He was older and more mature than the rest of the unit. He was the daddy, the rock. The other soldiers came to Wolter with problems. One of the men had just received a Dear John e-mail.

"We had one soldier whose girlfriend broke up with him," Wolter explained. "He wanted somebody to talk to. I talked to him for a while. He wanted to talk with a chaplain. So we went over, got a chaplain. I don't know what the conversation was after that, but whatever the chaplain said, it seemed to work because the guy is back to normal again. But we definitely keep a close eye on everybody, you know, sleeping habits, eating habits, things like that, making sure that people are acting normal.

"When we heard we were getting extended, you heard some grumbling, but nobody quit, nobody said, 'I'm not going to do this anymore.' Everybody just kinda put their shoulder down and said, 'Okay, this is what we gotta do, so let's do it.' "

Manning the Stryker's cannon was Staff Sergeant Jerami Harris, a good-looking man with short blond hair and an easy smile. He said his nine-year-old daughter, Jazmyne, and six-year-old son, Corbyn, were acting up back home. "My nine-year-old is kinda being rebellious," he said. "Her grades have dropped a little bit, and she's not listening to her mother as much as she usually does."

But Harris had the same grin-and-bear-it attitude as the rest. "I signed up for the army. I've been doing this almost twelve years now. I love my job. We have to take care of each other. It's one big happy family. I mean, if one person gets down, then the other person has to pick his buddy up."

The EOD team had a lot of practice at peer counseling. The platoon has been hit by IEDs thirty-four times. One of the blasts killed two members of the "big happy family."

I asked Harris how that made him feel. He paused and chose his words carefully.

"You gotta have control," he said. "It would be so easy to lash out, but you don't. You gotta realize it's not all the Iraqi people that are bad. If we go out and come in and nothing happens, then it's a good mission. That's how I shut the outside world off in the States and focus on what happens here. Make sure everyone comes back as a whole," Harris said.

After several hours inspecting piles of trash for hidden bombs along Baghdad's airport road, the patrol stopped at a small FOB at Baghdad's old Ministry of Defense. They took a twenty-minute break. It was another way the men coped with stress. The soldiers climbed out of their Strykers, played with stray puppies, and tossed around a Frisbee and Nerf football. When it started to rain, one of the soldiers tucked a yellow puppy under his poncho and fed him a muffin.

The men all carried good-luck charms.

Sergeant Gary Strakansky kept pictures of his wife and newborn son in his breast pocket. "The picture of my son has been in there since he was born in December, and my wife's since I got over here," he said. Strakansky also kept a pair of his wife's panties in another pocket, but he didn't let us film that.

Sergeant Anthony Santos from California wasn't shaving his mustache. "I guess we all carry something, have a little quirk or something, but the mustache is my thing."

The platoon had also rigged an iPod into the Strykers' comms system. They listened to the same ten songs every time they rolled out on a mission. The tenth song was "My Humps" by the Black Eyed Peas. When it came on, they danced. "It's kind of like a squad dance song," one of the soldiers said. "Even the driver dances in his hatch. Now everybody has got to dance because everyone is copying my squad, but it's all right."

There was one enemy, however, that the soldiers said they couldn't tolerate. They hated him more than the insurgents. They called him Jody.

"What is Jody? A Jody is the guy back home with your wife or your girlfriend. That is what a Jody is," Harris explained. "He's the guy hiding in a corner, behind the curtain, or hiding in the closet. How do I feel about Jody? I just hope that I never meet Jody, that's how I feel about it. You never want that to happen to you and you try not to be Jody yourself."

During basic training the soldiers sang cadences to Jody, the work songs they chant to keep time and rhythm as they run and do push-ups.

> *Used to date a beauty queen*
> *Now I date my M16*
>
> *Ain't no use in lookin' down*
> *Ain't no discharge on the ground*
>
> *Ain't no use in going back*
> *Jody's got your Cadillac*
>
> *Ain't no use in calling home*
> *Jody's got your girl and gone*
>
> *Ain't no use in feeling blue*
> *Jody's got your sister too*
>
> *Took away my faded jeans*
> *Now I'm wearing Army greens*

I wrote a blog about Jody for MSNBC.com. It obviously hit a nerve. Within twenty-four hours, we received hundreds of e-mails. Many of the comments were from soldiers and marines who'd met Jody in person.

"I lost my fiancée to Jody while deployed overseas. I received the Dear John letter while aboard the USS *Tarawa*, headed for a joint military exercise with South Korea. Words cannot express the pain and anger I felt at the time. I drowned my depression by crawling into a bottle for a while, but was lucky enough to crawl out again. When we got back to the States, I went home on leave, tracked Jody down, and let my fists do the talking for me. I felt so much better after that, like a great weight had been lifted from me." The e-mail was signed simply, Marine Corps Veteran.

Kyle offered her own unique advice on how soldiers should keep Jody away. "I have an answer for Jody. It's called BOB [battery-operated boyfriend]. Every serviceman that is married or has a girlfriend should buy her BOB before he leaves."

Callie from Bakersfield offered herself for comfort if Jody came knocking. "Any man having a problem with a Jody at home should look me up!!! I'm a woman who'd treat you like the man you are!!! Some women do cherish the man who loves them."

The Cisco Kid wrote to say that Jody also speaks Spanish. "I'm an American-born Hispanic. The term we use here for decades is not Jody but Sancho. That's the guy who goes out with your wife or girlfriend."

Mark from Kansas City offered a confession. "So I guess you could call me Jody. I have to confess that a couple of years ago when the war first started, we would go out to bars and there were all kinds of unattached women that we'd never seen before. Turns out most were attached, but their attachment was serving his country overseas. In all my time going to bars, I'd never had such good luck! I met four or five women who were alone. Most of the time I didn't know that they were wives/girlfriends of servicemen until later on. So am I to blame because I didn't ask? Maybe. I don't know. I do feel kinda guilty about it. So I guess consider this my public confession."

But my favorite was just a one-liner from someone who called himself "greglymon." I agreed with him. "Draft all Jodys!" he wrote.

21

Judge Munir Haddad sat on the edge of a sofa in the living room of his small villa in the Green Zone sipping a fifth cup of bitter Turkish coffee and looking expectantly at his watch. It was nearly midnight on December 29, 2006, but Judge Haddad was dressed in a black three-piece suit, the waistcoat buttoned to the top, his shoes freshly polished. The suit looked a few years old, and his stomach tugged at the vest's buttons. Haddad's suit seemed out of place for such a late hour. He was waiting for a call, dressed to leave at a moment's notice.

Haddad was full of nervous energy, almost giddy with expectation. He looked as if he were about to receive word that he'd won an Oscar or that his wife had just given birth. He had two phones on the coffee table in front of us. He opened and closed them several times, looked at the little screens, and held them up to the light to make sure the batteries were fully charged.

The Iraqi government had chosen Judge Haddad to preside over Saddam Hussein's execution. He was waiting for the call to tell him a car was on its way to pick him up. Saddam's zero hour was approaching, but no one knew exactly when it would finally happen. Saddam was still in American custody at Camp Cropper near Baghdad airport, held in solitary confinement for three years in a small cell with a cot, a table, a few books, a Koran, two washbasins, a prayer rug, two plastic chairs, and a window box full of weeds that he tended like a loving gardener.

Tonight, just four months ahead of his seventieth birthday, Saddam was being transferred in secret to an Iraqi facility with a renovated gallows. The Iraqi government's liaison to the trial, Bassam Ridha, had told me in vivid, breathless detail how Saddam would be led up the metal stairs of the gallows, marched onto a trapdoor on a metal platform fifteen feet above the floor, and have a noose tightened around his throat.

"Saddam will drop and his neck will snap," Ridha said. It would be faster than the "hoist and lift" method used by some of Saddam's hangmen, who pulled their victims off their feet, strangling them to death. Under Saddam, if the rope snapped, you were free. It was a sign of God's intervention. The new Iraqi government wasn't taking chances. Ridha said they had a new, thick rope. "It won't break."

Once Saddam was securely in place at the secret location, U.S. guards would surrender him to Iraqi custody, pull back, and allow Haddad to supervise the hanging, to be witnessed by about a dozen Iraqi government officials. "I could never have imagined Saddam's execution, not even in my dreams," Haddad said. He was a senior judge with the Iraqi Special Tribunal's court of appeals. He was one of the first judges to question Saddam after his capture. It was an honor to oversee the execution. There had been many volunteers.

Haddad didn't smoke. Instead, he talked in an incessant stream of chatter. He pointed out the lamps and books in the square living room. He introduced me to his two children. In our first hour together, he told me he was rich, had survived four assassination attempts, and had been a "brilliant" law student. He had no filter; perhaps it was all the coffee. He said he was a great ladies' man, and that his specialty was veiled women. "I know what to say to them," he boasted. Haddad said he was capable of immense self-discipline and concentration. "I could write a book in three weeks," he said, and looked down again at his watch.

"It could happen at any time and I have to be ready. Right now, right now, I bet Saddam is being moved to the secret location," he said. "It's the former military intelligence headquarters in Kazimiya."

So much for the secret.

It was my first meeting with Haddad. I had only just learned that he'd been picked to oversee the hanging. His identity had been kept secret, also unsuccessfully. It was a scoop. I was with *the* inside man, sitting in his house as he waited for *the* call. I knew I was in the right place. Sometimes, you can just feel it. I decided to stay with Haddad all night until he received the summons.

"Do you see that photograph?" he asked, and waved to his assistant to bring him another cup of coffee. "That's a very rare picture. Do you know why?"

The room was filled with photographs of Iraqi politicians and Saddam Hussein in court.

"That one," he said, pointing to a photo on the wall behind him. In the picture, Saddam was standing in front of a man sitting at a desk in a nondescript white room that looked like it could have been in a prison, hospital, or office building. I'd never seen the photograph before.

"What was he doing?" I asked.

"Saddam was giving a statement. I was taking it," Haddad said proudly. He stood up and walked over to the picture. "That's me," Haddad said, pointing to the man at the desk. "I was sitting and *Saddam* was standing. *He* was standing at attention in front of *me*," he said.

Haddad returned to the couch, sank into it, relishing the moment when the dictator had stood in front of him, like a child in the principal's office.

"Everything is ready," Haddad said. "All of the legal steps have been taken."

Iraq's prime minister, Nouri al-Maliki, had just signed the execution order. "He signed it in red ink," Haddad said. Iraq's president, Jalal Talabani, who opposed the death penalty on moral grounds, had refused to sign it. It was unclear if Maliki had the legal authority to authorize the execution, but he did so anyway.

Maliki had been Ibrahim al-Jaafari's deputy until he unseated the poetry-loving Shiite philosopher to take control of the Dawa party. Jaafari was an intellectual and hopelessly indecisive. Maliki was a party operative, an efficient, decisive bureaucrat. He was also known to be a Shiite hard-liner close to Moqtada al-Sadr and loyal to the Sadr family's ayatollahs and the howza.

As Haddad waited by the phone, Maliki was hosting a reception in another villa in the Green Zone. The party was code-named "the wedding," which was not a particularly stealthy name if you wanted to hide the fact that it was a celebration of Saddam's pending execution. The entire scenario was amazingly bizarre. Saddam Hussein was being held by American forces, his former enemies, while Maliki, the leader of the political party that tried to assassinate him, was celebrating in the Green Zone, Saddam's former palace complex. It was somehow poetically tragic, like one of the fantastic tales of the *Arabian Nights*.

If you had foretold that one day American troops would occupy Baghdad and that, in the name of democracy, supporters of Saddam's Iranian-backed assassins would convict him in a makeshift courtroom in the Baath party's former headquarters and sentence him to death specifically for cracking down on the village where the assassination attempt took place, I think the only person who would have believed it would've been Saddam himself. He believed in fortune-tellers, soothsayers, twists of fate, and the fables of power, war, and intrigue that have been told about Baghdad for centuries, evidently because they come true.

I waited with Haddad for another hour until our security consultants said it was time to go. I knew I was pushing it. They were like our chaperones and always made me feel like a naughty child. I increasingly resented them. They'd trapped us in a cycle of dependency. Would we be covered by health insurance if we fired them?

If we got hurt and didn't have security, we'd look irresponsible. I wanted to stay with Haddad, but accepted that it was getting late. American troops were about to close the bridges and checkpoints to the Green Zone. The castle's walls were shutting and we could be stuck in the Green Zone for the night. I needed to get back to the bureau at the Hamra to be close to our satellite uplink so I could broadcast that Saddam was dead as soon as the execution was carried out. Haddad promised to call me when it was done.

Back at the bureau, I paced and drank cup after cup of Nescafé with plenty of sugar. It was about 2 A.M. Baghdad time, 6 P.M. EST, and NBC was going crazy. When would it happen? How would we know? Who could confirm it? We'd interrupt programming and go to Special Events coverage. Campbell Brown, filling in for Brian Williams, and the president of the network were on standby and could be on air in seconds. I just needed a phone call, and to be right.

Iraqi television stations were broadcasting their own version of special coverage. It was more like Super Bowl Sunday. A Shiite TV station aired nothing but clips of Saddam-era abuses and mass graves. One station created a graphic of Saddam with a noose by his neck. Another channel broadcast pictures of Saddam's face in the crosshairs of a gun. The government's attitude had long been clear. It wanted Saddam to swing. This was as close to a public execution as the Americans were going to allow.

As I paced and gulped Nescafé, I gathered up my notes from the Saddam trial and went to our "live shot location," a little studio we'd built on one of the hotel's balconies. I was plugged in, notes and phone in hand, earpiece in, microphone on, ready to go.

It was a freezing cold night. As the hours passed, I shivered and made what must have been a hundred calls. I dialed Haddad, his assistant, and his driver like a stalker. I wanted to have the first confirmation that Saddam was dead.

I watched the sunrise from the balcony. Haddad told me the execution would likely take place just after the dawn call to prayer. The timing was important. A major Muslim holiday, Eid al-Adha, was starting that morning. Eid al-Adha is the Muslim Feast of the Sacrifice, when sheep are slaughtered to commemorate God's demand that Abraham sacrifice his son as a test of faith.

But in Iraq, Shiites and Sunnis celebrate holidays on different days. At sunrise, Eid had just started for Sunnis. Shiites still had another twenty-four hours. The government had decided to execute Saddam on the first day of the Sunni Eid, but before the Shiite Eid. It was highly insensitive—and symbolic. The government was killing Saddam on the day that more than 85 percent of the world's Muslims were celebrating the Feast of the Sacrifice. Saddam was the sacrifical beast. It seemed like another chapter from the *Arabian Nights*.

As the sun spread over Baghdad, I heard the lyrical call to prayer from my perch on the Hamra balcony.

"The call to prayer has just started," I told New York down the microphone. It was now nearly 6 A.M. Baghdad time, almost 10 P.M. in New York. "It could happen anytime now."

Campbell was in the studio, ready to go.

As I waited, I thumbed through my notes, preparing for questions she might ask.

The trial had been both fascinating and deadly. Three defense lawyers had been assassinated, including one I'd interviewed the day before he was shot dead. He told me he knew he was going to die.

As I'd suspected, Chief Judge Rizgar Mohammed Amin, the gentleman professor from Kurdistan, hadn't lasted long. He resigned after only two months on the bench, citing political pressure. Amin had been savaged in the local press, accused of being too soft on Saddam. The judge who replaced him, Ra'uf Rashid Abdul Rahman, got the message. He refused to allow Saddam to make his long, often incomprehensible tirades.

After the first few trial sessions, American advisors installed a kill switch on the judges' bench. Whenever he wanted, Judge Abdul Rahman could push the button and turn off Saddam's microphone. He used it so frequently, bleeping out Saddam's words and entire speeches, that his testimony was often difficult to follow. It was like listening to an Eddie Murphy stand-up routine broadcast on Saturday morning network television, censored beyond recognition.

When the defense lawyers, and once even Saddam himself, decided to boycott the trial, Judge Abdul Rahman continued the proceedings in their absence. As the trial progressed, Saddam seemed increasingly despondent and uninterested. The bags under his eyes grew deeper, his beard wilder, and his once smart Turkish suits looked increasingly crumpled and ill-fitting. In the final days, even Saddam's lawyers seemed to lose interest. During a witness's testimony, I watched one of his lawyers doodle on a stack of notes for fifteen minutes without looking up.

I was in court on November 5, 2006, when Saddam was sentenced to death. Like Saddam's case from the start, the timing was highly political. Since his capture, Saddam was a prop, a conquered beast, King Kong, brought out to amaze and entertain the masses. In July 2004, three days after taking office, Prime Minister Ayad Allawi tried to establish his bona fides by hauling Saddam into court. In October 2005, the next prime minister, Ibrahim al-Jaafari, carted out Saddam to soothe and reward his divided nation after the constitutional referendum. But in November 2006, it was the Bush administration that needed a Saddam boost.

Saddam Hussein was sentenced to death two days before the U.S. congressional midterm elections. The Republicans were getting creamed in the polls and looked like they were going to lose both houses of Congress. Yet again, Saddam was dragged out for political theater. The day before the sentencing, we spoke with a diplomat at the U.S. embassy in Baghdad, asking for an update on timing. When did the embassy expect it would happen?

"We're doing everything we can to make sure they're done by the midterm elections," he said. "We really hope they can do it by then." Then the diplomat realized what he had said and had second thoughts. "But don't report that," he added. "This is entirely an Iraqi process."

On the day of his sentencing, Saddam walked into the court-room like a tired old man. Guards held each of his arms. The gleam in his eyes was gone.

Judge Abdul Rahman got right down to business. He quickly read a list of crimes committed against the people of the village of Dujail, including torture through electric shocks, beatings, and forced enemas, "unlawful imprisonment," and "willful killing." He read the list in an emotionless, perfunctory way. It was as if he had a dozen more cases to get through that morning.

As Judge Abdul Rahman read the death sentence Saddam started to shout, but without passion. "Long live the people! Down with the occupiers and spies!" he yelled. It looked almost staged and stale, as if Saddam and the judge were actors playing roles that no longer inspired them.

"Take him out of here," the judge ordered the bailiffs, waving his hand dismissively, as if to say, take out this trash.

Saddam couldn't tolerate being touched or manhandled. As the guards took his arms, he yelled, but now for real. "Don't twist my arms!" he growled. One of the guards stood in front of Saddam and smiled in his face, slowly and deliberately chewing on a piece of gum. It was his moment to face the dictator and lord it over him. Saddam looked at the judge, the fire back in his eyes. "Go to hell!" he said.

Abdul Rahman didn't explain how he reached the verdict, or what evidence he'd used to convict Saddam. It was all over in less than an hour.

After that, the Iraqi government wanted blood, fast. Maliki promised that Saddam would hang before the New Year, less than two months away. The Eid holiday and Talabani's refusal to sign the death warrant were the only obstacles, both now clumsily over-come.

The Shiite-run TV stations were the first to break the news that Saddam was dead. They'd obviously received calls from Haddad or someone else in the execution chamber. When three Iraqi channels reported Saddam's death, we went with the story. It was about

6:15 A.M. on December 30 in Iraq, 10:15 P.M. on the 29th in New York, when Campbell broke into network programming for our Special Report from Baghdad, ironically interrupting NBC's drama *Law & Order.*

A few minutes later, one of our translators, Atheer Khatan, managed to speak with a witness, one of Maliki's advisors. Maliki himself had decided not to attend the execution. Atheer is the only self-proclaimed atheist I've ever met in Iraq. As a teenager, he was briefly attracted to Sunni fundamentalism. He joined what might be described as a gang. Mostly, they would hang out and interpret the Koran. It raised the suspicions of Saddam's security forces and, like so many, Atheer was arrested and tortured. His interrogators drilled holes in each of his shins with a power drill. The metal bit bored through the bone and left two perfectly round scars the size of pencil erasers, but amazingly no permanent damage.

Atheer came running down to the live shot as soon as he hung up the phone. "I spoke with a witness," he said, out of breath. Atheer smoked too much. "The guy, he was standing next to Saddam's body. He said, 'The son of a bitch is dead! He's at my feet now.' " Atheer said he could hear people cheering and dancing in the background. "It sounded like there were a few dozen people in the room. They were all yelling and shouting. It sounded like they were having a party."

It was a major development. We went back on air. Saddam was dead, but the execution had gone badly. A few hours later I managed to get Haddad on the phone.

"I can't talk now. Come back to my house," he said.

When I saw Judge Haddad he looked embarrassed. "It was ugly," he said. "They started to mock Saddam as he was standing on the gallows, waiting to be hanged."

Haddad said he and the chief prosecutor, Munqith al-Faroon, had tried to stop several of the fourteen of Maliki's advisors and half a dozen guards in the room from jeering Saddam.

"One of the guards shouted 'You destroyed Iraq!' " Haddad said. "It was not right. I said we needed to be professional. But they wouldn't stop."

"How was Saddam? Did he say anything? What did he do?" I asked.

"Saddam was very brave," Haddad told me. "I didn't think he would be brave like that, a man facing execution. It is a difficult thing. We thought he would beg for his life, or cry, or, you know, wet his pants. But he didn't. He was very brave."

Haddad said the guards were shouting out Moqtada al-Sadr's name, chanting: "Moqtada! Moqtada! Moqtada!"

"It was wrong," Haddad said. He told me that Iraq's national security advisor, Moufaq al-Rubaie, had asked Saddam why he killed the Grand Ayatollah Sayyid Mohammed Baqir al-Sadr, Moqtada al-Sadr's father-in-law, and the ideological founder of the Dawa party. He was executed by Saddam in 1980 for defending Iran's Ayatollah Khomeni and his Islamic Revolution. Mohammed Baqir al-Sadr was also a teacher of Ibrahim al-Jaafari, and Hezbollah's leader, Hassan Nasrallah.

I could imagine Saddam on the platform of the gallows, surrounded by executioners shouting the name of the leader of an Iranian-backed militia, and being asked why he killed a Shiite ayatollah. He'd been brought to the death chamber by the Americans. We had been used. Saddam must have died convinced that he was correct in believing that Iran, Shiite militias, and the Americans were all conspiring to kill him and destroy Iraq. I am sure he died believing himself to be a victim and a patriot.

Haddad admitted that while he tried to stop the other witnesses from taunting Saddam, he was also carried away by the moment. "As Saddam was about to drop, I said, 'This is for my brother,'" Haddad told me.

Haddad said his brother was killed by Saddam's security forces along with more than two dozen other relatives. I finally understood why he'd been chosen to oversee the execution. It was victims' justice.

Haddad walked me outside, where a new car was parked in front of his villa. It was an armored sedan with a cracked windshield. Haddad said Maliki had given him the hand-me-down vehicle as a reward for supervising the hanging.

Back at the bureau, I told Zohair, who knew something about executions himself, what I'd been told. He wasn't surprised. "The Kazimiya military intelligence headquarters was famous for executing Dawa party members. Many Dawa people were killed there."

Saddam's life had come full circle. Maliki's party had tried to assassinate him in Dujail in 1982 and failed. Now in power and backed by American forces, the Dawa party finished the job, making sure Saddam was tried for the relatively minor Dujail case—almost insignificant compared to his genocidal Anfal campaign against the Kurds—sentenced by a tough judge, and hanged in the same prison where Dawa party members were executed.

All day, I reported that Saddam had been taunted and jeered in his final moments. My stories didn't go over well with some people in the States. Right-wing bloggers immediately attacked me. Why was I crying for Saddam? He never gave his victims a trial at all. Saddam's execution was supposed to be a "good news" story, but yet again the freedom-hating media were determined to turn it into a scandal. They said I wanted to make the Bush administration look bad. I was anti-Republican and a liberal. Other e-mails were considerably less kind, and more colorful. I honestly couldn't have cared less about helping the Democrats or hurting the Republicans. It never crossed my mind. I was seven thousand miles away, busy with Iraq. As far as I was concerned, domestic politics were somebody else's problem. Tim Russert covered politics for us. He could have it.

The criticism stopped that night when a cell phone video of the execution aired on al-Jazeera. The shaky, two-minute, thirty-six-second video was a catastrophe for the Iraqi government and the Bush administration. In the video, Saddam looked oddly calm and slightly bewildered as he shuffled up to the gallows, his ankles in shackles. He was carrying his Koran, dressed in a black coat, white shirt, black pants, and black shoes. Saddam had prepared for his final moment, dying his hair, trimming his salt-and-pepper beard, and polishing his shoes.

The executioners wore leather coats and ski masks with gnarly holes cut out for eyes. They looked like terrorists, and cowards. Wearing a mask is considered a disgrace in the Arab world. If you are proud and in the right, why hide your face? Saddam looked like a victim surrounded by masked insurgents. For me, the most startling part of the video was how cooperative and dignified Saddam seemed. He never struggled. He politely but firmly refused to wear a hood. He wouldn't be blindfolded. He did allow the guards to tie a scarf around his neck. They told him it would prevent the thick noose dangling from the ceiling from tearing his skin and disfiguring his body. It didn't work.

Saddam stepped forward onto the platform and bowed his head, allowing the guards to put the rope around his neck. He didn't shake or tremble.

Suddenly one of the guards yelled out, "Moqtada! Moqtada! Moqtada!"

Another could be heard on the video praising the late Grand Ayatollah Sayyid Mohammed Baqir al-Sadr.

Saddam, the man Iraqis said no one could look in the eye, stared down the executioners. "Is this your manhood?" he asked, and smiled.

Then Saddam started to pray, reciting the *shahada*, the proclamation of faith Muslims hope will open the gate of paradise before they die. "There is no god but God, and Mohammed is His prophet," he said.

But the executioner didn't let Saddam finish his prayer. As Saddam repeated the *shahada*, a guard pulled the trapdoor open. "Mohammed" was his final word.

The crowd erupted in celebration. They were taking pictures, happy snaps, and the camera flashes gave the room the eerie, slow-motion effect of a strobe light.

"The tyrant has fallen," one of the onlookers shouted.

"Let him swing for three minutes," another voice called out as the video showed a close-up of Saddam's face as he swung from the rope.

The video spread on the Internet. In less than twenty-four hours, it had more than a million hits on YouTube. The site gave the video a four-star rating out of a possible five. It was the most widely watched execution in history.

Al-Jazeera hosted back-to-back guests who criticized the timing of the execution as a deliberate insult to Sunnis. Some were calling Saddam the Shiites' Eid sacrifice, slaughtered like a sheep. The network's more pro-American rival, al-Arabiya, gave airtime to Iraqi Shiite politicians to justify the hanging. It wasn't surprising. One of al-Arabiya's Iraq correspondents was one of Maliki's relatives.

Reaction on the streets in the Arab world was muted. There were only a handful of small protests in the West Bank (many Palestinians loved Saddam for having launched Scud missiles at Tel Aviv during the 1991 Gulf War) and near Saddam's hometown of Tikrit.

Libya took the most dramatic steps, declaring three days of mourning, ordering flags lowered to half-staff, and canceling all Eid celebrations.

Walid Abi-Mershed, a senior writer at the pan-Arab *Asharq al-Awsat* newspaper, said most Arabs hated Saddam and weren't prepared to demonstrate for him, but deeply resented the way he was "lynched." "There was resentment for making a TV show out of killing the head of a state," he said. "It was viewed in the Arab world as some kind of a belated assassination of a leader. He was a dictator. We don't argue about it. Everybody knows this. But showing it to the public in Arab society that still has tribal feelings and religious feelings was not at all a good idea.

"Why did they take the decision to hang Saddam Hussein on the first day of the most revered religious feast in the Muslim and Arab world? Why not postpone it a couple of days at least?" Abi-Mershed asked.

"Let us not forget that the Sunnis are not yet accepting that they are losing power in a country that they have governed since World War I, since 1918," he went on. "It's a long time to run a country by one establishment, and then this establishment is losing its grip on power, all of a sudden, because of a foreign intervention. So I don't think the stability of Iraq has been enhanced by the hanging of Saddam. Maybe to the Iraqi government, they were getting rid of an ex-dictator, but now they have a bigger issue on their hands. They have a martyr."

Most of my friends in the Arab world had the same reaction to the video of Saddam's execution. It reminded them of a movie.

The Lion of the Desert is one of the most popular, iconic films in the Middle East. It's the Arab equivalent of *Gone With the Wind*, or *Casablanca*. Everyone has seen it. *The Lion of the Desert* tells the story of Omar al-Mukhtar, a Libyan nationalist who fought Italian colonialists until they hanged him in 1931. Mukhtar's execution is the most famous scene in the movie. Mukhtar, played by Anthony Quinn, dies with composure and dignity on the gallows. Saddam seemed to show a similar stoicism. Perhaps he was even thinking of the movie as he prepared to die. If Saddam were shot in a toll booth, most Americans would have thought of *The Godfather*. Instead, he died coolly on the gallows, so Arabs thought of *The Lion of the Desert*. After the execution, Egyptian television aired *The Lion of the Desert* several nights in a row. Libyan leader Muammar al-Qaddafi promised to erect a statue of Saddam in Tripoli next to one of Omar al-Mukhtar.

The Mahdi Army and Maliki's government instantly knew they'd made a mistake and promised to investigate the execution. Moufaq al-Rubaie (who got on the next plane to London) told me over the phone that radical guards were to blame and that they would be punished. "I think these people are guards, which belonged to the Ministry of Justice. You know the militias, the Mahdi Army or other militias, have managed to infiltrate the security institutions," he said, calling the mob scene "disgusting."

It was an odd change of heart. After the execution, but before the video emerged, Rubaie had told British Sky News that the hanging had gone smoothly. "We followed methodically the international standards," he said. "Saddam was respected throughout when he was alive and when he became a body."

But the attempt at a cover-up was thin. The government didn't really seem to care that the execution was a farce. While al-Jazeera, which tends to be anti-Shiite, spent days analyzing the execution, Iraqi Shiite TV stations aired comedies.

After the video emerged, the Americans were scrambling to disentangle themselves from the mess. Ambassador Khalilzad said he'd advised Maliki to postpone the hanging by two weeks. Even U.S. military commanders seemed somehow sad. Saddam had earned their respect. Military spokesman Major General Caldwell said, "This is a sovereign nation and they made the decisions they made. We as a coalition force would have done things differently."

Caldwell described how at 5:30 A.M., U.S. troops handed over Saddam to the Iraqi government. He was in Iraqi custody for only forty-five minutes. Caldwell said Saddam even thanked his American guards as they parted. "He was dignified as always. He was courteous as he always had been to his U.S. police guards," Caldwell said.

But the most revealing statements came from Saddam's American nurse, Master Sergeant Robert Ellis. In an interview with the AP, Ellis said his job was to check on Saddam twice a day and write status reports on his condition. Ellis said Saddam believed cigars and coffee kept his blood pressure down, and that it appeared to work. Saddam would often insist that Ellis smoke with him.

"Saddam was at peace a long time ago, you know way before [he was hanged], because he never complained about anything," Ellis told the AP. "One thing he talked about was his little girl and how, when he used to read her bedtime stories, he'd give her half a Tums when she had an upset stomach. He didn't talk much about the boys."

But Ellis said Saddam did complain if he felt he wasn't being shown respect. "A door to the room where he was kept in had two slots. One at the top where you could see his eyes and one at the bottom where they'd put the food through. And he resented that because he felt like he was being treated like an animal and he kind of went on a hunger strike and I went to talk to him and he said,

'I'm not objecting to the food. I'm objecting to being fed through the slot in the door like a lion.' "

Ellis said Saddam spent his final days reading, writing, and feeding birds during his forty-five-minute daily walk in an exercise yard. He said that when he told Saddam he had to leave Iraq for the United States because his brother was ill, Saddam hugged him and said *he* would be his brother. Saddam, Ellis said, had once asked him why the United States invaded Iraq, saying the laws in his country were fair and the weapons inspectors didn't find anything.

"I told him that was politics, soldiers don't get caught up into politics," Ellis said.

I was amazed by Ellis's interview. Saddam Hussein, the butcher of Baghdad for twenty-four brutal years, died a hero, oddly respected by his American captors. It seemed possible only in the land of the *Arabian Nights*.

2007

THE SURGE

22

At the start of 2007, the Bush administration was facing a failed war in Iraq. The much-trumpeted two elections and constitutional referendum—purple-finger democracy—had produced an untrustworthy, sectarian government backed by Iran. Iran had known how to play local politics far better than Washington. There were 130,000 increasingly frustrated American troops in Iraq whose marriages were falling apart, or being picked apart by Jodys. The soldiers were fighting for a fourth year alongside unreliable allies against invisible enemies. More than three thousand American troops were dead, and ten times as many were injured. Conservative estimates said the military operations cost U.S. taxpayers $2 billion a week. A hundred Iraqis were being butchered and blown up each day in increasingly creative and abhorrent ways.

On a patrol in January 2007 in Ghazilya in west Baghdad with the military police, the MPs, the "mud puppies," I saw the body of an Iraqi man who'd been doused with acid and then shot in the back of the head. The killers had poured the acid on the man's face. It melted away one of his eyes and both of his lips, exposing his teeth like fangs. It looked like he was wearing a smiling, ghoulish

Halloween mask. The horrifying remains were in the back of an
Iraqi police pickup truck smeared with so much dried blood it
looked like the cops had been hauling joints of beef. The body and
truck were swarming with black flies.

"Don't let them land on you," one of the MPs told me. "They
love to feast on dead bodies." He carried a swatter in his Humvee,
along with Gatorade, Pop-Tarts, a copy of *FHM* magazine, tins of
chewing tobacco, and extra grenades. He'd painted smiley faces on
the tips of the grenades with a red Magic Marker.

By early 2007, more than three million Iraqis had escaped the
country, most of them to Syria, Jordan, and Iran. The refugee crisis
was breeding more frustration and extremism, and creating a new
pool of recruits for al-Qaeda.

On a windy night in the harsh desert cliffs outside Damascus, I
visited a club called the Lighthouse. The nightclub was a boxy white
building on a hilltop with a big parking lot out front. It looked like a
strip joint or Thai massage parlor on one of the back streets in Las
Vegas, the kind of place where bikers, truckers, and traveling sales-
men go alone at two in the afternoon after having lunch at a $6.95,
all-you-can-eat prime rib buffet, and where aging waitresses dance
topless after pouring pints of Coors Light. The Lighthouse was big,
square, and freshly painted, and screamed out, "Good times here!"
The building was covered in colored lights. Every few minutes, a
giant strobe light on the roof flashed to attract customers in passing
cars. There was a lot of competition. Starting in 2006, dozens of
clubs like the Lighthouse had opened on this desert strip. It was
Damascus's new red-light district.

Each club had a billboard outside showing a heavily made-up,
slightly pudgy woman with white fleshy arms and dyed blond hair
with black roots. The women in the pictures were all striking "sexy
poses," holding back their hair, pursing their lips, or running fin-
gernails down their craned necks. You could almost smell the cheap
perfume the women wore as the photos were taken, computer-
enhanced to buff out wrinkles and pimples, and blown up billboard
size.

But inside the Lighthouse, there was nothing sexy about the women at all. They were young girls—most looked around fifteen—parading on an elevated stage as a fat singer with acne scars wearing a shiny suit wailed out songs into speakers turned up so loud they crackled and hissed. The girls, dressed in tight belly-dancing costumes with turquoise, pink, and topaz sequins and matching ribbons in their hair, weren't even dancing. They marched in circles like prisoners in a small exercise yard, circling counter-clockwise on the stage. You could have attached them to a grinding wheel and made flour. Occasionally, some of the girls would shake their shoulders or shimmy their breasts for a few dozen middle-aged men from Syria, Kuwait, and Saudi Arabia sitting at tables around the stage.

One girl with a yellow sash in her black hair had a gold earring attached to a chain that draped across her cheek and connected to a stud in her nose. Some of the girls looked six or seven years old and wore tight jeans and T-shirts. They danced a little too, but were clumsy. Some of the other girls held the little girls' hands so they wouldn't fall down in their high heels. The club was as brightly lit as a gas station convenience store. The fluorescent lights were turned up full blast, yellow and sickly. The men wanted to see what was for sale. Nearly all of the girls were Iraqi refugees.

I sat at a front-row table with producer Madeleine Haeringer, cameraman Bredun Edwards, a photographer friend, Kate Brooks, and our local Syrian fixer who'd miraculously talked the club owner into letting us in to film and take pictures. He actually thought it would be good advertising.

Our table, draped in a red cloth, was pushed up against the stage. Waiters in black blazers brought us bowls of viciously salty popcorn and overpriced glasses of Johnnie Walker Black Label and arak. The owner also gave us a stack of about three hundred bills—play money printed by the club—to toss at the dancing girls. At nightclubs in Egypt, customers throw real money at the dancers, handfuls of ones or even five-dollar bills. Here it was all for show. For $50, the club gave you a bag of money, hundreds of bills, so you could make a big show of it, pretending to be spending sacks of cash.

The men at the Lighthouse seemed to love it. They puffed out their chests and threw fistfuls of the fake money at the girls, as if they had cash to toss into the wind. It left a mess, a constant ticker tape of dirty notes. Young boys with quick hands crawled on the floor, snapping up the play money. When the greasy-faced singer crooned songs praising the "resistance of Falujah!" or "the martyr Saddam Hussein!" the customers, including Syrian intelligence officers and gangsters, would cheer and stuff the faded bills down the girls' costumes. It was child abuse. It made me furious.

The girls were the daughters of Iraqi engineers, professors, and lawyers, anyone who had enough money to escape Iraq but couldn't afford the relatively high cost of living in a foreign country. They had rent to pay and furniture to buy, everything from scratch. Syria had allowed Iraqis in but refused to let them work. Local laws prohibited Iraqis from holding jobs. Syria already had about 20 percent unemployment before the influx of refugees. If the government allowed the 1.5 million Iraqis who'd just arrived to work, the economy might collapse. Most of the refugees lived on savings. When the money ran out, some were forced to send their daughters to do "unofficial work" like "dancing" in clubs like the Lighthouse, under the radar, all cash.

I managed to speak to one of the girls as she walked past our table on her way to the bathroom. She looked about fourteen but acted sassy and flirtatious, shoulders back, chest out, winking at men as she passed them like an old Playboy Bunny. She told me her name was Dunya and that she was from Mosul. When I said I was a journalist and wanted to tell her story, she pulled a cell phone from the top of her dress—they all kept mobiles in their bras—and gave me her phone number.

"Call me at 8:30 A.M.," she said.

"Eight thirty? It's already almost three in the morning."

"Yes. Call me at 8:30. I want you to speak to my father."

I was surprised. At seedy belly-dancing clubs in Egypt, if a customer—usually construction workers from Upper Egypt—wants to spend the night with one of the dancers, he has to negotiate with the owner. It can take days. If someone wanted to meet Dunya for "a date," he had to negotiate with her father. It seemed vile. Her father, a refugee, had now become his daughter's pimp.

I called Dunya a few hours later. She answered the phone and passed it to her dad.

"Good morning. I want to interview your daughter for a story I am doing about Iraqi refugees," I said. "You are more than welcome to come and be present during the interview."

He refused. He told me he didn't want to attract attention and that a TV interview wasn't worth the hassle. Dunya seemed disappointed, and promised to find a few of her friends for me to talk to on camera.

We went back to the Lighthouse for the next three nights trying to find someone who'd let us tape an interview. Eventually, one of the older girls, about twenty-three, agreed. Her hands shook as she chain-smoked throughout the interview, literally lighting one cigarette from the last. She told us how she'd been raped and often went unpaid.

I asked the owner of the Lighthouse, who said he employed seventy girls, if he thought what he was doing was exploitation.

"No, this is not abuse, this is work. They are paid for it in a normal way, like any artist," he said. "Most of the Iraqi refugees cannot work, they don't have jobs. These girls are the breadwinners. So the girls work in a nightclub, which is better than having a secret job that would be bad," he said. A "secret job" would be trolling the streets, where the girls could be beat up.

"How much do they make?" I asked.

"From $20 to $30 a day is the average wage," he said. "It depends on how she looks. When the clients throw money, if she is cute and they throw more money at her, then she will make more that evening. Some can make as much as $40 a night." He didn't mention how much they made from clients outside the club.

The owner, like the customers at the club, told me he blamed the Americans for the refugee crisis. The real criminal, he claimed, was the American war. It was a dubious argument from a dubious man, but he believed it. As I sat there watching six-year-olds shimmy and stumble in high heels as a singer praised the fighters in Falujah, I thought: "The next terrorist attack in the United States is going to be carried out by an Iraqi refugee. A new generation of suicide bombers is going to come from here. It will be one of these girls' brothers or fathers." I had been in Iraq for four years and I was starting to think like an Iraqi. If I were from Baghdad, forced to leave my country because of a Shiite or Sunni death squad that didn't exist before the war, and had watched my sister forced into prostitution, I might want revenge too.

But in Washington, President Bush was selling the war as a fight to spread moderation. It wasn't working. You can't beat and displace people into being moderates. Politically, he was getting hammered. The war had cost his party control of both houses of Congress. The Iraq Study Group, a bipartisan commission led by foreign policy veterans, former secretary of state James Baker III, and ex-congressman Lee Hamilton, called for a new strategy. Their eighty-four-page recommendation, *The Iraq Study Group Report: The Way Forward—A New Approach*, called for the troops to pull back to bases, Iraqi forces to stabilize their own country, and sweeping diplomacy from Tehran to Jerusalem.

"U.S. forces seem to be caught in a mission that has no foreseeable end," the report said. "The United States should embark on a robust diplomatic effort to establish an international support structure intended to stabilize Iraq and ease tensions in other countries in the region. This support structure should include every country that has an interest in averting a chaotic Iraq, including all of Iraq's neighbors—Iran and Syria among them. Despite the well-known differences between many of these countries, they all share an interest in avoiding the horrific consequences that would flow from a chaotic Iraq, particularly a humanitarian catastrophe and regional destabilization."

But the president seemed to have other plans. On January 11,

2007, he announced what came to be called the "the surge." Bush ordered an extra thirty thousand troops to Iraq, bringing the total to over 160,000. It was a white-knuckle decision. In blackjack terms, Bush decided to double down on what looked like a losing hand.

On Sunday, February 18, 2007, I was in Washington for an episode of *Meet the Press* with Tim Russert to discuss the surge. I thought the strategy would be a military success. U.S. troops have never had a problem winning street fights in Iraq. If you put more soldiers on the ground, you'll win more fights and the streets will be safer. That part of the surge was simple. But I told Russert I worried that the Iraqi government didn't have the same long-term interest as the administration. I thought the surge would be a Band-Aid. It would stop some of the bleeding, an urgent necessity, but Iraq needed complete reconstructive surgery. The surge would buy some time, but then what?

After *Meet the Press,* I flew from Washington to New York City, where I was working on a documentary for MSNBC about my experiences in Iraq.

At 8:30 the next evening, Monday, I received an unexpected e-mail on my BlackBerry. It was from Gordon Johndroe, a spokesman for the National Security Council. The e-mail said, "Richard . . . didn't know you were in the States this week. Do you want to come down to the White House and see some of our Iraq and Mideast policy people? Gordon."

I was surprised to have been contacted by the White House. I'd spoken to Johndroe only once on the phone from Baghdad, and rarely had access to policymakers in Washington. I wrote Johndroe to say I would be back in D.C. on Thursday to tape Russert's show on CNBC. Again, the topic was the troop surge. I asked Johndroe if the meeting could wait until then, and who I would be seeing. "Is it [Stephen] Hadley [the national security advisor]?" I asked.

"I'd like to set you up with J.D. Crouch, the deputy national security advisor. Hadley will be out of town. Does sometime after 3 P.M. work for you?" Johndroe asked. "Come to the West Wing lobby."

On Thursday morning, February 22, I flew back to D.C. We finished taping Russert's CNBC show around eleven, earlier than I'd expected. As usual after the show, Russert served elaborate snacks. We sat in the studio eating boiled shrimp, cheese and crackers, crudités, and fried crab cakes. I sent Johndroe a BlackBerry, asking if I could come by the White House before three to try to catch an earlier shuttle back to New York.

"No," he wrote back almost immediately. "The president would like to meet you and he's not back from North Carolina until three. Come to the WW lobby a little after three and maybe we'll start earlier."

"Tim, take a look at this," I said.

"Really?" he said, looking down at my BlackBerry. "They are really reaching out."

"What should I do?" I asked.

"Be careful. Don't tell them anything you wouldn't broadcast. This will become a brief. Say, 'As I said in my report,' or 'As I said on *Meet the Press*.' You want to make sure you stay a reporter."

It seemed like good advice. But first I had a more immediate problem. I wasn't even wearing a suit. Russert's program was taped in a studio where I sat at a table. I was wearing a dark blazer, but my pants didn't match. They were different shades of dark blue, not a good look. It didn't matter on TV. I could have been in my underwear behind the desk and no one would have noticed. But it was not the right outfit to meet the president.

I rushed to Nordstrom, ran up the escalator, and begged a salesman to fit me for a suit ASAP. He couldn't do it. By the time I arrived breathless in the store, I needed the suit in less than two hours. No way, he told me. I ended up buying a new tie and headed off to the White House.

I was about forty-five minutes early when the cab dropped me off in front of the Eisenhower Executive Office Building on the corner of 17th Street and Pennsylvania Avenue, next door to the White House. Now I was stuck. I was too early. I decided to walk in Lafayette Park in front of the White House to gather my thoughts. It was a warm winter day and I was hot and uncomfortable in a long black coat over my blazer. I paced back and forth on the closed road in front of the White House for about fifteen minutes before I started to worry that I was looking suspicious. Here I was, a young man, alone, in a black trench coat on a mild day, walking back and forth in front of the White House for no apparent reason. I thought Secret Service agents would jump me at any moment. I decided it would be better to head inside, even if I was still about half an hour early.

Johndroe, a young, all-American type from Texas with dark blond hair and a lean, athletic build, met me in the waiting area outside the Roosevelt Room in the West Wing. He gave me a ten-minute tour, showing me Teddy Roosevelt's Medal of Honor and Nobel Peace Prize. I've always been interested in Teddy Roosevelt. My mother lives in Oyster Bay, New York, just down the road from Sagamore Hill, Teddy Roosevelt's family home. As I looked at oil paintings of Native Americans and early European settlers, I asked Johndroe for a notebook in case I wanted to draw a map.

I have something of a map problem. Brian Williams ribs me about it all the time. Whenever I want to explain the situation in Iraq, I feel compelled to draw maps. It's a coping mechanism. I am dyslexic and I understand things better if they are visual. In middle school, my grades were so bad that one of the school administrators advised my parents to pull me out and enroll me in another school with a more developed "special learning program." They never did.

I am also convinced maps are essential to understanding the war in Iraq, which has always been more about geography, religion, and power than democracy. If you know where Shiites, Sunnis, and Kurds live, it's easy to understand their struggles for dominance. If you see on paper how Iran is wedged between U.S. bases in Iraq, Afghanistan, and the Persian Gulf, it helps explain why Tehran's foreign policy seems so aggressive. From where Iran sits, it looks like the country is being surrounded, which it is. Johndroe brought me a spiral notebook. I expected I'd draw a map for the president, explaining how Kurds, Sunnis, and Shiites interact and fight, and why. I was ready to give "the talk," my 1,300-years-of-Iraqi-history-in-thirty-minutes. It's a little speech I've used to bore countless NBC producers when they first arrive in Baghdad. I assumed I'd be doing it again, but for a much more influential audience.

At 3 P.M., I heard the president's chopper come in for a landing, right on time. Johndroe brought me to a narrow hallway outside the Oval Office. Bush's political advisor and deputy chief of staff Karl Rove was waiting there too. He didn't say hello. President Bush opened the door to the Oval Office and extended his hand.

"Sir, I'm Richard Engel," I said, and shook his hand. He had a good, firm grip.

"I know who you are," he said with a broad smile. He was wearing a suit. I wasn't. I was carrying a notebook like a schoolboy who'd gotten lost on a White House tour. I was thirty-three years old. My parents would have been proud of their dyslexic son, who they feared would end up pumping gas for a living.

President Bush showed me into the Oval Office and over to three chairs opposite the presidential desk. A photographer snapped pictures as we took our seats. There were about a dozen other men in the room. The only person who introduced himself was Dan Bartlett, presidential counselor, director of strategic communications, and speechwriter.

The others sat on couches flanking the chairs where I sat with the president and didn't say a word.

Bush was affable and friendly. He started the conversation. "So I think some journalists have spent time analyzing the situation. I met John Burns from *The New York Times*. I thought he had spent a lot of time thinking, reflecting on the situation."

I told him I respected John's work. John and I were together in the Palestine hotel during the invasion. We were among a handful of reporters who'd stuck it out. I told the president I've always tried to look at stories from an "on the ground" perspective.

"If I didn't think much of your work, you wouldn't be here," Bush said. He was very matter-of-fact. I liked it. He was easy to like.

Bush instantly seemed smarter than he appeared on television.

He didn't have the stammer or contorted facial expressions I'd seen countless times on TV, as if he were straining with his entire body to excavate the right words from a deep recess in his brain. In person, he was relaxed and cool, leaning back in his chair, legs crossed at his knees. He wasn't exactly poetic, but spoke in decisive, short, muscular sentences with engaging confidence. We were in his element. He had huge home court advantage.

Bush's small talk was direct, even somewhat rude. It was the opposite of the Arab style, where you sit, drink tea, smoke cigarettes, and talk around any sensitive issues for at least ten minutes until you reach a degree of comfort with each other's physical presence. Bush's small talk was the American original "let me get to know you in one minute or less so I know I'm not wasting my time." He shot rapid-fire, blunt questions.

"Where you from?"

"New York."

"You speak Arabic?"

"Yes."

"How long have you been over there?"

I told him I had moved to Cairo after graduating from Stanford University with $2,000 in my pocket. I explained how I learned Arabic while living in poor neighborhoods surrounded by the Muslim Brotherhood and working as a freelance print reporter. My first big story, I said, was the 1997 terrorist attack in Luxor, Egypt, where Islamic fundamentalists butchered fifty-eight tourists, most of them from Japan, Switzerland, and Germany, while they were visiting the Temple of the Pharaoh Queen Hatshepsut. Bush nodded as I spoke.

"So you speak Arabic, live in the Middle East. Are you Jewish?" he asked.

I was somewhat taken aback by the question. It is not something I publicize living in the Middle East, especially with some of the company I have to keep. But I wasn't going to lie to him. It's also a relevant, if impertinent question. How and why would a Jewish kid from New York learn Arabic and live and work with Muslim

fundamentalists in the Middle East for more than a decade? I'd
want to know.

"Half," I said. "My father is Jewish. My mother is not, but in the
region they would consider that not to be Jewish." Judaism is passed
through the mother's side.

"I get it," he said, and shifted in his chair. Small talk was evidently over.

"So what do you think?" he asked.

"I think this government does not have the same vision as you
do," I said. I told him I thought Prime Minister Maliki was part of
the problem. I told the president I thought he was overemphasiz-
ing the success of the elections, and that many Iraqis believed the
"purple-finger moment" was a disaster for the country. They liked
voting, but the wrong people won.

"Sistani, he's a good guy," Bush said. He seemed to jump
around from topic to topic. I do the same thing. I wondered if he
was dyslexic or had attention deficit disorder like me.

"But he's old," I said about Sistani, who was seventy-seven at
the time.

Sistani has long been the greatest stabilizer among the Shiites.
He could easily have rejected the American presence in Iraq after
the 2003 invasion and made the occupation impossible. That's
what happened to British forces after World War I. Once the Shiite
clergy turned on them, British troops didn't have a chance. Instead,
Ayatollah Sistani accepted the process and the American invasion
as a necessary step to get rid of Saddam, and then modified the political process to suit the Shiite community. Sistani kept the vast
majority of Shiites in line. But Sistani was the wizard behind the
curtain. He never spoke or appeared in public. He remained publicly silent, endorsing the broad strokes, while Sadr's Mahdi Army,
Iran, and Abdul Aziz al-Hakim's Badr Brigade were taking over.

I told the president that Sadr and Hakim had totally different
goals, and that there was another game under way in Iraq that had
nothing to do with his vision for a unified federal democratic Iraq
that is at peace with its neighbors and is a U.S. ally in the war on
terrorism.

Bush leaned in, his curiosity visibly piqued. He wanted to know more about Sadr and Hakim. He wanted details. He was much more in touch with the inner workings of Iraqi politics than I expected. He knew all the players, Maliki, Hakim, Allawi, Jaafari, and Sadr. I thought he'd delegated the political ins and outs to Iraq policy experts. Clearly, he hadn't.

"Sadr wants to be a nationalist leader along the lines of [Hezbollah leader] Hassan Nasrallah. He wants to unite all Iraqis," I said. "He wants to play a big role in Iraq. He wants to keep Iraq together so Shiites can run the whole country. Hakim is focused on the south. He wants to rule a small, oil-rich ministate allied with Iran."

"Well, that's not what he told me," Bush said with a laugh. Hakim had just visited the White House.

"I doubt he would," I said.

"Hakim sat right where you're sitting," Bush said. "I called him your excellence, no, your emine—"

He couldn't find the word.

"Your eminence?" I asked.

"That's it."

I told him Hakim had a reputation in Iraq as a liar. I'd interviewed him several times. He was terrible, always speaking in platitudes and slogans, never giving a straight answer. You couldn't have a conversation with him. When I asked Hakim a question, any question, he'd reflect in silence and eventually respond with a statement that sounded rehearsed and disingenuous.

I was laying it all out, insulting the men the president was counting on to democratize Iraq. Hakim, Sadr, Maliki and his aides weren't up to it, or interested. Maliki had been part of the Dawa party's secret "military planning wing" while living in Iran and Syria. Hakim was a member of the Badr Brigade. Sadr ran a death squad. Even Allawi's government, the most secular and pro-American of them all, was linked to dozens of corruption investigations.

But I hadn't come to the White House to tear apart the Iraqi politicians and the missteps of the Americans who believed them. I wanted information from Bush. What was his plan for the surge, and beyond?

The surge was a completely new strategy. It not only called for thirty thousand more troops, but envisioned a new approach to stabilizing Iraq. It was to be led by General David Petraeus, whom I'd first met in 2003 when he commanded the 101st Airborne Division in Mosul. Petraeus, a West Point graduate who'd also earned a Ph.D. in international affairs from the Woodrow Wilson School of Public and International Affairs at Princeton, wanted to push U.S. forces off the big Wal-Mart FOBs, and get them living in Baghdad and other hostile areas on small combat outposts. His plan was Death to the Fobits. Petraeus wanted to set up hundreds of tiny, lily pad bases across Iraq where U.S. and Iraqi troops would live together, doing joint patrols and training. The model, a commander told me, was like "oil on paper." Each little base would be like a drop of oil.

"When you drip oil on a piece of paper, the spots spread out and eventually connect into each other and cover the entire area. That's the plan for Iraq," the commander had said. To accomplish it, Petraeus needed more men. The thirty thousand extra troops the president had just committed were barely enough for the new strategy.

"Obviously you know the new security plan, it's your plan, but what I want to know is what's next?" I asked the president. "I think it will buy some calm, but then what?" Then I told the president what I'd wanted to say to him since the day I'd watched Saddam's statue fall in Baghdad on April 9, 2003. "Sir, you need to become a diplomat. Since you have been in office, you have focused on war. I think now you need to have a peace process and put the region back together," I said. "You have been a war president. You need to become a diplomat."

I told him I thought America needed a major diplomatic initiative on the scale of the historic negotiations that led to the treaties at the end of World War I that defined the modern Middle East. I told him I believed it was possible, and necessary, to try to rebuild the region, badly cobbled together after that war and then torn apart by the war in Iraq. The president had a war plan, but never a plan for peace. Bush needed to find one.

In my opinion, I told the president, the time to have reached a peace deal was right after the invasion. In the spring of 2003, the U.S. military destroyed Saddam Hussein's armed forces in twenty-one days. It sent an unmistakable message to our friends and enemies. Iran watched the U.S. military eliminate, with relative ease, the same army it had slammed its head against for a decade in the 1980s. Saddam's army killed a half million Iranians. We had eliminated the same army in less than a month and lost only 150 troops. Iran now had this devastatingly powerful force, the most technologically advanced in the history of warfare, on its border. After the invasion, we had Iran's attention. Iran was ready to talk and would have been flexible.

Syria had also watched U.S. troops flatten Iraq's army, roll up on its border, and turn the gun turrets toward Damascus. Syria was all ears too. But instead of taking the hard-fought opportunity, our message to Iran and Syria was "Shut up or you are next." I felt it was both arrogant and monumentally stupid. Not surprisingly, Syria and Iran sent their intelligence agents into Iraq to make U.S. troops stumble and stay bogged down in Mesopotamia. Keep Washington fighting in Iraq so they will leave us alone. If Iraqi troops were massing in Mexico and the U.S. military assessed that it couldn't defeat them, I imagine we'd also do everything in our power to keep them busy south of the border.

I told the president I thought he still had some time to negotiate and put the region he'd pulled apart back together, but that the price would be much higher. He would have been negotiating from a position of strength in 2003. Now in 2007, he was trying to dig himself out of the Iraq hole. In 2003, the United States could have dictated terms to Iran and Syria. Now we needed favors.

Bush didn't flinch. He didn't seem upset that I was presumptuous enough to suggest that he radically change course, or that I was effectively telling him that he didn't have a clue how to manage the aftermath of the Iraq war. But he did seem convinced that diplomatic conferences would be a waste of time. "We can have meetings. Talking is not the problem. We can talk to Iran," he said. "But Iran wants nuclear weapons and I'm not going to let that happen. Not on my watch. We tried to have dialogue with Syria, right after the war, didn't get much."

"You talked with them?" I asked.

"[Syrian President Bashar] Asad didn't deliver. We'd ask for ten al-Qaeda guys. They'd give us one."

I wasn't impressed. As far as I was concerned, a slow start with Syria was a positive development. The president said Damascus was handing over al-Qaeda suspects. Why not build on that? Why stop just because you are not happy with the pace of the cooperation? Of course they are going to lie, hide their intentions, and deliberately attempt to be confusing. It's part of negotiations in the Arab world. The president had obviously never bought any carpets in Damascus. It's a pain in the ass, but worth it.

"So you are a three-state guy?" he asked.

"No, I'm a federal guy. Three federal states with a weak central government that distributes resources and protects the borders."

"Me too."

"What I really am is a grand-bargain guy. I'm up for a 1919 Treaty of Paris deal."

"It's too much. Too complicated. Too broad."

He said his mission was for Condi to keep up shuttle diplomacy, Petraeus to stabilize Iraq and contain Iran, maintain troops in Iraq, and support moderates in the region like Lebanese prime minister Fouad Siniora. It seemed like it would take a long time. The status quo never lasts that long. It's a Rumsfeldian known unknown.

"I don't think you are going to have a chance to wait it out," I said. "I think there will be another 9/11-type attack and it will probably be carried out by an Iraqi."

"We are all very worried about that."

I'm not sure if he meant that he was worried about another

massive terrorist attack, or that it would be carried out by a disgruntled Iraqi.

"You know many people in the region liked the Baker-Hamilton report?" I asked. I was trying to say, I'm not alone. Many academics and newspaper editors I'd spoken to in the region were calling for sweeping negotiations, a grand Middle East swap meet, the Grand Bargain. What did we have to lose? We had no peace in Iraq, and no peace process. Without a peace process there can be only more war.

"I want to get to Baker-Hamilton, we're just not there yet," Bush said. "I didn't agree with pulling back to bases. It didn't make sense to me."

I agreed with him on that. What was the point to having troops in a country and not doing anything with them? As long as the soldiers were in Iraq, they had an obligation to make the country safer. The troops wouldn't like being ordered to hide on the FOBS and listen to the screams outside. They would feel like cowards. It would have destroyed their morale. Troops want to fight when they are deployed in a war zone. That's what soldiers do.

The president told me the surge would lead to negotiations and bring him to Baker-Hamilton. It sounded good. If the surge brought calm, and he followed it up with a major diplomatic push, he might, just maybe, be able to pull himself out of this mess. But I wanted proof. If he wanted peace and negotiations, why wasn't he already working for it?

"I think the Israeli-Palestinian crisis is your way out of this thing," I said.

"Condi is having talks with [Palestinian president Mahmoud] Abbas and [Israeli prime minister Ehud] Olmert. But you can't rush it. It can't be done on our timetable. Look what happened last time when everything was rushed," Bush said.

He was talking about the July 2000 Camp David peace talks under President Bill Clinton when Palestinian leader Yasser Arafat and Israeli prime minister Ehud Barak came close to reaching a final status peace agreement. After it failed, the peace process died. Critics said Bush then ignored the issue. I asked him why.

"I didn't trust Arafat," Bush said.

"Yes, it was clear you didn't want to deal with him."

"No, I didn't."

"But now you have Hamas in power."

Hamas won the Palestinian general elections in January 2006, in part because there was no progress with peace talks. Whenever there was progress, Arafat's more moderate Fatah party had the upper hand. After the talks failed, Hamas, a militant offshoot of the Muslim Brotherhood, offered itself as the Islamic alternative. Islamic resistance, Hamas promised, was the solution.

"I think the election of Hamas was a good thing," Bush said. I wasn't sure I'd heard him correctly.

"It was, why?" The Israeli and U.S. governments classify Hamas as a terrorist group. How could a U.S. president, especially Bush, consider the election of a declared enemy to be a good thing?

"It proved to Abbas he was failing," Bush explained. "I told Abbas, 'You lost the election because you aren't providing for your people, jobs, education, what people want.' Now they know they have to compete."

It seemed to be a remarkably idealistic way of looking at world politics. Bush was saying democracy was worth almost any cost, even the election of Hamas in the backyard of a U.S. ally and in one of the most volatile regions in the world. He was saying Hamas's election was a good thing because, in the long run, it would teach Abbas and other moderates the lessons of democracy and good governance.

"But in the Middle East, the Islamic parties have faith and Islam," I argued. "They have the pulpit. It's an unfair advantage in elections."

"In Egypt, [President Hosni] Mubarak has the pulpit, the TV," he said. It wasn't convincing. In Egypt, the president does control the media, which gives him an advantage over political rivals. But the increasingly irrelevant and little-watched state television can't compete with the power of mosques and preachers on every street corner who promise salvation and eternal paradise. The Muslim Brotherhood, by far the most powerful political organization in Egypt, has a slogan that is simple and all-encompassing, "Islam Is the Solution." It's the party's universal answer to any question or political grievance.

Egyptian politicians are corrupt.

Islam is the solution.

There are no jobs in Cairo.

Islam is the solution.

Israel is on our border.

Islam is the solution.

Dirty water from the Nile is making my child sick.

Islam is the solution.

Islam trumps Mubarak TV any day of the week.

I asked the president if he was going to restart the Israeli-Palestinian negotiations. Arafat had been dead for more than two years. If he was the problem, the problem was gone.

"The problem is Olmert. This is a man who came to power on a promise that he was going to unilaterally define a Palestinian state. You can't pressure democracies," Bush said.

"Why? Because they fall apart?"

"Yeah. I was the first president to call for Palestine. I think I deserve some credit for that. [Israeli prime minister Ariel] Sharon was here and we talked about the withdrawal from Gaza and he said the only two people who support it are in this room."

"Do you think the Saudis will develop a nuclear weapon?" I asked. I was also jumping back and forth. We had a good rhythm together. It felt like a real conversation. The meeting was supposed to have lasted fifteen minutes. We were forty-five minutes into it.

"Not as long as we are in Iraq," he said. "The Arab states, they want us to stay."

"Many people in the region believe you have helped the Shiites by bringing them to power in Iraq and that they are being used to help Iran," I said. Iraqi Sunnis, Jordan, and Saudi Arabia all worried, with reason, about Iran's expansion after the collapse of Iraq.

"Me? I'm Iran's worst nightmare," Bush said. He seemed genuinely surprised that anyone could think he was helping Iran.

"Would you attack Iran?" I asked.

"[Leading Israeli politician and former Soviet dissident Natan] Sharansky told me, if a man is holding a gun and pointing it at you, you don't help him. Don't hold up his gun," Bush said, pantomiming someone holding up a shotgun.

Sharansky's book *The Case for Democracy: The Power of Freedom to Overcome Tyranny and Terror* argued that freedom leads to stability. The book made a tremendous impact on the Bush administration.

"You'd make [Iranian president Mahmoud] Ahmadinejad a hero if you attacked, even with a few missiles, you know that?" I asked.

"Yes, but you can't rule anything out. As a president I can't rule out any option," Bush said, and sat back in his chair. At that moment I was convinced that if intelligence reports indicated that Iran was close to developing a nuclear weapon, he'd pull the trigger and launch an attack.

"There are a lot of people in Iran who are pro-American, who don't support Ahmadinejad," Bush explained. "We have a lot of supporters in Iran."

Again, he was stressing the value of democracy, as if it were a panacea for the world's ills. It struck me as similar to the Muslim Brotherhood's universalistic argument that "Islam Is the Solution." For Bush the mantra was "Democracy Is the Solution."

The Palestinian authority has collapsed.

Democracy is the solution.

Iran is belligerent.

Democracy is the solution.

Iraq is in chaos.

Democracy is the solution.

"Maliki has always been scared that you are going to remove him, or that there will be a coup," I said.

"I guess that's good that he's worried. If he's not getting it done, someone else will."

In public Bush had called Maliki "the right man for Iraq." In private, he didn't seem to have the same confidence.

I told him about a conversation I'd had with Iraq's national security advisor, Moufaq al-Rubaie. Along with the U.S. troop surge, the Iraqis were starting their own offensive in Baghdad. "Iraqis are calling their new Baghdad security plan 'Operation Law Enforcement.' The name is critical," I said. "It is not 'Operation Dismantle Militias' or anything like that. They have no intention of dismantling them. Rubaie told me his plan is to incorporate the militias into the security services."

"Who told you that? That's not my understanding." Bush seemed annoyed for the first time.

"You are creating a leaner, meaner Mahdi Army. The plan of the Mahdi Army is to stop fighting and lay low. They know if they hide, they won't be chased down. Rubaie made it clear the government would not confront the militia head on, but 'prune it' by arresting or killing the really radical elements that the Mahdi Army can't control anyway. The plan is to cut away the deadwood, then incorporate the militia into the security services. They are using you, Mr. President, to make the militia leaner and stronger and become Hezbollah.

"I think they have a very different vision than you do. So what *is* your vision?" I asked again.

"Petraeus is now over there with his new plan in Iraq, which I think is going to work."

"Are you going to make Casey the fall guy?"

"No, not me. I wouldn't do that, and I told him that."

"Okay, so the new Baghdad security plan, then what?"

"Why are you so pessimistic? You make it sound impossible."

"I don't get to meet you often. This is the first time and I don't know if I will meet with you again, so I want to be frank with you, otherwise I'd be wasting your time."

"Okay," he said, and smiled. "I know people are saying we should have left things the way they were, but I changed after 9/11. I had to act. I don't care if it created more enemies. I had to act."

I don't know if he meant he'd created more political enemies, or real enemies. I certainly had the impression he was talking real enemies, the kind who shoot and bomb you. I wondered how a president could say he didn't care if his defense strategy created more enemies. It didn't make sense to me; neither did his argument about the intrinsic value of democracy in the Middle East.

"In the Middle East, democracy is a tool, especially among Shiites," I said. "They are not egalitarians. In the United States, democracy is based on a belief that if you get a group of average people together, they will collectively come up with a just solution. There is a belief that all people are equal. For religious Shiites in Iraq it is different. There is an ayatollah who is inspired by God, and people who surrender their decision-making authority to him. It is not democracy. The elections are a tool to obtain power. If you asked them to jump up and down on one foot for ten minutes and promised that it would give them power, they would have done it, but I don't think it makes them great democrats. I really think you need to get the peace process with the Israelis and Palestinians moving."

"Condi goes back and forth."

"Mr. President, you need to get involved. It's your vision. You're the president. It has to be you. Condi doesn't have the juice. You're the one in charge. You're the one they want to deal with."

"Maybe we should have some more meetings, but they are too broad. Nothing will get done."

"I understand they can be too broad, too much on the agenda, too much to handle. So do it one-on-one. But you've got to do it."

I asked him how long the United States would stay in Iraq.

"We're not leaving Iraq for a long time. This is the great struggle of our times. This is the great war of our times. It is going to take forty years."

"Forty years?"

Bush said in forty years the world would know if the war on terrorism, and conflicts in Iraq and Afghanistan, had reduced extremism, helped moderates, and promoted democracy.

"I'm sort of jealous," he told me, suddenly turning the conversation personal again. "I'm envious of what you've been doing." He said he liked that I was able to travel and explore, the adventurous nature of it. I thought, Here was a man who hadn't traveled much before he was president and had suddenly woken up to the world and wanted to explore and change it.

"Are you some sort of thrill seeker?" he asked.

"No, no thrill seeker. I don't like driving fast or bungee jumping. I just think this is important."

"It is. You ever been to Iran?" he asked me. "I haven't."

"Yes, I know. We would have noticed."

"Yes, but not even in my somewhat wayward youth," he joked, and looked down at his watch. It was time to wrap it up. We'd been together for an hour and a half without pausing for a second. Bush's detractors say he doesn't have an attention span. He does.

"Be careful out there. Keep safe," he said.

I thanked the president for his time, picked up my unused notebook, and left. My mind was swirling with thoughts as I took a taxi to the airport to fly back to New York. Could this work? I wondered. Could we all look back in forty years and think perhaps President Bush was on to something? He was clearly counting on it and wanted to be vindicated by history. My impression was that Bush thought of himself as a visionary, a bold statesman like Winston Churchill, and that he believed passionately that democracy and personal freedom led to stability. I feared he wanted to be a martyr for democracy; that he believed he was a victim, sacrificing himself for the cause at the expense of popularity. He seemed willing to go down fighting, hoping that history would prove him right. It seemed to me that he was not, as many had accused, a front man for Dick

Cheney's policies. This was his policy. He was the skipper. We were just passengers.

The president had done a lot of reading. Since he'd invaded Iraq, he'd earned two Ph.D.s' worth of information about the country and the Middle East. He'd met all the players and had access to information that only a president could have. But he still had no idea how to deal with Arabs.

23

General Petraeus was a rock star from the moment he assumed command in Iraq. Soldiers would line up in the Green Zone to have photographs taken with the four-star general. Colonels and brigadier generals competed to join him for morning jogs. Petraeus was the only celebrity general, the military's golden boy, and everyone wanted to be close to the rising star.

Petraeus didn't look the part of a commanding general. He wasn't barrel-chested with a crew cut. The general, who wrote his 328-page Ph.D. thesis on the lessons of the Vietnam War, looked more like a professor than someone who spent his vacations stalking deer and shooting ducks from the sky. He had a medium build, straight, longish hair, and a bashful, toothy smile. Petraeus was the opposite of General Casey, the shy, inaccessible, officious bureaucrat who was generally unknown and unpopular with other senior officers for his cold distance and the fact that he'd never served in command in an active combat zone. Most of Casey's experience before Iraq had been in Colorado, Texas, Bosnia, and Germany. General Petraeus had led the fabled 101st Airborne Division, the Screaming Eagles, into Mosul in 2003. His tour was considered so

successful that before he returned to Iraq to lead the training of the
new Iraqi army, *Newsweek* put him on the cover in July 2004, asking, "Can This Man Save Iraq?"

Petraeus understood how to use the media. He could boil down
his thoughts to fifteen-second sound bytes, and always tracked the
camera during interviews. Whenever we did a "walk and talk," the
little parade television reporters do to show that we actually meet
the person we're interviewing, I watched Petraeus focus on the
cameraman and time his answers to catch the moving lens. He had
what actors call "camera awareness." Casey had no camera or media
awareness at all. I had what might have been considered a good relationship with Casey. At least I had some access to him. Most reporters were completely shut out. I still had to request interviews,
in writing, weeks in advance, which were almost always off camera.
When General Petraeus took command in February 2007, nearly
every reporter, including journalists from tiny foreign television
stations and even American college newspapers, could be guaranteed an on-the-record interview within a few days.

I returned to Iraq after my meeting with President Bush intensely curious. Would his surge, his gamble with thousands of
lives, America's credibility, and billions of dollars, pay off? Or was it
just part of a trillion-dollar folly in Mesopotamia? Was he a losing
gambler who couldn't walk away from the table?

In early 2007 I made several trips to a combat outpost in west
Baghdad led by Lieutenant Colonel Dale Kuehl of the 1st Battalion,
5th Cavalry Regiment. The outpost was an abandoned two-story
wedding hall surrounded by a few blast walls. Vagrants and Iraqi
soldiers had used it as a toilet. When American soldiers moved in,
the building was full of cigarette butts and piles of shit. I watched
them muck it out with shovels and paint over urine stains on the
walls. The outpost was one of the new lily pad bases, the core of Petraeus's strategy, the ink stains on paper. In typical military jargon,
it was known by an acronym, JSS (joint security station). It was considered "joint" because U.S. and Iraqi troops shared the same compound: Iraqis downstairs, Americans upstairs. "Don't go down

there by yourself at night," a soldier warned me. "We still don't know these guys. If you go downstairs, make sure you go with one of us."

I was with our ever-calm-and-quiet Australian cameraman, Bredun Edwards, and Kianne Sadeq, a young, attractive Kuwaiti producer. The soldiers loved her. They hardly saw any women, especially at frontline outposts. Within minutes, soldiers were streaming into the room where we were staying with coffee, Pop Tarts, Otis Spunkmeyer premium chocolate muffins, and seemingly endless offers of help. Did we need anything? Did we have enough power cables? Had someone shown us the bathrooms? Mostly they just wanted a little female attention. Having a woman on a frontline base always helped. A pretty woman on a base is a military PAO's worst nightmare. The soldiers would tell her anything. Kianne, fluent in Arabic and Farsi, was our secret weapon.

The JSS was in the center of Khadra, a middle-class Sunni neighborhood. Our local staff had long stopped coming here. It was overrun by al-Qaeda supporters. The soldiers called the main commercial street Phone Card Road because many of the shops had once sold scratch-off cards for pay-as-you-go cell phones. Now, nearly every store on Phone Card was bombed out and covered with graffiti praising insurgents. Residents used the twisted, burned wrecks of cars that had been bombed to block the entrances of their homes. There were several potholes from roadside bombs on every block. Phone Card looked like south Lebanon after the 2006 Israeli bombardment. Phone Card looked like Falujah after the 2004 Marine offensives.

"Stay away from the window," a soldier told Kianne as we were setting up our cots. "There are a lot of fucking snipers around here."

He showed us another room where we could store our camera, lights, and viewing decks. I was surprised to see an Iraqi detainee inside, sitting alone on a folding chair. He'd been blindfold with a bandage. His wrists were bound behind his back with a zip tie. The man was slumped forward, bleeding from his lips, and had a gash in his forehead like he'd been punched by someone wearing a chunky ring. He'd clearly been worked over.

"What happened to this guy?" I asked. "Somebody beat him up?"

"The Iraqis don't have the same procedures as we do as far as questioning detainees," the soldier said. "We're working with them on that."

We left our gear in the room with the detainee. He didn't move or seem to notice as we pushed our heavy boxes against the wall next to him. He may have been pretending not to hear, afraid of what might happen if he moved. He may have been too tired to react.

I felt uncomfortable leaving our equipment next to the detainee. It made me feel like we were part of the abuse. The soldier told me he also worried about living with the Iraqis. They often roughed up detainees. "It's the Iraqi way, I get that. But this shit is going to come back on us," he said.

It was all up close and personal. Like the marines at Combat Outpost in Ramadi way back in 2004, the army had finally caught on. The soldiers in Baghdad were now, finally, living in the war zone. They weren't commuting from FOBs anymore. The outposts were leading the fight. Life here was tough and ugly—full of snipers, shit, horny soldiers, and bleeding detainees—but that's what the war looked like up close. It was about time they faced it. Lieutenant Colonel Kuehl was a new type of army field commander. He lived at the JSS with his men and understood the science-fiction nightmare Baghdad had become.

"This is what we should have been doing from the start," he said. "If we'd been out here, living in the city like this back in 2003, things would have been different."

It felt like the war was starting over and that the Americans were trying to implement the strategy they should have used in 2003. For four years, American soldiers patrolled, kicked down doors, rolled up "bad guys," and then returned to bases, assuming Iraqi police and soldiers would hold the areas they'd just cleared. It rarely happened. Petraeus finally decided to keep American troops in the field all the time. It seemed like an obvious change of tactics.

I don't know why it took four years to figure it out. As time passes, Casey and his advisors will have to answer tough questions about their performance in Iraq.

I went with Kuehl on a patrol in Mansour, another mostly Sunni neighborhood near the JSS. Mansour had been one of Baghdad's most upscale addresses. U.S. administrator Paul Bremer had considered renting a villa in Mansour after the fall of Baghdad. Saddam Hussein's favorite restaurant, As-Seaa, "The Clock," was here until U.S. troops obliterated it with JDAMS in a failed assassination attempt during the 2003 invasion. Saddam had just left the restaurant when the bombs crashed through the roof. When I arrived a short time later, I saw a crater as deep as a swimming pool.

Kuehl was talking to the owner of a furniture store, handing out tip cards, when a group of young men desperately tried to flag us down, waving their arms and urging us to come to a bakery a few doors down.

"Gunmen entered in the bakery. We heard shots," a man said. "The gunmen might still be inside."

Kuehl and his soldiers crept up to the door, guns on their chests. They stacked against a wall and streamed in. Bredun and I slipped in behind them. I saw a man's body on the floor behind a glass display case filled with sugar cookies and date cakes. He had been executed with a single shot to the head. Blood was still pooling around the body, spreading into a sticky puddle. It was obvious he'd been shot only moments before. By now I could tell.

"More back here!" a soldier yelled from the kitchen.

There were three more bodies on the kitchen floor. One of the men had tried to hide behind a big oven. His body was curled up, wedged in the corner, head facing the wall. The gunmen had killed him too with a single shot to the head. But what struck me most was the smell. Cakes were baking in the oven next to the body. They smelled delicious. I thought they were angel food cakes. The scent of warm vanilla made me hungry. I suddenly became very concerned about the cakes and wanted to turn off the ovens. I didn't want the cakes to burn. I don't know why I cared so much. The bodies didn't interest me. They were just rubbery, leaking corpses. Perhaps it was compassion fatigue, the emotional detachment that emergency-room doctors experience after treating hundreds of car crash victims. There were stacks of peanut-and-pistachio cookies on a counter next to the oven. I considered taking a cookie, but felt guilty and stopped myself. I thought it would have been looting from the dead. Then one of the dead men's cell phones started to ring. I jumped a bit. The ring tone was a loud, annoying jingle, happily beeping and buzzing in the dead man's pocket. I wondered who was trying to call. Was it his mother? Perhaps his wife? The ringing phone made us all uncomfortable. None of us answered it. I forgot to turn off the oven. The wonderful cakes burned and started to smoke as a man outside told Kuehl the bakery was owned by Shiites. He said a Shiite milkman and three bread makers had been gunned down on the same street earlier that week.

"It's all about power," Kuehl said. "The Shiites are trying to gain power in Baghdad and the Sunnis are trying to hold on to power. Where you have mixed communities that are butting up against each other, Sunni or Shiite, that's where you have the biggest point of conflict."

A police pickup truck, as usual its flatbed already painted with dried blood from other stops, eventually arrived to collect the bodies. On our way back to the JSS, the convoy passed yet another body in the street. The soldiers didn't slow down or call it in.

I thought I had an interesting story about the fleeting nature of life and death in Baghdad, featuring the symbolism of a dead man's phone ringing after he'd been executed in a sectarian killing. It was the new face of the civil war in Iraq. My editors liked the story, but wanted to hold it for another day. It was February 2007, and the former Playboy Playmate Anna Nicole Smith had just been found dead in the Bahamas. I told Kuehl we were bumped by Anna Nicole Smith. He laughed.

I almost didn't survive the next morning. I went to visit a patrol base—an outpost smaller than a JSS—that Kuehl's men were set-

ting up in an empty shopping center in Adel, another neighborhood where Sunnis and Shiites were crashing into each other. I was
in the lead vehicle in a convoy of Humvees, sitting in the backseat
behind the driver. I always feel vulnerable in Humvees, even wearing my black Kevlar helmet, ballistic anti-shrapnel sunglasses, ear
plugs, and a sky-blue flak jacket. It's basically just a hard hat, plastic
glasses, two pieces of foam, and a couple of ceramic tiles strapped
to my chest.

The convoy stopped at an intersection. The driver wasn't sure
which way to go. On our left was a trash dump, another killing field
like the one in Dora where insurgents and militias dumped bodies.
In front of us the road continued straight. Was the driver supposed
to turn right at the intersection, or keep going straight? We sat there
for about a minute while the staff sergeant, Chris Copley, checked a
satellite map. I was staring blankly out the window, looking at the
trash. The world turns down a notch when you have earplugs in.
Everything is muted. You can hear yourself breathing and feel the
saliva in your mouth. It's relaxing. I was half asleep. Copley told the
driver to turn right. As we started moving, I heard the explosion.

It wasn't a roaring boom, or a deep growl. It was a quick and
nasty pop, shallow and high-pitched like a scream. The bomb was
most likely an artillery shell buried in a trash mound, the standard
IED that had by now killed more than 1,500 soldiers. It exploded
just a few feet from my door. Dust and white smoke poured into the
Humvee through the gunner's turret. The smoke smelled bitter-
sweet, like gun powder. It smelled good. I felt the shock wave pass
through my body, a surge of pure energy. It's a hard feeling to describe. The force hits you, ripples through, and keeps going like a
noise. It feels like you are being slapped by a ghost.

"Holy shit!" the driver yelled.

"Push through! Push through!" Copley ordered, and started
shouting into the radio. "IED. Contact. IED."

The driver hit the gas, speeding out of the kill zone.

"Everybody okay?" Copley asked.

"I'm good," I said.

The gunner wasn't sure. He started to pat himself down, feeling for blood. He didn't find any.

"Nothing," he said. "I'm surprised. I'm checking myself. Nothing. Whoo-hoo!" he cheered.

"You okay?" I asked Copley.

"I'm a little shook up, but I'm good," he said.

We were saved by technology. Every year the Humvees were hardened with extra armor, especially on the doors and around the gunner's turret. If I'd been in an older Humvee, I might not have survived. My door was flecked with shrapnel, but I was fine. All I had was a ferocious headache that lasted three days and a sore lower back for a week.

We pushed on to the shopping center. The soldiers were fired up, juiced, full of adrenaline, and hungry. IEDs make you hungry. Adrenaline needs to be fed.

While eating an MRE, Copley said the bomb was most likely "command detonated."

The militants had been watching us, and detonated the IED as we passed it.

"How many times has this happened to you?" I asked. "How many times have you been blown up?"

"Me personally? About two in the past week and a half," Copley said.

"That sucks."

"Yeah. It's starting to become pretty common. It's pretty much a daily thing. Hopefully we can just get the sectarian violence to stop so we can get out of here."

"You ready to go home?" I asked.

"Oh yeah. Ready for the war to end, ready to go home. It's pretty much almost a lost cause. I mean it seems like nothing we do is doing any good. The sectarian violence, we can't stop it. Every country goes through a civil war, so maybe it would be better for them to have a civil war and hash it out and then help them after that."

Oddly, I was more angry than shaken up—angry that the war was taking so long, angry that soldiers and Iraqis were being killed and injured. For what? In an empty room in the shopping mall, next to a shop filled with mannequins dressed in women's bras and underwear, I took out my camera and recorded another of my video diary entries.

"Why are we out here dealing with this? Why are we putting ourselves between a Sunni and Shiite civil war?" I asked the camera.

"This is going to sound weird, but I knew this was going to happen. I knew it. I had a feeling when we rolled out that this was going to happen. They said, 'Richard, why don't you ride up in the lead vehicle.' I had a moment of hesitation. I had a feeling that today is gonna be the day that they are going to hit the lead vehicle. I don't know why I felt that. Maybe I should have listened to it. But I was lucky, nothing happened.

"But you wonder, are you going to stay lucky forever? A soldier asked me, 'You've been here four years. How much longer are you going to keep doing this?' I told him, 'Well, you're asking me on the wrong day.' I think maybe I've done enough. But this war is not over and it's going to take a long time.

"While I was in the vehicle just after the attack, I was thinking about a soldier who was on the base where I'm staying. Just a few days ago, he was hit by a roadside bomb. It was much worse than today. The bomb tore off the door and badly damaged his legs. The soldier fell out of the vehicle and then was shot. He was shot three times, twice in the chest, once in the scrotum. They evacuated him to a medical facility, but they couldn't save his legs. He had to have a double amputation. I was thinking, 'I don't want this to happen to me.' I got lucky today, but how many times can you get lucky? How many times do you push it? The IED could have been a lot closer. Maybe next time it will be a lot closer.

"What really upsets me about this war is that there are no efforts to make peace. There's no peace process. Four years into this conflict and all they seem to be coming up with are new military strategies, a new security plan, a new tactic to battle the militias and insurgents. But you can't end war without some sort of peace process. The U.S. has gone to war without a plan for peace.

"Where does this go? How much longer does this war go on? This strategy of U.S. troops trying to keep the two sides apart, pushing them

*back, you could do this for years. You could do this for decades even.
What we need is a solution to end this war."*

By the middle of 2007, the extra surge troops were still arriving
in Baghdad. The Petraeus plan was taking shape, but so far it wasn't
making a difference. In March, April, and May, there were more
than 1,400 bomb, mortar, and sniper attacks per month, including
120 "high profile" car bombings and suicide attacks. More than
2,500 civilians were being killed every month. There were sixty IED
attacks across Iraq every day. Violence was at near-record levels, and
it seemed that Iraqis were increasingly fighting a war that had little,
if anything, to do with President Bush's vision for a moderate, democratic Iraq. The president had described to me a fight between
moderates and radicals, freedom lovers versus freedom haters. It
wasn't what I was seeing.

Everyone in Iraq had an agenda and a war to fight, and none of
it seemed to match President Bush's vision.

Moqtada al-Sadr wanted to equal or surpass the influence of
his father and unite Iraq's poor, uneducated, and unemployed Shiite community, which was increasingly fed up with the continued
presence of U.S. troops.

Iraqi Kurds wanted independence and control of the oil-rich
city of Kirkuk. They were busy consolidating their control and driving Arabs out of Kurdistan. They wanted to establish what they'd
been denied for centuries, an autonomous, prosperous, oil-rich
state. For Kurds, the fighting in Iraq was never about democracy,
but self-determination.

Abdul Aziz al-Hakim, the leader of the Supreme Council for Islamic Revolution in Iraq, the man President Bush called "his eminence," wanted to control southern Iraq and carve out a ministate
allied with Iran.

Ayad Allawi wanted to overthrow Prime Minister Maliki, unite
Sunnis and Shiites under his secular rule, and bring back divisions
of the Iraqi army dissolved by Paul Bremer.

U.S. politicians and military commanders were forever complaining that the Iraqi government refused to "step up and do its

job." The impression they gave was that Iraqi officials sat around smoking hookah pipes, and that if they would just pull themselves up by their bootstraps, gosh darn it, U.S. troops wouldn't have to fight to get the job done. U.S. soldiers always asked me when the Iraqis would step up and fight for their own country. The problem was, they were fighting for their country. Iraqi officials, clerics, militia groups, Syria, Iran, and al-Qaeda were all struggling and dying to get a job done in Iraq; it just wasn't the same job the White House wanted them to be doing.

In April 2007, Defense Secretary Robert Gates said on a visit to Iraq that America's "patience is running out." I thought, If he and President Bush were waiting for Iraqis and the wider Middle East to start fighting the White House's fictional battle between good and evil, democracy and tyranny, they would need a lot more patience.

2008

THE TURNING POINT?

24

I was on home leave at my mother's house in Oyster Bay, Long Island, on an unseasonably cool spring day in 2007 when I received a cell phone call from Ali. I was surprised when I heard his voice. He rarely called when I was out of Baghdad. Ali had told me he was going to Iran to help his mother have eye surgery. I assumed he'd run into some bureaucratic troubles with the authorities in Tehran.

"Ali, my brother, how are you? Can I call you right back so you don't have to pay for the call?"

"No, it's okay. I'm fine."

"Where are you?"

"I'm in Sweden."

"Sweden?"

"Yes, Sweden."

"I thought you were in Tehran finding a clinic for your mother."

"I didn't go to Iran."

"You didn't?"

"No."

"What are you doing in Sweden?"

"I'm here," he said.

"Yes, I understand that. Why?"

"I'm trying to get refugee status."

"Are you there legally?"

"I'm working on it."

"And your mother, what about her surgery?"

"She's okay."

I was angry with Ali for the first time. I was silent on the phone for about thirty seconds.

"Why did you tell me you were going to Iran? You lied to me," I finally said. The word "lied" stuck in my throat like a bitter aspirin tablet.

"I know. I am very sorry. I didn't even tell my family. Even my brother thought I was going to Iran. I packed and left, telling everyone I was going to Iran. After I was kidnapped, the Mahdi Army wouldn't leave me alone. They kept coming to my house, asking about me, checking in. They wanted me to work for them and pass on information about the bureau and about you. I didn't want to do it."

"They wanted you to become a spy for them, an inside man in our office?"

"Yes."

"Did they want to kidnap any of us?"

"I don't know what they wanted. They want to know everything. They have to have a person in every place. That's their way."

I wasn't sure if I should believe him. I was still upset. "But why make up a story about Iran and your mother? Why not just leave? Why didn't you tell me?" I asked, my tone somewhat accusatory.

"If the Mahdi Army knew I was leaving for Sweden, they would have become suspicious. They would have known I was leaving for good. They would have stopped me. But the Mahdi Army people go to Iran all the time. It is something normal for them. I told everyone I was going to Iran and then went to Syria."

"And from Syria, how did you get to Sweden?"

"I paid a broker $10,000. You pay half when you leave and half when you arrive. If you don't make it or get arrested, you don't pay the second half. There are many, many Iraqis here."

"What do you need now?" I asked.

"I don't need anything. I just wanted to tell you that I am here. Everything is okay."

"Does your family know where you are?"

"No. You are the first person I am telling."

The more I spoke to Ali, the more I became convinced he was telling the truth. The Mahdi Army typically demanded favors. Like with the Mafia, once you are affiliated, it's hard to break away. What convinced me most, however, was that Ali didn't want anything. He wouldn't even let me pay for the phone call. He could have played up that he had fled to protect me and the office and asked for help and money. He never did. I wasn't angry with him anymore. I don't know many people who give up everything and ask for nothing in return. He had refused to cooperate with a militia that had tortured him. I was so proud of him.

"How the hell did you end up in Sweden? What does Sweden have to do with anything?" I asked, the anger gone from my voice. "Isn't it cold for you?"

"It's not too cold now. I'm living with another Iraqi in a government apartment for refugees. He's older than me. He's a doctor and very nice. But the language is difficult. I can't communicate."

"You are learning Swedish?" I asked. Ali hardly ever spoke more than a few sentences in a row in Arabic or mumbled more than a couple of words in English. I couldn't see him chatting away in Swedish with all its perky "hej-hej"s, "ya-ya"s, and fifteen-letter words with umlauts.

"They give us classes in Swedish, but they are difficult."

Ali told me he was in a quiet town called Alvesta, a hundred miles north of Malmö. I'd never been to Alvesta, with a population of fewer than eight thousand, but know the area of lakes and forests. My mother is Swedish, born in Göteborg. She met my father when he was a young army officer in Germany. She was a strikingly beautiful eighteen-year-old exchange student, studying in Germany. He was a twenty-five-year-old lieutenant, the son of a Long Island businessman, and a member of the army golf team with a single-digit handicap. When my father's deployment ended, he asked my mother to come back with him to the States. She refused unless they were married first. Although they'd known each other for only a few months, they married in a tiny church in Sweden. In New York, she found a job as a translator and secretary at the Swedish consulate while my father looked for work on Wall Street. He eventually went to work for Goldman Sachs. They were together for thirty years until they divorced amicably in 2000. I remain very close to both.

I pictured Ali in a sparsely furnished refugee-processing apartment in rural Sweden, the land of orderly lines, pickled herring, snowdrifts, Christian hymns, and gravlax. I'd spent a summer in Sweden visiting relatives when I was a teenager, fishing for cod, eating boiled shrimp, and picking wild mushrooms with my aunt and cousins in the forest. I couldn't think of a more unfamiliar place for Ali, so different from the mean urban sprawl of Sadr City with its militias, guns, and open sewers. While I was surprised he'd suddenly popped up in Sweden, I was relieved that he'd left Iraq. I recalled our last conversation in my office in Baghdad.

Ali walked in, quiet as always. His hair was thinning more by the week and his black shirt was speckled with dandruff. His face was thin and his eyes seemed to have sunk deep in the back of his head. He showed me another one of the videos he kept on his cell phone. It was the execution of a Nepalese contractor, beheaded by Ansar al-Sunna, Zarqawi's old group. A man with a long knife was straddling the screaming, shirtless Nepalese man. The murderer slit his throat, sawed off his head, held it up for the camera, and then placed it on top of the dead man's back. Other masked gunmen yelled, "*Takbeer!*

"*Allah u Akhbar!*

"*Takbeer!*

"*Allah u Akhbar!*"

Ali showed me another video of a man in a white plastic lawn chair. I watched as a militant chopped at his neck with a knife. It looked as if he was swinging an ax, crashing blow after blow on the man's throat, until his head fell to the ground.

"That's enough. I don't want to see that," I said. I'd seen too many of these videos. When they first started to circulate in 2004, I felt that I had to watch them to understand. Now I thought they were an affront to what little humanity I was trying to hang on to. Watching the videos can be like breathing in a smelling salt or a bottle of ammonia. If you do it once, you remember the experience for the rest of your life. If you do it every day, you'll cause brain damage and lose your sense of taste and smell forever.

Ali had seen too many horrors. I don't think human beings are wired for it. He was once again blaming his religion. It was not healthy. "Take Islam, I am innocent of it," he said. "It's all hypocrisy. In Karbala, I could get you a thirteen-year-old girl to have fun with. This is in Karbala. Karbala the holy! It's all bullshit. All in the name of religion," he said.

Zohair walked in and heard the tail end of Ali's conversation. Unlike Ali, Zohair had long been a cynic. "Of course it's bullshit," he said. "I am a believer. I have faith and believe in God, but I threw out my wife's prayer rug and destroyed her veil. I just tore it up and tossed it in the street. I told her it's ugly. 'The veil is ugly,' I said. Then, I took a bottle of whiskey and left it on the table in front of the door. When you open the door, it's the first thing you see when you come in," Zohair said, and laughed. "I am a believer, but what is this Islam, only slaughtering? We're all going to end up in the nuthouse."

Zohair had come by to show me a fatwa from the howza in Najaf. It was a public health advisory, warning Iraqis not to eat fish.

"Do not eat river fish because of the danger of water infected by rotting bodies," it said. The fatwa advised against eating the Iraqi national dish, *masgouf*, smoked carp. "As a bottom feeder, this fish is especially susceptible to diseases from the water," the fatwa explained. The Tigris and Euphrates, the Fertile Crescent's ancient rivers that had given life to civilization, had become so full of rotting human flesh that the clerics condemned them. Compared to that, Sweden's pickled herring didn't sound so bad.

I told my mother about Ali and his flight to Sweden. Her sister, whom Ali had no way of knowing, works with refugees for the Swedish government. A few days later, my aunt met Ali with a translator to help him sort out his paperwork.

I spent most of the summer of 2007 doing investigative stories about al-Qaeda. I wanted to know whether the anger I felt in the Lighthouse in Damascus, the humiliation I saw as the young girls danced onstage, was widespread across the Islamic world and al-Qaeda had been able to exploit it. I interviewed active and former al-Qaeda members and their supporters in Jordan, Saudi Arabia, Pakistan, Iraq, and Lebanon, and talked to American intelligence officials in New York and at the National Counterterrorism Center, an unmarked office building in Washington, D.C. My interviews suggested that al-Qaeda's central command was regrouping in the lawless tribal areas in Pakistan and that the militant group had changed its basic management structure. When al-Qaeda carried out the 9/11 atrocities, it was a small, disciplined group based in Afghanistan. By the end of 2007, it had transformed itself into a franchise with dozens of small, self-sufficient cells across the Islamic world. Al-Qaeda had become like McDonald's. It supplied the formula, brand name, and advertising strategy to local groups that found their own recruits and funding, and picked their own targets. As McDonald's and other franchises well know, it's a powerful, adaptive business model.

In the fall of 2007, I shuttled between Iraq and Pakistan, reporting on former prime minister Benazir Bhutto's return from exile to challenge President Pervez Musharraf. I wasn't surprised when she was assassinated by Islamic militants. She wanted to be a public hero, the Princess Diana of Pakistan, but Pakistan had changed in the eight years she was away. I don't think she understood how dangerous it had become.

I returned to Baghdad in January 2008. It was clear to me that the city had changed even before I landed. As I sat at gate six in Amman's Queen Alia International Airport, I was struck by the number of American contractors waiting to fly to Iraq. There were so many middle-aged men with badges in plastic pouches around their necks, potbellies, and golf shirts emblazoned with company logos, I couldn't even find a seat. Royal Jordanian Airlines had increased its schedule to three flights a day and put bigger planes on the route to Baghdad, but the flights were still full. Nobody smiled or spoke at gate six. The men all looked tired, haggard, and resigned, like convicts waiting for the last bus back to jail after a weekend furlough.

When I landed at Baghdad International Airport, I walked past an American contractor sitting on a chair in a waiting area. He was wearing blue jeans with a big turquoise New Mexico–style belt buckle, boots, and a cowboy hat. "What is this guy doing in Baghdad?" I thought as I waited in line to clear customs, behind a small army of private security guards in matching shirts from West Africa. All the reports from Iraq over the last several months had said that security was improving. They opened the floodgates for foreigners hoping to earn three times their salaries at home.

Zohair was waiting for me at the bureau.

"I hear things are better. Has security really improved? What's going on?" I asked before he even had a chance to sit down.

"Yes, it's much better. You could say violence is down 60 percent. People are out at night until 1 A.M. Restaurants are full. We can go in my car like we used to. You remember when we would go downtown and buy old records? We can go again. Come now and I'll show you. Even a Chinese restaurant opened up in Karadah."

"Is it any good?"

"Yes. They make these bread balls filled with a little meat and vegetables. They're very good."

"They're called dumplings," I said.

"The kids love them. There are kids who go every day just to eat them."

"I'll have to try them," I said. I was happy a restaurant had opened in Karadah near our bureau. It was as if my own neighborhood was improving. I'd been in Karadah so long that the chairman of the local council had given me a framed certificate naming me an "honorary council member" and a "friend of Karadah." I proudly display the certificate in my office, not that anyone can see it amid the clutter of newspapers, notebooks, half-full mugs of Nescafé, dusty Beta tapes, and a gas mask, which I keep nearby in case there's a fire.

"What happened? Why are things better?" I asked Zohair.

"The Mahdi Army has called a cease-fire and the Awakening forces are hitting al-Qaeda hard. But I don't think it will last."

The Awakening movement was what the Americans called Sunni tribesmen, many of them former insurgents, who'd turned on al-Qaeda and were now fighting alongside U.S. troops. The Americans called it the Awakening to signify that the Sunnis had symbolically woken up to the danger of al-Qaeda and changed sides.

"How's Najaf?" I asked.

"Najaf is more of an Iranian city than an Iraqi one," Zohair said.

"I want to go."

"No problem. I'll set it up."

I hadn't been to Najaf in three years. If Iraq had really changed, I believed I would see it in Najaf, home of the howza, the Shiites' brain trust and central command. As always, transportation was a problem. Although security had improved, there were still suicide

Overall Weekly Iraq Attack Trends
(Includes Found and Cleared Bombs)
September 2004 – November 2007

Department of Defense, "Measuring Stability and Security in Iraq," Report to Congress, December 2007, p. 16.

bombings and mortar attacks every day. There just weren't as many of them. General Petraeus's office gave me several charts that showed clearly how violence had dramatically decreased since the summer.

In January 2008, the total number of sniper, rocket, bomb, and mortar attacks was down to six hundred a week, compared to nearly 1,600 a week at the peak of the violence during the early summer of 2007. The chart tracking the violence looked like an ocean wave. I had surfed it for five years. Here in PowerPoint was my experience. I wondered if the wave I'd watched rip through Iraq and displace millions had enough force and momentum to create new waves like tides slapping at the beach. Was the violence self-sustaining?

Although attacks were down, our security consultants still didn't feel it was safe enough to drive to Najaf. I asked the U.S. military for a lift. Colonel Ed Cardon, who'd impressed me by being so forthright in 2005 when he helped confirm Ali's story about U.S. troops unwittingly helping insurgents round up Shiites in

Dora, was now back in Iraq as Brigadier General Cardon, the deputy commander of the southern belt of Baghdad, Najaf, and Karbala. He had an upcoming meeting with the governor of Najaf and
let me tag along.

Cardon's Black Hawk landed on a small base in the desert outside Najaf. Along with a small group of U.S. Special Forces, it was
the only remaining American presence in the Shiite city, now under
the sovereignty of the Iraqi government.

General Cardon drove to meet the governor at his office downtown. I didn't feel any tension as the general's convoy of Humvees
twisted through the city. No U.S. troops had been killed in Najaf
in over a year. Iraqis lined the streets, shopping and fixing cars. But
no one waved at us. It was as if we were invisible. No one wanted to
see us.

When General Cardon walked into his office, the governor
wanted to talk about one thing: the airport. He said Najaf needed an
international airport to receive pilgrims and tourists from around
the Shiite world. For centuries, Najaf has lived off caravans of
Shiite pilgrims who come from Iran, India, Lebanon, and the Gulf
to worship and bury their dead. The airport was under construction
next to the small American patrol base, but the governor needed
U.S. help to finish it quickly. He told Cardon he wanted the Americans to reinforce the runways so they could accommodate heavy
jumbo passenger jets. The concrete on the runways now was too
thin and would crack under the weight of the planes.

"I want to open flights from Najaf to New York," the governor
said. "They should be direct flights."

Cardon told the governor that the airport contract was "in process" and that the Iraqis needed to locate international advisors and
technical experts, and put together a tender for the best bid. He was
telling him to go through American bureaucratic channels, which
everyone knows are tedious, frustrating, time-consuming, and
often dead ends. Even General Cardon didn't look convinced, and
seemed to be apologizing for having to refer the governor to an endless paper trail, an accounting nightmare, and, more than likely, a
money pit.

"It's infuriating," Cardon told me when we were alone. "If we really wanted to get this airport open for them, we could do it. We have the means. We could get some army bulldozers down here with some engineers and have it done in no time."

But America doesn't work that way in Iraq. It works through the Green Zone and its web of paperwork, forms, rules, and checkpoints run by bullies and pencil pushers, civilian Fobits. Imagine rounding up the most inflexible employees from the Department of Motor Vehicles in New York City and flying them all to Baghdad where they live, away from their families, in trailers surrounded by high gray concrete walls for months or even years at a time. Add to the mix roving bodyguards dripping with weapons, their eyes invisible behind Oakley wraparound sunglasses, and guards from Peru whose English is limited to phrases like "Step forward," "One at a time," "Raise your hands," "Empty your pockets," "Where's your badge?" and "You can't come in here."

I agreed completely with the general. If the Americans just did what was needed and avoided the Green Zone bureaucracy, they could have finished the runway and won goodwill in a strategically important city without spending much money.

Iran, however, knew how to do business in Iraq. Iran had already built the airport's control towers, no tender necessary. Iran was also building a power plant and had even connected parts of southern Iraq to the Iranian electrical grid, effectively running an extension cord across the border. The Iraqis loved it.

The governor begrudgingly accepted Cardon's explanation and politely changed the conversation to preparations for the upcoming Arbayeen, the Shiite ceremony commemorating the end of the forty-day mourning period for the martyr Hussein. Shiites march to Karbala during Arbayeen. This year the Shiite-led government was putting first aid stations along the roads and hundreds of rest stops serving free lamb stew. In some towns, the state was even providing masseuses to treat the pilgrims' tired feet.

"We're expecting six or seven million visitors," the governor said, and took out his cell phone. He showed Cardon a video of a man using a blowtorch to light a fire under a cauldron of lamb stew at one of the rest stops. "You see the torch? It isn't attached to a gas tank," the governor said. The flame did indeed seem to be burning without fuel. In one hand, the man held the flaming torch. In the other, he held a dangling tube that was supposed to be connected to a propane tank.

"You see this miracle?" the governor asked me.

"Yes. I see the flame is burning without gas."

"There are many miracles. Since this man is cooking for Hussein, he is blessed," the governor said.

Zohair, also a big believer in miracles, claims that during Arbayeen men have stood up from their wheelchairs or been cured of cancer. I'd sent Zohair to Najaf a few days earlier to set up contacts and interviews. He was waiting at the governor's office as Cardon finished his meeting. While the war had broken and nearly killed Ali, Zohair had become a powerful man. He'd met the prime minister several times, knew the howza, and was one of the leading members of the Iraqi journalist association. The man who'd almost been executed for deserting the army under Saddam had learned to adapt and thrive. He was a survivor.

For the next several days I traveled with Zohair in Najaf, walking the narrow alleys filled with howza students in turbans and women in black capes. I didn't have any security consultants with me. I was free. Like I'd been just after the 2003 invasion. I ate kebaabs in restaurants and did interviews outside. I was with one of our Shiite cameramen and our indefatigable producer, Madeleine Haeringer, wrapped in so much black cloth she was barely recognizable. Like all women in Najaf, she wore both a veil and an all-encompassing cape similar to the Iranian chador. Madeleine's job is like a movie director. She thinks about television. Do we have all the angles and shots we need? Can we tell a story with the pictures that have actually been recorded on our tapes? While I enjoy spending hours discussing the history of the howza with clerics and miracles with the governor, Madeleine makes sure we have enough material to produce television packages for the *NBC Nightly News*, the *Today* show, and MSNBC, which after all are paying the bills.

Our first stop was to the center of Najaf, the exquisite Imam Ali mosque. The mosque is not a single building like a church. It looks more like a fortress with high walls covered in calligraphy and azure tiles. The walls enclose a wide internal courtyard. At the center of the courtyard is the mosque itself, with a dome and doors encased in gold. Inside the mosque, under a massive crystal chandelier, is the tomb of Ali Ibn Abi Talib, the founder of Shiite Islam and the son-in-law of the Prophet Mohammed. The mosque also houses a treasury, which holds donations left by pilgrims. General Cardon said the United States estimated the shrine collected upward of $5 billion a year.

Outside the mosque, I saw cranes, scaffolding, and workmen with shovels and wheelbarrows. An engineer told me they were starting a massive project to expand the mosque complex, doubling its size. The mosque and internal courtyard could already hold thousands of worshippers. No one could give me an exact count. They just pack them in until it is full. The engineer said the plan was to make the mosque complex big enough to hold at least 100,000 worshippers.

Islam's holiest and biggest mosque is the Masjid al-Haram, the Sacred Mosque, in Mecca, Saudi Arabia. Like the Imam Ali mosque, the Masjid al-Haram is also a sprawling complex of courtyards and domed buildings. It is constructed around the Kaaba, which all Muslims face to pray. The Masjid al-Haram has been expanded con-tinuously over the centuries and covers more than 350,000 square meters. Its prayer areas can accommodate hundreds of thousands of worshippers during the Hajj. While Mecca is holy to both Sunnis and Shiites, dating back to a time before the split, it is firmly under Sunni control. Shiites are welcome to the annual Hajj pilgrimage, but have long been considered second-class citizens by Saudi Arabia's purist Wahabi monarchy and clergy. Wahabis consider Shiites to be infidels. In 1802, Wahabi warriors captured and dese-crated the Shiite shrine of Karbala.

In Najaf I was watching Shiites build their own version of Mecca. The significance cannot be overstated. After thirteen centuries of persecution, Shiites were in charge of a powerful nation and its holiest site, the Imam Ali mosque. I could understand why the governor was seeing miracles everywhere he looked.

"We want the Imam Ali shrine to be bigger than the Masjid al-Haram," an official from the governor's office told me. He pointed out rows of hotels and an open market of shops selling turquoise rings and white burial shrouds that would be flattened to make room for the mosque expansion. The official said the government in Baghdad had just finished compensating the hotel owners for their land and that construction would soon begin.

No one could tell me how much the mosque project would cost. All I was told by engineers and local officials was that some of the budget had come from the central government and that the rest was from Iran. I shook my head in disbelief. As the Americans were bickering with the governor about the correct procedure to reinforce a few runways, Iran was helping to expand the center of Shiite worship and redeem centuries of persecution.

"We still don't get this place even after five years," I thought.

I asked the American soldiers on the patrol base outside Najaf if they knew an Iranian-funded Islamic revolution was under way just down the street.

The commander of a U.S. Military Transition Team, Major Michael Crane, told me that U.S. troops no longer patrolled Najaf and that his job was limited to training the Iraqi army.

"Do you have any sense of what is going on in the city, in terms of the power plays of the religious leadership? Are you able to follow that, or is it something you don't focus on?"

"We honestly don't focus too much on it," Crane said. "We have a little bit of interaction with the Iraqi government as far as revolving around security, but when it comes to actually how the religion plays off of politics, no sir, we don't get too involved in that."

"What about Iranian influence? Do you track Iranian influence? Are you concerned about Iran's influence in Najaf?" I asked.

"I can't say that we really track it, no," he said.

I understood Major Crane's dilemma. His responsibility was to train and equip the Iraqi army, not to follow the howza and Iran. But I was surprised that the Americans living in Najaf didn't appear to notice the momentous changes going on outside the base.

———————

After Najaf, I wanted to see the Awakening movement. The Shiite militias had stopped fighting as they consolidated their gains and built their power base, but what about the Sunnis? Had they truly ended their support for al-Qaeda?

Again General Cardon let me join him on a trip to a rural village south of Baghdad where he was meeting the local Awakening leaders.

Twenty-nine-year-old Oday Karim claimed to command one thousand men in his area. He had been a university student under Saddam. After the U.S. invasion, Oday told me he joined the Islamic Army, a Sunni militant group with ties to the Baath party. "My goal was to fight the occupation," he said as he showed me his men lined up along a dirt road winding through a palm grove. Some were just fourteen- or fifteen-year-old boys carrying AK-47s. Oday had an athletic build and wore a dark overcoat, which he pulled back to show me a pistol on his hip. "I was an ambush specialist," he said, nodding his head with cocky self-satisfaction. "I led many operations."

"I am happy to meet you, but I have a personal grudge with you. Why did you, the Islamic Army, kidnap journalists? We were trying to talk to your movement and you kidnapped us. Why? Journalists have met al-Qaeda members and even Osama bin Laden, but when we tried to talk to you, you kidnapped us. It was stupid."

The Islamic Army had held two French journalists for four months in 2004, including my friend Georges Malbrunot.

"We made many mistakes and didn't know how to deal with the media," Oday said. "But we got a great benefit from kidnapping the French reporters. The money we got for their release helped the Islamic Army very much." (The French authorities, for their part, have always firmly denied that any money was in fact paid.)

"So now you work with the Americans. It's a 180-degree change. You were fighting the Americans, now you are helping them. Why?"

"The Americans are weak. Fighting them is easy. The only thing they have is helicopters. If they didn't have helicopters, we could defeat them. They are not fighting for their country or principles. We are fighting for our land and our faith."

"But why are you helping the Americans now?" I asked.

"We discovered that there is a more dangerous enemy than the Americans and that is Iran. There has been an occupation within the belly of the occupation. The bigger enemy is Iran."

"What about the government in Baghdad? Are you with it or against it?"

"The government in Baghdad is made of foreign political entities."

"Is this just a truce with the Americans?"

"Yes. It is a tactic. Even the Prophet Mohammed made peace treaties to defeat his enemies. This is a transition period. We will say when it is time for the Americans to leave. If they don't, we will fight them."

Oday was standing next to a small Shiite shrine in the palm grove that had been destroyed by al-Qaeda. His men were picking up bricks and tossing them into a pile, clearing away the rubble.

"What about al-Qaeda. They destroyed this shrine. Now you are rebuilding it. Have you stopped supporting al-Qaeda?"

"Many of them have left. But there are some members of al-Qaeda who didn't fight their Muslim brothers, so we have nothing against them," he said.

"And those al-Qaeda members are still here?"

"Yes, but we watch them. They could be useful to us in the future."

"How could they be useful? Do you mean if you were to return to fight the Americans you would use them?"

"Exactly."

I wasn't sure why Oday was telling me this. I think he didn't want anyone to think he'd gone soft and given up on the resistance. He wanted people to know he wasn't a traitor or on the take from the Americans. It was an intensely strange moment. A few minutes after Oday told me he maintained contacts with al-Qaeda members in case he needed to use them to kill Americans, he was shaking General Cardon's hand. Oday walked up to one of the general's aides and gave him a list of detainees he wanted the Americans to release. The aide took the list and promised to follow up on it.

The Americans had to keep these former fighters happy because they were exceptionally effective. The men who had until recently put IEDs in the roads knew exactly where to find them. Another slide from General Petraeus's office showed that in 2008, U.S. troops were finding four times as many IEDs and weapons caches as they had in 2006.

The Awakening councils first started in Anbar at the end of 2005, but spread much more quickly than the U.S. military expected. By 2008, there were nearly 100,000 men like Oday operating under a new name, the Sons of Iraq. The Sons of Iraq (SOIs in military jargon) didn't like to be called the Awakening. It made them sound as if they'd been asleep. It was insulting. General Petraeus had formed a private Sunni army. It was effective, but a huge gamble.

"Is he just setting up a bigger civil war?" I wondered.

I told Cardon about my conversation with Oday. "A lot of people are worried that this could blow up one day," I said.

"They are right to be worried," he said.

General Petraeus, however, told me when I saw him a few weeks later he was confident the Sons of Iraq would remain loyal. "You have to negotiate with your enemies," he said. Petraeus is a pragmatist.

As the fifth anniversary of the start of the Iraq war was approaching, I went back to the Palestine hotel, where I'd watched the invasion begin from my balcony. The lobby was as empty and lifeless as a mausoleum when I walked in. My footsteps echoed on the polished floor. I wanted to go back to my old room. I hadn't seen it in five years. I had my small camera with me, ready for another installment of my video diary. The deputy manager almost jumped out of his seat, rushed toward me, and slipped into the elevator with me as the doors were closing.

"I am not sure if you remember me," I asked. "I was here back during—"

"Oh yes, I remember you," he interrupted. "I remember you when you were here with the journalists."

"You have been here the whole time?"

"Yes, all of it."

"How are you holding up?" I asked.

He didn't want to talk about himself. "Let me show you the rooms. We have done many nice renovations and redecorated rooms. There is a gym and Internet. Very, very nice."

"I'd like to see my old room. I was on the fourteenth floor," I said, and reached out to push the elevator button. The deputy manager stopped me, taking my hand and holding it like an old friend.

"But not the fourteenth floor," he said with a smile. "That floor was damaged and still has to be renovated."

The fourteenth floor, along with several others, was destroyed by the bomb in the cement truck that exploded outside the Palestine hotel in October 2005.

"Let me show you the fifteenth floor," the deputy manager said, still holding my hand. He pushed the button for 15, and up we went. "There are suites. Two-room suites, big ones, small ones, you decide. Whatever you want. Why don't you come back here? Why don't you move your bureau here? We can give you an entire floor. You will like it."

"How much does it cost?"

"Whatever you like."

"I'll think about it. We can talk about it later. I just came today to see my old room," I said, and pulled my hand from his grip. "I don't mind if it was destroyed. I want to see what it's like now."

"Of course, but look at this room," he said, and opened the door to a corner room on the fifteenth floor.

I remembered the room instantly.

"Is this the room where the journalists were killed during the invasion?" I asked.

"Yes," the deputy manager said, completely nonplussed. "Look, there are new curtains, and the furnitures, they are new," he said, pulling back the curtains so I could get a better look. They didn't look new to me.

On April 8, 2003, an American tank fired a shell at this room, killing cameramen Taras Protsyuk, thirty-five, and José Couso, thirty-seven, from Reuters and Spain's Tele 5, respectively. Both men were married with children. I remembered seeing a sweep of blood on the floor, shattered glass, a destroyed camera, and blood-soaked sheets. Now the bed was neatly made. But I could still see the blood in my mind.

"Come, I show you another room, a nice suite," the deputy manager said. I barely heard him. I was almost in a trance.

"No thank you," I eventually said. "I'm going to look at my old room."

"Okay, then we talk about moving the bureau back here."

I started to laugh. The guy was persistent. He'd just showed me a room where my colleagues were killed, tells me my old room was gutted by a bomb blast, and thinks I'm going to seriously consider moving back. But he needed the business. The Palestine was now an abandoned relic.

"What's your occupancy now?" I asked.

"Fifty percent," the deputy manager said. It was impossible. The entire time I was there I never saw a single guest.

The deputy manager had the front desk bring me all the keys to the rooms of the fourteenth floor. I took a handful and went down to find my old room. The floor was dark when the elevator doors opened. I turned on a flashlight on my keychain and carefully walked over chunks of plaster and pieces of metal that once held up the ceiling. I had no trouble finding my old room. I could have found it with my eyes closed. With my flashlight in my teeth, I tried the keys, most of which weren't labeled. After trying five or six, I felt the key turn in the lock. I was excited. But the door was jammed. The bomb had twisted the frame. The door wouldn't open. I took a step back and tried to kick it in. After three hard kicks, it opened with a crack. Light was pouring in through the sliding glass balcony door.

The room was blanketed in a thick layer of dust. Mattresses from other rooms were piled in a corner. I was immediately drawn to the balcony with its sweeping view of Saddam's former palace complex across the Tigris, now the Green Zone. The last time I was in the room, I'd been on the balcony filming the U.S. bombings. I was back in the moment. I opened the balcony door and took a deep breath. I remembered seeing the oil fires Saddam lit to try to cover the city in black smoke to confuse U.S. bombers. I remembered the hotel shaking and swaying like an earthquake during the air strikes. I remembered covering the windows with tape to prevent them from shattering. I was suddenly emotional, in a fragile, alert state. If someone had come up behind me and put his hands on my shoulders, I would have jumped out of my skin. I hadn't expected coming back would affect me. I sat down on the floor against the stack of mattresses and turned the camera on myself. As I stared into the camera's viewfinder, I wondered if I looked any different. I certainly had more gray hairs.

"I didn't think it would be, but it is emotional for me to come back here," I said. "I remember I was sitting outside on this balcony, crunched down watching the destruction of Baghdad, watching this incredible military assault. I was watching the invasion happen right in front of me. I had no idea that I would still be here.

"Five years later so much has changed for me, for this country, even for this room. Back then, it was clear something big was happening. 'Decisive days,' that's what Saddam called the war, were upon us and the Americans were advancing to Baghdad to overthrow the regime. Now, it feels we are once again at a turning point. There is the surge and the new security plan and it feels like we are starting over again. Violence is down, but there is still a war going on.

"Am I going to be here in another two, three, or five years still report-

ing about the war in Iraq? One of the biggest changes is when I was here initially watching Shock and Awe, the world wanted to know what was going on, hungry for every detail, picture, and sound. Now, we have crews and bureaus here, but the world has moved on. People don't want to hear about Iraq anymore. It's frustrating. Sometimes I wonder why I have done all this. Why have I dedicated five years to covering this conflict if people just want to turn off the light and not listen anymore?

"I still want to stay. I still think this is the story of my generation.

"I have learned a few things since I came here, but they weren't what I expected. I thought war would make me harder, make me tougher, and, initially, it did. I'd see bodies and conflict and it gave me thick skin. But then after a certain point, it starts to hurt."

I turned off the camera and sat in the room for another ten or fifteen minutes. An hour could have passed and I wouldn't have known it. I was lost in time. A few days later the four thousandth American soldier was killed in Iraq.

Special thanks to:

Madeleine Haeringer, ML Flynn, Bob Windrem, Kadri Cetin, Brian Williams, Alice Mayhew, Steve O'Neil, Steve LoMonaco, Kevin Burke, Martin Francis, Rob Moro, Brendun Edwards, Karl Bostic, Steve Wende, John Kooistra, Sohel Uddin, Carla Marcus, Kianne Sadeq, Truus Bos, Michele Neubert, Ghazi Balkiz, and all of the editors and producers without whom this would not have been possible.

Index